D1168701

BANNED BOOKS

Literature Suppressed on

RELIGIOUS GROUNDS

Ken Wachsberger, General Editor

BANNED BOOKS

Literature Suppressed on

RELIGIOUS GROUNDS

Margaret Bald

Introduction by
Ken Wachsberger

Foreword by
Siobhan Dowd

Facts On File, Inc.

For Jonathan, André and Daniel

Banned Books: Literature Suppressed on Religious Grounds

Facts On File, Inc.
11 Penn Plaza
New York NY 10001

**Library of Congress
Cataloging-in-Publication Data**

Bald, Margaret.
Banned books: literature suppressed on religious grounds /
Margaret Bald: introduction by Ken Wachsberger : foreword by Siobhan Dowd.
p. cm. — (Banned books)
Includes bibliographical references and index
ISBN 0-8160-3306-4
1. Censorship—Religious aspects. 2. Censorship—Religious aspects—Christianity.
3. Prohibited books—Bibliography.
4. Religious literature—Censorship. 5. Censorship—History.
I. Title. II. Series.
BL65.C45B35 1998
016.098′11—dc21 97-43638

Facts On File books are available at special discounts when purchased in bulk quantities for businesses, associations, institutions or sales promotions. Please call our Special Sales Department in New York at 212/967-8800 or 800/322-8755.

You can find Facts On File on the World Wide Web at http://www.factsonfile.com.

Text design by Cathy Rincon
Cover design by Whizbang! Studios

Printed in the United States of America

MP FOF 10 9 8 7 6 5 4 3 2 1

This book is printed on acid-free paper.

Contents

There is no freedom either in civil or ecclesiastical [affairs], but where the liberty of the press is maintained.

—Matthew Tindal

One idea can only be opposed by another idea

—Naguib Mahfouz

ACKNOWLEDGMENTS

Credit and thanks are due to Jonathan Pollack, for his contribution of research and writing for the entries on Erasmus Darwin, John William Draper, John Eliot, Anatole France, Sigmund Freud, William Penn, William Pynchon and Roger Williams. Thank you also to Ken Wachsberger for his keen editorial eye and unflagging encouragement and enthusiasm, to Bert Holtje, Siobhan Dowd, George Calvert, Elizabeth Stuart Calvert and my colleagues in the National Writers Union. A special thanks to Jonathan Calvert for the constancy of his loving support and to my children, André MacLeod Calvert and Daniel Ian Calvert, young opponents of censorship, for their understanding and affection.

INTRODUCTION

We Americans are proud of our Constitution, especially its Bill of Rights. The First Amendment right to freedom of speech and religion has inspired dissenters and nonconformists everywhere. Censored writers such as Salman Rushdie, Pramoedya Ananta Toer and Aleksandr Solzhenitsyn have looked to our country's example for strength as they battled for their right to express their own thoughts, and that of others to read them, even at the risk of their lives.

Yet censorship has been a major part of American history, from the time of Roger Williams and other early colonial freethinkers. Many of our richest literary works—*The Adventures of Huckleberry Finn*, *The Color Purple*, *Grapes of Wrath*, *The Jungle*, *Uncle Tom's Cabin*, *Tropic of Cancer*—have been censored at one time or another. Even today school boards, local governments, religious fanatics and moral crusaders attempt to restrict our freedom to read. Advancing technology has provided more diverse targets—the record, film and television industries, and the Internet—for the censors and would-be censors to aim for, as they work their strategies to restrict free expression and the freedom to read, watch and listen, dumbing us all down in order to shield their children, and you, from original or disturbing thoughts.

Fortunately, our country has a strong tradition of fighting censorship as well. Groups such as the National Coalition Against Censorship, the American Library Association's Office for Intellectual Freedom, People for the American Way, the American Civil Liberties Union and the PEN American Center exist to defend the First Amendment, through legal action and by raising public awareness. They deserve our moral, political and financial support.

The four volumes in this collection add to that rich tradition by spotlighting more than 400 works that have been censored for their political, social, religious or erotic content, in the United States and around the world, from biblical times to the present day. While many of these have been legally "banned"—or prohibited "as by official order"—all indeed have been banned or censored in a broader sense: targeted for removal from school curricula or library shelves, condemned in churches and forbidden to the faithful, rejected or expurgated by publishers, challenged in court, even voluntarily rewritten by their authors. Censored authors have been verbally abused, physically attacked, shunned by their families and communities, excommunicated from their religious congregations and shot, hanged or burned at the stake by their enemies, who thus made them heroes and often enough secured their memory for posterity. Their works include novels, histories, biographies, children's books, religious and philosophical treatises, dictionaries, poems, polemics and every other form of written expression.

It is illuminating to discover in these histories that such cultural landmarks as the Bible, the Koran, the Talmud and the greatest classics of world literature have often been suppressed or censored from the same motives, and by similar forces, as those we see today seeking to censor such books as *Daddy's Roommate* and *Heather Has Two Mommies*. Every American reading these volumes will find in their pages books he or she loves and will be thankful that their authors' freedom of expression and their own freedom to read are constitutionally protected. But at the same time, how many will be gratified by the cruel fate of books we detest? Reader-citizens capable of acknowledging their own contradictions will be grateful for the existence of the First Amendment and will thank its guardians, including the authors of this series, for protecting us against our own worst impulses.

To prevent redundancy, works banned for multiple reasons appear in only one volume apiece, based on the judgment of the editor and the volume authors. The alphabetical arrangement provides easy access to titles. Works whose titles appear in SMALL CAPS within an entry have entries of their own elsewhere in the same volume. Those whose titles appear in *ITALICIZED SMALL CAPS* have entries in one of the other volumes. In addition, each volume carries complete lists of the works discussed in the other volumes.

—Ken Wachsberger

Foreword

The reason why all mortals are so gripped by fear is that they see all sorts of things happening on the earth and in the sky with no discernible cause, and these they attribute to the will of a god.

—Lucretius, *On the Nature of the Universe**

The word *religion* has its roots in the Latin verb *religo*, "to bind," and the *Oxford English Dictionary*'s primary definition is an "obligation or bond between man and the gods." However, belief in and fear of divine beings is at least as old as the city-state itself and may go back as far as our hunting-and-gathering ancestors. In fact, it is probably safe to say that our preoccupation with conceptions such as immortality, infallibility and omnipotence is as old as our perception of our own mortality, fallibility and relative impotence. Lucretius, who lived between about 100 and 55 B.C., was one of the first to plead that gods either did not exist or were irrelevant to our lives, and that we should abandon belief in divine beings as mere superstition and be satisfied with our humble place within nature.

The word *censorship* also has Latin roots: the censor was one of two Roman magistrates who drew up the census of citizens and supervised public morals, and *censeo* meant "to estimate" or "appraise."

Notions of what we owed to a divine order and what we owed to our fellow citizens quickly became entangled. Adherence to one formal belief system, in which articles of faith were codified, became intimately allied with government of the state. Perhaps we believed that there was no other way to control vast populations and prevent anarchy than to have everyone follow precisely the same rules of conduct, based on one construct of the universe, in which a perfectly good, all-knowing God communicated to us in some way

*Translated by Ronald Latham

what the rules were. Arguably, the two faiths that have been the most widespread, the most codified and the most embraced by governments over the ages as official state religions are Christianity and its various denominations and Islam. The God of both had prophets or messiahs to communicate the rules. Bodies of elders were set up to interpret the Scriptures on a day-to-day basis, and the function of such bodies quickly became censorial, in both the Roman and the modern sense. It is thus no surprise that the majority of cases in this volume of books running afoul of religious authorities were perceived as critical in some way of these two faiths (although note the exceptions, such as Lindsey Collen's *Rape of Sita*, which was deemed offensive to Hindus, and Moses Maimonides's *Guide of the Perplexed*, which was deemed offensive to Jews).

Subsequently, during the Enlightenment, there emerged a different system of government, in which the freedom of the individual was paramount and in which secularism was mandatory in all public fora, allowing all citizens to be free to practice whatever religion they wished. The United States is the best example of this alternative approach; its constitutional separation of church and state and simultaneous injunction against Congress's passing laws abridging the freedom of speech, was truly revolutionary. The First Amendment was not adopted out of a Lucretian cynicism about religion; on the contrary, it was deemed necessary for the flourishing of many differing approaches to religion, in a country where immigrants from widely differing backgrounds were still arriving. Their diverse creeds and cultural backgrounds needed equal protection before the law.

In the 19th and 20th centuries, many of the West's great thinkers declared religion outmoded. Marx dismissed it as "opium," Freud as "immature delusion" and Nietzsche even declared it "dead." However, while these three men may have affected our ways of viewing the world, they have failed to convince most of us that belief in God is fatuous. Islam and Christianity thrive, as do other faiths—and nowhere more strongly than when atheism is itself enforced, as has been the case in this century in communist countries. Science and a purely utilitarian approach to our human lot has failed to satisfy most of us; faced for the first time this century by televised proof of our worst atrocities—the Holocaust, Apartheid, ethnic cleansing, genocide—many of us feel a new sense of the need to impose fresh checks on the basest of instincts. Some suggest international tribunals; others turn back to religion.

In every censorship controversy of a religious nature lie two elements: dissent and offense. The dissenter examines the religious construct and suggests that it is man-made, and therefore at best faulty, at worst an entire artiface. He or she might press for an updating of old tenets; or a revision of a law that is seen as out of touch with the times. The religious authorities, often backed overwhelmingly by the population at large, respond by expressing their offense. They castigate the dissenter as an unbeliever whose notions are corrosive and pernicious. An enforced silencing, whether it takes the form of excommunication, imprisonment or even execution, follows—although the ensuing controversy, so far from creating silence, instead causes the views of the dissenter to be on everyone's lips. The dissenters, whatever their personal fates, are thus aided in their quests to make their views known.

Those of us who believe in defending freedom of expression roundly condemn all actions aimed at silencing dissent. However, in reading through the entries in this timely and germane book, we might find ourselves reconsidering how we should proceed in our mission in the next millenium. Perhaps we should demonstrate more persuasively than hitherto that burning books and branding authors as apostates has only ever served to sell more copies, not fewer, as Graham Greene once wryly observed of his own work. We might also appreciate more thoroughly that, where an entire and cherished belief system is abruptly called into question, alarm and anger are natural. Those who defend the dissenter should neither deride nor ignore these most human of reactions.

But, over and above this, we must be on the sharp lookout for political expedience masquerading as religious outrage. In such unresolved cases as *The Satanic Verses*, perhaps the heart of the problem lies not with the views of the author, nor in the words, for the most part unread, of his fiction; nor with those many sincerely devout Muslims who took to the streets without ever having set eyes on the book; nor, in fact, with religion at all. The controversy would have been resolved years ago had there been the requisite political will.

No; the problem here, and in other cases, lies rather with governments, who find it expedient to have a symbolic football to kick extravagantly up and down the playing field of international relations, so that everyone is distracted from the real transactions that are occurring behind the scenes. Such governments are masters of manipulation and disguise: and the only way to consign such controversies to history is to expose the players in the very act of lining their own pockets, negotiating lucrative deals and strengthening their hold on power and privilege. It is incumbent on all of us, whether dissenter, defender or offended, to be less susceptible to such manipulation and more alert to the cruder, greedier motives that often underlie the pious rhetoric of our leaders.

—Siobhan Dowd

Siobhan Dowd, former program director of PEN American Center's Freedom-to-Write Committee and the founder of the Rushdie Defense Committee USA, is the editor of *This Prison Where I Live: The PEN Anthology of Imprisoned Writers* (Cassell, 1996).

PREFACE

In 1989 an edict from Tehran brought a shocking reminder of religious censorship, regarded by many as a spectre from the distant past of the Inquisition and the burning of heretics. The Ayatollah Khomeini's death decree against author Salman Rushdie and the widespread banning of Rushdie's novel, *The Satanic Verses*, for blasphemy against Islam was a startling example of a phenomenon that is as old as history and, with the current wave of religious fundamentalism, as recent as today's headlines.

Censorship has existed in every society to protect the prevailing moral and social order. Book censorship in Western culture can be traced to the earliest years of Christianity, when the church began to suppress competing views as heretical. In the second century, the Council of Ephesus burned superstitious works and prohibited the *Acta Pauli*, a history of St. Paul, and in the fifth century, the pope issued the first list of forbidden books.

The flood of unauthorized Bible translations and religious tracts that followed the invention of the printing press in 1450 and the rise of religious dissent during the Protestant Reformation motivated the church to expand its censorial functions. In 1559 Pope Paul IV published the first *Index Librorum Prohibitorum* (Index of Forbidden Books). The Index, sometimes referred to as the Roman Index, was administered by the Roman Inquisition. It was binding on all Roman Catholics, who represented most of the population of continental Europe, and was enforced by government authorities. At the same time, similar Indexes were also prepared by theological faculties in Paris and Louvain and by the Spanish Inquisition.

As church and state in Europe began to separate in the 16th century, national monarchies instituted their own mechanisms of religious and political censorship to supplement or substitute for that of the church. In the areas where they had political control, the new Protestant faiths began to ban the writings of Catholics or dissenters.

From the earliest times religious orthodoxy and politics have been intimately connected. To be a heretic was often to be considered a traitor, subject to punishment by secular authorities. And manipulation of religious sensibilities for political purposes has a long and sordid history, with recorded examples dating to the trial of Socrates in 399 B.C.

As Europe became more politically fragmented and means of communication more sophisticated, state censorships were rarely thorough enough to prevent forbidden books from circulating. By the 18th century, the proliferation of underground publishing, as France's book censor Malesherbes said, meant that "a man who had read only books that originally appeared with the formal approval of the government would be behind his contemporaries by nearly a century."

It is impossible to discuss religious censorship of books without referring to the Index of Forbidden Books, described as the most successful censorial device of modern times, undoubtedly the most enduring. Sixty-one of the 100 books discussed in this volume, many subject to multiple forms of censorship, were listed on the Index. When it was finally abolished by the Vatican in 1966 after four centuries of existence, however, it had outlived its effectiveness. The church had long before lost the authority to enforce it and the list was widely viewed as anachronistic.

In the forty-second and final Index issued in 1948 and in print until 1966, a total of 4,126 books were still prohibited to Catholics: 1,331 from the 17th century or earlier, 1,186 from the 18th century, 1,354 from the 19th and 255 from the 20th century. Though many were obscure theological titles or works that were controversial in their day but had been forgotten for centuries, literary and philosophical classics by dozens of authors representing a Who's Who of Western thought were also included: among them, Bentham, Bergson, Comte, Defoe, Descartes, Diderot, Flaubert, Gibbon, Hobbes, Hume, Kant, Locke, Mill, Montaigne, Montesquieu, Pascal, Rousseau, Sand, Spinoza, Stendhal, Voltaire and Zola. Rather than banning books, the church's post-Index book censorship has focused primarily on sanctioning dissident Catholic theologians for their writing or pressuring the occasional Catholic author to hew to orthodoxy.

Though the First Amendment prevents government authorities from practicing religious censorship in the United States, individuals and organized religious fundamentalists have successfully pressed to remove books viewed as anti-Christian from public and school libraries and curricula. The majority of these instances have focused on perceived immorality, profane language or treatment of sexuality, rather than religious content per se, and have been discussed in another volume in this series. Their targets, however, have included textbooks that teach evolution without presenting the alternative theory of "creationism," books said to promote the religion of "secular humanism" and, in a growing trend, material with references to Eastern religions, "New Age" thought, witchcraft or the occult.

Although Rushdie's *Satanic Verses* is the most notorious international case of book censorship in this century, it is not unique. Authors in Muslim countries face increasing threats to their freedom of expression and their safety both from governments that censor or prosecute those whose writing is offensive to Islamic religious authorities and from unofficial militant Islamic groups.

Egyptian intellectual Farag Fouda and Algerian novelist and journalist Tahar Djaout, among scores of Algerian intellectuals, were murdered during the 1990s by fundamentalist terrorists. In 1994, the Egyptian Nobel laureate Naguib Mahfouz was stabbed and seriously wounded. Other writers, such as Taslima Nasrin of Bangladesh, have been driven into exile by death threats or, like Egyptian novelist Alaa Hamed, sentenced to prison for blasphemy. The writing of feminists such as Nasrin, Nawal El Saadawi of Egypt and Fatima Mernissi of Morocco, who challenge interpretations of Islamic dogma that restrict women, has particularly angered both governments and Islamist fundamentalists.

The 100 books discussed in this volume represent a sampling of the thousands that have been targets of religious censorship over the centuries. They include texts of the world's major religions, novels and classic works of philosophy, science and history representing the intellectual heritage of Western civilization. They also include contemporary works that offended church authorities, governments or Christian, Muslim or Hindu fundamentalists. A few entries—such as those on Laurence Yep's *Dragonwings* and Dickens's *Oliver Twist*, for example—chronicle censorship attempts in the United States that were ultimately unsuccessful but that merit attention because they involved legal challenges.

Many of these books were branded with the charge of heresy. Heresy is defined as opinion or doctrine that is at variance with orthodox religious teaching, or, as religious historian David Christie-Murray observed, "the opinion held by a minority of men which the majority declares is unacceptable and is strong enough to punish." Others were tarred with the brush of blasphemy, speaking in a profane or irreverent manner of the sacred. All were censored because they were seen as dangerous—to orthodoxy, to faith and morals or to the social and political order.

Some authors—Henry Cornelius Agrippa, Erasmus, Cyrano de Bergerac, Blaise Pascal, Bernard Mandeville, Jonathan Swift, Daniel Defoe, Montesquieu, Voltaire, Anatole France and Salman Rushdie—ran afoul of censors for what Swift called "the sin of wit": irreverence in the form of satire, parody, irony or mockery, in combination with dissenting ideas on religion or philosophy.

Philosophers, scientists and historians—from Abelard in the 12th century to Galileo, René Descartes, John Locke and Charles Darwin—who advocated the use of reason or the experimental or scientific method, were condemned for what might be called the sin of thinking.

The works of Sebastian Castellio, Thomas Helwys, Hugo Grotius, Pierre Bayle, Roger Williams and Baruch Spinoza were censored for advocating religious freedom, the sin of tolerance. And the sin of disputation was committed by dissidents and reformers such as John Wycliff, John Hus, Martin Luther, John Calvin, William Tyndale, William Penn, John Toland, Matthew Tindal, Emanuel Swedenborg and contemporary theologians Leonardo Boff and Hans Küng.

Some writers paid for their sins against orthodoxy with silencing, prison or banishment. Others, notably John Hus, Michael Servetus, William Tyndale and Giordano Bruno, were victims of what George Bernard Shaw called the ultimate form of censorship, assassination.

The history of censorship is one of inhumanity, of lives and livelihoods lost, talent or genius snuffed out, work unfinished, withheld, deleted or destroyed. Literary history and the present are dark with silences, Tillie Olsen has written. It is also a history of rebellion, of defiance in the face of mortal danger and perseverance against harassment, discouragement and disdain.

Yet to review the censorship of the books discussed in this volume is to be struck by the futility of religious censorship. As historian Leonard W. Levy observed, the verdicts of time mock judgments and alter sensibilities. Insurgent faiths become established and revolutionary ideas lose their power to shock. For centuries censorship has created bestsellers because, as Montaigne said, "To forbid us anything is to make us have a mind for it." Like water leaking slowly through a dike to become a steady trickle or a flood, words and ideas inexorably elude the censor's grasp.

"A book cannot be killed," commented Moroccan writer Nadia Tazi on Rushdie's censorship, "it lives and dies on its own. Once the 'vases' are 'broken,' the fragments of life spread throughout the world; voices escape, going their adventurous ways; and there are always encounters, mutations, and festivals of the spirit."

—Margaret Bald

WORKS DISCUSSED IN THIS VOLUME

ADDRESS TO THE CHRISTIAN NOBILITY OF THE GERMAN NATION
Martin Luther

THE ADVANCEMENT OF LEARNING
Francis Bacon

THE AGE OF REASON
Thomas Paine

ALCIPHRON, OR THE MINUTE PHILOSOPHER
George Berkeley

THE ANALECTS
Confucius

ARCANA COELESTIA
Emanuel Swedenborg

THE BABYLONIAN CAPTIVITY OF THE CHURCH
Martin Luther

THE BIBLE

THE BLOUDY TENENT OF PERSECUTION
Roger Williams

THE BOOK OF COMMON PRAYER
Thomas Cranmer and others

CHILDREN OF THE ALLEY
Naguib Mahfouz

THE CHRISTIAN COMMONWEALTH
John Eliot

CHRISTIANITY NOT MYSTERIOUS
John Toland

CHRISTIANITY RESTORED
Michael Servetus

CHURCH: CHARISM AND POWER: LIBERATION THEOLOGY AND THE INSTITUTIONAL CHURCH
Leonardo Boff

COLLOQUIES
Desiderius Erasmus

COMMENTARIES
Averroës (Ibn Rushd)

COMPENDIUM REVELATIONUM
Girolamo Savonarola

CONCERNING HERETICS
Sebastian Castellio

THE COURSE OF POSITIVE PHILOSOPHY
Auguste Comte

CREATIVE EVOLUTION
Henri Bergson

THE CRITIQUE OF PURE REASON
Immanuel Kant

DE ECCLESIA
John Hus

DE INVENTORIBUS RERUM
Polydore Vergil

DE L'ESPRIT
Claude Adrien Helvétius

DIALOGUE CONCERNING THE TWO CHIEF WORLD SYSTEMS
Galileo Galilei

DIALOGUES CONCERNING NATURAL RELIGION
David Hume

DISCOURSE ON METHOD
René Descartes

DON QUIXOTE
Miguel de Cervantes Saavedra

DRAGONWINGS
Laurence Yep

ÉMILE
Jean-Jacques Rousseau

ENCYCLOPÉDIE
Denis Diderot and Jean d'Alembert, eds.

AN ESSAY CONCERNING HUMAN UNDERSTANDING
John Locke

ESSAYS
Michel de Montaigne

ETHICS
Baruch (Benedict) Spinoza

THE FABLE OF THE BEES
Bernard Mandeville

THE GUIDE OF THE PERPLEXED
Moses Maimonides

THE HIDDEN FACE OF EVE: WOMEN IN THE ARAB WORLD
Nawal El Saadawi

HISTORICAL AND CRITICAL DICTIONARY
Pierre Bayle

HISTORY OF THE CONFLICT BETWEEN RELIGION AND SCIENCE
John William Draper

THE HISTORY OF THE DECLINE AND FALL OF THE ROMAN EMPIRE
Edward Gibbon

INFALLIBLE? AN INQUIRY
Hans Küng

AN INQUIRY CONCERNING HUMAN UNDERSTANDING
David Hume

INSTITUTES OF THE CHRISTIAN RELIGION
John Calvin

INTRODUCTION TO THEOLOGY
Peter Abelard

AN INTRODUCTION TO THE PRINCIPLES OF MORALS AND LEGISLATION
Jeremy Bentham

INTRODUCTORY LECTURES ON PSYCHOANALYSIS
Sigmund Freud

THE KORAN

LAJJA (SHAME)
Taslima Nasrin

THE LAST TEMPTATION OF CHRIST
Nikos Kazantzakis

LETTER ON THE BLIND
Denis Diderot

LETTERS CONCERNING THE ENGLISH NATION
Voltaire (François Marie Arouet)

LEVIATHAN
Thomas Hobbes

THE LIFE OF JESUS
Ernest Renan

MEDITATIONS ON FIRST PHILOSOPHY
René Descartes

THE MERITORIOUS PRICE OF OUR REDEMPTION
William Pynchon

THE METAPHYSICS
Aristotle

THE NEW ASTRONOMY
Johannes Kepler

THE NEW TESTAMENT
William Tyndale, trans.

NINETY-FIVE THESES
Martin Luther

OF THE VANITIE AND UNCERTAINTIE OF ARTES AND SCIENCES
Henricus Cornelius Agrippa

OLIVER TWIST
Charles Dickens

ON CIVIL LORDSHIP
John Wycliff

ON JUSTICE IN THE REVOLUTION AND IN THE CHURCH
Pierre-Joseph Proudhon

ON MONARCHY
Dante Alighieri

ON THE INFINITE UNIVERSE AND WORLDS
Giordano Bruno

ON THE LAW OF WAR AND PEACE
Hugo Grotius

ON THE ORIGIN OF SPECIES
Charles Darwin

ON THE REVOLUTION OF HEAVENLY SPHERES
Nicholas Copernicus

OPUS MAIUS
Roger Bacon

PENGUIN ISLAND
Anatole France (Jacques Anatole Thibault)

THE PERSIAN LETTERS
Charles-Louis de Secondat de Montesquieu

PHILOSOPHICAL DICTIONARY
Voltaire (François Marie Arouet)

THE POLITICAL HISTORY OF THE DEVIL
Daniel Defoe

POPOL VUH

THE POWER AND THE GLORY
Graham Greene

THE PRAISE OF FOLLY
Desiderius Erasmus

PRINCIPLES OF POLITICAL ECONOMY
John Stuart Mill

THE PROVINCIAL LETTERS
Blaise Pascal

THE RAPE OF SITA
Lindsey Collen

THE RED AND THE BLACK
Stendhal (Marie Henri Beyle)

RELIGIO MEDICI
Sir Thomas Browne

RELIGION WITHIN THE LIMITS OF REASON ALONE
Immanuel Kant

THE RIGHTS OF THE CHRISTIAN CHURCH ASSERTED
Matthew Tindal

THE SANDY FOUNDATION SHAKEN
William Penn

THE SATANIC VERSES
Salman Rushdie

A SHORT DECLARATION OF THE MISTERY OF INIQUITY
Thomas Helwys

THE SHORTEST WAY WITH THE DISSENTERS
Daniel Defoe

THE SOCIAL CONTRACT
Jean-Jacques Rousseau

THE SORROWS OF YOUNG WERTHER
Johann Wolfgang von Goethe

THE SPIRIT OF LAWS
Charles-Louis de Secondat de Montesquieu

SPIRITS REBELLIOUS
Khalil Gibran

THE STORY OF ZAHRA
Hanan al-Shaykh

A TALE OF A TUB
Jonathan Swift

THE TALMUD

THEOLOGICAL-POLITICAL TREATISE
Baruch (Benedict) Spinoza

THREE-PART WORK
Meister Eckhart

THE VEIL AND THE MALE ELITE: A FEMINIST INTERPRETATION OF WOMEN'S RIGHTS IN ISLAM
Fatima Mernissi

VOYAGES TO THE MOON AND THE SUN
Savinien Cyrano de Bergerac

ZOONOMIA
Erasmus Darwin

LITERATURE SUPPRESSED ON RELIGIOUS GROUNDS

ADDRESS TO THE CHRISTIAN NOBILITY OF THE GERMAN NATION

Author: Martin Luther
Original date and place of publication: 1520, Switzerland
Literary form: Theological tract

SUMMARY

The German monk and theologian Martin Luther was the founder of the Protestant Reformation. His NINETY-FIVE THESES, posted on the door of Wittenberg Castle church in 1517, marked the beginning of a movement that would shatter the structure of the medieval church.

On August 18, 1520, he published *Address to the Christian Nobility of the German Nation*, an open letter to the ruling class of the German-speaking principalities advocating control by the nobility of German ecclesiastical matters and calling for the help of the princes in reforming the church. The *Address*, called "a cry from the heart of the people" and a "blast on the war-trumpet," was Luther's first writing after he was convinced that his breach with the Roman Catholic church was irreparable.

He expressed his anger at corruption of the Renaissance papacy and exploitation of Germans by the church and proposed reforms to severely limit the pope's power and authority over secular rulers. Each local community, he believed, should take charge of its own affairs and elect its own ministers and bishops. He denied that the pope was the final interpreter of Scripture and enunciated his doctrine of the priesthood of all believers.

"To call popes, bishops, priests, monks and nuns the religious class, but princes, lords, artisans and farm-workers the secular class," Luther wrote, "is a specious device. . . . The fact is that our baptism consecrates us all without exception and makes us all priests." Moreover, the claim that the pope alone can interpret Scripture or confirm any particular interpretation is a "wicked, base invention, for which they cannot adduce a tittle of evidence in support."

Luther detailed a sweeping program of church reorganization and purification to strip away its temporal power so that it could better perform its spiritual functions. Recalling the example of Christ on foot and comparing it to the image of the pope in a palanquin, he recommended that the papacy return to apostolic simplicity. The number of cardinals should be reduced, the temporal possessions and claims of the church abandoned and its income from fees and indulgences curtailed. Monks should be relieved of hearing confession and preaching. The number of monastic orders should be cut and the practice of irrevocable monastic vows eliminated. The clergy should be permitted to marry. Litigation by church courts involving Germans should be tried under a German primate. Luther urged the German states to refuse to pay papal taxes and exactions and to expel papal legates from their territories.

"Heretics should be vanquished with books, not with burnings," Luther recommended. The church's response to the *Address* and his next major tract of 1520, THE BABYLONIAN CAPTIVITY OF THE CHURCH, was hostile. Shortly after the publication of the two tracts, Luther received word that the pope had pronounced him a heretic and ordered the burning of his books.

CENSORSHIP HISTORY

See NINETY-FIVE THESES.

FURTHER READINGS

Bainton, Roland H. *Here I Stand: The Life of Martin Luther*. New York: Penguin Group, 1995.

Bokenkotter, Thomas S. *A Concise History of the Catholic Church*. Garden City, N.Y.: Doubleday and Co., 1977.

Christie-Murray, David. *A History of Heresy*. Oxford: Oxford University Press, 1989.

Haight, Anne Lyon. *Banned Books: 387 BC to 1978 AD*. Updated and enlarged by Chandler B. Grannis. New York: R. R. Bowker, 1978.

Putnam, George Haven. *The Censorship of the Church of Rome*, Vol. 1. New York: G. P. Putnam's Sons, 1906–07.

Spitz, Lewis W., ed. *The Protestant Reformation*. Englewood Cliffs, N.J.: Prentice-Hall, 1966.

Wilcox, Donald J. *In Search of God and Self: Renaissance and Reformation Thought*. Boston: Houghton Mifflin Company, 1975.

THE ADVANCEMENT OF LEARNING

Author: Francis Bacon
Original date and place of publication: 1605, 1623, England
Literary form: Scientific treatise

SUMMARY

English philosopher and statesman Francis Bacon was a pioneer in the use of the modern inductive method and the logical systemization of scientific procedures. He is credited with the slogan, "Knowledge is power." He planned the writing of a large scientific work, the *Instauratio Magna*, or Great Restoration of Science, but completed only two parts. The first part, *The Advancement of Learning*, a sketch in English of his key ideas, was published in 1605 and expanded in Latin in 1623 as *De Augmentis Scientiarum*. The second part, the *Novum Organum*, was published in 1620.

In *The Advancement of Learning* Bacon explained his intention to survey the sciences and methods of attaining truth in order to develop a system of classifying the various branches of knowledge. But first he had to deliver scientific learning from "the discredits and disgraces which it hath received, all from ignorance, but ignorance severally disguised, appearing sometimes in the zeal and jealousy of divines, sometimes in the severity and arrogancy of politiques, and sometimes in the errors and imperfections of learned men themselves."

Bacon believed that knowledge was best attained through what he called the "initiative method," as opposed to the "magistral method." "The magistral method teaches," he wrote; "the initiative intimates. The magistral method requires that what is told should be believed; the initiative that it should be examined." As opposed to the prevailing deductive Aristotelian Scholastic approach to knowledge, Bacon advocated an empirical and inductive method, which began with observations of particular things and events and moved toward wider and wider generalizations. He recommended investigation as the key to knowledge, rejecting theories based on insufficient data and, as he described further in the *Novum Organum*, ideas drawn from individual propensities and prejudices, "the idols and false notions which are now in possession of human understanding."

He proposed a strict separation of the study of nature from the study of the divine, opposing St. Thomas Aquinas's doctrine that knowledge of the supernatural was sought through the natural. "We do not presume, by the contemplation of nature to attain to the mysteries of God," he declared. Rather, the value and justification of knowledge, he believed, consisted in its practical application and utility. The function of knowledge was to achieve material progress by extending the dominion of human beings over nature.

CENSORSHIP HISTORY

Bacon is often described as the father of modern empiricism. The clear functional style of his writing and his advocacy of sober and dispassionate inquiry free of preconceived notions had a powerful impact on the generation that followed him. His rejection of prevailing Aristotelian orthodoxy and the a priori method of medieval Scholasticism was strongly opposed by 17th-century clerics, who believed that it was sinful to inquire into nature.

While medieval Scholastics argued from premises established by past authority and religious revelation, Bacon bypassed the tenets of received knowledge to recommend the discovery of general principles through observation. In 1640, all of Bacon's works were banned by the Spanish Inquisition, and in 1707 the Spanish Index of Forbidden Books condemned Bacon's *opera omnia* (all his works). In 1668, *De Augmentis Scientiarum* was placed on the Index of Forbidden Books in Rome, listed with the notation *donec corrigantur* (until corrected). Bacon's work remained on every edition of the Index until the latter was abolished in 1966.

FURTHER READINGS

Bacon, Francis. *Francis Bacon: A Selection of His Works*. Ed. by Sidney Warhaft. Indianapolis: Odyssey Press, 1981.

Collinson, Diané. *Fifty Major Philosophers: A Reference Guide*. London: Routledge, 1988.

Copleston, Frederick. *A History of Philosophy*. Vol. 3, *Late Medieval and Renaissance Philosophy*. New York: Doubleday, 1993.

Haight, Anne Lyon. *Banned Books: 387 BC to 1978 AD*. Updated and enlarged by Chandler B. Grannis. New York: R. R. Bowker, 1978.

THE AGE OF REASON

Author: Thomas Paine
Original date and place of publication: 1794–95, France
Literary form: Philosophical treatise

SUMMARY

The Anglo-American political theorist, writer and revolutionary Thomas Paine was one of the greatest pamphleteers in the English language. *The Age of Reason*, an uncompromising attack on Christianity based on the principles of rationalism, became the most popular deist work ever written.

The son of an English Quaker, Paine emigrated to America in 1774 and became active in the independence movement. His pamphlet, *Common Sense*, published in January 1776, called for the founding of an American republic and galvanized the public toward independence.

In 1787 Paine returned to England, where he published in 1791–92 *THE RIGHTS OF MAN*, a work defending the French Revolution and attacking social and political inequities in Britain. It was to sell an estimated half-million copies in the next decade and become one of the most widely read books in England. Indicted for seditious libel by the British government for *The Rights of Man*, Paine fled to Paris, where he participated in the French revolution as a member of the National Convention. For 10 months in 1794, during the Reign of Terror, he was imprisoned by Robespierre and the Jacobins before being rescued by the American ambassador to France, James Monroe.

On his way to prison Paine delivered to a friend the manuscript of part one of *The Age of Reason*, which was published in Paris in 1794. After his release from prison he completed part two, which appeared in 1795. During his stay in France, Paine became convinced that popular revulsion against the reactionary activities of the French clergy, who plotted against the Revolution in alliance with the forces of aristocracy and monarchy, was leading the French people to turn to atheism. In *The Age of Reason*, Paine resolved to rescue true religion from the Christian system of faith, which he regarded as a "pious fraud" and "repugnant to reason."

Paine, in common with many prominent American and European intellectuals, such as Benjamin Franklin, Thomas Jefferson, Voltaire and Rousseau, was a deist. Deism, a religious expression of scientific rationalism, proposed that the existence of God could be inferred from the order and harmony of creation. Deists saw formal religion as superfluous and scorned claims of supernatural revelation as a basis for belief. God's creation, deists believed, was the only bible.

In *The Age of Reason*, Paine popularized deism, removed it from the sphere of the intellectual elite and made the philosophy accessible to a mass audience. Though the book was described as "the atheist's bible" by the book's critics, Paine repudiated atheism. He opened the book with a profession of faith: "I believe in one God, and no more; and I hope for happiness beyond this life."

Paine's declared objective in all his political writings, beginning with *Common Sense*, was to rescue people from tyranny and false principles of government. *The Age of Reason* was written in the same vein. "Of all the tyrannies that affect mankind," Paine wrote, "tyranny in religion is the worst; every other species of tyranny is limited to the world we live in; but this attempts to stride beyond the grave, and seeks to pursue us into eternity." Organized religion was set up to "terrify and enslave mankind, and monopolize power and profit." The only true theology was "natural philosophy, embracing the whole circle of science."

Paine criticized insincere claims of belief as "mental lying." Every national church or religion claims some special mission from God, communicated to certain individuals, and every church proclaims certain books to be revelation or the word of God. "It is a contradiction to call anything a revelation that comes to us second-hand, either verbally or in writing," Paine wrote.

Paine believed that mystery, miracle and prophesy were three frauds and that the Old and the New Testaments could not be attributed to revelation. "I totally disbelieve that the Almighty ever did communicate anything to man . . . other than by the universal display of Himself in the works of the creation, and by that repugnance we feel in ourselves to bad actions, and the disposition to do good ones." It was the "Bible of Creation," not the "stupid Bible of the Church," to which men should turn for knowledge. "My own mind is my own church," he proclaimed.

While in part one of *The Age of Reason* Paine disputed in general terms the tenets of Christianity, in part two he attacked both the Old and the New Testaments in tones of ridicule and sarcasm. Challenging the authenticity of the five books of Moses, Paine asserted that they had not been written in the time of Moses; rather, they represented an "anonymous book of stories, fables and traditionary or invented absurdities, or of downright lies." He described the Old Testament as being full of "obscene stories, the voluptuous debaucheries, the cruel and tortuous executions . . . a history of wickedness that has served to corrupt and brutalize mankind; and for my part, I sincerely detest it as I detest everything that is cruel."

Criticizing the New Testament, Paine wrote that the Gospels, having appeared centuries after the death of Christ, were not written by the apostles. He admitted that Jesus was a virtuous and honorable man, but denied that he was God. He took offense at the Christianity of the church, "a religion of pomp and revenue" contradictory to the character of Jesus, whose life was characterized by humility and poverty. He described the story of the Immaculate Conception as "blasphemously obscene." He deplored the depiction of miracles for "degrading the Almighty into the character of a showman."

Of all the systems of religion that ever were invented, none is "more derogatory to the Almighty, more unedifying to man, more repugnant to reason, and more contradictory in itself, than this thing called Christianity," Paine wrote. "As an engine of power, it serves the purpose of despotism; and as a means of wealth, the avarice of priests; but so far as respects the good of man in general, it leads to nothing here or hereafter."

As Christianity worships a man rather than God, it is itself a species of atheism, a religious denial of God, Paine contended. "The creation is the Bible of the Deist. He there reads, in the handwriting of the Creator himself, the certainty of his existence and the immutability of His power, and all other Bibles and Testaments are to him forgeries."

CENSORSHIP HISTORY

The Age of Reason was written in an accessible, easy-to-read style and was distributed free of charge or at low cost in America and Europe by deistic organizations. In America, in the mid-1790s, Paine's book went through 17 editions, selling tens of thousands of copies. *The Age of Reason* became the bible of American deists, Paine their hero and deism a mass movement allied with republicanism.

However, the book also aroused the hostility of clergy and believers on both sides of the Atlantic—a hostility that endured even long after Paine's death. A century later, for example, Theodore Roosevelt referred to Paine as "a filthy little atheist." *The Age of Reason* outraged the leaders of the religious establishment. But it also angered religious reformers who shared Paine's critique of religious conservatism but who parted company with him when he rejected the Bible and all forms of Christianity.

Like its seditious predecessor, *The Rights of Man*, *The Age of Reason* was regarded by the British government as genuinely dangerous, because it appeared in the context of mass unrest stirred by the French Revolution. Though Paine was out of reach of British law in France and America, his publishers and booksellers in Britain were not. They were relentlessly prosecuted and imprisoned by the British government over a period of more than 25 years.

In 1797, Thomas Williams of London was tried by a special jury before the Court of King's Bench and found guilty of the crime of blasphemy for having published *The Age of Reason.* The prosecution contended that Paine's book, by subverting the truths of Christianity, undermined the government and the Constitution, both of which rested on Christianity. Further, *The Age of Reason* robbed the poor by depriving them of a belief in a happier afterlife. Williams was sentenced to a year at hard labor and a £1,000 fine.

In 1812, the British Crown prosecuted publisher Daniel Isaac Eaton for blasphemy for publishing and selling a new edition of *The Age of Reason.* Eaton had earlier been imprisoned for publishing *The Rights of Man.* "Our civil and religious institutions are so closely interwoven together," the prosecutor told the jury, "that they cannot be separated—the attempt to destroy either is fraught with ruin to the state." Eaton was sentenced to stand in the pillory and to serve 18 months in Newgate Prison. Upon his release from prison he again defied authorities by publishing *The Age of Reason*; once again, he was prosecuted and convicted of blasphemy. However, because of his age and poor health, he was not sentenced.

The highest price for the defense of Paine's right to publish his ideas was paid by publisher Richard Carlile, a radical exponent of freedom of the press, who between 1817 and 1835 served more than nine years in prison for publishing *The Age of Reason* and other deist tracts. In 1818, he read *The Age of Reason* for the first time and became a deist. He decided to republish the book knowing that its previous publishers had been imprisoned for blasphemy. Indicted for blasphemy, Carlile defiantly kept selling the book. He was brought to trial in October 1819 and in his own defense read the entire book to the jury, taking 12 hours the first day of the trial. By reading it into the court proceedings, he ensured that the work would be republished as part of the public record. It sold 10,000 copies in this form thanks to publicity surrounding the trial.

Carlile was found guilty of blasphemy and sentenced to two years in prison and a £1,000 fine for publishing *The Age of Reason*, and a year in prison and a £500 fine for publishing Elihu Palmer's deist book, *The Principles of Nature.* Within an hour of his conviction, government officers seized the contents of his shop and closed it down. Carlile was bankrupted and spent six years in prison, as he could not pay his fines. His wife, his sister and more than 20 of his workers were also prosecuted and jailed in the years that followed for continuing to publish *The Age of Reason* and other material judged blasphemous.

Rather than succeeding in suppressing Paine's work, Carlile's prosecution aroused interest in it. Four years later more than 20,000 copies were in circulation in England. According to the philosopher John Stuart Mill, writing in 1824, "as among the poorer classes it is notorious that there are several readers to one purchaser, it may be estimated that at least one hundred thousand persons have been led to the perusal of that work under circumstances highly favourable to its making an impression on their minds."

FURTHER READINGS

Foner, Eric. *Tom Paine and Revolutionary America.* London: Oxford University Press, 1976.

Levy, Leonard W. *Blasphemy: Verbal Offense Against the Sacred, from Moses to Salman Rushdie.* New York: Alfred A. Knopf, 1993.

Paine, Thomas. *The Age of Reason.* Intro. by Philip S. Foner. Secaucus, N.J.: Citadel Press, 1974.

ALCIPHRON, OR THE MINUTE PHILOSOPHER

Author: George Berkeley
Original date and place of publication: 1732, Ireland and England; 1803, United States
Literary form: Philosophical dialogue

SUMMARY

The Anglo-Irish philosopher and Anglican bishop George Berkeley is regarded as among the outstanding and influential classical British empiricists. Among his most important works, written in his younger years, were *An Essay Towards a New Theory of Vision* (1709), *A Treatise Concerning the Principles of Human Knowledge* (1710) and *Three Dialogues Between Hylas and Philonous* (1713).

Berkeley's philosophy of subjective idealism held that matter does not exist independent of perception, and that the observing mind of God makes possible the continued apparent existence of material objects. Qualities, rather than things, are perceived and the perception of qualities is relative to the perceiver. Berkeley characterized his immaterialism with the phrase, "*esse est percipi*"—to be is to be perceived.

The most popular and accessible of his works was *Alciphron, or the Minute Philosopher*, published in Dublin and London in 1732 and in the Hague in French in 1734. A third edition was published in London in 1752, the year before Berkeley's death. *Alciphron* was directed against freethinkers—English deists and atheists—and attempted to vindicate Christianity. Berkeley believed that the growth of atheistic freedom from religious restraints was the primary cause of England's social maladies, because atheism withdraws the strongest motive for promoting the common good. He charged the "minute" (meaning "small") philosophers with anticlericalism, intellectual arrogance and contempt for religion, attributing their atheism to their limited intellectual vision.

"The Author's design being to consider the Free-thinker in the various lights of atheist, libertine, enthusiast, scorner, critic, metaphysician, fatalist, and sceptic," Berkeley wrote in the introduction to *Alciphron*, "it must not therefore be imagined that every one of these characters agrees with every individual Freethinker; no more being implied that each part agrees with some or other of the sect. . . . Whatever they pretend, it is the author's opinion that all those who write, either explicitly or by insinuation, against the dignity, freedom, and immortality of the Human Soul, may so far be justly said to unhinge the principles of morality, and destroy the means of making men reasonably virtuous."

The seven dialogues comprising *Alciphron* occur over the seven days of one week, during which Euphranor, a prosperous farmer, and Crito, a neighboring distinguished gentleman, debate the tenets of "minute philosophy" with Alciphron and Lysicles, both confirmed freethinkers. Their conversations are reported in a letter to a friend by Dion, who observes but does not participate in the discussions. Alciphron and Lysicles are depicted as comic figures. The pedantic Alciphron is influenced by the deistic philosophy of the third earl of Shaftesbury, who posited that true morality was found in a balance of egoism and altruism. Lysicles is a follower of the philosophy of Bernard Mandeville, who, in his FABLE OF THE BEES, argued the social utility of vice.

In Berkeley's view, neither Shaftesbury nor Mandeville understood the function of reason in moral life, nor did they provide a motive for altruistic conduct. In the dialogues, Berkeley defends the individual and social utility of Christianity and declares the universal providence of God as indispensable to the vitality of virtue and the practice of morality.

CENSORSHIP HISTORY

Unlike many other British thinkers of the period, Berkeley was a devout Christian. Predictably, freethinkers attacked *Alciphron* soon after its appearance. Bernard Mandeville, in his *Letter to Dion*, complained of misrepresentation by Berkeley. A number of other books and tracts critical of *Alciphron* were published. But Berkeley's censors were not the freethinkers.

In *Alciphron*, Berkeley, who used the terms "popery and papists" when referring to Catholicism and Catholics, suggested that the "minute philosophers" might be dupes of the Jesuits. At the end of the second dialogue, Euphranor argues that if the opinions of freethinkers were to prevail and destroy the Protestant church and clergy, they would leave way for "a harvest by popery."

"I am credibly informed there is a great number of emissaries of the church of Rome disguised in England," Euphranor says. "[W]ho can tell what harvest a church so numerous, so subtle, and so well furnished with arguments to work on vulgar and uneducated minds, may be able to make in a country so despoiled of all religion, and feeling the want of it?" In effect, one of Berkeley's arguments against freethinking was that it would lead to a resurgence of Catholicism, which he, as an Anglican, abhorred.

In 1742, despite Berkeley's defense of Christianity against deism and atheism, his anti-Catholic views led the Catholic church to place *Alciphron* on the Index of Forbidden Books. It was retained on the Index of Pope Leo XIII in 1897 and remained listed through the last edition, compiled in 1948 and in print until 1966. Mandeville's *Fable of the Bees*, which Berkeley attacked in *Alciphron*, was also placed on the Index and was still listed in the last 20th-century edition.

FURTHER READINGS

Berkeley, George. *The Works of George Berkeley*. Vol. 2, *Philosophical Works, 1732–33*. Preface by Alexander Campbell Fraser. Oxford: Clarendon Press, 1931.

Collinson, Diané. *Fifty Major Philosophers: A Reference Guide*. London: Routledge, 1988.

Cook, Richard I. *Bernard Mandeville*. New York: Twayne Publishers, 1974.

Copleston, Frederick. *A History of Philosophy*. Vol. 5, *Modern Philosophy: The British Philosophers from Hobbes to Hume*. New York: Doubleday, 1994.

THE ANALECTS

Author: Confucius
Original date and place of publication: Third–fourth century B.C., China
Literary Form: Religious and philosophical text

SUMMARY

The Analects is a collection of sayings and short dialogues attributed to Confucius (551–479 B.C.) and first compiled after his death by his disciples during the third and fourth centuries B.C. Confucius was China's greatest philosopher and founder of the ethical and religious system known as Confucianism, which dominated China's social and political thinking for millennia. *The Analects* was learned by heart by all educated men in China as a guide to ethics and morality in personal and political life.

Though it is chiefly through *The Analects* that Confucianism has been known to the West, many of the pithy maxims and remarks in *The Analects* are extracts from longer discourses found in other works of the Confucian canon. In the centuries after Confucius's death, five works attributed to Confucius, but most likely compiled by his followers, were collected into the *Five Classics*: one on ritual, two on history, one on poetry and one book of changes (*I-Ching*) on cosmology and divination. In the 12th century A.D. selections from the *Five Classics*, including *The Analects*, the sayings of Confucius's follower Mencius and two selections from the book on ritual dealing with human nature and moral development, were formed into the *Four Books*. The *Four Books* were thought to embody the essence of Confucius's teachings. The *Five Classics* and the *Four Books* became the basis for state examinations required for government service in China. Until the second half of the 19th century, China's educational system was based entirely on the Confucian classics.

The Analects emphasizes rational thinking rather than dogma and stresses the virtue of altruism. In Confucius's dialogues with statesmen and students, he is portrayed as a shrewd and modest teacher who tested himself and others for character flaws while sustaining faith in the power of moral example and virtuous action.

Social relations function smoothly by a strict adherence to *li*, a term denoting a combination of etiquette and ritual. Filial piety—the hierarchical code governing behavior among family members—required respect of son for father, wife for husband and younger brother for older brother. This code extended homage to the emperor, who was regarded as the embodiment of wisdom and moral superiority.

Confucius, it says in *The Analects*, taught four subjects or precepts: literature, personal conduct, being one's true self and honesty in personal relationships. He denounced arbitrary opinions, dogmatism and egotism and was described as gentle but dignified, austere but not harsh, polite and completely at ease. "Whenever walking in a company of three," Confucius said, "I can always find my teacher among them (or one who has something to teach me). I select a good person and follow his example, or I see a bad person and correct it in myself." He advised his followers to criticize their own faults rather than those of others. When asked if there was one single word that would serve as a principle of conduct for life, Confucius replied, "Perhaps the word *reciprocity* (*shu*): Do not do unto others what you do not want others to do unto you."

The golden mean—moderation in all things—and the golden rule are essential principles expressed in *The Analects*. "To go a little too far is as bad as not going far enough." Many of the maxims of *The Analects* describe the qualities of the superior man. "To know what you know and know what you don't know is the characteristic of one who knows," Confucius said. "A man who has committed a mistake and doesn't correct it is committing another mistake. . . . The superior man understands what is right; the inferior man understands what will sell. . . . The superior man blames himself; the inferior man blames others."

Confucius's views of political ethics were extensions of his view of personal ethics. "When wealth is equally distributed, there is no poverty; when the people are united, you cannot call it a small nation, and when there is no dissatisfaction (or when the people have a sense of security), the country is secure," he said. When a ruler does what is right he will have influence without giving commands, and when the ruler does not do what is right, his commands will be of no avail.

CENSORSHIP HISTORY

The first ruler of the Qin dynasty, Shih Huang Di, unified all of China in 221 B.C. The system of warring feudal states was abolished in favor of a centralized feudal system known as Legalism, with an appointed bureaucracy, laws and standardized currencies, weights and measures. In 213 B.C., the emperor, who saw the traditional culture of China as a challenge to Legalism and the centralized state, ordered all Confucian books burned. He also threatened to execute anyone who dared to quote them. Only practical works on agriculture, medicine and divination were exempted from the burning and preserved in the imperial library. In the following year, 460 Confucian scholars were buried alive. The imperial library was destroyed during a civil war in 206 B.C.

In 191 B.C., the book-burning edict was rescinded by the rulers of the Han dynasty. Because the teachings of Confucius were memorized and handed down orally from master to disciple, scholars were able to reconstruct the texts from memory and from manuscripts that had been hidden and escaped destruction.

In the 20th century, *The Analects* and the Confucian canon were again subject to attack. During the Great Proletarian Cultural Revolution of 1966–74, Mao Zedong and the leaders of the Chinese Communist party called for a comprehensive attack on the "four old" elements within Chinese society—old customs, old habits, old culture and old thinking. Youths organized as Red Guards charged intellectuals with feudal or reactionary modes of thinking and destroyed libraries and art collections. Though Mao previously had quoted aphorisms of Confucius in his essays and poems, possession of Confucian writings became dangerous during the early years of the Cultural Revolution when Red Guards were on the rampage.

During 1973–74, the Communist party launched a major propaganda campaign against the teachings of Confucius as well as against Former Defense Minister Lin Biao, who was considered a reactionary parallel to Confucius. The party criticized Confucian thinking as promoting an ideology of exploitation, elitism, social hierarchy and preservation of a status quo in which people knew and kept their place in a static society and obeyed the prescribed rites for their station in life. Party leaders asserted that Lin Biao promoted Confucian ideology and had opposed Mao Zedong, just as conservative Confucianist thinking opposed the politically centralizing policies of the first emperor in the third century B.C. The anti–Lin Biao, anti-Confucius campaign was the focus of mass rallies and discussions in party cells, the army, agricultural communes and factories. The burning of Confucian books and the execution of scholars in the third century B.C. were defended in the campaign as historically necessary to overthrow the feudal landlords of the slave-owning aristocracy.

FURTHER READINGS

Lin, Yutang, ed. *The Wisdom of Confucius*. New York: Random House, Modern Library, 1966.

Spence, Jonathan D. *The Search for Modern China*. New York: W. W. Norton & Co., 1990.

ARCANA COELESTIA

Author: Emanuel Swedenborg
Original date and place of publication: 1747–58, England
Literary form: Theological treatise

SUMMARY

The writings of Emanuel Swedenborg, the Swedish scientist, philosopher and theologian, form the doctrinal basis of the church of the New Jerusalem, or New Church, founded after his death. Swedenborg was an engineer and assessor of the Swedish Royal Bureau of Mines. He wrote many notable scientific volumes between 1720 and 1745, including *Principia*, a groundbreaking mathematical, rational explanation of the universe, the first part of a three-volume *Philosophical and Mineralogical Works*.

Swedenborg adopted his religious philosophy, generally called Swedenborgianism, during 1744 and 1745, when he had a number of dreams and mystical visions in which he believed God directly called him to bring a new revelation to the world. In 1747, he resigned his post of assessor to dedicate himself to spiritual matters and, for the next quarter century, wrote voluminous theological works expounding "the true Christian religion," a body of spiritual law meant to revivify all churches.

In his theosophic teachings he declared that two worlds exist, both emanating from God. The "New Jerusalem" is the spiritual world to which man will ultimately be restored by a process of purification through divine love. The second is the world of nature in which human beings live. A symbolic counterpart to everything in our world exists in the spiritual world. All creative forces, both in the spiritual and in the natural kingdom of consciousness, flow from the divine center of the universe. Man's spirit or soul was created to be a receptacle of divine life, whose essence is love and wisdom.

Between 1747 and 1758, Swedenborg wrote and published the eight-volume *Arcana Coelestia*, or *Heavenly Secrets*, his first major theological work, a 7,000-page, three-million-word commentary on the books of Genesis and Exodus. *Arcana*, as well as his other theological works, Swedenborg believed, were dictated to him by God. Between his chapters of biblical exegesis, Swedenborg inserted his personal accounts of experiences "from the other world," copied or transposed from his own spiritual diaries.

In *Arcana*, Swedenborg interpreted the Bible according to the doctrine of correspondences, by which everything that is outward or visible has an inward or spiritual cause. "The universal heaven is so formed as to correspond to the Lord, to His Divine Human; and man is so formed that all things in him, in general and in particular, correspond to heaven, and through heaven, to the Lord," he wrote. He believed that God inscribed within the historical narratives of the Bible an interior spiritual sense. The early chapters of Genesis, for example, were allegorical and did not literally describe the creation of the universe and the origins of the first human beings. He interpreted Genesis as descriptive of man's spiritual regeneration. Adam and Eve represented the human race or human nature in the abstract, Adam standing for its intellectual qualities and Eve for its emotional side. Through the language of correspondences, the familiar Bible stories revealed basic divine teachings on life after death, relationships between the spiritual and natural worlds, human nature and religion. In the preface to *Arcana*, Swedenborg maintained that without an understanding of the internal meaning of the Scriptures, they were like "a body without a soul."

Central elements of Swedenborg's theology diverged from both Catholic and Protestant doctrines. He taught that rewards and punishments have no place as incentives to virtue. He denied that there were three persons in the Holy Trinity, believing instead in the exclusive divinity of Jesus Christ. He also took issue with the doctrine of Atonement and called the Catholic church "Babylon" for its desire for dominion over men's souls. He attacked the Lutheran belief that faith without works is sufficient for salvation, holding that true faith could not be disassociated from a life of charity and active usefulness. He saw good in all churches and criticized Protestants for their self-righteousness.

In 1758, Swedenborg published the three-volume *Heaven and Hell*, extracts from *Arcana* describing the nature of heaven and hell, as well as the world of the spirits, the transitory state between natural life and heaven or hell, where human beings prepare for their ultimate fate. Whether human beings go to heaven or hell depends on the quality of their lives in the natural world. Swedenborg believed that spirits go to hell when their selfish lives on earth cause them to find the unselfish love of heaven oppressive.

CENSORSHIP HISTORY

The eight volumes of *Arcana Coelestia*, written in Latin, were published anonymously during the years 1749 to 1756 in London, where Swedenborg had settled. Despite its size, Swedenborg insisted that the book be sold cheaply. He advanced the money for its publication, dedicating all profits to "the propagation of the gospel."

As only the second volume was issued with an English translation, the book appealed primarily to the learned, and few copies were sold. Swedenborg gave away many copies anonymously to clergymen, including the bishops of Sweden, England, Holland and Germany, as well as to universities and libraries. Though his expectation was that some would accept his teachings and spread them, most of the clergy either ignored his doctrines or regarded them with contempt.

Swedenborg's efforts to remain anonymous in his theological writings lasted until 1759. That year in Stockholm, in a well-publicized incident, Swedenborg apparently demonstrated clairvoyance by correctly predicting a fire.

As a result of the general curiosity about this and other examples of his unusual abilities, he became a public figure. He became known in Sweden as the author of *Arcana Coelestia* and *Heaven and Hell* and copies published in London began to trickle into Sweden.

His theological writings caused great controversy in Gothenburg's Lutheran Consistory. In September 1768, a country parson introduced a resolution objecting to Swedenborg's writings and calling for measures to stop the circulation of works such as Swedenborg's that contradicted Lutheran dogma. However, some members insisted that Swedenborg's works should not be judged until the entire membership had studied them. But Dean Ekebom, the ranking prelate, announced that, even though he was unacquainted with Swedenborg's religious system and had not read much of it, he found Swedenborg's doctrines to be "corrupting, heretical, injurious, and to the highest degree objectionable." He concluded that Swedenborg's views on the nature of the divine, the Bible, the Holy Supper, faith and other basic teachings should be suppressed as dangerous to established religious concepts. He also charged Swedenborg with the anti-Trinitarian heresy of Socinianism.

Swedenborg, who had gone to Amsterdam in 1769 to publish a new book, replied by letter in his own defense, stating, "I look upon the word Socinian as a downright insult and diabolical mockery." The clergy, however, regarded Swedenborg's letter as "sinister," because he also argued that his doctrine of the New Church had come directly from God, who had asked his servant Swedenborg to introduce it to the world.

The case of Swedenborg's heresy was brought before the Swedish Diet. The chief prosecutor urged that "the most energetic measures be taken to stifle, punish and utterly eradicate Swedenborgian innovation and downright heresies by which we are encompassed . . . so that the boar which devastates and the wild beast which desolates our country may be driven out with a mighty hand."

The royal council, appointed through the Diet, issued its final report in April 1770. It "totally condemned, rejected and forbade the theological doctrines contained in Swedenborg's writings." Swedenborg's supporters among the clergy were forbidden to read or propagate his teaching, and customs officials were directed to impound his books and stop their circulation unless the nearest Lutheran consistory granted permission.

Swedenborg continued to protest the council's decision. The royal council referred the matter to the Gotha court of appeals, which asked several universities to thoroughly study his ideas. The universities found nothing objectionable in his writing, but asked to be excused, as they were not inclined to put bishops and consistories on trial for false accusations. Eventually the controversy abated. Some Lutheran clergymen preached Swedenborgian ideas without interference and Swedenborg continued to write and speak, dividing his time among Sweden, London and Amsterdam. But because of censorship in Sweden, his religious ideas found the most fertile ground elsewhere. Toward the end of his life, Swedenborg's works were widely translated and circulated. In a letter written in 1771 he stated that the Arcana "can no longer be obtained either here in Holland or in England, as all the copies are sold." He was most influential in England, where societies formed for the study of his works.

Swedenborg had not intended to establish a religious sect, for he saw his ideas as relevant to all Christians. However, after his death in 1772, his English followers began to organize the New Church. The first public services of its congregation were held in 1788 in London. Swedenborg's teachings were introduced into the United States in 1784 and a congregation of the New Church was formed in Baltimore in 1792.

Swedenborg's reputation increased in the 19th century, when he was admired by many European and American intellectuals. His book on marriage and sex, *Conjugal Love*, condemned by Swedish authorities shortly after its publication in 1768, became popular in Germany and France. It attracted public attention in the United States in 1909 when it was seized by Philadelphia post office authorities on grounds of obscenity.

Despite Swedenborg's divergence from Catholic dogma as expressed in such works as *Arcana*, the Catholic church condemned only Swedenborg's early scientific work, *Principia; or the First Principles of Natural Things*, published in 1721. It was placed on the Index of Forbidden Books in 1738 and remained there through the final edition of the Index compiled in 1948 and in effect until 1966. In the Soviet Union, all of Swedenborg's works were banned in 1930 in an effort to suppress mystical and religious works generally.

FURTHER READINGS

Haight, Anne Lyon. *Banned Books: 387 BC to 1978 AD*. Updated and enlarged by Chandler B. Grannis. New York: R. R. Bowker, 1978.

Synnestvedt, Sig. *The Essential Swedenborg*. New York: Twayne Publishers, 1970.

Toksvig, Signe. *Emanuel Swedenborg: Scientist and Mystic*. Freeport, N.Y.: Books for Libraries Press, 1972.

Trowbridge, George. *Swedenborg, Life and Teaching*. New York: Swedenborg Foundation, 1938.

THE BABYLONIAN CAPTIVITY OF THE CHURCH

Author: Martin Luther
Original date and place of publication: 1520, Switzerland
Literary form: Theological tract

SUMMARY

In 1520, Martin Luther, the German founder of the Protestant Reformation, published a radical tract whose uncompromising assault on Roman Catholic church doctrine led to an irreparable breech with the church hierarchy. In *The Babylonian Captivity of the Church*, Luther definitively abandoned traditional Catholicism and presented a new theory about the nature of the church and its sacramental system. He denied the authority of the priesthood to mediate between the individual and God and rejected the sacraments except as aids to faith.

On the grounds that a sacrament must have been directly instituted by Christ and based on the authority of Scripture, Luther reduced the number of the sacraments from seven to two. Confirmation, marriage, ordination, penance and extreme unction were eliminated. Only baptism and the Eucharist, radically transformed, remained. Luther's repudiation of ordination, the sacrament granting priests the power to celebrate the Eucharist and marking them with an indelible character, provided the basis for Luther's priesthood of all believers, ending the "detestable tyranny of the clergy over the laity."

Ordination as a sacrament, Luther wrote, "was designed to engender implacable discord whereby the clergy and the laity should be separated farther than heaven and earth. . . . All of us who have been baptized are priests without distinction, but those whom we call priests are ministers, chosen from among us so that they should do all things in our name and their priesthood is nothing but a ministry."

In eliminating the sacrament of penance, Luther recognized the usefulness of confession, but believed that it could be made to any Christian rather than only to a priest. He regarded confirmation, the rite that confirms the initiation into the church by baptism, and marriage, which he felt should be allowed to priests, as useful ceremonies rather than as sacraments.

He proposed that the efficacy of extreme unction, or anointing of the sick, depended on the faith of the recipient. The church taught that a sacrament's benefits could not be impaired by any human weakness, as it operates by virtue of itself. Luther viewed this interpretation of the sacraments as mechanical and magical. "I may be wrong on indulgences," Luther declared, "but as to the need for faith in the sacraments I will die before I will recant."

Luther accepted the scriptural origins of baptism, but believed that no vow beyond the baptismal vow should ever be taken, thereby repudiating the vows taken by monks. Although he retained the sacrament of the Eucharist, he held that the Mass is not a repetition of Christ's sacrifice. Thus he rejected the doctrine of transubstantiation, by which the bread and wine are held to be transformed into the Body and Blood of Christ. He proposed instead his doctrine of consubstantiation, meaning that after their consecration the substances of bread and wine remain along with the Body and Blood of Christ. The priest does not "sacrifice Christ" and effects no miracle because Christ is present everywhere and at all times.

CENSORSHIP HISTORY

See NINETY-FIVE THESES.

FURTHER READINGS

Bainton, Roland H. *Here I Stand: The Life of Martin Luther.* New York: Penguin Group, 1995.

Bokenkotter, Thomas S. *A Concise History of the Catholic Church.* Garden City, N.Y.: Doubleday and Co., 1977.

Christie-Murray, David. *A History of Heresy.* Oxford: Oxford University Press, 1989.

Haight, Anne Lyon. *Banned Books: 387 BC to 1978 AD.* Updated and enlarged by Chandler B. Grannis. New York: R. R. Bowker, 1978.

Putnam, George Haven. *The Censorship of the Church of Rome.* Vol. 1. New York: G. P. Putnam's Sons, 1906–07.

Spitz, Lewis W., ed. *The Protestant Reformation.* Englewood Cliffs, N.J.: Prentice-Hall, 1966.

Wilcox, Donald J. *In Search of God and Self: Renaissance and Reformation Thought.* Boston: Houghton Mifflin Company, 1975.

THE BIBLE

Literary form: Religious text

SUMMARY

The Bible is a collection of books containing the sacred writings of the Jewish and Christian religions. Both religions regard the Bible as inspired by God. The Christian Bible has two parts: the Old Testament, which includes the Hebrew Bible that is sacred to Jews, and the NEW TESTAMENT, which includes specifically Christian writings. The Hebrew Bible is divided into three sections: the Law, or Torah (also known as the Pentateuch), consisting of the first five books—Genesis, Exodus, Leviticus, Numbers and Deuteronomy; the Prophets, books of history and prophecy; and the Writings, containing prayers, poems and maxims.

The books of the Bible were written over centuries by many different authors. The authorship of the Old Testament was traditionally attributed to great Jewish leaders, among them Moses, Samuel, David, Solomon and various prophets. Modern scholars, however, have concluded that many of the books are later compilations of early traditions and writings. Scholars believe that the earliest books of the Bible began as oral literature and were first written down following the reign of King David, after 1000 B.C. The Book of Genesis, for example, contains passages that may date to the 10th century B.C., but the entire book was probably not written down in its present form until the fifth century B.C. The whole Torah, or first five books of the Bible, was in use by about 400 B.C.

The Old Testament—written in Hebrew, with some sections in Aramaic—tells the story of Creation and provides information on pre-Israelite times and the history and religious life of ancient Israel from about 1300 B.C. to the second century B.C. Christians and Jews regard the Old Testament as the record of a covenant or testament made by God with man and revealed to Moses on Mount Sinai.

The canonical books of the Old Testament and their order vary within the Jewish, Catholic and Protestant religions. The Hebrew Bible revered by Jews consists of 24 books. The Christian Old Testament divides some of the books, increasing their number to 39. The Catholic Bible also includes as authentic seven books of the Old Testament that Protestants consider to be of doubtful authority and refer to as the Apocrypha.

The 27 books of the New Testament, sacred only to Christians, chronicle the years from the birth of Jesus Christ to about A.D. 100, and comprise the earliest documents extant on the life and teaching of Jesus and the establishment of the Christian church. Christians believe that Jesus Christ proclaimed a new covenant or new testament that both fulfilled and superseded the covenant revealed to Moses.

The New Testament is divided into four sections: the Gospels or biographies of Jesus; the Acts of the Apostles; the Letters or Epistles of the apostles; and Revelation, a book of prophecy. Written in Greek between A.D. 70 and 100, the New Testament was compiled in the second century. Although the New Testament is traditionally considered to have been written by the apostles and disciples of Jesus, modern scholars have questioned the apostolic authorship of some of the books.

Both the Old and New testaments were translated into Latin by Saint Jerome in about A.D. 400 and compiled as the standard and definitive text in the sixth century. His translation, known as the Vulgate, was designated as the authorized Bible of the Roman Catholic church and remained so for 1,000 years, up to the time of the 16th-century Reformation. The first book printed in Europe, the famous Gutenberg Bible of 1456, was an edition of the Vulgate.

CENSORSHIP HISTORY

"Both read the Bible day and night, But thou read'st black where I read white." These words of the poet William Blake aptly describe the origins of censorship of the Bible over the centuries. Battles over the correct version of the Bible began in the early years of Christianity, when many of the church's first decrees established certain books as acceptable parts of the Bible and disclaimed others. Throughout the later Middle Ages, the Catholic church discouraged translation of its official Latin Vulgate edition for fear that the text might be corrupted or misinterpreted. In the late 14th century, in defiance of the church's restrictions, the first complete translation of the Vulgate into English appeared, the work of the scholar and reformer John Wycliff and his followers.

Wycliff, whose treatise ON CIVIL LORDSHIP was condemned for heresy, maintained that all people had the right to read the Gospel "in that tongue in which they know best Christ's teaching." Reading the Wycliff Bible was forbidden in England except by ecclesiastical permission. In 1409, the Synod of Canterbury at Saint Paul's in London issued a decree forbidding translation of the Scriptures or the reading of any new translations without a special license, under penalty of excommunication. Although Bible translations were undertaken in other European countries, no others appeared in England until the Protestant Reformation. Despite the ban, the Wycliff Bible was frequently copied and some portions of it were later adopted by William Tyndale, the first of the Reformation translators.

The 16th-century Protestant reformers held that, because God speaks directly to human beings through the medium of the Bible, it is the right and duty of every Christian to study it. They either sponsored or undertook themselves translations of the Bible into their own languages. By 1522, when Martin Luther's German translation was published, or shortly thereafter, there were already 14 printed German Bibles, and vernacular versions had appeared in France, Italy, Spain, Portugal, Bohemia, the Netherlands and Scandinavia.

Protestant reformers believed that the Bible should be understood literally and historically by readers without interpretation by church authorities. This doctrine, *sola scriptura* (the Bible alone), was seen as threatening by the Catholic church, faced with a widespread loss of its authority as the Protestant revolt spread throughout Europe. Catholic censorship focused on the burgeoning number of Protestant vernacular versions of the Bible, notably Martin Luther's in Germany, William Tyndale's in England and Robert Estienne's in France. Protestants also censored biblical material, banning titles by dissenting Protestants as well as by Catholics. But Protestants could only censor within their own political boundaries. Because of the fragmentation of Protestant Europe, Protestant censorship was not as comprehensive as that of the Catholic church.

The most violently suppressed Bible translation was Tyndale's. He was the first person to translate the Bible into English from its original Hebrew and Greek, and the first to print it in English. His translation of the New Testament, printed in Cologne and Worms, Germany, in 1524–26, was smuggled into England, where it was banned and publicly burned by the church. His translations of the Pentateuch in 1530, the book of Jonah in 1531 and a revised New Testament in 1534 were also prohibited and burned. Despite the bans, many reprints of Tyndale's translations were smuggled into the country and circulated.

In a plot masterminded by English authorities, Tyndale was arrested by authorities in Antwerp, Belgium, tried for heresy and strangled and burned at the stake near Brussels in 1536 with copies of his Bible translation. Despite its repression, Tyndale's translation survived to form a considerable portion of later Bibles, including the Authorized or King James Version published in 1611.

Miles Coverdale, Tyndale's colleague, produced a complete English Bible in 1535. Because it could not be licensed to be printed in England, it was published in Germany. The popular demand for the Bible in English and the growing difficulty of suppressing its publication led King Henry VIII to name an authorized version, Matthew's Bible, based on Tyndale's and Coverdale's work. It appeared in 1537 with prefaces and annotations by John Rogers, who used the pseudonym John Matthew. Rogers was a Catholic priest who converted to Protestantism and a friend of Tyndale. Matthew's Bible was the first in English to be licensed by the government. But on the accession of the loyal Catholic Queen Mary I, Rogers was among the first of 300 martyrs to be imprisoned and burned as heretics in 1554.

Bans on new Bible versions were not confined to England. In 1539, Henry VIII issued his own Great Bible, a revision by Coverdale of his earlier work, which was to be the official version in the newly reformed Church of England. When he decided to print it in Paris, authorities moved to stop it. Regnault, the famous Parisian printer of English books, was seized by the Inquisition and imprisoned. Sheets of the Great Bible were smuggled out of France in hats and taken to every church in England with the king's directive that each man should interpret Scripture for himself.

In 1546, the doctors of theology at the Sorbonne secured the condemnation in the Louvain Index of Forbidden Books of a Bible edition printed by the renowned humanist Robert Estienne, the official printer of King Francis I. The king responded by prohibiting the printing or circulation in France of the Louvain Index and ordering the withdrawal of strictures on the Estienne Bible. With the death of the king in 1547, however, the prohibition was renewed and Estienne had to move his press to Geneva. But Protestant Geneva, under the authority of the Protestant reformer John Calvin, was not a bastion of religious toleration. The Calvinists also condemned the Estienne Bible.

Spain under the Inquisition moved to suppress Bible editions influenced by Protestantism. In 1551, the Index of Valladolid listed 103 editions condemned because of errors and heresies to suppression, correction or cancellation.

The restoration of papal authority, ecclesiastical courts and the laws against heresy in England under the Catholic regime of Mary I reconfirmed the ban on Protestant Bibles. In 1555, a royal proclamation commanded "that no manner of persons presume to bring into this realm any manuscripts, books, papers ... in the name of Martin Luther, John Calvin, Miles Coverdale, Erasmus, Tyndale ... or any like books containing false doctrines against the Catholic faith." Protestants from England who took refuge in Frankfurt and Geneva published the Calvinist "Breeches Bible" in 1560. Although its use was forbidden in churches in England, it went into 140 editions between 1560 and 1644.

In 1546, the Catholic church's Council of Trent declared the Latin Vulgate of Saint Jerome to be the sole canonical text of the Bible. In opposition to the Protestant reformers, the council decreed that dogma is transmitted through the church's teaching, whose authority is equal to that of the Bible, and forbade the reading of any unapproved translation. The first English version approved for Catholics was a translation of the New Testament from the Vulgate by church scholars published in Rheims in 1582 and printed in 1610 with an approved Old Testament as the Rheims-Douay version.

In 1631, the word "not" was inadvertently omitted from the seventh commandment, "Thou shalt not commit adultery," in an edition of 1,000 copies of the Bible printed in England by R. Barker. The printers were heavily fined and the edition, known as the "wicked Bible," was so vigorously suppressed that few copies have survived.

Because the copyright of the Authorized (King James) Version was held by the British Crown, the right to print it in England in the 17th century was held by the royal printers. Only the universities of Oxford and Cambridge were exempt from the restriction. This meant that no authorized Bible could be printed in the American colonies until after their independence. The first Bible printed in America was not the King James Version, but the *Up-Biblum God*, John Eliot's Bible translation for the Algonquian Indians, published in 1661–63. The Bible in English was probably not published in the United States until 1782 in Philadelphia, though historians have found evidence that a Bible may have been secretly printed in Boston about 1752.

The prudish sensibilities of the Victorian period in England and the United States produced a new kind of censorship of the Bible—the publication of expurgated editions. *The Holy Bible, Newly Translated*, by John Bellamy, a Swedenborgian, was published in 1818. Declaring that no major biblical figure could have committed actions he found unacceptable, Bellamy decided that the translation from Hebrew must be at fault, and he revised passages he considered indecent. *The New Family Bible and Improved Version*, by Dr. Benjamin Boothroyd, a Congregationalist who wanted to circumvent "many offensive and indelicate expressions" in the Bible, was published in several editions beginning in 1824. That year, in *The Holy Bible Arranged and Adapted for Family Reading*, John Watson, a Church of England layman, replaced offensive sections with his own writing and dropped the numbering of traditional chapters and verses so that it was difficult for readers to notice what had been cut. In 1828, William Alexander, a Quaker printer, published *The Holy Bible, Principally Designed to Facilitate the Audible or Social Reading of the Sacred Scriptures*. He changed words and passages "not congenial to the views and genius of the present age of refinement."

The first expurgated Bible in America was published in 1833 by the lexicographer Noah Webster, who made thousands of alterations in material he considered indecent. Although his Bible was adopted by the state of Connecticut in 1835, endorsed by Yale and widely used in Congregational pulpits for about 20 years, Webster's desire to make changes even in "decent" parts of the Bible met with criticism. The third edition, published in 1841, was the last.

Twentieth-century government censorship of the Bible has been most widespread in socialist countries. In 1926, the Soviet government instructed libraries throughout the U.S.S.R. to remove all religious books such as the Bible. It was allowed to remain only in the country's largest libraries. Its importation was forbidden and it was not printed again in the Soviet Union until 1956. In China, during the Cultural Revolution of the 1960s and 1970s—a campaign to destroy "the four olds" of culture, thinking, habits and customs—Bibles were burned and all places of Christian worship were closed.

A 1986 government-authorized printing of a Bible used by the Baptist church in Romania marked the first time since 1951 that the Bible had been printed there. The socialist military government of Ethiopia in 1986 banned several books of the Bible as "contrary to the ongoing revolution." A shipment of over 45,000 Bibles destined for a church in Ethiopia was held indefinitely in customs.

Many attempts to censor the Bible have been recorded in the United States. Parents or religious groups who denounced the teaching of the Bible as comparative literature or believed it should be taught only as the sacred word of God from their own perspective and interpretation have attempted to remove it from school libraries or curricula. Challenges to the Bible have also often been based in misunderstanding of Supreme Court decisions prohibiting prayer in the public schools. In 1963 in *District of Abington Township v. Schempp*, the U.S. Supreme Court prohibited devotional exercises in public schools. The court, however, did not forbid the study of the Bible as literature, or of religion in historical or social studies. In its decision the court declared, "In addition, it might well be said that one's education is not complete without a study of comparative religion or the history of religion and its relationship to the advancement of civilization. Nothing we have said here indicates that such study of the Bible or of religion, when presented objectively as part of a secular program of education, may not be effected consistently. . . ."

In an early challenge to the Supreme Court decision, a conservative religious organization sued the University of Washington for having offered an elective course on the Bible as literature. It argued that such a course could not be offered in a public institution and that the approach taken conflicted with its religious views. The Washington state courts upheld the inclusion of the course in a broad curriculum.

A 1982 study of 17 surveys conducted of school libraries during the previous two decades found that the presence or use of the Bible in schools had been challenged by students, parents or teachers who thought it was illegal or who objected to the interpretation used. Similar challenges were reported during the 1980s and 1990s. For example, in 1989 an elementary school student in Omaha, Nebraska, was forbidden to read the Bible in school or to have it on the premises. In a settlement of a suit in Federal District Court that never came to trial, it was agreed that the student could read the religious literature of his choice at school during his free time. In 1991, a library patron who believed that public funds could not be expended on religious books challenged the presence of the *Evangelical Commentary on the Bible* and the *Official Catholic Directory* in the Multnomah, Oregon, public library. The books were retained by the library. In May 1981, Christian fundamentalists burned copies of The Living Bible in Gastonia, North Carolina.

A spate of attempts during the 1990s to restrict access to the Bible, reminiscent of Victorian-era attempts to bowdlerize it, have been motivated by the view that it contains indecent material. In 1992 in the Brooklyn Center, Minnesota, independent school district, an atheist "seeking to turn the tables on the religious right" challenged use of the Bible, declaring that "the lewd, indecent, and violent contents of that book are hardly suitable for young children." In 1993, the Bible was challenged as "obscene and pornographic," but retained, at the Noel Wien Library in Fairbanks, Alaska. Near Harrisburg, Pennsylvania, protestors attempting to remove it from the West Shore schools cited "more than 300 examples of obscenities in the book" and objected that it "contains language and stories that are inappropriate for children of any age, including tales of incest and murder."

Though the Bible is among the most censored books in history, it has been translated more times and into more languages than any other and has outsold every book in the history of publishing. In the English language alone, 450 different editions are in print. The long history of Bible censorship has had little impact on its availability and influence today.

FURTHER READINGS

Burress, Lee. *Battle of the Books: Library Censorship in the Public Schools, 1950–1985.* Metuchen, N.J.: Scarecrow Press, 1989.

Daniell, David. *Let There Be Light: William Tyndale and the Making of the English Bible.* London: British Library, 1994.

———. *William Tyndale: A Biography*. New Haven: Yale University Press, 1994.

Doyle, Robert P. *Banned Books 1996 Resource Guide*. Chicago: American Library Association, 1996.

Haight, Anne Lyon. *Banned Books: 387 BC to 1978 AD*. Updated and enlarged by Chandler B. Grannis. New York: R. R. Bowker, 1978.

Hentoff, Nat. *Free Speech for Me, but Not for Thee*. New York: HarperCollins, 1992.

Jenkinson, Edward B. "The Bible: A Source of Great Literature and Controversy." In *Censored Books: Critical Viewpoints*. Ed. by Nicholas J. Karolides, Lee Burress and John M. Kean, 98–102. Metuchen, N.J.: Scarecrow Press, 1993.

Lofmark, Carl. *What is the Bible?* Buffalo, N.Y.: Prometheus Books, 1992.

Manguel, Alberto. *A History of Reading*. New York: Viking, 1996.

New York Public Library. *Censorship: 500 Years of Conflict*. New York: Oxford University Press, 1984.

O'Neil, Robert M. "The Bible and the Constitution." In *Censored Books: Critical Viewpoints*. Ed. by Nicholas J. Karolides, Lee Burress and John M. Kean, 103–08. Metuchen, N.J.: Scarecrow Press, 1993.

Perrin, Noel. *Dr. Bowdler's Legacy: A History of Expurgated Books in England and America*. Anchor Books, 1971.

Putnam, George Haven. *The Censorship of the Church of Rome*. Vol. 1. New York: G. P. Putnam's Sons, 1906–07.

Tinguet, Margaret. "Ethiopia: Destroy the Muslims." *Index on Censorship* 16:4 (April 1987): 33–35.

THE BLOUDY TENENT OF PERSECUTION

Author: Roger Williams
Original date and place of publication: 1644, England
Literary form: Religious text

SUMMARY

Roger Williams, a founder of the Massachusetts Bay Colony, brought a radical liberty of conscience to the shores of New England. In *The Bloudy Tenent of Persecution* he espoused the ideas of religious toleration and intellectual freedom under both secular and ecclesiastical governments. The trajectory of Williams's life represented the dissenting currents in British Protestant thought. Born into a family that belonged to the Church of England, he became a Puritan while at Cambridge in the 1620s and was a Separatist Puritan by the time he joined the Massachusetts Bay Colony in 1631.

In 1635, his disenchantment with the Separatists in Massachusetts led to his exile to Rhode Island, at that time a wilderness between the British colonies of Massachusetts and Connecticut. Williams was dissatisfied with the way churches began as fundamentalist, back-to-basics movements and gradually developed their own orthodoxies. His desire for a pure church led him to question the idea of an official church decreed by a political entity, such as a local or colonial government.

In the summer of 1643, Williams returned to England to persuade Parliament to grant him a charter for Rhode Island, which would establish it as an official colony, free to govern its own affairs. England in this period was racked with religious controversy, particularly over the boundaries between church and state authority and individual liberty. By the spring of 1644, Williams had made a name for himself arguing for a balance of church, state and individual interests that would favor individual conscience. Observing the proliferation of new Protestant sects, he believed that no church or state power could control this impulse toward fragmentation. Liberty of conscience, which Williams defined as the freedom to worship as one saw fit, should not be restricted.

Williams published his ideas in *The Bloudy Tenent of Persecution*, officially a rebuttal to John Cotton, the most powerful Puritan minister in Massachusetts and a skillful politician who wanted to curry favor with Parliament. Cotton had endorsed new legislation that increased the church's power in civil affairs. Williams's book argued against the right of Parliament to demand and enforce conformity in interpretation and practice of Scriptural principles. He claimed that the Massachusetts Puritans were trying to build a modern state based on the Ten Commandments. He criticized the idea that the abstract and absolute principles of Moses could be used to govern society thousands of years later.

Williams had his own religious and philosophical reasons for opposing Cotton's ideas. Williams believed that the British government's enforcement of the First Commandment, that there is one God to be obeyed, was offensive to Christian tradition, because the New Testament superseded Mosaic law; Williams also objected because, as he put it, prayer offered insincerely "stinks in God's nostrils."

The Bloudy Tenent of Persecution continued in this vein, offering copious evidence from religious and secular history that the state and the church had separate realms. Williams denounced the philosophy and practice of religious repression. The earth has been "made drunk with the bloud of its inhabitants," he wrote, slaughtering each other with indiscriminate zeal as each sect seeks to aggrandize itself at the expense of others. "Those churches cannot be truly Christian . . . which either actually themselves, or by the civil power of kings and princes . . . doe persecute such as dissent from them or be opposite against them." Unless reason and charity prevail, the result will be the ruin of the church and the devastation of civil society.

Williams was all too familiar with the power of an official church. In *The Bloudy Tenent* he stated that his exile to Rhode Island was a result of his campaigning for liberty of conscience and that the Puritans sent him to a remote outpost to silence him. The example of his own life, he hoped, would persuade readers of the harm of religious doctrine enforced through civil punishment.

Williams wrote *The Bloudy Tenent* in the form of a dialogue between Peace and Truth, as a parable about his fight with the established churches of his day. He was particularly troubled by the role of nonbelievers in English and colonial society. He wondered what was to be gained in forcing someone who was not a sincere Protestant to mouth the words of Protestant doctrine. Williams believed that the salvation of nonbelieving individuals would come from their own conversion experiences, rather than through the commands of a religious orthodoxy.

To Williams, religion was primarily an inner belief, as opposed to the outward expression of religion practiced by most Puritans in Massachusetts and Presbyterians in the English Parliament. Official religion, state celebration of religious holidays and courts empowered to enforce religious doctrine offended his religious sensibilities. Mixing the private religious sphere and the public governmental sphere resulted in a cheapening of religion: religious doctrine came straight from divine sources, while political leaders were merely appointed or elected by other humans. This latter idea offended King Charles I, who still clung to the idea that his power could be traced to divine origins.

Williams's ideas in *The Bloudy Tenent*, as they attacked the relationship between church and state—which most Britons took for granted—became infamous. But his inflammatory language won few converts to his ideas. However, his book did not hinder his achieving another goal. One month after its publication, he returned to the wilderness of Rhode Island with the charter in hand that established Rhode Island as a British colony.

CENSORSHIP HISTORY

Upon its publication in July 1644, *The Bloudy Tenent of Persecution* failed to persuade Parliament and the British reading public of the importance of separating religious doctrine from civil policy. Given the imperative that Parliament placed on religious conformity, it is hardly surprising that Parliament ordered all copies of Williams's 400-page book to be burned publicly in August 1644.

Williams's style of organization was partly to blame as well. He had composed his book in fits and starts over nearly 25 years. This gradual formation of a religious philosophy showed up in the muddled prose of the original work. It is unlikely that most members of Parliament, or anyone else, read far enough into the book to be persuaded by Williams's defense of his ideas through painstaking analysis of scriptural passages.

Hostility toward this book may also have been generated by its subtitle: "for cause of Conscience." Liberty of conscience was a radical concept in England at this time. When members of such dissenting sects as the Quakers were jailed for their beliefs and Catholics and Jews faced more violent suppression, a plea for complete religious tolerance was unlikely to be persuasive.

By the time Williams's book was burned, he was on a ship bound for New England. He never faced jail or other personal punishment for writing *The*

Bloudy Tenent of Persecution. He did, however, have to answer attacks on his ideas. In 1647, his old nemesis John Cotton wrote *The Bloudy Tenent, Washed, and Made White in the Bloud of the Lamb*, in which he denied that Williams had been expelled from Massachusetts for religious reasons. He contended, rather, that Williams had spoken against the Boston government, preaching sedition, and had to be punished. Explicit in Cotton's argument was the idea that there was no separation between religious and civil authorities, that a dispute with the religious practice of civil leaders was tantamount to a civil dispute and this constituted advocating rebellion. Cotton attacked Williams as self-serving, and dismissed Williams's claims that he was persecuted for his religious beliefs.

Five years after Cotton's rebuttal, Williams published *The Bloudy Tenent yet More Bloudy: by Mr. Cotton's endeavour to wash it white in the Bloud of the Lambe*. Williams stood by his original principles, especially the scriptural justification for religious tolerance. In his opinion, forcing people to worship in churches against their will resulted in the sin of hypocrisy. Thus, the Massachusetts authorities were requiring their citizens to sin. Forcing nonmembers to attend a church was to Williams a greater sin than was lack of belief in Christianity.

While Parliament's burning of *The Bloudy Tenent of Persecution* did not stop Roger Williams from publishing his ideas or from prospering in his colony of Rhode Island, this censorship signalled the beginning of an era of religious intolerance in both England and New England. Respect for Williams's belief in freedom of conscience grew, however, over the following 150 years. His philosophy of religious tolerance inspired the rights to "life, liberty, and the pursuit of happiness" in the Declaration of Independence, as well as the Constitution's First Amendment guarantees of freedom of religion and speech. In 1936, 300 years after Williams's exile to Rhode Island, the state of Massachusetts pardoned him for his offense.

FURTHER READINGS

Covey, Cyclone. *The Gentle Radical: A Biography of Roger Williams*. New York: Macmillan Co., 1966.

Gaustad, Edwin S. *Liberty of Conscience: Roger Williams in America*. Grand Rapids, Mich.: Wm. B. Eerdmans Publishing Co., 1991.

Green, Jonathon. *The Encyclopedia of Censorship*. New York: Facts On File, 1990.

Haight, Anne Lyon. *Banned Books: 387 BC to 1978 AD*. Updated and enlarged by Chandler B. Grannis. New York: R. R. Bowker, 1978.

Jordan, W. K. *The Development of Religious Toleration in England*. Vol. 3. Gloucester, Mass.: Peter Smith, 1965.

Morgan, Edmund S. *Roger Williams: The Church and the State*. New York: Harcourt, Brace & World, 1967.

Polishook, Irwin H. *Roger Williams, John Cotton, and Religious Freedom: A Controversy in New and Old England*. Englewood Cliffs, N.J.: Prentice-Hall, 1967.

THE BOOK OF COMMON PRAYER

Author: Thomas Cranmer and others
Original date and place of publication: 1549, England
Literary form: Religious text

SUMMARY

The Book of Common Prayer contains the prescribed forms of public worship for the Church of England and the churches of the Anglican Communion around the world. Known for the beauty of its language and its comprehensiveness as a source of religious thought, it was produced mainly by Thomas Cranmer, archbishop of Canterbury, who served King Henry VIII and his successor, Edward VI. Cranmer shaped the doctrine and liturgical transformation of the Church of England during Edward's reign.

In 1548, Cranmer presided over an assembly of scholars that convened to discuss the draft of the book he had prepared, which was based mainly on translations from the Sarum or Salisbury Missal rendered in Cranmer's sonorous prose. The book approved by the assembly reflected liturgical reforms based on Lutheran influences, such as the abolition of the elevation of the host during the Mass and elimination of the Mass's sacrificial nature. Cranmer's intention was to purge the service of innovations that had crept into it over the centuries and to return to the old practices of the primitive church. It also provided that the whole of the Mass was to be said in English, rather than in Latin, so that it could be better understood. This change was among those that aroused conservative religious revolts against the prayer book when it was put into use throughout England.

The Book of Common Prayer, brought into compulsory use in the Church of England in 1549 by act of Parliament, was the first complete service book in English to be published under one cover. It was revised by Cranmer in 1552, with the aid of Protestant reformers from the Continent, as the Second Prayer Book. This substantial revision altered baptism, confirmation and funeral services and swept away all traces of the old Mass.

It has been periodically revised over the centuries both in England and in the United States, where it is the prayer book of the Episcopal church. Controversial modern revisions have changed the language of Cranmer to make the book more relevant to contemporary concerns. It includes prayers, liturgies and scriptural readings for the sacraments, for all occasions, seasons and holy days. It also contains a catechism, historical documents of the church, including the Articles of Religion, and tables for finding the date of holy days.

CENSORSHIP HISTORY

Upon her accession to the throne in 1553, the Catholic Queen Mary I legally restored the Roman Catholic church in England and banned use of the Prayer Book. Cranmer was convicted of treason, then tried for heresy in 1555. He was excommunicated, degraded from his office as archbishop and sentenced to death. Cranmer signed six documents admitting the supremacy of the pope and the truth of all Roman Catholic doctrine except transubstantiation, but when asked to repeat his recantation in public at the stake, he refused. Along with two other leading Protestant reformers, Hugh Latimer and Nicholas Ridley, he was burned at the stake in Oxford on March 21, 1556.

In 1559, under Queen Elizabeth I, the Prayer Book of 1552 was restored in altered form. From 1645 to 1660, under the Puritan Commonwealth Protectorate and the rule of Oliver Cromwell, it was suppressed again. Despite government prohibition of its use, Anglican services were held freely and no systematic effort was made to enforce the ordinances against it.

In 1662, a new post-Restoration revision of the book was declared by King Charles II to be the only legal service book for use in England. It remains in use today in revised form. The Book of Common Prayer, adapted to fit the needs of the American community, was adopted in 1789 by the first general convention of the Protestant Episcopal church of the United States and is today the standard of faith and worship among Episcopalians.

Because it promulgated non-Catholic religious devotions, the Book of Common Prayer was placed on the Catholic Church's Index of Forbidden Books, where it remained through the first 20th-century edition prepared under Pope Leo XIII in 1897.

In 1975 the Prayer Book Society was formed in Britain to uphold the use of the 1662 edition and protest modern changes in Cranmer's language.

FURTHER READINGS

The Book of Common Prayer. New York: Seabury Press, 1977.

Jordan, W. K. *The Development of Religious Toleration in England.* Vol. 3. Gloucester, Mass.: Peter Smith, 1965.

Ridley, Jasper. *Thomas Cranmer.* Oxford: Clarendon Press, 1962.

Welsby, Paul A. *A History of the Church of England 1945–1980.* Oxford: Oxford University Press, 1984.

CHILDREN OF THE ALLEY

Author: Naguib Mahfouz
Original date and place of publication: 1959, Egypt; 1988, United States
Original publisher: *Al-Ahram* newspaper, Egypt; Three Continents Press, United States
Literary form: Novel

SUMMARY

The Egyptian author Naguib Mahfouz, awarded the Nobel Prize in literature in 1988, is the most celebrated contemporary Arab writer, with 35 novels and over a dozen collections of stories to his credit over the last half century. Many of Mahfouz's richly detailed novels portray life in Cairo's teeming working-class neighborhoods. Among them are the three novels of his masterpiece, *The Cairo Trilogy*, written between 1945 and 1957, chronicling the fortunes of three generations of a Cairo family.

Children of the Alley (also known by the title *Children of Gebelawi*) is the history of an imaginary Cairo alley and a retelling in allegorical form of the lives of Adam and Eve, Cain and Abel, and Moses, Jesus and Muhammad. The novel can be read on many levels. It is an evocative account of the vanished world of Mahfouz's childhood in the alleys of Gemalia in Cairo and an engrossing fictional narrative. It is also a fable that echoes the history of Judaism, Christianity and Islam, as well as a critique of religious intolerance and political and economic repression.

Narrated by an unnamed resident of the alley who is a professional writer, the story begins in the shadow of the mansion of Gabalawi, master of the estate at the foot of Muqattam mountain. Gabalawi, whose despotic presence looms over generations of his descendants, represents God, or as Mahfouz has said, a certain idea of God that people have created.

Gabalawi's son, Adham, and Adham's wife, Umaima, tempted and tricked by Adham's dissolute brother, Idris, are permanently expelled by Gabalawi from the mansion and its fragrant gardens for seeking a look at his forbidden book. One of their two sons, Qadri, kills the other, Humam, in a fight. Qadri marries Hind, the daughter of Idris. They have several children and from these ancestors all the people of the alley descend.

Gabalawi shuts himself away in his mansion and is not seen again. The management of his estate subsequently becomes a source of conflict. Though the estate's overseer at first follows the good example of Gabalawi, sharing its benefits with all the descendants, greed eventually gets the better of him and he exploits the poor. The neighborhood is run by young gangsters in the overseer's employ, who extort protection money from its hard-working inhabitants.

The first to rise up and rebel against injustice in the alley is the snake charmer Gabal, who defeats the gangsters and takes over leadership of the quarter. Gabal, who applies eye-for-an-eye justice, is honest and upright and shares the estate revenues equally, but he is also feared. He is a symbol of justice and order, but after his death, the era of the dishonest overseers and their threatening gangsters returns.

In another generation, a new leader—Rifaa, the carpenter's son—comes forth to preach against violence and materialism. He calls on Gabal's followers to trust him so that he can deliver them from evil spirits. Rifaa is murdered by the overseer and his gangsters, who see him as a threat to their social order.

A third leader, Qassem, eventually emerges from among the Desert Rats, the poorest and most wretched people of the neighborhood. He says that the people of the alley are all equally Gabalawi's children and the rule of gangsters must end. Following Rifaa's example, he ushers in an era of brotherhood and peace among the followers of Gabal, Rifaa and his own disciples. He proclaims that no neighborhood is more closely related to Gabalawi than any other and that the estate belongs to everyone.

But those who succeed Qassem as overseer return to the old system of violence and exploitation. The alley is again divided against itself, with separate quarters for the followers of Gabal, Rifaa and Qassem. "Gabalawi," the old man Shakrun cries out facing the mansion, "how long will you be silent and hidden? Your commandments are ignored and your money is being wasted. . . . Don't you know what has happened to us?"

Arafa, a magician, resolves to liberate the alley from the overseer's tyranny. He wants to find Gabalawi's book, the cause of Adham's exile, believing that it holds the magic secret of Gabalawi's power. When he breaks into the mansion to search for the book, he kills a servant. Having come in a quest for power to use against evil, he has turned into an evildoer.

In murdering a servant, Arafa indirectly kills Gabalawi, who dies from the shock of the murder in his house. The followers of Gabal, Rifaa and Qassem squabble over where Gabalawi should be buried, each group believing they have a closer relationship with their ancestor. The overseer instructs the storytellers to sing the story of Gabalawi, emphasizing how he died at the hands of Arafa. But the people favor Arafa and his magic, exalting his name above those of Gabel, Rifaa and Qassem. Gabalawi is dead, the people of the alley say: "We have nothing to do with the past. Our only hope lies in Arafa's magic, and if we had to choose between Gabalawi and magic, we'd choose magic." The final line of the book looks to the future with hope: "Injustice must have an end, as day must follow night. We will see the death of tyranny, and the dawn of light and miracles."

CENSORSHIP HISTORY

Children of the Alley was serialized in 1959 in the semiofficial Cairo newspaper *Al-Ahram*. Devout Muslims took to the streets in protest, demanding a ban because Mahfouz had suggested in allegorical fashion that the God of Adam, Moses, Jesus and Muhammad might be dead. It was only upon the intervention of Egypt's president, Abdul Nasser, a friend of *Al-Ahram*'s editor, Mohammed Heikal, that the serialization was published uncut to the end. However, the scholars of Cairo's powerful government-recognized religious authority, Al-Azhar University, banned *Children of the Alley*, condemning it as "blasphemous," and calling its author a heretic for causing offense to the prophets of Islam and for misrepresenting the character of Muhammad.

Since that time, militant Islamic groups have sustained a relentless campaign against the book and its author, which successfully ensured its banning for over three decades. *Children of the Alley* was passed from hand to hand in its newspaper version until 1967, when a pirated edition of the novel was published in Beirut, Lebanon, in slightly expurgated form. Smuggled into Egypt, it was sold under the counter at some Cairo bookstores.

In 1979, Mahfouz again incurred the wrath of Islamic fundamentalists in Egypt and elsewhere in the Arab world when he was among the first to support the peace treaty between Egypt and Israel. His novels were banned for several years in many Arab countries.

In 1988, Mahfouz won the Nobel Prize. Fundamentalists, who had never forgiven him for writing *Children of the Alley*, renewed their attacks, fearing that the prize would be used as a pretext to remove the book from the proscribed list. "The novel had basically been forgotten for a period of 30 years," Mahfouz said in a 1989 interview, "but following the prize it was subjected to very heavy attack in all the Islamicist-oriented newspapers and magazines. So the idea of publishing it here isn't even a topic for discussion."

Bolstered by Egyptian President Hosni Mubarak's statement that the novel should be published and the fact of its availability in much of the rest of the Arab world, renewed attempts were made to lift the ban on the book. But when the Egyptian monthly, *Al-Yasar*, began to serialize it in 1989, the Islamic press campaigned so virulently against it that Mahfouz himself asked the magazine to stop the serialization.

Mahfouz again ran afoul of militants that same year when he spoke out against Iran's Ayatollah Khomeini's edict calling for the death of British author Salman Rushdie for having written THE SATANIC VERSES. Sheikh Omar Abdel Rahman, the Egyptian fundamentalist leader of the militant Gamaat Islamia sect (who was later convicted in a plot to blow up New York City landmarks and assassinate U.S. political leaders), issued a statement calling on both Mahfouz and Rushdie to repent. "If they do not, they will be killed," he said. "If this sentence had been passed on Naguib Mahfouz when he wrote *Children of the Alley*, Salman Rushdie would have realized that he had to stay within certain bounds."

In June 1992, Islamist terrorists in Cairo shot and killed Farag Fouda, a prominent Egyptian secular writer, who, like Mahfouz, had spoken out against violent censorship. Shortly after Fouda's slaying, the Egyptian government uncovered a death list including Mahfouz and several other leading writers and intellectuals. Mahfouz was offered but declined police protection.

In early 1994, the weekly magazine *Rose el-Youssef* published extracts from several banned works, including *The Satanic Verses* and *Children of the Alley*, accompanied by a statement in defense of freedom of expression. Most Arab countries, with the exception of Egypt and Kuwait, banned the magazine's distribution. In October 1994, Mahfouz was stabbed several times in the neck as he sat in a car outside his Cairo home. (Two Islamic militants were convicted of attempted murder and executed, and others received lesser sentences.) Mahfouz has not regained full use of his right arm and hand since the assault and dictates his writings.

Shortly thereafter, the government's minister of information, speaking from Mahfouz's hospital bed, said the government did not support a ban on any of his works. His statement was interpreted as ending the official prohibition of *Children of the Alley*. As Egyptian newspapers rushed to serialize the novel, Mahfouz asked that publication come at a later time, fearing that his life would be further endangered. "The issue is diverting attention from a crime against my life to whether this novel is, or is not, against religion," he said. But his request was ignored. A few weeks after the attack, the novel was published in the Egyptian press for the first time in 35 years. As of mid-1997, however, the novel had not been published in book form in Egypt.

FURTHER READINGS

Appignanesi, Lisa, and Sara Maitland, eds. *The Rushdie File*. Syracuse, New York: Syracuse University Press, 1990.

Pipes, Daniel. *The Rushdie Affair*. New York: Carol Publishing Group, 1990.

Weaver, Mary Anne. "The Novelist and the Sheikh," *The New Yorker* (January 30, 1995): 52–59.

THE CHRISTIAN COMMONWEALTH

Author: John Eliot
Original date and place of publication: 1659, England
Literary form: Religious text

SUMMARY

John Eliot, who succeeded Roger Williams as the Anglican minister of the First Church of Roxbury, Massachusetts, gained fame for his missionary work among the Algonquian Indians, the original inhabitants of what became the Boston metropolitan area. While he is most widely known for translating the Bible into Algonquian, he also worked with Algonquian leaders to create a society run according to legal principles of the Old Testament. Eliot wrote the blueprint for such a government in a tract titled *The Christian Commonwealth: or, the Civil Policy of the Rising Kingdom of Jesus Christ.*

Eliot wrote *The Christian Commonwealth* before 1650, shortly after he learned Algonquian and began preaching to the Indians of the area in their own language. Perhaps as a way of discounting local chiefs' authority, Eliot's book emphasizes the ultimate power of God over all civil governments. For Eliot there is no separation of church and state. Because civil authorities acknowledge God's power, God's laws are the underpinning of laws passed by governments.

Yet Eliot did not intend for his work to convert only the Algonquians. In his preface, he exhorts his audience to "set the Crown of England upon the head of Christ, whose only true inheritance it is, by the gift of his father." In the same chapter, Eliot addresses the British tradition of the rights of elected governments when he writes, "It is the holy Scriptures of God only that I do urge, to be your only Magna Charta, by which you should be ruled in all things; which being, Christ is your King and Sovereign Lawgiver, and you are his people ruled by him in all things." Eliot uses specific examples of British laws to prove the importance of the Bible in underpinning earthly governments.

As Eliot wrote *The Christian Commonwealth*, Oliver Cromwell's reign as lord protector had brought radical changes to England. The English Revolution expanded political liberties and overthrew the monarchy, and Eliot took occasion to address those who might look for salvation in democracy. Eliot warns them: "And when a Christian people are to choose their Government, should they take their Patern from the Nations of the World, we know what an offence that would be to Christ, who intends to rule them himself, by his own Divine Patern and Direction."

Eliot stands clearly against democracy and secular government as an ideal. For these reasons, he was much more acceptable to the Puritan leadership of Roxbury than was the more radically democratic Roger Williams, whose BLOUDY TENENT OF PERSECUTION was burned in London by order of the British Parliament in 1644.

In the eight chapters of *The Christian Commonwealth*, Eliot discusses exactly how a political and legal system could be set up under biblical guidelines. He begins by stressing the hierarchy of the household, where the wife and children serve the husband. In Exodus 18:25, Jethro advises Moses on how the Israelites should govern themselves: They should elect men to represent groups of ten, 50, 100 and 1,000, with the rulers of ten handling the least consequential decisions, and the rulers of 1,000 responsible for the most important decisions. Eliot's belief in the Old Testament as a literal document led him to think that such a government could work for England, Ireland and Scotland.

Eliot's role as a missionary to the Algonquians gave him an opportunity to create a "Christian commonwealth" of his own. In 1651, he helped the Algonquian Speene family organize the Christian Indian village of Natick, near Boston. Fewer than 150 people lived in Natick, a population small enough to experiment with Eliot's Old Testament system of governance. According to the few surviving mentions of life in Natick, the system worked for the small community. The Indians who settled Natick had lived among the English for several decades and had already begun to adopt English dress and language. The community agreed with Eliot's idea that all true governing power comes from a divine source, and in September 1651 they assembled to take an oath affirming their status as a holy town. Their special form of governance lasted until 1675–76, when white settlements took over the village.

CENSORSHIP HISTORY

In 1651, Eliot sent *The Christian Commonwealth* back to England, hoping to publish it there, but the book did not appear until eight years later. However, King Charles II, who was restored to the throne in 1660, did not appreciate a religious work which stated that even royal authorities owed their power to a higher source.

Livewell Chapman, Eliot's publisher, tried to avert censorship by including a disclaimer on the book's title page. Under Eliot's full title, Chapman included a note that the book was "Written Before the Interruption of the Government. . . . And Now Published by a Server of the Season." By 1661, copies of the book had made their way back to Massachusetts and, in spite of Chapman's efforts to appease royal suspicions, the Massachusetts general court feared that Eliot's ideas could be misconstrued by the king or his ministers. On May 30 of that year they ordered the book suppressed. Within two weeks, any Massachusetts citizen who owned copies of the banned work had to "cancel or deface" them or bring them to local judges, who would then dispose of them.

Eliot admitted that he had made some mistakes in his work, but stood by his original principles, claiming in a statement to the Massachusetts general court that "All forms of Government . . . [are] from God . . . and whatsoever in the whole epistle or book is inconsistent therewith, I do at once most cordially disown." While the judges had hoped that he would admit guilt for denying the king's power, Eliot apologized only for any errors he might have made in his interpretation of Scripture.

Evidently, Eliot's nonadmission of guilt satisfied the court. There is no further record of Eliot being punished by Massachusetts authorities for *The Christian Commonwealth*. He continued to live and work in Roxbury for almost 30 years after his trial. The residents of Roxbury and Natick regarded him fondly for his deep religious faith and his service to the members of the two communities. As in the case of Springfield merchant and amateur theologian William Pynchon, whose MERITORIOUS PRICE OF OUR REDEMPTION was the first work to be publicly burned in North America, Eliot's experience shows how even the most upstanding citizen of early Massachusetts could become a victim of censorship.

FURTHER READING

Winslow, Ola Elizabeth. *John Eliot, "Apostle to the Indians."* Boston: Houghton Mifflin Company, 1968.

CHRISTIANITY NOT MYSTERIOUS

Author: John Toland
Original date and place of publication: 1696, England
Literary form: Religious treatise

SUMMARY

The Irish deist John Toland was brought up as a Roman Catholic and became a Protestant at age 16, before later declaring his affinities for deism and pantheism. He studied at the universities of Glasgow, Edinburgh and Leiden and earned his living as a writer and publicist for radical Whig causes. Toland wrote nearly 200 works The most important of these is *Christianity Not Mysterious*, published in 1696, a book that launched the deist controversy. Deists held that the course of nature alone was sufficient to demonstrate the existence of God. Formal religion was superfluous and the claims of supernatural revelation were scorned as spurious.

In *Christianity Not Mysterious*, Toland attempts to reconcile the scriptural claims of Christianity with John Locke's theory of knowledge as revealed in AN ESSAY CONCERNING HUMAN UNDERSTANDING, asserting that neither God nor revelation is above the comprehension of human reason. The book's purpose is indicated in its subtitle: *A Treatise Shewing, That There is Nothing in the Gospel Contrary to Reason, Nor Above it; And That No Christian Doctrine Can Be Properly Call'd A Mystery*.

On the title page Toland quotes Archbishop Tillotson, a liberal Anglican admired by deists: "We need not desire a better Evidence that any Man is in the wrong, than to hear him declare against Reason, and thereby acknowledg[e] that Reason is against him." Toland believed that revelation is a "means of information," rather than a "motive of assent." The Bible should be assessed critically by each person who reads it. "Since Religion is not calculated for reasonable Creatures," he wrote, "'tis Conviction and not Authority that should bear Weight with them. A wise and good Man will judg[e] of the Merits of a Cause consider'd only in itself, without any regard to Times, Places, or Persons."

Toland insists that everything, including religious revelation, must pass the test of reason or be rejected: "I hold nothing as an Article of my Religion, but what the highest Evidence forc'd me to embrace." Only reason enables people to distinguish between fact and fancy, between what is certain and what is only probable. Toland suggests that God, who endowed human beings with the faculty of reason, would not require belief in the irrational as a condition of salvation. Much of the Bible must be interpreted symbolically, otherwise "the highest Follies and Blasphemies" can be drawn from the letter of Scripture.

Toland concludes *Christianity Not Mysterious* with an expression of the deist's credo: "I acknowledge no ORTHODOXY but the TRUTH; and,

I'm sure, where-ever the TRUTH is there must also [be] the CHURCH, of God. . . ."

CENSORSHIP HISTORY

Christianity Not Mysterious was published anonymously in 1695, after expiration of the book censorship provisions of the Licensing Act of 1662. Though Toland insisted that he was a sincere Christian who wished only to purge Christianity of its mysteries and restore it to a rational condition, his critics saw *Christianity Not Mysterious* as a blasphemous expression of the Socianian heresy, which denied the doctrine of the Holy Trinity. The book was described as the first act of warfare between deists and those who held more orthodox Christian views.

By the late summer of 1696, Toland decided to allow his name to be attached to the book, which was rapidly becoming notorious. By publicly claiming authorship, Toland became a visible target for the heretic hunters. The book was presented by the grand jury of Middlesex, England, but Toland fled to Ireland and escaped criminal or civil penalties. Intense hostility against him in Ireland, led by clergy who viewed the book as denying Christ's divinity, resulted in action by an Irish grand jury. The archbishop of Dublin called on the civil arm of government to "suppress his Insolence." In 1697, the Irish Parliament, acting on the report of an investigating committee, condemned *Christianity Not Mysterious* as heretical and ordered it burned by the public hangman. The government also ordered Toland's arrest and prosecution by the attorney general. He returned in haste to England, where he remained in hiding.

Toland's book infuriated orthodox Christians. The profusion of deistic, anti-Trinitarian books such as *Christianity Not Mysterious* led the House of Commons to press for the passage of a new anti-blasphemy statute. The act, adopted in 1698 "for the more effectual suppressing of Blasphemy," provided that any person who professed to be a Christian would be convicted of blasphemy if he denied in conversation or in writing that any one of the persons of the Holy Trinity was God, that the Christian religion was true or that the Bible had divine authority. The punishment for a first offense was denial of civil, military or ecclesiastical employment. A second offense would cost the loss of all civil rights and three years in prison without bail. In 1699 Toland decided to take a journey to Holland until the furor over his book had abated.

The act of 1698 remained in effect until 1967, when it was revoked by Parliament. The common law of blasphemy, however, based on judicial precedents dating from 1676 to 1921, still existed. It became a subject of debate in Britain in the 1980s during the controversy over the censorship of Salman Rushdie's SATANIC VERSES, when an unsuccessful campaign was launched by Muslim organizations in Britain to extend the common law against blasphemy to protect all religions.

FURTHER READINGS

Levy, Leonard W. *Blasphemy: Verbal Offense Against the Sacred, from Moses to Salman Rushdie*. New York: Alfred A. Knopf, 1993.

Smith, George H. *Atheism, Ayn Rand and Other Heresies*. Buffalo: Prometheus Books, 1991.

Sullivan, Robert E. *John Toland and the Deist Controversy. A Study in Adaptations*. Cambridge, Mass.: Harvard University Press, 1982.

CHRISTIANITY RESTORED

Author: Michael Servetus
Original date and place of publication: 1552, France
Literary form: Theological treatise

SUMMARY

The Spanish theologian and physician Michael Servetus earned his reputation for religious deviationism at the age of 20. During his law studies at Toulouse, France, he had discovered in the Scriptures the historical person of Jesus of Nazareth, leading him to reject traditional formulations of the nature of Christ and the relationship of the three persons of the Trinity.

Servetus believed that Protestant reformers Luther, Calvin and Zwingli were not revolutionary enough, because they accepted the doctrine of the Trinity, which he viewed as incomprehensible. Failing to convince the reformers in Basel and Strasbourg of his ideas, Servetus decided to write a book that would persuade all Christians of the truth of his discoveries.

In 1531, he published *On the Errors of the Trinity*, a treatise asserting that traditional Scholastic theology introduced Greek philosophical terms and nonbiblical concepts into the definitions of the Trinity that were abstract, speculative and unrelated to the living God. "Not one word is found in the whole Bible about the Trinity, nor about its Persons, nor about an Essence, nor about a unity of the Substance, nor about one Nature of the several beings," he wrote. Orthodox Catholics and many Protestants viewed Servetus's theology as having revived the fourth-century heresy of Arianism, which denied the doctrine of the Trinity by teaching that Jesus as the Son of God was neither equal to nor eternal with God the Father.

In 1552, Servetus recast his earlier tracts in a new book, *Christianity Restored*. It contained a revised edition of *On the Errors of the Trinity* and new material, including 30 letters on theology that he had sent to John Calvin. In *Christianity Restored* Servetus challenged the established churches, both Catholic and Protestant, to return Christendom to the purity of its origins: "A calling of the whole apostolic church to make a fresh start, restored completely in the knowledge of God, the faith of Christ, our justification, regeneration, baptism, and the Lord's Supper. Our restoration finally in the kingdom of heaven, with the loosing of the captivity of ungodly Babylon and Antichrist and his own destroyed."

In the new work he claimed that Christianity had failed because it had become corrupted in the early fourth century by pagan doctrines and by the church's acquisition of temporal power. He attacked the definition of the Trinity established by the church's Council of Nicaea in the fourth century, as well as the practice of infant baptism, which he termed as unchristian. He accepted the heretical Anabaptist tenet that baptism should be deferred until maturity, when a sinner has experienced Christ and repented. Christ himself was not baptized until he was an adult, Servetus wrote, and becoming a Christian meant sharing a spiritual communion that an infant could not understand.

CENSORSHIP HISTORY

The publication in 1531 of *On the Errors of the Trinity* made Servetus notorious and a hunted man, threatened by both the French and Spanish Inquisitions and the Protestants, who banned his book and closed cities to him. In 1532, the Inquisition in Toulouse issued a decree ordering his arrest. He went underground in Paris and assumed a new identity, adopting the name of Michel de Villeneuve, from the family home of Villanueva, Spain. Fear of persecution in Paris drove him to Lyons, where he worked as a printer's editor, eventually settling in 1540 in the Lyons suburb of Vienne.

Using his own name, Servetus began to correspond with Protestant reformer John Calvin in Geneva, instructing him on theology. In all he sent 30 epistolary discourses to Calvin. Calvin sent him a copy of his INSTITUTES OF THE CHRISTIAN RELIGION, which Servetus boldly returned annotated with criticisms. Servetus also presented Calvin with a manuscript copy of part of *Christianity Restored*, apparently hoping that Calvin would view it favorably.

A thousand copies of *Christianity Restored* were printed anonymously and in secret in Vienne by the publishers Arnoullet and Guéroult in 1552 after publishers in Basel refused to have anything to do with the book. Some copies were sent to the Frankfurt book fair and others to a bookseller in Geneva. There a copy came into the hands of Calvin's colleague, Guillaume Trie, who forwarded the first four leaves of the book to a Catholic cousin in Lyons, revealing Villeneuve's identity and location in Vienne. The cousin placed the material in the hands of the Inquisition, which began an investigation.

Servetus and his publisher Arnoullet denied any knowledge of the book. But at the request of the Inquisition, Trie provided the investigators the manuscript copy of the book sent by Servetus to Calvin, implicating Servetus. Servetus was arrested and held for trial, but escaped. In June 1553, the civil tribunal of Lyons condemned him in absentia for heresy, sedition, rebellion and evasion of prison, fining him 2,000 *livres* and sentencing him to be burned. In his absence, bales of copies of his books were incinerated with his effigy. His publisher was imprisoned.

In August, on his way to seek refuge in Italy, Servetus passed through Geneva, Calvin's stronghold. There he was recognized and, on Calvin's orders, arrested. Charged with 39 counts of heresy and blasphemy, for more than two months he stood trial before the judges of the Geneva city council. The verdict of the council was that the book Servetus had secretly printed in Vienne had spread "heresies and horrible, execrable blasphemies against the Holy Trinity, against the Son of God, against the baptism of infants and foundations of the Christian religion." The Geneva authorities consulted the magistrates of all the Swiss cantons, who unanimously agreed on the verdict.

Servetus was sentenced to be burned to ashes with his book for trying "to infect the world with [his] stinking heretical poison." The verdict stated further, "And so you shall finish your days and give an example to others who would commit the like." Servetus's last request was to see Calvin. "I told him to beg the pardon of the son of God, whom he had disfigured with his dreams . . .," Calvin reported. "But when I saw that all this did no good I did not wish to be wiser than my Master allows. So following the rule of St. Paul, I withdrew from the heretic who was self-condemned."

Servetus asked to die by the sword, rather than by burning. Although Calvin supported this request for mercy, it was denied by the magistrates. "He asked forgiveness for his errors, ignorance and sins, but never made a full confession," wrote Calvin's colleague, Guillaume Farel. "But we could never get him openly to admit his errors and confess that Christ is the eternal son of God." On October 27, 1553, Servetus was burned at the stake.

Calvin urged the destruction of *Christianity Restored* in Protestant countries, as it contained "prodigious blasphemies against God." Only three copies survived. In part the tragic result of a power struggle between Calvin and his opponents, Servetus's execution damaged Calvin's reputation. As church historian Roland H. Bainton wrote, Servetus had "the singular distinction of having been burned by the Catholics in effigy and by the Protestants in actuality." Servetus was the first person to be executed as a heretic on the authority of a reformed church. His martyrdom came to have a significance greater than any other in his century, as it marked the first important controversy over the issue of toleration within Protestantism.

The movement on behalf of toleration, reflected in Sebastian Castellio's CONCERNING HERETICS AND HOW THEY ARE TO BE TREATED, was galvanized by widespread revulsion at Servetus's punishment. Yet the systematic repression of *Christianity Restored* minimized Servetus's posthumous influence on religious thought. Almost two centuries later, Richard Mead, the physician to the king of England, tried to publish Servetus's work. In 1723, the government seized and burned the whole printing and imprisoned Mead and his printer.

FURTHER READINGS

Bainton, Roland H. *Hunted Heretic: The Life and Death of Michael Servetus.* Gloucester, Mass.: Peter Smith, 1978.

Christie-Murray, David. *A History of Heresy.* Oxford: Oxford University Press, 1989.

Haight, Anne Lyon. *Banned Books: 387 BC to 1978 AD.* Updated and enlarged by Chandler B. Grannis. New York: R. R. Bowker, 1978.

Levy, Leonard W. *Blasphemy: Verbal Offense Against the Sacred, from Moses to Salman Rushdie.* New York: Alfred A. Knopf, 1993.

Parker, T. H. L. *John Calvin.* Batavia, Ill.: Lion Publishing Corporation, 1975.

Smith, George H. *Atheism, Ayn Rand, and Other Heresies.* Buffalo: Prometheus Books, 1991.

Spitz, Lewis W., ed. *The Protestant Reformation.* Englewood Cliffs, N.J.: Prentice-Hall, 1966.

CHURCH: CHARISM AND POWER: LIBERATION THEOLOGY AND THE INSTITUTIONAL CHURCH

Author: Leonardo Boff
Original date and place of publication: 1981, Brazil; 1985, United States
Original publisher: Editora Vôzes, Brazil; Crossroad, United States
Literary form: Theological essays

SUMMARY

The Brazilian Catholic theologian Leonardo Boff is among the leading exponents of liberation theology, an interpretation of Christian faith drawn from the experience of the poor. *Church: Charism and Power*, a collection of essays, speeches and lecture notes, contains some of the sharpest criticisms of the Roman Catholic church to come from Latin America. Boff argues from his experience with the poor in Brazilian base communities—grassroots, Catholic communities led by laity. He urges institutional reform of Catholicism and its transformation into a "liberation Church," not simply *for* the poor, but *of* the poor. Criticizing abuse of hierarchical power, he calls for a return to the collegial structure of early church communities, in which both clergy and laity exercised power.

Boff's central thesis is that the struggle for justice and human rights cannot be separated from a similar struggle within the church itself. The preferential option for the poor demands shifts within Catholicism. The institutional church must move away from its reliance on power and coercion and toward a democratic model of openness and tolerance, the original model upon which Christ founded the church. Boff contends that the church hierarchy took its form only after Jesus' death. When Christianity became the official religion of the Roman empire, the church began to reflect the empire's feudal structure of authority, including its institutions, laws and bureaucratic centralization.

Boff distinguishes between two kinds of power: *exousia*, the power of love employed by Jesus, and *potestas*, the power to dominate and rule that characterized Roman officialdom. He describes the exercise of *potestas* by the clergy and the division between the clergy and the laity as a cancer within the church. The charismatic essence of the church, in which everyone has a charism, or gift, to offer, has been extinguished. "Christianity is not against power in itself," Boff writes, "but its diabolical forms which show themselves as dominion and control." Using Marxist terminology, Boff refers to the "gradual expropriation of the spiritual means of production from the Christian people by the clergy."

The church must contain charisms, such as teaching, serving, preaching and administering, as well as power. The papacy does have a special position within the church in maintaining doctrinal unity based on the emerging consensus of the community. Power can be a charism, Boff believes, as long as it serves everyone and is an instrument for building justice in the community.

CENSORSHIP HISTORY

Boff's orthodoxy already had been investigated by the Vatican in 1976 and again in 1980 on suspicion of doctrinal deviation. The 1980 investigation centered on his book *Jesus Christ, the Liberator*. But the Vatican had been generally willing to leave the question of orthodoxy of individual Latin American theologians to their own bishops.

When *Church: Charism and Power* was published in Brazil, Spain and Italy in 1981, it was not expected to spark widespread debate. It was a further development of ideas expressed in Boff's doctoral thesis and in a previous book on ecclesiology, or the study of the structure of the church. Boff was not optimistic that the book, a loosely connected collection of disparate writings and talks rather than a comprehensive analysis, would find an audience.

Almost immediately, however, the book provoked an unusual amount of discussion. Boff had applied the insights of liberation theology, previously directed at the reform of secular society, to the church itself. His choice of the words "symbolic violence" to refer to the Vatican's methods for discouraging dissent and his use of quasi-Marxist terminology to analyze the church's structure angered critics.

In the book, he quotes at length a Brazilian Catholic who makes a point-by-point parallel between Kremlin and Vatican styles of governance. In another highly controversial passage, he writes: "It is strange to see that the Church institution has developed into exactly that which Christ did not want it to be."

Boff had earlier described the Vatican's Congregation for the Doctrine of the Faith as relying on procedures that are unacceptable in civil society, a "Kafkaesque process wherein the accuser, defender, the lawyer and judge are one and the same." In 1982, a similar process was initiated to investigate Boff's views.

In February 1982, Boff, who knew that his critics had already complained to the Vatican, mailed to Rome as a courtesy a copy of some negative reviews of his book and a response by Father Urbano Zilles of Brazil. Three months later, he received a letter from Joseph Cardinal Ratzinger, Prefect of the Congregation for the Doctrine of the Faith, asking him to respond to criticisms. He wrote a response and published it.

In May 1984, Boff received a six-page letter from Ratzinger criticizing Boff's views as expressed in the book and saying they "did not merit acceptance." The letter referred to Boff's theological method, his analysis of church structure, his concepts of dogma and revelation and his description of the exercise of power in the church. It criticized his "ecclesiastical relativism" and his "sociological" analysis. Ratzinger accused Boff of using language that was "polemic, defamatory and pamphleteering, absolutely inappropriate for a theologian," drawing on "ideological principles of a certain neo-Marxist inspiration," proposing "a certain revolutionary utopia which is foreign to the church" and holding a "relativizing conception" of church structure and doctrine.

Boff replied with a 50-page document, insisting that he wrote "only to right the balance in the direction of the experience of the laity, the poor, and the contributions of the social sciences." He concluded, "Of one thing I am sure: I prefer to walk in the church than go it alone with my theology. The church is a reality of Faith that I assume. Theology is a product of reason that I discuss."

Rather than going through the Brazilian bishops, who would have supported Boff, Ratzinger summoned him to Rome for a "colloquy" in September 1984. Boff took with him to Rome petitions signed by 50,000 Brazilians and was accompanied by two Brazilian cardinals, who came to show their support. Although Boff would not have selected *Church: Charism and Power* to fully represent his ideas, the colloquy turned out to be a full-scale interrogation on his views as expressed in the book.

In March 1985, the congregation published a Notification, making public the letter Ratzinger had sent the previous year and labeling it an official public notification approved by the pope. The congregation stated that its reservations about his book "had not been substantially overcome" and that Boff was guilty of three errors: his statement that the church borrowed societal characteristics from contemporary Roman and later feudal society; his relativistic interpretation of dogma as good for specific circumstances and times; and his statements that clergy had expropriated spiritual means of production from the laity. "The options of Leonardo Boff analyzed herein endanger the sound doctrine of the Faith which this congregation has the task of promoting and safeguarding," the Notification concluded.

In May 1985, Boff received an official notice from the congregation ordering him to begin immediately to observe an "obedient silence" for an unspecified period of time. The notice stated that the period of silence "would permit Friar Boff a time for serious reflection." It required him to abstain completely from writing and publishing, from his duties as editor of the *Revista Ecclesiastica Brasileira*, the most influential theological journal in Brazil, from his work as editor of books on theology at the publishing house Editora Vôzes and from teaching or lecturing. Boff submitted to the silencing, saying, "As a Christian, Franciscan friar and theologian, it is for me to listen and adhere."

Ten Brazilian bishops, who viewed the Vatican's attack on one of liberation theology's most prominent figures as an unwelcome intrusion of Rome into Latin American matters and a threat to the right of Catholics to think and write freely, took the highly unusual step of publicly criticizing the Vatican's treatment of Boff. Senior Brazilian bishops met with Pope John Paul II in Rome during March 1986. That month, after ten months of the silencing, Boff's punishment was lifted. Boff said he received the news of the lifting of the silence "as an Easter present" and was sure that it was a gesture of good will on the part of the Vatican toward the bishops of Brazil.

In 1991, Boff published a series of articles calling for change in the church's prohibition against marriage for priests. When church officials denied approval for publication of his next manuscript, he resigned from the priesthood. In an open letter to his followers he wrote, "I am leaving the priestly ministry, but not the church. . . . I continue to be and will always be a theologian in the Catholic and ecumenical mold, fighting with the poor against their poverty and in favor of their liberation."

FURTHER READINGS

Cox, Harvey. *The Silencing of Leonardo Boff: The Vatican and the Future of World Christianity*. Oak Park, Ill.: Meyer Stone Books, 1988.

Sigmund, Paul E. *Liberation Theology at the Crossroads: Democracy or Revolution?* New York: Oxford University Press, 1990.

COLLOQUIES

Author: Desiderius Erasmus
Original date and place of publication: 1518–33, Switzerland
Literary form: Essays

SUMMARY

The Dutch writer and biblical scholar Desiderius Erasmus, an influential proponent of the values of Christian humanism, was a critic of abuses within the Catholic church. He advocated the practice of a simpler, purer Christianity, purged of superstition, corruption and meaningless ceremonies. Among his main works were *Adages* (1500), a collection of classical proverbs; *The Handbook of the Christian Soldier* (1503), a manual of piety taken from Christ's teachings; THE PRAISE OF FOLLY (1511), a satire on theologians and church dignitaries; *Education of a Christian Prince* (1516) and a translation into Latin of the Greek New Testament (1516).

Colloquies, a collection of informal conversations or dialogues on contemporary issues, had its origins during the years 1495 to 1499 when Erasmus supported himself in Paris by tutoring Latin. He prepared some simple exercises for his pupils to improve their writing and conversation. Some 20 years later, in 1518, to Erasmus's surprise and annoyance, the exercises were published in Basel without his authorization by Johannes Froben, then reprinted in Paris and Antwerp. The book became a popular textbook for the study of Latin.

Erasmus wrote in 1523: "There had also appeared a small book of 'Colloquies' pieced together partly from familiar conversation and partly from my notes, but with a certain amount of nonsense thrown in which was not only foolish but bad Latin and simply packed with blunders; and this worthless piece was given a surprisingly warm welcome. . . . At length, by taking more than ordinary pains, I added a good deal, to bring it up to the right size for a book." In 1519, Erasmus had the thin volume reissued, with some corrections and his own preface.

Beginning with the 1522 edition, the character of the book changed as Erasmus began to make significant additions to the text, with new dialogues containing elements of social criticism directed as much to adults as to students. Between 1522 and 1533, 12 new expanded editions of the book were published.

The final edition contained some 50 colloquies. Many of them were humorous diversions; others represented lively debates on the moral, religious and political issues of the day, from discussions of methods of study, sleep and diet and amusing accounts of the passing scene to sober and provocative reflections on ethics, government, marriage and money. "Socrates brought philosophy down from heaven to earth," Erasmus said of his *Colloquies*. "I have brought it even into games, informal conversations, and drinking parties."

Many pages in the *Colloquies* made pointed reference to the religious controversies of the day and criticized superstition and lack of spirituality in the church. In "Cyclops," a character who refers to the calamities of the times says, "Kings make war, priests are zealous to increase their wealth, theologians invent syllogisms, monks roam throughout the world, the commons riot, Erasmus writes colloquies."

In "The Godly Feast," in a passage that was censored by the Sorbonne, Erasmus wrote, "Hence those who adorn monasteries or churches at excessive cost, while meanwhile so many of Christ's living temples are in danger of starving, shiver in their nakedness, and are tortured by want of necessities, seem to me almost guilty of a capital crime." It was this thread of social criticism running through many of the dialogues of the *Colloquies* that led to its censorship.

CENSORSHIP HISTORY

Colloquies became a bestseller in Europe, with at least 100 editions printed before Erasmus's death in 1536. Erasmus wrote of the book, "And to be sure, as long as there was nothing in that book but the merest trifles, it found surprising favour on all sides. When it began to be useful in many ways, it could not escape the poison-fangs of slander."

After the emergence of Lutheranism, whatever he wrote that related to criticism or reform of the church was closely scrutinized. Erasmus was repeatedly compelled to defend the *Colloquies*. Its critics alleged that certain passages were indecent and that his portrayals of the hypocrisy of monks, friars and prelates and his attacks on superstition and ignorance were irreverent and heretical.

In 1526 the Sorbonne, the theological faculty of the University of Paris and the most influential body of theologians in Europe, took action. In a petition to the Parlement of Paris, it formally censured *Colloquies*, along with passages from other writings by Erasmus viewed as promoting Lutheranism. Condemning 69 pages as "erroneous, scandalous or impious," it described Erasmus as "a pagan who mocks at the Christian religion and its sacred rites and customs." The Sorbonne recommended that the book be forbidden to all, especially to youth, lest it corrupt their morals. In 1528, the university forbade regents to use the *Colloquies* in their teaching.

In 1535, King Charles V of Spain made it a capital offense to use *Colloquies* in schools. Three years later, an eccesiastical commission appointed by Pope Paul III recommended that the *Colloquies* "and any other book of this sort" be prohibited as "injurious to youthful minds." When the Index of Forbidden Books was established in 1559 by Pope Paul IV, the *Colloquies* was included, along with all of Erasmus's other work. The Tridentine Index of 1564, issued by the Council of Trent, removed some of Erasmus's writings from the proscribed list, but the *Colloquies* remained condemned.

Subsequent Indexes in Rome and Spain maintained the bans on the *Colloquies*, and Erasmus was listed on the Index of Forbidden Books until 1930. Nevertheless, the book continued to be widely read and translated for three centuries, as long as Latin was the basis of study in schools and the accepted international language among the educated.

FURTHER READINGS

Erasmus, Desiderius. *The Colloquies of Erasmus*. Trans. and intro. by Craig R. Thompson. Chicago: University of Chicago Press, 1965.

———. *Ten Colloquies of Erasmus*. Trans. and intro. by Craig R. Thompson. New York: Liberal Arts Press, 1957.

Rummel, Erika, ed. *The Erasmus Reader*. Toronto: University of Toronto Press, 1990.

COMMENTARIES

Author: Averroës
Original date and place of publication: 1168–90, Spain and Morocco
Literary form: Philosophical commentaries

SUMMARY

The 12th-century Spanish-Arab philosopher and physician Ibn Rushd, known as Averroës, is among the outstanding figures of medieval philosophy. Born in Córdoba, Spain, into a family of distinguished judges, Averroës was trained in the legal tradition and in theology, medicine and philosophy. He held judicial posts under the Almohad dynasty (Arab Islamic rulers of Spain and Morocco), first in Seville and later in Córdoba, and became physician to the caliph in 1182.

His extensive commentaries on the works of Aristotle, translated into Latin in the early 13th century, had a great influence on the development of medieval Scholasticism. Averroist schools sprang up at many of the leading universities of Europe. His commentaries rendered Aristotle accessible at a time when knowledge of his writing in the Western world was fragmentary. He also played a crucial role in the transmission of classical philosophy to Islam. In less technical works, such as the *Incoherence of the Incoherence and the Decisive Treatise*, he defended philosophy against charges that it opposed the teachings of the Koran.

Convinced that the genius of Aristotle represented the model of human perfection, Averroës devoted many years to writing his greatest work, in the form of commentaries presenting and interpreting the thought of Aristotle. They can be categorized in three classes: the greater commentaries, in which Averroës presents Aristotle's original text along with comments on it; the middle or lesser commentaries, reproducing only the opening words of particular paragraphs of the Aristotelian text, with extensive interpretation by Averroës; and the little commentaries or paraphrases, in which Averroës gives only Aristotle's conclusions, omitting proofs and historical references.

In his interpretation of Aristotle, Averroës contributed his own philosophy. As a Muslim who believed that philosophy was the highest form of inquiry and Aristotle the author of a system representing the supreme truth, he attempted to delimit the separate domains of faith and reason. He held that the two need not be reconciled, because they did not conflict but rather followed parallel paths, arriving at the same goals. The same truth is expressed allegorically in theology and understood clearly in philosophy.

Religious teaching expresses truth to the unlettered ordinary person, while philosophy attains it through the use of pure reason for those with the mental ability to understand it. Averroës's theory, later described as a doctrine of "double truth," allowed science to advance and the free mind to inquire without fetters imposed by either Islam or Christianity.

CENSORSHIP HISTORY

While the Almohad monarch Youssef the Wise ruled in Spain and Morocco, Averroës was protected from orthodox Islamic theologians who opposed the study of philosophy. When rule of the empire passed to Youssef's son, Yacoub el Mansour, Averroës at first continued to hold positions of honor as either *cadi* or court physician in Seville and in Morocco. El Mansour, however, succumbed to the pressure of theological scholars and the reaction against philosophy. Averroës was stripped of his honors, banished from court and imprisoned until a few years before his death in Marrakesh in 1198, when he was reinstated and his honors restored.

The Averroistic interpretation of Aristotle remained influential in western Europe long after his death. By the end of the 12th century, most of his works were available to the Christian world in Latin translation and he was widely known as "the Commentator." His admirer, the Franciscan philosopher Roger Bacon, recommended the study of Arabic at 13th-century Oxford so that students could read Averroës in the original. Emperor Frederic II welcomed Michael Scott, the first translator of Averroës into Latin, to his Sicilian court in defiance of the church, which was alarmed by Averroist thinking.

The dissemination of Aristotelian thought, accompanied by Averroës's commentaries emphasizing its nonreligious character, precipitated a grave crisis for the church. Averroism represented a challenge to religious authority, for it allowed philosophy to claim access to truth outside established religious sources. One of the central controversies of 13th-century thought concerned his theory of "double truth." Saint Thomas Aquinas, Italian philosopher and theologian and the greatest figure of Scholasticism, was respectful of Averroës, but attacked the Averroist contention that philosophical truth is derived from reason and not from faith. While Aquinas vindicated the rights of reason against those who wished to suppress Aristotle's thought, he opposed the Averroist views that would separate faith and truth absolutely.

He held that reason and faith constitute two harmonious realms and that reason gives a rational content to faith.

Thirteenth-century Scholastics concluded, from reading Averroës's commentary on Aristotle's *De Anima*, that Averroës rejected the reality of individual intellect, thus denying personal immortality. Averroës was led by his understanding of Aristotle to postulate that there is one intellect for all people, which is not a soul. The soul does not survive the death of the body and the world has not been created, but is eternal.

In *De unitate intellectus contra Averroistas* Aquinas argued that if the Averroistic theory is accepted, "it follows that after death nothing remains of men's souls but one intellect; and in this way the bestowal of rewards and punishments is done away with." Averroistic theory was incompatible with Christian doctrines of immortality and of sanctions in the next life.

In 1210, bishops who were gathered at the Provincial Council of Paris forbade the public or private teaching of the natural philosophy and THE METAPHYSICS of Aristotle, or commentaries on them. The ban applied to instruction at the University of Paris, the most important center of higher education in Christendom, and was imposed under penalty of excommunication. The ban was reiterated by the papal legate, Robert de Curzon, in 1215. Averroës's commentaries were condemned as the "unholy gloss of infidels." In 1231, Pope Gregory IX prohibited the reading of the works of Aristotle until they were purged of heresy and appointed a commission of theologians to correct them. By 1245, the prohibition was extended to Toulouse by Innocent IV.

These interdictions were gradually lifted when they became impossible to enforce. It is recorded that Roger Bacon lectured on Aristotle as a member of the arts faculty at Paris between 1241 and 1247. By 1255, all the known works of Aristotle and the commentaries on them were officially taught there. Though Averroist doctrines on "double truth," personal immortality and eternity of matter were again condemned by the pope in 1263 and by the bishop of Paris in 1277, his interpretations of Aristotle remained influential throughout the later Middle Ages and the Renaissance.

FURTHER READINGS

Bokenkotter, Thomas. *A Concise History of the Catholic Church*. New York: Doubleday, 1977.

Copleston, Frederick. *A History of Philosophy*. Vol. 2, *Medieval Philosophy*. New York: Doubleday, 1993.

Hoffman, Eleanor. *Realm of the Evening Star: A History of Morocco and the Lands of the Moors*. Philadelphia: Chilton Books, 1965.

Landau, Rom. *Morocco*. New York: G. P. Putnam's Sons, 1967.

Urvoy, Dominique. *Ibn Rushd (Averroës)*. Trans. by Olivia Steward. Cairo: American University in Cairo Press, 1993.

Wippel, John F., and Allan B. Wolter, eds. *Medieval Philosophy: From St. Augustine to Nicholas of Cusa*. New York: Free Press, 1969.

COMPENDIUM REVELATIONUM

Author: Girolamo Savonarola
Original date and place of publication: 1495, Italy
Literary form: Religious treatise

SUMMARY

Dominican monk and religious reformer Girolamo Savonarola, perhaps the best known heretic of the Renaissance, made his mark as a charismatic preacher in Florence soon after he was sent there by the Dominican order in 1490. Calling for a regeneration of spiritual and moral values, he warned in his fiery sermons that a great scourge was about to descend on the city. He declared that the wickedness he observed in Florence—the corruption of the church, the excesses of the wealthy and their exploitation of the poor—was proof that the message of the Apocalypse was soon to be fulfilled.

After the expulsion in 1494 of the Medicis, Florence's ruling family, Savonarola became the spiritual leader of the city and wielded great influence in the new government. Savonarola urged the Florentines who had ejected the Medici tyranny to establish a model government to regulate the moral and religious life of the city and help convert its citizens to the life of the spirit. He saw Florence as a new Zion, the center of a reform that would spread throughout Italy, to all Christendom and ultimately to the entire world.

Savonarola had earlier predicted that Charles VIII of France would invade Italy to wield the sword of God's wrath, and he warned Florentines to repent. When Charles VIII marched through Florence in 1494, Savonarola's prophecies were fulfilled and his reputation in the city was enhanced. Savonarola and the city of Florence supported Charles's invasion, which was opposed by Pope Alexander VI in league with Milan, Venice, Spain and Holy Roman Emperor Maximillian. Savonarola hoped that the advent of the French king would lead to the establishment of a democratic government in Florence and the reform of the corrupt and morally lax court of Pope Alexander VI, the ambitious Rodrigo Borgia, of whom Savonarola was an outspoken critic.

Savonarola's enemies sent reports of his preaching and prophecies to the pope. Alexander VI summoned Savonarola to Rome, writing that he had heard that Savonarola "dost assert that thy predictions proceed not from thee but from God." Savonarola asked to be excused from appearing at that time because he had been ill and his absence from Florence would be detrimental to his reforms. He recommended, instead, that as the pope had expressed the desire to be more fully informed of Savonarola's predictions, he could refer to the *Compendium Revelationum*, a new book Savonarola was printing, which would summarize his visions and prophecies. As God had confided in him in secrecy, he was not at liberty to reveal more than what he had written in his book.

In the *Compendium* that Savonarola sent to the pope, published in Latin and Italian in 1495, he explained that God had arranged for his superiors in the Dominican order to send him to Florence on a divine mission to begin the work of conversion that would lead to the reform of the church and of the world. “Almighty God, seeing that the sins of Italy continue to multiply, especially those of her princes, both ecclesiastical and secular, and unable to bear them any longer, decided to cleanse His church with a mighty scourge,” he wrote. God wanted the impending scourge to be foretold by Savonarola so that Florence might prepare better to withstand it.

At first, Savonarola wrote, he did not reveal to the people that he had learned these things directly from God, “since it seemed to me that your minds were not ready for a revelation of mysteries.” His predictions initially referred to information provided by the Scriptures alone. But later, when he concluded that the minds of the people were better prepared to believe, he began to reveal that he knew of these future events through divine inspiration.

Savonarola described a dramatic vision that came to him during Advent in 1492. A hand brandished a great sword of judgment, filling the air with dense clouds, hail, thunder, arrows and fire, while wars, plagues and famine arose upon the earth. Savonarola explained that he was “compelled to write about my public prophecies, especially the more important ones, because many who have heard them from me in the pulpit have tried to describe them, but being inexpert writers in Latin they have butchered the truth or contaminated it with many errors. . . .”

He recounted some of his earlier predictions that had proven to be correct, such as the time of the deaths of Pope Alexander VI’s predecessor, Pope Innocent VIII, and Lorenzo de’ Medici, as well as Charles VIII’s invasion of Italy and many others, “which, if I wished to recount them now would perhaps not be believed, since they were not generally made known at the time.”

As Charles VIII approached Florence, Savonarola recalled, he had preached from the pulpit that these adversities had come to Italy because of its sins. Further, he predicted that Florence would be reformed to a better way of life and that the city would be “more glorious, richer, more powerful than ever before.” He said that events had proven the divine will of God, as it was through Savonarola, speaking with divine authority, that the peace of the city had been restored and constitutional reforms adopted.

CENSORSHIP HISTORY

When Pope Alexander VI received his copy of the *Compendium Revelationum*, he was already angered by Savonarola’s role in mounting Florence’s support for the French invasion. He was infuriated by Savonarola’s claim in the *Compendium* that his illumination came directly from God and, no doubt, also by Savonarola’s thinly veiled attack on the papacy in his references to God’s punishment for the sins of “ecclesiastical princes.”

The pope sent a brief to the Dominican friars of San Marco in Florence. "We are informed," it read, "that a certain Fra Hieronymo of Ferrara . . . has been led by the disturbed condition of affairs in Italy to such a pitch of folly as to declare that he has been sent by God and that he holds converse with him." The pope had hoped by "patient forbearance" to persuade the friar to acknowledge the folly of his prophecies. Instead Savonarola had written a book for "uninformed readers," in which he had written down the ideas that previously he was bold enough to disseminate only by word of mouth. The pope commended Savonarola's case to Fra Sebastiano Maggi, the vicar general of the Dominican order for the province of Lombardy. Pending examination by Maggi, Savonarola was forbidden to preach.

Savonarola sent a letter to the pope describing himself as "deeply grieved that the malice of men had gone to such lengths that certain people had not scruples to suggest to His Holiness a brief so full of false statements and perverse interpretations of his conduct and motives." He said that his enemies made it impossible for him to emerge from his monastery without taking extraordinary precautions, and that he trusted the Holy Father would not consider him disobedient if he prudently refrained for the moment from complying with the pope's wishes that he come to Rome.

If the pope demanded of him that something he had written should be retracted, he would do so, he wrote, as he submitted himself and all his writings to the correction of the Holy Roman church. The pope agreed to suspend the investigation of Savonarola, on the condition that he cease preaching until it was possible for him to come to Rome.

During Lent of 1496 he was allowed to preach again. Later that year, the pope tried to bring him under more direct control by commanding that he unite the Dominican monastery of San Marco in Florence, of which Savonarola was prior, with the Tuscan Roman congregation that was more directly subject to the Vatican. Savonarola defied the pope's orders and the following Lent preached boldly against the evils of the church. On May 13, 1497, Savonarola was excommunicated by Alexander VI for having ignored the pope's first brief summoning him to Rome and for refusing to bring San Marco under Roman control.

In response to his excommunication, Savonarola published "Epistle against Surreptitious Excommunication" addressed to "all Christians and believers of God," in which he claimed that the pope's excommunication was based on false insinuations devised by his enemies and thus it had no value in the eyes of God or the church. He also published a letter citing church canon law experts to bolster his claim that he was not obliged to honor an unjust excommunication.

Savonarola continued preaching until the pope threatened Florence with an interdict unless the city silenced Savonarola and sent him to Rome to be tried. At the request of the leaders of the Florentine republic, he stopped preaching in March 1498. Savonarola called upon the sovereign powers of Europe to summon an ecumenical council, declaring that Alexander was neither a true Christian nor a true pope, as he had committed the sin of simony by paying for his election to the office of the papacy.

In the meantime, Florentines began to grow weary of Savonarola's demands for asceticism. He had pressed for the passage of laws against "all those things which are pernicious to the soul's health," including gambling, drinking and indecent dress in women. He organized bands of children to confiscate volumes of works by Ovid, Dante and Boccaccio, as well as paintings, cards, dice, mirrors, makeup and carnival masks, which were burned in gigantic bonfires of vanities erected in the Piazza della Signoria.

Hostility against him grew, led by members of the Franciscan religious order, who used the enmity of the pope and local officials to their advantage. Savonarola's downfall came in April 1498 when one of his disciples accepted the challenge of an ordeal by fire to prove Savonarola's holiness. When rain cancelled the event, there were riots and Savonarola and two of his followers were arrested and put on trial for heresy and schism.

Alexander VI sent judges from Rome with instructions to find Savonarola guilty. Under torture, Savonarola was said to have confessed that he was a false prophet who committed heresy in demanding church reforms and denouncing papal corruption. In May 1498 he was hanged and burned with all of his writings.

Fourteen years after his death, renewed circulation of Savonarola's writings led the vicar of the Florentine archdiocese to issue proclamations against unlicensed preaching and the persistent cultic veneration of Fra Girolamo. The authorities believed that the continuing influence of Savonarola's prophetic writings was the root cause of the ferment of apocalytic sects, preachers and tracts.

The Tridentine Index of Forbidden Books, issued by the Council of Trent in 1564 and effective in Belgium, Bavaria, Portugal, Italy and France, listed the complete writings of Savonarola. A revised Index in 1612 confirmed the banning of Savonarola's work in the most severe category of *opera omnia*, or all works condemned.

The 19th century saw a revival of interest in Savonarola and the growth of a cult of Savonarola followers who regarded him as a saint, a prophet and a martyr. Calling themselves the New Piagnoni, after the friar's original followers, they gathered at the Dominican Convent of San Marco in Florence. Though Savonarola's writings were eventually eliminated from modern editions of the Index of Forbidden books, efforts to rehabilitate Savonarola's reputation within the Catholic church and elevate him to sainthood were unsuccessful. Savonarola is remembered today more for his censorial bonfires of the vanities than for his martyrdom and the banning of his writings.

FURTHER READINGS

Burman, Edward. *The Inquisition: Hammer of Heresy*. New York: Dorset Press, 1992.
Christie-Murray, David. *A History of Heresy*. Oxford: Oxford University Press, 1976.
Erlanger, Rachael. *The Unarmed Prophet: Savonarola in Florence*. New York: McGraw-Hill, 1988.
George, Leonard. *Crimes of Perception: An Encyclopedia of Heresies and Heretics*. New York: Paragon House, 1995.
Weinstein, Donald. *Savonarola and Florence: Prophecy and Patriotism in the Renaissance*. Princeton: Princeton University Press, 1970.

CONCERNING HERETICS

Author: Sebastian Castellio
Original date and place of publication: 1554, Germany
Literary form: Theological treatise

SUMMARY

The French Protestant theologian Sebastian Castellio deserves to be called the founding father of toleration. As a refugee from the French Inquisition, he moved to Geneva and became a teacher. When he split with Protestant reformer John Calvin over doctrinal differences, he left Geneva and became a professor of Greek at the university in the more tolerant city of Basel. Castellio wrote epic poems in Greek and Latin and translated the Bible. The preface to his Latin Bible translation published in 1551 contained a notable defense of religious toleration.

In 1553, at the instigation of the Calvinists, the young Spanish theologian Michael Servetus was burned at the stake in Geneva for his unorthodox views on the Trinity and the efficacy of infant baptism expressed in his treatise CHRISTIANITY RESTORED. The execution of Servetus prompted Castellio to write *Concerning Heretics, Whether They Are to Be Persecuted and How They Are to Be Treated*, the most important book favoring religious toleration to be published on the Continent during the 16th century.

Published in Latin and in French and German translations in 1554 under three different pseudonyms, *Concerning Heretics* courageously protested cruelty and persecution carried out by Christians in the name of religious doctrine. The book included selections from the writings of the early church fathers and contemporary religious writers on the subject of toleration, with commentary by Castellio.

In the book's preface, addressed to the evangelical prince Christoph of Wuerttemberg, Castellio presented a parable illustrating that tolerance and mutual love are imperative to Christians. He asked the prince to imagine that he had instructed his subjects to prepare to meet him clad in white garments whenever he might appear. When he returned, he found instead that they were disputing among themselves. Suppose further, he asked the prince, that the controversy was being conducted not only verbally, but also by blows and swords and that one group wounded and killed those who disagreed with them. And what if those who killed others claimed to have done it in his name and in accord with his commands, even though he had previously expressly forbidden it?

"Although opinions are almost as numerous as men, nevertheless there is hardly any sect which does not condemn all others and desire to reign alone," Castellio continued. "I ask you, then, most Illustrious Prince, what do you think Christ will do when He comes? Will He commend such things? Will He approve of them?"

Castellio declared that he wrote to "stanch the blood" so wrongfully shed by those called heretics. After investigating the meaning of heresy, he concluded that heretics are those with whom we disagree. Each sect views the others as heretical, "so that if you are orthodox in one city or region, you must be held for a heretic in the next."

The points of religion over which Christians disagree and persecute one another are uncertain, he wrote. "Were these matters obvious, that there is one God, all would agree." The wisest course is to condemn no one who believes in God, whatever their religion. Because people will never agree on religious matters, conduct alone should be punishable, never religious belief or worship. On such matters as the doctrine of the Trinity, "each may be left to his own opinion and revelation of the Savior." Religion resides "in the heart, which cannot be reached by the sword of kings and princes." Since faith cannot be compelled, coercion is futile.

Christ and his disciples died as heretics and seditious blasphemers, Castellio reminded his readers. "This ought to fill us with fear and trembling when it comes to persecuting a man for his faith and his religion." Servetus had fought with "reasons and writings" and should have been answered the same way, Castellio declared. Now that Servetus has been burned, everybody desires to read his books. "To kill a doctrine is not to protect a doctrine, but it is to kill a man. When the Genevans killed Servetus, they did not defend a doctrine, but they killed a man."

CENSORSHIP HISTORY

In 1544, Calvin had Castellio dismissed from his teaching position in Geneva for questioning the inspiration of the Song of Songs and for disagreeing with Calvin's interpretation of Christ's descent into hell. After Castellio's preface to his Bible translation espousing toleration was published in 1551, Calvin, who regarded Castellio as a follower of Servetus, urged the authorities at Basel to punish Castellio as an enemy of religion. Harassment of Castellio increased after the publication of *Concerning Heretics*, when the Calvinists discovered that Castellio was the author and condemned him as a blasphemer deserving of Servetus's fate.

Calvin assigned the task of responding to the book to his disciple, Theodore Beza. Toleration, Beza wrote, is a diabolical doctrine. Its defenders are "emissaries of Satan." Castellio replied to Beza in 1555 in a satirical polemic, *Against Calvin's Book*. Calvin was able to ensure, however, that no publisher would print it. It circulated only in manuscript form until 1612, when it was published for the first time in the Netherlands.

"If Servetus had attacked you by arms, you had rightly been defended by the magistrate," Castellio wrote in his reply to Calvin. "But since he opposed you in writings, why did you oppose them with iron and flame? . . . Does your piety consist only in hurrying to the fire strangers passing peacefully through your city?" For the next decade, the Calvinists hounded Castellio. In 1563, they finally were able to bring him to trial for heresy, but Castellio died during the proceedings.

In spite of Calvinist efforts to suppress *Concerning Heretics*, it was popular and widely influential in Western Europe in inspiring other tracts in favor of toleration and sparking the first great controversy over the issue within Protestantism. Many Polish students attending the University of Basel were influenced by Castellio and returned home imbued with his spirit. Poland in the 16th century became the first country to establish a policy of religious toleration.

FURTHER READINGS

Castellio, Sebastian. *Concerning Heretics, Whether They Are to Be Persecuted and How They Are to Be Treated.* Trans. and intro. by Roland H. Bainton. New York: Columbia University Press, 1935.

Christie-Murray, David. *A History of Heresy*. Oxford: Oxford University Press, 1989.

Levy, Leonard W. *Blasphemy: Verbal Offense Against the Sacred, from Moses to Salman Rushdie*. New York: Alfred A. Knopf, 1993.

Smith, George H. *Atheism, Ayn Rand, and Other Heresies*. Buffalo: Prometheus Books, 1991.

Spitz, Lewis W., ed. *The Protestant Reformation*. Englewood Cliffs, N.J.: Prentice-Hall, 1966.

THE COURSE OF POSITIVE PHILOSOPHY

Author: Auguste Comte

Original date and place of publication: 1830–42, France; 1855, United States

Literary form: Philosophical text

SUMMARY

The French philosopher Auguste Comte was the founder of the school of philosophy known as positivism. *The Course of Positive Philosophy*, Comte's main contribution to intellectual history, began as a series of public lectures and was published in six volumes between 1830 and 1842.

In *The Course*, Comte systematized all of science based on two general laws: the Law of the Three States and the Classification of the Sciences. The Law of the Three States, scientifically derived from Comte's observations of patterns of human intellectual development, consists of three progressive stages: the theological, metaphysical and positive states. In the theological state, events are explained by spiritual forces; in the metaphysical state, natural phenomena are considered to be the result of fundamental energies or ideas; and in the positive state, phenomena are explained by observation, hypotheses and experimentation.

Comte believed that the science of society had already passed through the first two states and was about to enter the third, definitive state based on positive philosophy. The educational system should be structured along the lines of these stages of intellectual development, and *The Course* would provide the text.

In *The Course*, Comte proposed that the natural hierarchy of the sciences provides a useful classification system. He ranked the sciences according to their complexity. Mathematics was the first science and the basis of natural science, followed by astronomy, physics, chemistry, biology and, finally, social physics, or sociology, a term that Comte originated. Because each science depends in part on the science preceding it, all the sciences contribute to sociology. The new science of sociology would be created by extending scientific methodology to social phenomena.

Comte believed that the moral and political anarchy he observed in his society was caused by intellectual confusion resulting from the outmoded remnants of theological and metaphysical thinking. The first step toward the achievement of social unity was the creation of a unified set of beliefs. Comte's systemization of the sciences and the application of the scientific method to society would supply the intellectual basis of such unity. In Comte's view, only positivism could provide a firm foundation for belief and action. As a science-based philosophy, it was accessible to all reasonable people who assess facts positively, or scientifically, and who respect scientific observation and natural law.

The Course of Positive Philosophy represented Comte's first major step in his program for the reorganization of society. In other works—the four-volume *System of Positive Polity* (1851–54), the *Positivist Catechism* (1852) and the *Subjective Synthesis* (1856)—he presented positivism as a religion, the Universal Church of the Religion of Humanity. In Comte's religion, the Great Being of Humanity was the object of worship. This religion without metaphysics had its own catechism, sacraments, priesthood and rituals, modeled on those of the Catholic church, but without God. As the writer T. H. Huxley said, it was "Catholicism minus Christianity."

CENSORSHIP HISTORY

In France the publication of the six-volume *Course of Positive Philosophy* during the years 1830 to 1842 elicited little critical attention. However, in the preface to volume six, published in 1842, Comte wrote a vituperative attack on the "establishment" of the École Polytechnique in Paris, where he was admissions examiner. From that time on, Comte's reappointment was uncertain and in 1844 his position was not renewed. In 1851, he lost the position of assistant lecturer that he had held since 1832.

What Comte described as persecutions were due in part to the resistance of the intellectual establishment to his ideas. His contemporaries reported, however, that he was an exceedingly difficult person (particularly during the times when he struggled with mental illness), that he did not properly fulfill his academic duties and that he brought many of his troubles on himself.

It was not until the end of 1844, when the eminent academic and journalist Emile Littré published six articles about Comtean philosophy, that his positivist ideas began to be widely disseminated in France. Comte's thought influenced the work of his contemporary, the English philosopher John Stuart Mill, and such writers as Edward Bellamy, George Bernard Shaw and George Eliot.

In 1869, the Catholic church placed the third edition of *The Course of Positive Philosophy* (with a preface by Émile Littré) on the Index of Forbidden Books. It was still prohibited when the last Index was compiled in 1948. Because Comte's positivist philosophy viewed Catholicism as retrograde, excluded metaphysics and revealed religion and substituted a new religion of humanity and sociological ethics, it was not surprising that the church found it offensive.

The Course of Positive Philosophy, however, was the only work of Comte's to be placed on the Index, though in several later works Comte framed in more detail his plans for a new positivist religion that adapted and parodied many Catholic rituals. Ironically, Comte believed that the church's attempts to impose unity by insisting on absolute faith and repressing dissent were not only necessary, but a real advance. The organization of the church impressed him with its effectiveness in providing unifying beliefs, education and worship for its vast community. Mirroring the church's efforts to censor books that challenged its doctrine, Comte himself in *The System of Positive Polity* proposed "the systematic destructions of the accumulations which now compress or misdirect thought." He drew up a list of 150 books he felt deserved to survive as part of the Positivist Library and suggested that all others be destroyed.

FURTHER READINGS

Putnam, George Haven. *The Censorship of the Church of Rome*. Vol. 2. New York: G. P. Putnam's Sons, 1906–07.

Standley, Arline Reilein. *Auguste Comte*. Boston: Twayne Publishers, 1981.

CREATIVE EVOLUTION

Author: Henri Bergson
Original date and place of publication: 1907, France
Literary form: Philosophical treatise

SUMMARY

The publication in 1907 of *Creative Evolution* established the worldwide reputation of the French philosopher Henri Bergson as one of the most influential thinkers of his time. In *Creative Evolution* he sought to reconcile Darwin's theory of evolution with his own beliefs about the nature of the universe. He held that matter is propelled by an internal *élan vital*, or life-force, the eternally creative source of being that permeates the universe and guides the evolutionary process.

The *élan vital* is present in all species and organisms and works unconsciously with internal purposefulness to produce progressively higher variations of instinct and intelligence. "The more we focus our attention on the continuity of life," Bergson explains, "the more we see how organic evolution comes closer to the evolution of consciousness where the past presses the present to give birth to a new form which is incommensurable with its antecedents." Bergson believed that this process could only be explained as the work of divine energy. It is through intuition that we are able to discern the divine impulse in evolution.

Bergson rejects both materialist and mechanistic accounts of reality, along with theories that propose that an individual goal or purpose controls the functioning of each organism. Speaking of the *élan vital* as God, he writes: "Thus defined, God has nothing of the ready-made, he is uninterrupted life, action, freedom. And the creation, so conceived, is not a mystery: we experience it in ourselves when we act freely." For Bergson, God is not a thing or a substance, but creativity itself. God is timeless, living in the eternal present.

Bergson's dynamic vision of the universe was regarded as a bold attempt to reconcile the theory of evolution with Christian traditions of creation. *Creative Evolution* offered a system of thought that mediated between rigid scientific determinism and a Christian worldview. Recent scientific discoveries, Bergson believed, did not conflict with the concept of the immateriality of consciousness and the idea of God's presence in the universe.

CENSORSHIP HISTORY

Bergson was the target of many attacks after the publication of *Creative Evolution*. Rationalists viewed his philosophy as opposing analytical reason and attempting to replace the scientific method with quasi-mystical insights. Catholic theologians, who saw him as allied to the pernicious movement of modernism, took issue with what they described as his pantheism and anti-intellectualism.

The influential French Catholic philosopher Jacques Maritain led the critical opposition to Bergson. In his 1913 anti-Bergsonian work, *La philosophie bergsonienne*, he asserted that Bergson's thinking was incompatible with Christian belief, as Bergson regarded faith as purely an inner experience, rather than an assent to revealed truth.

"The Bergsonian doctrine leads imperceptibly and infallibly to a view of dogmas as transitory," Maritain wrote. "If there is no eternal truth and if axioms evolve, why should dogmas not evolve as well?" Bergson promoted the destruction of both faith and reason, Maritain believed. Bergson denied that God could be understood through intellectual efforts and also challenged the concepts of divine creation, free will and the substantial unity of the human soul. His ideas could not be reconciled with the Catholic concepts of the Eucharist or revelation.

Bergson's thought was seen as being in sympathy with a modernist movement among Catholic intellectuals that questioned the church's system of authority and emphasized the importance of personal religious experience. Modernists argued that revelation is transmitted through enlightenment of the individual consciousness by God, rather than by sacred texts. They saw the church's dogmas as provisional and changeable, affected by historical circumstances.

The campaign against modernist heresy was a primary preoccupation of the church of the time. In 1907, the Vatican's Holy Office condemned 65 erroneous statements by modernists. This pronouncement was confirmed the same year in Pope Pius X's encyclical, *Pascendi*, in which he called for disciplinary measures to stamp out what he termed "the synthesis of all heresies." Catholic scholars who held modernist views were excommunicated and all Catholic priests were required to take an anti-modernist oath. This practice remained in force until the mid-1960s, when it was ended by the reforms of the Second Vatican Council.

In 1914, *Creative Evolution* was placed on the church's Index of Forbidden Books, where it remained through the last edition, published until 1966. Bergson was also elected in 1914 to the prestigious French Academy, and in 1927 he received the Nobel Prize in literature. Despite church opposition, Bergson was regarded as the chief intellectual spokesman of his era. His philosophy continued to be read and admired, exercising an important influence on European thinkers before World War Two.

Ironically, though his work was condemned by the church, he moved closer to the Catholic faith in his personal beliefs. He had not intended to undermine Catholicism, as it was his conviction that philosophical illumination could in the end only purify and enhance any religious doctrine. In 1937, in his last will and testament, Bergson, whose father was Jewish, stated that he had wished to be baptized as a Catholic, but noting the growth of anti-Semitism, preferred to remain among the ranks of the persecuted. On January 3, 1941, he died of pneumonia in occupied Paris after standing in line for many hours to be registered as a Jew.

FURTHER READINGS

Collinson, Diané. *Fifty Major Philosophers: A Reference Guide*. London: Routledge, 1988.

Kolakowski, Leszek. *Bergson*. Oxford: Oxford University Press, 1985.

THE CRITIQUE OF PURE REASON

Author: Immanuel Kant
Original date and place of publication: 1781, Prussia
Literary form: Philosophical treatise

SUMMARY

Kant's most important work, *The Critique of Pure Reason*, marked the birth of the critical philosophy known as transcendental idealism. It is regarded as one of the most difficult and controversial works in philosophy. To make the ideas of the *Critique* more accessible, Kant wrote a shorter work, *Prolegomena to Any Future Metaphysics*, published in 1783, which is often read in place of the longer, more demanding *Critique*.

Kant recognized the validity of the empiricist claim that sense experience is the source of belief, but could not accept its skeptical conclusion that those beliefs cannot be justified. "Although all our knowledge begins with experience," he declared, "it does not follow that it arises from experience."

The rationalists, beginning with Descartes, posited that systematic knowledge can be derived from reason and that sense perception is a secondary, less certain source of knowledge. The opposing movement of British empiricism began with John Locke's refutation of Plato's doctrine of innate ideas and led finally to the skepticism of David Hume, who denied the possibility of any valid knowledge. In the *Critique*, Kant identifies the merits and defects of both approaches to thought and offers an alternative approach mediating between the two. He criticizes rationalistic claims that reason can know what is beyond sense experience, but defends the possibilities of knowledge from the skepticism of Hume.

Kant's concern in the *Critique* is to discover the extent of a priori knowledge, that is, knowledge that is necessary and independent of experience. The first step in this process is to distinguish between ultimate realities, things in themselves, and phenomena, things as they appear to human minds. Kant finds that metaphysical knowledge—knowledge of such matters as the existence of God, free will and the immortal soul—cannot be attained through speculative thought. Things lying beyond the realm of experience are unknowable. Their existence is, nevertheless, a necessary proposition, which Kant demonstrates through his moral philosophy. Kant's conception of the "categorical imperative" convinces him by practical reasoning of man's moral nature, freedom and immortality.

Kant calls his basic insight into the nature of knowledge "the Copernican revolution in philosophy." Copernicus reversed the commonly accepted theory of planetary revolution by removing the earth from the center of creation. By proposing the theory that objects conform to the mind, rather than assuming that ideas must conform to an external independent reality, Kant removes sense experience from the center and makes it peripheral. Objective reality is known only as it conforms to the structure of the mind. "All objects of any experience possible to us," he writes in the *Critique*, "are nothing but appearances, that is, mere representations which . . . have no independent existence outside our thoughts."

CENSORSHIP HISTORY

Kant's work influenced almost every area of philosophy. *The Critique of Pure Reason* was immediately recognized as a work of major importance, but it was not well understood when it first appeared. Because of Kant's cumbersome and technical style, it proved difficult to translate from German and its influence spread slowly. Because Kant was a prominent author who enjoyed the confidence of the king, and the *Critique* was not intended for and not likely to be read and understood by the general reader, it was spared the censorship that affected Kant's RELIGION WITHIN THE LIMITS OF REASON ALONE, published in 1793, 12 years after the appearance of the *Critique*.

In October 1794 the Prussian king, Frederick William II, wrote a personal letter to Kant accusing Kant of having "misused" his philosophy over a long period of time and of "the destruction and debasing of many principal and basic teachings of the Holy Scripture of Christianity." He warned Kant not to write or publish any similar works on religion, or "otherwise you can unfailingly expect, on continued recalcitrance, unpleasant consequences." *Religion Within the Limits of Reason Alone* was banned by the Lutheran church in Prussia.

Kant promised "to refrain entirely in the future from all public discourse concerning religion, natural or revealed, in lectures and in writing alike," and published no further philosophical writing until after the king's death.

The Critique of Pure Reason came to the attention of the Catholic church in 1827, when an Italian translation was published. Kant's contention that the existence of God can be neither confirmed nor denied through the use of reason caused the book to be placed on the Index of Forbidden Books, where it remained through the last edition, compiled in 1948 and in effect until 1966.

In 1928 *The Critique of Pure Reason*, along with all of Kant's writing, was also prohibited in the Soviet Union—presumably because the metaphysical and transcendental themes of Kant's works were thought to conflict with Marxist-Leninist ideology. All of the works of "such disgraceful writers" as Kant and Goethe were also purged from the libraries of Spain under the Franco dictatorship in 1939.

FURTHER READINGS

Appelbaum, David. *The Vision of Kant*. Rockport, Mass.: Element Books, 1995.

Cassirer, Ernst. *Kant's Life and Thought*. Trans. by James Hader. Intro. by Stephan Korner. New Haven: Yale University Press, 1981.

Collinson, Diané. *Fifty Major Philosophers: A Reference Guide*. London: Routledge, 1988.

Copleston, Frederick. *A History of Philosophy*. Vol. 6, *Modern Philosophy: From the French Enlightenment to Kant*. New York: Doubleday, 1994.

Green, Jonathon. *The Encyclopedia of Censorship*. New York: Facts On File, 1990.

Kant, Immanuel. *The Philosophy of Kant: Immanuel Kant's Moral and Political Writings*. Ed. and intro. by Carl J. Friedrich. New York: Modern Library, 1993.

———. *The Critique of Pure Reason*. Trans. by N. Kemp Smith. New York: St. Martin's Press, 1965.

Popkin, Richard, and Avrum Stroll. *Philosophy Made Simple*. New York: Doubleday, 1993.

Wolff, Robert Paul, ed. *Ten Great Works of Philosophy*. New York: New American Library, 1969.

DE ECCLESIA

Author: John Hus
Original date and place of publication: 1413, Bohemia
Literary form: Theological treatise

SUMMARY

The Czech religious reformer John Hus, a Catholic priest and theologian, was a forerunner of the Protestant Reformation. He was influenced by the views of English heretic John Wycliff and became the leading exponent of Wycliff's teaching in Bohemia. In his sermons in Prague's Bethlehem chapel, Hus attacked the worldliness and corruption of the Catholic clergy and advocated the purification of the church and a return to the simplicity of its origins. He opposed the condemnation in 1403 of Wycliff's doctrines by the University of Prague, and translated Wycliff's writing into Czech.

A formal complaint against Hus was brought to the archbishop of Prague and, with the support of the pope, he was deprived of his position as preacher in the Bethlehem chapel. In 1410, the archbishop ordered the burning of Wycliff's ON CIVIL LORDSHIP and the following year excommunicated Hus and his followers. Hus left Prague in 1412, but continued preaching his opposition to the sale of indulgences and asserting the primacy of Scripture as the chief authority on doctrinal questions.

During two years of exile from Prague he wrote his chief works, including his treatise *De Ecclesia*, in which he denied the infallibility of the pope and proposed that the state had the right and duty to supervise the church. He allowed for private interpretation of the Bible and declared that it was correct to resist church authority on matters of conscience. In contradiction to Catholic theology, he advocated more frequent communion, claimed that the efficacy of the sacraments depended on the worthiness of the minister and declared that only the predestined elect, not sinners, belonged to the true church. *De Ecclesia* was publicly read in the Bethlehem chapel upon Hus's return to Prague on July 8, 1413.

CENSORSHIP HISTORY

In 1414, the church convened the Council of Constance in Germany at the request of Holy Roman Emperor Sigismund. The aim of the four-year-long council was to reform Christian life, extirpate heresy and resolve a schism in the church in which three men—Gregory XII (since recognized as canonical pope), John XXIII and Benedict XIII—all claimed to be the true pope. The council was organized as a convention of the nations of Germany, Italy, France, England and, later, Spain, with each nation having one vote.

Emperor Sigismund, anxious to bring the unrest caused by Hus's preaching to a swift end, invited Hus to justify his views before the council, promising him a safe conduct and suspension of his excommunication if he would appear to present his case. Upon Hus's arrival in Constance, however, on the principle that faith cannot be kept with heretics, his safe conduct was ignored and he and his follower Jerome of Prague were arrested and put on trial.

The council had already condemned Wycliff as a hesiarch, or archheretic, and ordered his bones exhumed and burned and his ashes thrown into a running stream. Hus was charged with 42 errors extracted from his own writing, among them the charge that *De Ecclesia* reflected Wycliff's views. Hus denied that he accepted all of Wycliff's teachings, but refused to disavow the extracts from his own works that the council claimed were heretical. He maintained that the Scriptures were the only test of doctrine and that he would submit to the judgment of the council only if it did not offend God or his conscience.

The council condemned Hus for both his written errors and those recounted by witnesses, and declared him an incorrigible heretic who did not desire to return to the church. His books were ordered burned, he was removed from the priesthood and, with Jerome of Prague, he was sentenced to be executed for heresy. Seven bishops warned him to recant, but Hus declared that he was unable to confess to errors he had not committed, lest he should lie to God. On July 6, 1415, he was burned at the stake and his ashes were thrown into the Rhine.

Hus became a Czech national hero. He was declared a martyr by the University of Prague and the day of his execution was inserted into the calendar of saints. In 1418, a papal bull condemned the followers of the "arch-heretics" John Wycliff, John Hus and Jerome of Prague, declaring that they "cease not to blaspheme the Lord God" and that their "heretical pravity" must be extirpated. Hus's writings and those of other pre-Reformation heretics were included in the first Index of Forbidden Books compiled by the church in 1559. Over the centuries, Hus became a central symbol of the Czech nation and his proclamation, "Truth prevails," has been adopted as a slogan by every popular Czech revolutionary movement since that time.

FURTHER READINGS

Burman, Edward. *The Inquisition: Hammer of Heresy*. New York: Dorset Press, 1992.

Christie-Murray, David. *A History of Heresy*. Oxford: Oxford University Press, 1989.

George, Leonard. *Crimes of Perception: An Encyclopedia of Heresies and Heretics*. New York: Paragon House, 1995.

Haight, Anne Lyon. *Banned Books: 387 BC to 1978 AD*. Updated and enlarged by Chandler B. Grannis. New York: R. R. Bowker, 1978.

Lea, Henry Charles. *History of the Inquisition of the Middle Ages*. Vol. 2. New York: Russell & Russell, 1955.

Levy, Leonard W. *Blasphemy: Verbal Offense Against the Sacred, from Moses to Salman Rushdie*. New York: Alfred A. Knopf, 1993.

DE INVENTORIBUS RERUM

Author: Polydore Vergil
Original date and place of publication: 1499, Italy
Literary form: Reference book

SUMMARY

Polydore Vergil was an Italian humanist who for many years lived in England, where he served as the archdeacon of Wells cathedral. His small book of proverbs, the *Adagia*, was one of the most widely read books of the 16th century. Vergil is also remembered for two influential works: *Anglica Historia*, a history of England, and *De Inventoribus Rerum*, his account of the beginnings of things, a bestselling book of popular scholarship. First published in three volumes in 1499, *De Inventoribus Rerum* traced the inventions and discoveries of civilization to their original inventors. Designed to provide scholarly information in a compact and accessible form, it was among the first of many popular reference books published during the 16th and 17th centuries.

Vergil's work was translated into all the major European languages and was familiar to most literate persons in 16th- and 17th-century Europe, as indicated by the comical reference to it in Cervantes's DON QUIXOTE. "Another work which I soon design for the press I call a 'Supplement to Polydore Vergil, concerning the Invention of Things,' " the clerk tells Cervantes's knight, "a piece, I will assure you, sir, that shows the great pains and learning of the compiler, and perhaps in a better style than the old author. For example, he has forgot to tell us who was the first that was troubled with a catarrh in the world. Now, sir, this I immediately resolve, and confirm my assertion by the testimony of at least four-and-twenty authentic writers. . . ." The clerk later rejoices at his discovery of the first inventor of playing cards, a fact which will be included in his supplement to Polydore Vergil.

Vergil's method was to state a subject, such as music or geometry and arithmetic, and examine the possible claims of its origins in pagan antiquity, ancient Greece, Rome, Egypt, Syria or in Jewish culture. He cited as sources the Greek and Latin classics, the New and Old Testaments and early Christian, medieval and contemporary writers. Vergil's copious use of references, satirized by Cervantes, marked the transition to the scholarly methods that distinguished the later Renaissance. It also provided a valuable guide for later historians to the knowledge of classical texts in the early Renaissance.

His aim was to list all those "who first invented or began all things or arts; who first established particular provinces or towns; by whom the names come of provinces, towns, peoples, islands, rivers, mountains and other matters; in what places, provinces, islands or towns various things were first hit upon; who first held certain offices and dignities; who first did anything splendid or unusual."

Indeed, Vergil's compendium was eclectic and diverse, full of illustrative material drawn from contemporary life, ranging from the marriage customs of Germany and Italy to the gambling games of Flanders and the differences between ale and beer in northern Europe. In Book One, he examined the origins of the word *God* and of creation, language, marriage, divorce and science; in Book II, law, administration, time, books and military science; and in Book III, agriculture, architecture, navigation and prostitution.

In 1521, Vergil revised the book, adding five volumes on Christianity that discussed the sacraments, church services and festivals, monastic vows, relics, indulgences, papal titles, heresy, schisms, church councils and martyrs. In these new volumes, Vergil, allying himself with the moderate proponents of church reform associated with the humanist scholar Desiderius Erasmus, advocated a return to the simple purity of the early days of Christianity. He criticized corruption in the church and the attention to ceremony and external form which he felt violated the spirit of Christ's teaching, condemning veneration of relics and statues as "not far removed from impiety." He attacked the immorality of monks and advocated marriage for priests. He also argued that the church's failure to call regular church councils was responsible for a decline in religious belief.

CENSORSHIP HISTORY

For well over a century after its publication, *De Inventoribus Rerum* was unrivaled as a work of popular scholarship. Before Vergil's death in 1555, it appeared in some 30 editions published in Latin in Venice, Strasbourg, Basel and Lyons. It was translated into English, French, Italian, German, Spanish and, in the 18th century, Dutch and Russian. The "battle of the books" of the 17th century—the debate that opposed the knowledge of antiquity and that of modern times—renewed interest in the book. In all, at least 100 editions were issued over the centuries.

The publication of the expanded version of *De Inventoribus Rerum* in 1521, including Vergil's account of Christian institutions and his criticisms of church practices, aroused the interest of church authorities. Vergil's *Commentary on the Lord's Prayer*, which accompanied the 1524 Basel edition of *De Inventoribus Rerum*, was also viewed with suspicion. As the Counter-Reformation intensified at mid-century and the Catholic church moved to suppress reform elements within its ranks, Vergil's writing was condemned for having criticized the morality of the Catholic clergy and the policies of the pope and for passages suggesting that the church's discovery of Purgatory stimulated a market for indulgences. *De Inventoribus Rerum* was included in a 1551 list of books condemned by the Sorbonne, then in the Spanish Index of Forbidden Books in 1559, the Index of Forbidden Books issued by Pope Paul IV in Rome in 1564 and the Liège Index of 1569.

An indication of *De Inventoribus Rerum*'s continued popularity despite its censorship was the Catholic church's decision in 1576 to publish its own expurgated edition in Rome, more than two decades after the author's death. Many passages were removed or altered in the censored version: Vergil's views on the meaning of Christ's baptism and mission on earth; his discussion of circumcision; his exposition on the practices of the primitive church as being without ritual confession, monastic rules or an organized priesthood; his attacks on worldly monks, ignorant priests and the sale of indulgences; and his criticism of the church for failing to hold general councils every 10 years. The expurgated version was translated into Italian and Spanish, but all other unexpurgated editions remained on the Index of Forbidden Books.

The 1546 English-language translation, which enjoyed considerable success and was reprinted in several editions, was subjected to another form of censorship. Its translator, Thomas Langley, heavily abridged it, reducing it to less than a tenth of its original size, and added his own commentaries. This gave the work, written from the perspective of a Catholic reformer, a more Protestant flavor. All critical comments on Luther and Lutheranism were excised, as were references that emphasized pagan, rather than Christian, sources.

FURTHER READINGS

Haight, Anne Lyon. *Banned Books: 387 BC to 1978 AD*. Updated and enlarged by Chandler B. Grannis. New York: R. R. Bowker, 1978.

Hays, Denys. *Polydore Vergil: Renaissance Historian and Man of Letters*. Oxford: Clarendon Press, 1952.

DE L'ESPRIT

Author: Claude Adrien Helvétius
Original date and place of publication: 1758, France
Literary form: Philosophical treatise

SUMMARY

Claude Adrien Helvétius was a French philosopher of the Enlightenment and a contributor to the famous ENCYCLOPÉDIE. His utilitarian theories influenced the work of British philosophers Jeremy Bentham, James Mill and Adam Smith. Helvétius held the lucrative post of farmer-general, or tax collector, a position to which he was appointed through his father's influence with the queen. His first major work was *De l'esprit* (Essays on the Mind), published in 1758, which proposed that self-interested pursuit of pleasure and avoidance of pain is the sole motive for human actions.

De l'esprit divided into four discourses. The first presents the epistemological foundation of his system; the second and most influential deals with ethics; the third explains his educational ideas, later amplified in a posthumously published work, *De l'homme* (A Treatise on Man); and the fourth concerns aesthetics.

Helvétius maintains that since consciousness is derived from sensation and is the same in everyone, all forms of intellectual activity originate in sensation. Self-love, directed toward the acquisition of pleasure, is the universal basis of human conduct. Even benevolent virtues can be attributed to self-love. "What is a benevolent man?" Helvétius asks. "One in whom a spectacle of misery produces a painful sensation."

Although self-interest is the fundamental motive of conduct, "the public good is the supreme law." The criterion for the morality of an action is its usefulness to the community. Altruism is psychologically possible if education is directed toward developing benevolent impulses. If children are taught to empathize with those who are unfortunate, for example, the misfortune of others will arouse in them painful sensations and self-love will stimulate a desire on their part to relieve misery.

"To love one's fellow-men, one must not expect much of them," Helvétius believed. Justice and the happiness of the greatest number can be obtained through education and legislation that manipulate and condition people to treat one another well through a system of rewards and punishments. All progress depends on education. "Destroy ignorance, and you will destroy all the seeds of moral evil."

Helvétius felt that the entire educational system of France had to be reconstructed, freed from the control of the church and assigned to the state. Catholic control of education, he charged, impeded the technical advance of the nation and subjected the minds of children to priestly domination. "There is nothing which the sacerdotal power cannot execute by the aid of superstition. For by that it robs the magistrates of their authority and kings of their legitimate power; thereby it subdues the people, and acquires a power over them which is frequently superior to the laws; and thereby it finally corrupts the very principles of morality."

CENSORSHIP HISTORY

Few books of the 18th century provoked greater opposition from religious and civil authorities than *De l'esprit*. It was condemned as atheistic, materialistic, sacrilegious, immoral and subversive, the epitome of all the dangerous philosophical trends of the age. The Catholic church saw Helvétius's theories as antireligious, because earthly happiness, rather than salvation, was the object of his ethical theory. Theologians objected to his reduction of all the powers of the human understanding to sense perception, and to his materialistic ethic of self-interest that posited social utility as the only criterion for morality. The Jesuits objected to his proposals to remove education from their control. The church charged that his deterministic philosophy rejected the doctrine of free will and denied the soul's spirituality and immortality.

De l'esprit was published in 1758 with a royal privilege or permission from the official censor, Tercier, a principal secretary at the foreign office. "I have found nothing in it which in my judgement ought to prevent its publication," Tercier declared. Soon after its publication, however, the Jesuits at court, the queen and the Parlement of Paris made official complaints about it to Malesherbes, the director of the book trade. Malesherbes ordered sale of the book suspended until a second censor could examine it.

The second censor detected improper criticism of the church and asked for cuts in the manuscript. Helvétius was ordered to write a retraction. Instead, he provided an introduction defending his writing against charges of heresy. "Of what impiety can they accuse me?" he protested. "I have in no part of this work denied the Trinity, or the divinity of Jesus, or the immortality of the soul, or the resurrection of the dead, or any other article of the papal creed; I have not therefore in any way attacked religion."

Durand, the printer, put the original typesetting aside and printed a second, anonymous version with the changes ordered by the censor and with Helvétius's introduction. This version was approved for publication, but it also met with condemnation. In a futile effort to deter the censors, Helvétius wrote two more submissive retractions disavowing his work and explaining his desire not to offend the church. Jesuits and Jansenists alike attacked it in periodicals and pamphlets, bishops lambasted it from the pulpit and in November 1758, *De l'esprit* was prohibited by the archbishop of Paris.

Only three weeks before the book's publication, Pope Clement XIII, who was determined to stamp out the new materialistic thought, succeeded the more moderate Benedict XIV. In January 1759, the new pope banned it in a special brief forbidding—under pain of excommunication—the printing, reading or possession of the work. The pope described Helvétius as doing Satan's work and opening "the broadest possible path to lead souls to perdition." The book was also placed on the Index of Forbidden Books.

In February the Parlement of Paris, having extended its authority to censor books on its own initiative, without waiting for the verdict of the faculty of theology at the Sorbonne, ordered *De l'esprit* to be burned by the public hangman and prohibited in Paris and in the provinces. In April the Sorbonne finally weighed in with its own condemnation.

Despite its banning, *De l'esprit* became an underground bestseller in pirated and clandestine editions. Twenty editions appeared in France within six months, and the work was translated into English and German. Though Helvétius was dismissed from his sinecure as major domo to the queen, he escaped further punishment by virtue of his personal relationships with high-level persons in the court and government, such as Madame de Pompadour and Choiseul, the foreign minister, who interceded on his behalf. He was ordered, instead, to retire to his estate for two years. It was said that the penalty might have been more severe if the king had not remembered that his life had been saved by Helvétius's father, who had been physician to the queen.

In 1772, the year following Helvétius's death, *De l'homme* was published. In it he attacked political despotism and called for a more equitable distribution of the national wealth. He also assailed the detrimental influence of revealed or "mysterious" religion, declaring that the power of the church and the Catholic clergy were impediments to reforming education and insuring the smooth running of society. In 1774, *De l'homme* was also condemned and burned in Paris.

FURTHER READINGS

Copleston, Frederick. *A History of Philosophy*. Vol. 6, *Modern Philosophy*. New York: Doubleday, 1994.

Curtis, Michael, ed. and intro. *The Great Political Theories*. Vol. 1. New York: Avon Books, 1981.
Durant, Will, and Ariel Durant. *The Age of Voltaire*. New York: Simon and Schuster, 1965.
Smith, D. W. *Helvétius, a Study in Persecution*. Oxford: Clarendon Press, 1965.

DIALOGUE CONCERNING THE TWO CHIEF WORLD SYSTEMS

Author: Galileo Galilei
Original date and place of publication: 1632, Italy
Literary form: Scientific monograph

SUMMARY

The work of the great Italian astronomer, mathematician and physicist Galileo had a profound effect on the development of science and philosophy, laying the foundations for modern experimental science and enlarging human understanding of the nature of the universe. Although the Polish astronomer Copernicus had argued in ON THE REVOLUTION OF HEAVENLY SPHERES, published in 1543, that the sun was the center of the universe and the earth a planet that moved, belief in the geocentric Ptolemaic system (named for the second-century astronomer Ptolemy) remained prevalent in the early 17th century. The Ptolemaic theory placed the earth motionless at the center of the universe, with the sun, the moon and the five planets moving around it in complex circular motions.

When Galileo, a professor of mathematics at the University of Pisa, first gazed at the sky through the refracting telescope he had designed, it had been a half-century since Copernicus introduced his theory of a heliocentric, or sun-centered, universe. For the first time, however, actual observations of the heavens through a telescope seemed to confirm Copernicus's hypothesis. In 1610, Galileo published *The Starry Messenger*, a 24-page pamphlet reporting his astronomical observations of the moon and the planets. Galileo recounted his discovery of four previously unknown heavenly bodies moving around the planet Jupiter, proof that Copernicus's theory was correct. He also noted that the moon was not a self-luminous body, but was lit by the sun.

The Venetian senate granted Galileo a salary for his discoveries, and he was appointed mathematician to the Duke of Tuscany. In 1613, he published *Letters on the Solar Spots*, in which he declared his belief in the Copernican theory. Galileo was convinced that "the Book of Nature is written in mathematical symbols," and that in observation and quantification lay the science of the future. In 1632, Galileo published the work which was to mark a turning point in the history of science, *Dialogue Concerning the Two Chief World Systems, Ptolemaic and Copernican*.

In this dialogue in the Platonic tradition, Galileo allowed arguments for and against the Copernican system to emerge from a conversation among three friends: a Florentine who believes in the Copernican system, an Aristotelian supporter of the geocentric theory and a Venetian aristocrat for whose benefit they propose their arguments. Galileo wrote in Italian for the nonspecialist, rather than in Latin, the language of scholars and intellectuals.

In structuring the *Dialogue*, Galileo complied with the church's orders that the heliocentric theory be discussed as a useful mathematical hypothesis, rather than as a representation of physical reality. But the views he expressed in the *Dialogue* were clearly supportive of the Copernican system. Galileo found that the earth, like the other planets, rotated on its axis, and that the planets revolved around the sun in elliptical paths determined by gravity. The idea of a finite universe bounded by an outer sphere of unchanging perfection was rejected. By showing that the earth was not the center of creation but, rather, an insignificant part of it, Galileo overturned the medieval system of cosmology based on Aristotelian theories of the motion of bodies.

Galileo expressed two principles in the *Dialogue* that have become the guiding principles of modern science. First, statements and hypotheses about nature must always be based on observation, rather than on received authority; and second, natural processes can best be understood if represented in mathematical terms.

CENSORSHIP HISTORY

In 1616, the system of Copernicus was denounced as dangerous to the faith and Galileo, summoned to Rome, was warned by Pope Paul V not to "hold, teach or defend" Copernican theories. Galileo promised to obey the papal injunction and returned to Florence. Similar theories, published by the German astronomer Johannes Kepler in THE NEW ASTRONOMY were banned by the pope in 1619. According to the papal bull accompanying these bans, teaching or even reading the works of Copernicus and Kepler was forbidden.

In 1624, Galileo went to Rome again to pay his respects to the newly annointed Pope Urban VIII. Despite the prohibition of 1616, he requested papal permission to publish a book comparing Ptolemaic and Copernican doctrines. The pope refused his request.

Despite warnings by the Vatican, which had cited numerous corrections required before any of Copernicus's theories might be promulgated, in 1632 Galileo published *Dialogue Concerning the Two Chief World Systems*. He attempted to satisfy the authorities by including a preface by a leading Vatican theologian describing Copernican theory as merely an interesting intellectual exercise. But the pope was unconvinced. The book had attracted the attention of all of Europe. The rising threat of Protestantism spurred the pope to respond aggressively to preserve the integrity of the church's dogmas.

Further, Galileo's enemies at the Vatican implied that by publishing the book under the colophon of three fishes—the usual imprint of the Florentine press of Landini—Galileo had made a libelous reference to Pope Urban VIII's three incompetent nephews, whom he had promoted to the church hierarchy. They further suggested that one of the characters in the dialogue, Simplicio, the conservative defender of the geocentric view of the universe, was meant to be a caricature of the pope himself.

In February 1633, Galileo was summoned to Rome. Although he was gravely ill in Florence and his doctors warned that a journey in the dead of winter might prove fatal, the pope threatened to forcibly remove him in chains if he did not appear. The grand duke of Florence provided a litter to carry Galileo to Rome, where he was imprisoned. In June he was put on trial for heresy.

The trial focused on technicalities regarding what he had been told by church authorities during his visit to Rome in 1616 and on how clearly he had understood the papal disapproval of Copernican doctrines. The Inquisition's verdict was that Galileo was "vehemently suspected of heresy, namely of having believed and held the doctrine which is false and contrary to the sacred and divine scriptures that the sun is the center of the world and does not move from East to West and that the earth moves and is not the center of the world and that an opinion may be held and defended as probable after it has been declared and defined to be contrary to Holy Scripture. . . ."

Galileo was sentenced to prison for an indefinite period and required to make a public and formal abjuration. On the morning of June 22, 1633, at the age of 70, Galileo knelt before the court and declared, "With sincere heart and unpretended faith I abjure, curse, and detest the aforesaid errors and heresies and also every other error and sect whatever, contrary to the Holy Church, and I swear that in the future I will never again say or assert verbally or in writing, anything that might cause a similar suspicion toward me. . . ." "And yet it [the earth] moves," he is said by legend to have muttered after his recantation.

In 1634, the *Dialogue* was formally condemned and banned along with all of Galileo's works. Galileo was confined to a secluded house in Arcetri, outside Florence, where he was allowed no visitors except with the permission of the pope's delegate. During his confinement Galileo was able to complete a new work, *Dialogue Concerning Two New Sciences*, which was smuggled out of Italy and published by the Protestants in Leiden in 1638, four years before his death. During the last four years of his life, Galileo was blind. Eventually the pope allowed him the companionship of a young scholar, Vicenzo Viviani. Still in seclusion, Galileo died on January 8, 1642, a month before his 78th birthday.

The Index of Forbidden Books of 1664 confirmed the condemnation of the works of Copernicus and Galileo and of all other writings affirming the movement of the earth and the stability of the sun. In 1753, the Index of

Benedict XIV omitted the general prohibition covering books that teach the heliocentric theory.

However, it was not until 1824, when Canon Settele, a Roman astronomy professor, published a work on modern scientific theories, that the church finally announced its acceptance of "the general opinion of modern astronomers." In the next papal Index of 1835, the names of Galileo, Copernicus and Kepler were removed. On October 31, 1992, Pope John Paul II formally rehabilitated Galileo—359 years, four months and nine days after Galileo had been forced to recant his heresy that the earth moved around the sun.

FURTHER READINGS

Boorstein, Daniel J. *The Discoverers: A History of Man's Search to Know His World and Himself.* New York: Random House, 1983.

Collinson, Diané. *Fifty Major Philosophers: A Reference Guide*. London: Routledge, 1988.

Garraty, John A., and Peter Gay. *The Columbia History of the World*. New York: Harper & Row, 1972.

Green, Jonathon. *The Encyclopedia of Censorship*. New York: Facts On File, 1990.

DIALOGUES CONCERNING NATURAL RELIGION

Author: David Hume
Original date and place of publication: 1779, England
Literary form: Philosophical treatise

SUMMARY

Dialogues Concerning Natural Religion was the last work of the Scottish philosopher and historian David Hume, one of the great empiricists of the 18th-century Enlightenment. Published posthumously in 1779 because Hume felt it was too controversial to be released during his lifetime, it distills his thought on religious skepticism and is regarded as among the most important works on the philosophy of religion.

In earlier works Hume contributed several influential arguments against both revealed religion and the rationalist arguments for belief. The most famous was his celebrated attack on miracles in AN INQUIRY CONCERNING HUMAN UNDERSTANDING, published in 1748. *Dialogues Concerning Natural Religion* contains a full development of many of the arguments introduced in the notorious sections X and XI of the *Inquiry*.

In the *Dialogues*, Hume examines the rational claims for religious belief. Through the differing views of three characters whose conversations are reported by Pamphilus, the narrator—Philo, the skeptic, Cleanthes, the empirical or rational theologian, and Demea, the orthodox defender of revealed religion—Hume analyzes the arguments that have been advanced to prove God's existence and benevolence.

His primary target in the *Dialogues* is "the argument from design," advanced by deists and theists alike, which proposes that because the universe works like a machine, showing signs of a designing intelligence, a perfect and immutable designer must have created it. This argument is advanced by Cleanthes in the *Dialogues*. "Look around the world, contemplate the whole and every part of it," he says, "you will find it to be nothing but one great machine, subdivided into an infinite number of lesser machines, which again admit of subdivisions to a degree beyond what human senses and faculties can trace and explain."

The argument is challenged by Philo, the skeptic, who objects to Cleanthes's logic and demonstrates the faultiness of his experimental reasoning. Philo shows that the basic analogy of the argument comparing the universe and a machine is exceedingly weak, that alternative hypotheses not considered by Cleanthes explain the data equally well and that Cleanthes's conclusion is incompatible with the existence of evil.

Even if we accept the basic premises of the argument from design, Philo points out, it provides no basis for making assumptions about the nature of the designer. It is pure conjecture to state that the designer is necessarily morally perfect or even good. "But were this world ever so perfect a production, it must still remain uncertain whether all the excellence of the work can justly be ascribed to the workman. . . . Many worlds might have been botched and bungled, throughout an eternity, ere this system was struck out; much labor lost, many fruitless trials made, and a slow but continued improvement carried on during infinite ages in the art of world-making."

The argument for design proceeds from the existence of an effect, a designed universe, to the existence of a cause, God the designer. In Philo's view, Cleanthes's data do not support his conclusions. His argument simply rationalizes what he already believes independently of the data. The existence of God is a hypothesis and the argument from design does not provide the evidence necessary to demonstrate its truth.

CENSORSHIP HISTORY

Although Hume did not state which of the views expressed in the *Dialogues* were his own, it is clear that his position was represented primarily by the arguments of the skeptic, Philo. Hume was a resolutely secular thinker who felt that religion was a negative influence on both individuals and society. Though many British intellectuals were hostile to revealed or organized religion, most believed in God. Atheism was unthinkable in the culture of the day and could not be put forward as a serious option, even by deists or freethinkers. In the *Dialogues*, Hume skirted dangerously close to atheism by taking issue with both the tenets of revealed religion and deists' claims on behalf of "natural religion."

Hume believed not only that the arguments put forth for God's existence and benevolent nature did not meet the tests of empirical investigation, but also that religion impeded morality. It encouraged people to act for motives other than love of virtue for its own sake and caused anxiety, intolerance and persecution. In *The Natural History of Religion*, published in 1755, Hume observed that fanaticism and bigotry increased with the development of monotheism and that in the Christian world philosophy was misused in the service of theological doctrines.

The torrent of criticism Hume faced after publication of *An Inquiry Concerning Human Understanding* in 1748, particularly of the two sections discussing philosophy of religion, "Of Miracles" and "Of a Particular Providence and of a Future State," led Hume to decide that he could not publish *Dialogues Concerning Natural Religion* during his lifetime.

Hume had been rejected for appointments at the universities of Edinburgh and Glasgow, and a formal attempt had been made to excommunicate him from the Church of Scotland. The Vatican placed a French version of his first philosophical work, *A Treatise of Human Understanding*, on the Index of Forbidden Books in 1761, and a flood of widely circulated attacks on Hume were published during the years after the appearance of the *Inquiry*.

The manuscript of *Dialogues Concerning Natural Religion* had been largely completed by 1751. He circulated it to a few friends, including the philosopher and economist Adam Smith, who advised him not to publish it. More than 20 years later, in a 1776 letter to his publisher, Hume indicated that he planned to print 500 copies of the work. But the decline of his health led him with "abundant prudence" to prepare instead for its posthumous publication.

The book appeared in late 1779, three years after Hume's death. Hume had tried to convince Adam Smith to guarantee its publication, but Smith was reluctant to become involved because of its highly controversial nature. Hume's printer, also a friend, refused to publish it. Finally Hume's nephew, David Hume, had it published anonymously without a publisher's imprint. A French edition appeared the same year and a German one in 1781. The book sold well in Britain and a second edition was published in 1779.

In 1827, Hume's *History of England* and all his philosophical works, including *Dialogues Concerning Natural Religion* and *An Inquiry Concerning Human Understanding*, were placed by the Catholic church on the Index of Forbidden Books, where they remained through the last edition of the Index compiled in 1948 and in effect until 1966.

In 1986, more than 200 years after the publication of *Dialogues Concerning Natural Religion*, the work was censored again—this time by the government of Turkey. A translation by Mere Tuncay of Hume's writing on religion was banned under the Law to Protect Minors. This legislation was enacted in

1985 to allow for restriction of "items of a political nature which may affect minors adversely." Also included in the proscription were the film *Gandhi* and the television program "Dallas."

FURTHER READINGS

Boyle, Kevin, ed. *Article 19 World Report 1988*. New York: Times Books, 1988.

Collinson, Diané. *Fifty Major Philosophers: A Reference Guide*. London: Routledge, 1988.

Copleston, Frederick. *A History of Philosophy*. Vol. 5, *Modern Philosophy: The British Philosophers from Hobbes to Hume*. New York: Doubleday, 1994.

Gay, Peter. *The Enlightenment: An Interpretation. The Rise of Modern Paganism*. New York: W. W. Norton & Co., 1995.

Penelhum, Terence. *David Hume: An Introduction to His Philosophical System*. West Lafayette, Ind.: Purdue University Press, 1992.

Popkin, Richard H., and Avrum Stroll. *Philosophy Made Simple*. New York: Doubleday, 1993.

Price, John V. *David Hume*. New York: Twayne Publishers, 1968.

Scott-Kakures, Dion, Susan Castegnetto, Hugh Benson, William Taschek and Paul Hurley. *History of Philosophy*. New York: HarperCollins Publishers, 1993.

DISCOURSE ON METHOD

Author: René Descartes
Original date and place of publication: 1637, Holland
Literary genre: Philosophical text

SUMMARY

Discourse on Method outlined the philosophy of René Descartes, the founder of modern philosophy and mathematics. Published in 1637 along with other important essays on optics, meteorology and analytical geometry, *Discourse on Method* established Descartes's reputation throughout Europe and introduced philosophy as a field of intellectual inquiry open to all self-critical thinkers. His MEDITATIONS ON FIRST PHILOSOPHY, published four years later, offered a more complete exposition of the ideas introduced in *Discourse on Method.*

Descartes's method of philosophical inquiry was to proceed by rigorous deduction from self-evident premises. He claimed that this method provided a foundation for solving on the basis of available facts any problem that could be resolved by human reason.

Descartes divided *Discourse on Method* into six parts to make it more accessible to the reader. In part one, "Some Thoughts on the Sciences," Descartes stated that the ability to distinguish true from false is the same by nature in all men. Differences of opinion are due not to variations in intelligence, but rather to different approaches to arriving at the truth.

In part two, "The Principal Rules of the Method," Descartes resolved to reject all the opinions he had received since birth until he determined how they fit into a rational scheme. He outlined four rules: First, never accept anything as true unless you recognize it to be so. Second, divide difficulties into as many parts as possible. Third, think in an orderly fashion, beginning with the simplest and most easily understood ideas, gradually reaching toward more complex knowledge. Fourth, make complete enumerations and general reviews to be sure that nothing has been omitted.

In part three, "Some Moral Rules Derived from the Method," Descartes recounted the personal code of morality he followed while he was discarding his own opinions in order to reexamine them. He obeyed the laws and customs of his country, retaining the religion of his upbringing. He acted resolutely on all his decisions, even those he was unsure of. He sought to conquer himself and change his desires rather than the established order, believing that nothing except our thoughts is wholly under our control.

In part four, "Proofs of the Existence of God and of the Human Soul," Descartes noticed that while he wished to think everything false, "it was necessarily true that I who thought so was something." Since this truth, "I think, therefore I am" (*Cogito ergo sum*), was so firm and assured, he judged he could accept it as the first principle of the philosophy he was seeking. In ascertaining how he had learned to think of something more perfect than himself, it appeared evident to him that it must have been from some more perfect nature, which was God.

In part five, "Some Questions of Physics," Descartes recounted the discovery of certain laws established by God in nature, the idea of which he had fixed in our minds, leading him to conclude that the soul is immortal. In part six, "Some Prerequisites for Further Advances in the Study of Nature," Descartes outlined his own procedure. He first tried to discover the general principles or first causes of existence. Next he examined the first and most common effects that could be deducted from these causes. But when he wanted to descend to particulars, he found it impossible to distinguish the forms or species of objects found on earth from an infinity of others which might have been there if God had so willed. It thus appeared impossible to proceed further deductively. To reach understanding, causes would have to be discovered by their effects, through experimentation.

Descartes did not claim that his ideas were original. He asserted, rather, that he did not accept ideas simply because they were maintained by others, but only because reason persuaded him of their truth. "As for my real opinions," Descartes concluded, "I do not apologize for their novelty, especially since I am sure that anyone who attends to the argument will find them so simple and so comfortable to common sense that they will seem less extraordinary and strange than any other opinions that can be held on the same subjects."

CENSORSHIP HISTORY

By attempting to apply the methods, standards and concepts of mathematical and natural sciences to philosophic inquiry, Descartes launched an intellectual revolution. He changed the emphasis in philosophical inquiry from metaphysics, the study of the ultimate nature of existence, to epistemology, the study of the origins and grounds of knowledge, thereby ushering in a new philosophical era. Descartes's rationalist approach to knowledge, whereby reason alone, unaided by experience, can arrive at basic truths about the world from self-evident premises, challenged Catholic church doctrine.

As expressed by Saint Thomas Aquinas, church doctrine asserted that not all articles of faith were demonstrable by reason. Descartes, in common with many individuals in his period, discarded the authoritarian system of the Scholastics, the medieval philosophy synthesizing faith and reason that dominated the thinking of the church. He adopted instead the concept of universal doubt and belief in the unique adequacy of each individual's reason to discover truth.

Descartes was a devout Catholic and accepted the existence of God, but he considered moral questions to be separable from the process of scientific observation. The church attacked the scientific method as a form of atheism, and branded Descartes's methodology as dangerous to the faith.

Though Descartes's philosophy, as expressed in *Discourse on Method* and *Meditations on First Philosophy*, made rapid advances, it was attacked by church, state and universities. In France, an officially Catholic country governed by an absolute monarchy, as well as in liberal Holland, his rejection of Scholasticism was regarded as threatening. In 1641, in Holland, the senate of the University of Utrecht voted to condemn his philosophy. At the University of Leiden, any mention of Descartes's philosophy in lectures was forbidden. In 1643, civil authorities in Utrecht took direct action against Descartes, and the open letters he published in his own defense were declared defamatory. Two years later, Descartes was ordered by the city magistrate to appear in person to answer libel charges. An appeal to the French ambassador, who exercised his influence with the Dutch Prince of Orange, led to the charges being dropped.

In France, where all universities were subject to royal and ecclesiastical authorities, repression of Descartes's ideas was particularly severe under the Catholic absolute monarchy of Louis XIV (1643–1715). Catholic opinion in France was particularly disturbed by the question of whether his philosophy of matter could be reconciled with the dogma of transubstantiation. This dogma holds that the substances of bread and wine of the sacrament of the Eucharist are turned miraculously into the substance of Christ himself. Cartesians attempted to explain the Eucharist using Descartes's philosophy, rather than declaring it a mystery to be accepted on faith.

The debate on the Eucharist after Descartes's death in 1650, led by advocates of Cartesian philosophy who promoted his views on transubstantiation, resulted in further repression of his philosophy. It is thought that Jesuit hostility to Cartesian ideas, particularly the suspicion that Cartesians favored a purely symbolic interpretation of the Eucharist, was responsible in 1663 for the placement on the Index of Forbidden Books of all Descartes's philosophical writings. They were listed on the Index with the notation *d.c.* (*donec corrigantur*), meaning "until corrected," a qualification used to express condemnation in milder form.

In 1671, the debate on the Eucharist again resulted in censure of Cartesian philosophy. A Benedictine monk, Desgabets, published a book offering a Cartesian interpretation of the Eucharist. The king took offense and mounted a major campaign against Cartesianism in French universities. That year the University of Paris complied with a royal ban on teaching of his philosophy, and other French universities followed suit. Religious orders also imposed bans on teaching of Cartesian philosophy.

Despite such bannings, Descartes's philosophy and science won many converts in Holland and France. Cartesian views circulated in informal settings such as the salons of Paris and in universities, where professors were able to find ways to discuss Cartesian ideas while technically complying with official bans. By the mid-18th century, Descartes's ideas had become the philosophy of the establishment.

In 1722, Descartes's 1641 *Meditations on First Philosophy* was prohibited unconditionally in the Index. In 1948, when the last revision of the Index was made by the church, Descartes's philosophical works, including *Discourse on Method*, were still listed. It was not until 1966, when the Vatican abolished the Index, that Catholics were officially allowed to read Descartes.

In 1926 in the Soviet Union, many philosophical works were suppressed, including those of Descartes.

FURTHER READINGS

Descartes, René. *Discourse on Method.* Trans. and intro. by Laurence J. Lafleur. Indianapolis: Bobbs-Merrill Company, 1956.

Green, Jonathon. *The Encyclopedia of Censorship.* New York: Facts On File, 1990.

Jolley, Nicholas. "The Reception of Descartes' Philosophy." In *The Cambridge Companion to Descartes.* Ed. by John Cottingham, 393–423. Cambridge: Cambridge University Press, 1992.

DON QUIXOTE

Author: Miguel de Cervantes Saavedra
Original date and place of publication: 1605, 1615, Spain
Literary form: Novel

SUMMARY

One of the greatest and most enduring classics of European literature, *Don Quixote de la Mancha* is a burlesque of the popular romances of chivalry. Cervantes's masterpiece tells the story of Don Quixote, a country gentleman of La Mancha in central Spain, whose mind has become unbalanced by his reading of too many tales of chivalry. He sees himself as a knight-errant whose mission is to travel the world in rusty armor in search of adventure, riding a decrepit horse, Rosinante, and accompanied by his squire, the peasant Sancho Panza. He selects as his knightly belle a country girl, Aldonza Lorenza, and dubs her Dulcinea del Toboso, though she remains unaware of the honor bestowed upon her.

Don Quixote embarks on a series of absurd and extravagant adventures, as in his disordered imagination the land is transformed into a knightly landscape where the most commonplace objects assume fantastic forms. Windmills become giants; an inn, a castle; and a flock of sheep, a great army. Concerned about his safety, his friends trick him into returning to his home, where he recovers his health. Don Quixote's misadventures continue, as he endeavors to free Dulcinea from what he believes is an enchantment by a wicked spell. Finally Don Quixote is induced to abstain from his chivalrous exploits for a year and resolves to live a pastoral life as a shepherd. But falling sick upon his return to his village, he regains his sanity and, renouncing his fantasies of chivalry, he dies.

CENSORSHIP HISTORY

Through Cervantes's vivid portrayal of the panorama of 16th-century society, *Don Quixote* explores two conflicting attitudes toward the world: idealism and realism. Cervantes's brilliant humanistic study of illusion and reality is considered by many critics to be the first modern novel in its pioneering effort to reveal the variety of the individual and translate all human experience into the novel form.

Immediately upon its publication in 1605, *Don Quixote* became a bestseller. It was reprinted in six editions in Spain during the first year of its publication and translated into all the major languages of Europe. The popularity of a pirated edition of his idea spurred Cervantes to publish a sequel in 1615. Part two also sold well and was soon bound and marketed together with the first part.

The censorship of *Don Quixote*, though minor in scope and impact, was a notorious example of the fastidious and thorough nature of the Spanish Inquisition's control over book publishing and distribution. Under penalty of confiscation and death, no bookseller could sell or keep any work condemned by the Inquisition. Agents searched bookstores and private libraries and a commissioner was appointed to survey ships docked at Spanish ports to prevent the importation of offensive literature. The examiners of the Inquisition read every book published in Spain or imported from abroad for heretical ideas, but allowed certain books to circulate if offensive passages were expurgated. Under this system, permission could be given for publication of books that were absolutely prohibited by the Roman Index of Forbidden Books. But the heavy financial loss incurred by printers by suppression of the original edition often discouraged investment in a second, expurgated text and effectively halted publication altogether.

In part one of *Don Quixote*, the knight-errant tears off the tail of his shirt and ties knots in it to serve as a rosary in the wilderness of the Sierra Morena. This passage was pronounced indecent by the church's Holy Office, and in a second edition the shirt-tail was changed to a chapelet of corn-tree nuts. "I would have made the book more amusing," Cervantes commented on the church's restrictions, "had it not been for the Holy Office."

But unaccountably the censors let pass Cervantes's satire on ecclesiastical censorship in chapter six of part one, in which the priest and the barber set themselves up as inquisitors and purge Don Quixote's library of its most deleterious works on chivalry.

In 1640, 25 years after the first publication of part two of *Don Quixote*, the book was placed on the Spanish Index for a single sentence extracted from the half-million words of one of the world's longest novels: "Works of charity performed negligently have neither merit nor value." The church viewed this statement as reflecting Lutheran beliefs. Removal of the sentence in a reprinted edition satisfied the censors and allowed the novel's continued circulation.

In Chile in 1981, the military junta led by General Augusto Pinochet banned *Don Quixote* because the general believed it contained a plea for individual freedom and an attack on authority.

FURTHER READINGS

Boorstein, Daniel J. *The Discoverers: A History of Man's Search to Know His World and Himself.* New York: Random House, 1983.

Burman, Edward. *The Inquisition: Hammer of Heresy.* New York: Dorset Press, 1992.

Manguel, Alberto. *A History of Reading.* New York: Viking. 1996.

Putnam, George Haven. *The Censorship of the Church of Rome.* Vol. 1. New York: G. P. Putnam's Sons, 1906–07.

Roth, Cecil. *The Spanish Inquisition.* New York: W. W. Norton & Co., 1964.

DRAGONWINGS

Author: Laurence Yep
Original date and place of publication: 1975, United States
Original Publisher: Harper & Row
Literary form: Novel

SUMMARY

Dragonwings is a critically praised, Newbery Honor award-winning novel for young adults by Laurence Yep. Yep has written more than 20 books inspired by the Chinese-American immigrant experience and legends of Chinese folk tales. *Dragonwings*, about a boy who emigrates from China to San Francisco in 1905 to join the father he has never met, is a coming-of-age story and a celebration of the courage and industry of the Chinese-American community of the early 20th-century.

Eight-year-old Moon Shadow lives with his mother and grandmother in a small village in China. One day he receives a letter from his father, who emigrated years before to the Golden Mountain, or America, asking that Moon Shadow sail to San Francisco to join him. Upon Moon Shadow's arrival in the Land of the Demons, as the people of his village refer to the United States, he meets his father. He is brought to the Company of the Peach Orchard Vow, the laundry that serves as the family headquarters in the neighborhood of the Tang people, San Francisco's Chinatown.

He is soon exposed to the difficult conditions under which Chinese immigrants must live and work. Moon Shadow's own grandfather had been lynched 30 years before by a mob of white demons. Now a brick shatters the laundry window, as a racist mob of drunken white men roam through the neighborhood.

His father, who is called Windrider, was known in China as a master kitemaker. He shows Moon Shadow the electrical devices he has invented and recounts the story of how he received the name Windrider. In a former life the father was the greatest physician of all the dragons. His skill at kitemaking is only a remnant of his former powers.

As Moon Shadow grows to love and respect his father, he studies English and begins to learn the strange customs of the American people. After Windrider fights with a member of the criminal brotherhood in Chinatown and kills the man as he is about to shoot Moon Shadow, he and Moon Shadow must leave the Tang neighborhood. They move to rooms in the house of a landlady, Miss Whitlaw, on Polk Street, where Windrider has found work as a handyman.

Moon Shadow becomes friends with Miss Whitlaw's niece, Robin, the first non-Chinese child he has ever met. With Robin's help, Moon Shadow learns to read and write English. Moon Shadow and his father begin a correspondence with the Wright brothers on the mechanics of flying machines, and Windrider begins to build large glider models.

By 1906, Windrider is saving money, looking forward to opening his own fix-it shop and thinking of the day when he might be able to bring Moon Shadow's mother over from China. One morning in April a great earthquake shakes the city. Moon Shadow, his father, Miss Whitlaw and Robin survive; Miss Whitlaw's well-constructed house is the only one still standing on their street. When fires sweep the city, they flee by wagon to Golden Gate Park, then to the Oakland foothills, where they make a home in an abandoned barn.

Windrider dedicates his time and resources for the next three years to building Dragonwings, his flying machine. He makes a successful test flight, but the plane is destroyed and he is injured when it crash-lands. As his broken bones mend, Windrider and Moon Shadow rejoin the company, moving into its sturdy new building in San Francisco. Finally, Moon Shadow's father sails for China to bring Moon Shadow's mother to America.

Moon Shadow knows that many problems and challenges lie before him, but "I knew I could meet them," he says, "with the same courage with which Father had pursued his dream of flight and then given it up, or the same courage with which Mother had faced the long separation from us."

CENSORSHIP HISTORY

Dragonwings was inspired by historical accounts of Fung Joe Guey, a young Chinese man who improved upon the Wright brothers' original airplane design and flew in the hills over Oakland on September 22, 1909, for 20 minutes before a mishap brought his biplane down.

In *Dragonwings*, the author wished to breathe life into the dry historical facts of the experience of Chinese immigrants. "At the same time," Yep wrote, "it has been my aim to counter various stereotypes as presented in the media. . . . I wanted to show that Chinese-Americans are human beings upon whom America has had a unique effect."

Because the novel is written from the point of view of a recently arrived boy, Moon Shadow refers to white Americans as "demons." The Tang word for demon can mean many kinds of supernatural beings, Moon Shadow explains. "A demon can be the ghost of a dead person, but he can also be a supernatural creature, who can use his great powers for good as well as for evil, just like the dragons."

Such allusions to the customs and beliefs of the Chinese immigrants portrayed in *Dragonwings* led to an attempt to ban the book in May 1992. Sylvia Hall, a Pentecostal minister, approached the Apollo-Ridge School Board in Kittanning, Pennsylvania, to ask that *Dragonwings* be removed from the eighth-grade curriculum. She objected to the use of the word "demon" in the book, references to reincarnation and other allusions to Eastern religion and what she described as content relating to the occult and satanism.

When the school board rejected Hall's request to ban the book by a vote of 9–0, she took her case to court, asking for an injunction prohibiting the use of the book. The complainant told the court, "There may be children who will commit suicide because they think they can be reincarnated as something or someone else."

Hall contended the reading of the book in a public school violated the First Amendment prohibition against the establishment of religion. *Drag-*

onwings, she argued, advanced the religion and beliefs of Taoism and reincarnation. It also promoted the religion of secular humanism by implying that people can achieve their goals without God's intervention.

In a September 15, 1992 ruling, Armstrong County Judge Joseph Nickleach denied the request to ban the book. In his opinion, Nickleach wrote: "The fact that religions and religious concepts are mentioned in school does not automatically constitute a violation of the establishment clause." He stipulated that the book was used for a purely secular purpose and that neither the book nor the teachers who taught it promoted a particular religion as the only correct belief or even the preferred belief. He found that the complainant failed to sustain her burden of proof that Apollo-Ridge School District violated the U.S. constitution by assigning the book to be read in school.

FURTHER READINGS

American Library Association. *Newsletter on Intellectual Freedom* 42.1 (January 1993): 18.

Yep, Laurence. *Dragonwings*. Afterword by Laurence Yep, New York: Scholastic, 1990.

ÉMILE

Author: Jean-Jacques Rousseau
Original date and place of publication: 1762, France
Literary form: Novel

SUMMARY

An intimate in the circle of French intellectual Denis Diderot and contributor of music articles to the famous Encyclopédie, Jean-Jacques Rousseau launched his own literary career in 1750, when he unexpectedly won the prize of the Dijon Academy for his essay, "Discourse on the Influence of Learning and Art." Rousseau had been encouraged to enter the competition by Diderot, whom Rousseau had visited when Diderot was imprisoned after the publication of LETTER ON THE BLIND. In his essay Rousseau first expressed the visionary theories that would generate the romantic movement in literature—a belief in human goodness and a call for a return to nature and the primitive virtues corrupted by society.

In 1761, he published an epistolary novel, *Julie, or the New Héloïse*, a love story that popularized the moral beauty of simple living and unaffected virtue. The following year his two greatest and most influential works appeared: THE SOCIAL CONTRACT, explaining his political philosophy, and *Émile*, a pedagogical novel exemplifying his ideas on education.

In *Émile*, which Rousseau considered to be his best work, he presents a plan for the upbringing of male children based on the principle of the natural goodness of man. The book was first intended to be a "memoir of a few pages." When Rousseau introduced the fictional element of the characters of the Tutor, Émile and Sophie, the work expanded. In *Émile* Rousseau discourses on a great variety of subjects, including language, history, politics, society and religion, within a loose fictional framework.

Rousseau structured the book in five parts: the first, on the "age of nature," covering infancy; the second on boyhood; the third on the "age of reason"; the fourth on adolescence; and the fifth on love and society. In Rousseau's theory of "negative education," giving free reign to nature will result in the best development of human potential. "Nature wants children to be children before being men," Rousseau wrote.

Education is seen not simply as imparting or imposing information; rather, it requires a gentle nurturing of what is already within the child. Instruction should proceed by stimulating curiosity and intelligence; the growing child should learn by experience, rather than by rote. The child's mind should develop through conversations and experiments arranged by his tutor that will assist him to use his senses and imagination.

The best preparation for development of healthy, self-reliant children begins in infancy. Babies should be nursed by their own mothers and kept free of swaddling clothes so that the body's natural movements are not impeded. Doctors should be called in as little as possible in order to allow nature's healing powers to operate. As the child grows up, he should participate in athletic activities and commune with nature.

Rousseau was opposed to book learning in childhood. "Reading is the curse of childhood," he believed. The first book he would prescribe for reading at age 12 was Defoe's *Robinson Crusoe*, the story of a man who faced nature with steadfastness and self-reliance. As the child matures, relationships with others begin to be more important and moral and political awareness follows. "The only moral lesson which is suited for a child—the most important lesson for every time of life—is this: 'Never hurt anybody.' "

A child's religious education should begin only when he is familiar with the wonders of the universe. Rousseau would substitute for the dogmas of the church a natural religion based on the principles of deism, in which God's creation is the only Bible and the existence of God is inferred from the order and harmony of the universe, rather than from formal religious teachings.

He recommended against religious books, ritualistic observances or church attendance. "If I had to depict the most heart-breaking stupidity I would paint a pedant teaching children the catechism," he wrote. As an example of what Émile should learn, Rousseau included a long statement of his own religious belief, "Profession of Faith of a Savoyard Priest," an open attack on Christianity. Book Five opens with a section called "Sophie, or Woman," devoted to the education of women, in which he proposed that a woman's place is in the home and subordinate to that of man.

If his education has spared him unnatural stimulations and energies, eventually the individual is able to exercise his natural powers within a community of rational beings. The child raised according to these methods will become the man who is fit to live in Rousseau's good society, which he analyzed in *The Social Contract.*

CENSORSHIP HISTORY

The deistic religious views expressed by Rousseau in *Émile* offended ecclesiastical authorities. The archbishop of Paris issued a mandate against the book, condemning it for its "abominable doctrines," and prohibited the residents of his diocese from reading or possessing it. In 1762, the Parlement of Paris ordered that the book be publicly torn up and burned. The parlement condemned *Émile* for its proposals "to re-establish natural religion . . . that criminal system." It also cited its opposition to the idea of an education based on nature, "the kind of knowledge which instinct alone" suggests. It further took issue with the way the author did "misrepresent sovereign authority," destroying "the principles of obedience which is due to kings." The book was also prohibited at the Sorbonne and by the Inquisition.

When the French government ordered his arrest on June 11, 1762, Rousseau fled Paris for Berne, but was refused permission to remain there. He took refuge in the Swiss canton of Neuchâtel, then a Prussian possession under the protection of Frederick the Great, king of Prussia. In 1763, *Émile* and *The Social Contract* were attacked by Protestant authorities and condemned by the council of Geneva; copies of the book were burned for having "confused anarchy and liberty, [for having] brought the chaos of the state of nature into the system of civil societies, put an axe to the root of all governments, and in turn exalted and insulted Christianity." An order was given for Rousseau's arrest if he entered the city.

Rousseau was outraged that Geneva, the city of his birth, known as a just and free state, could condemn his work and order his arrest without trial. "I trembled with fear that such an evident and obvious breach of every law, beginning with that of common sense, would throw Geneva upside down," he wrote. When there was little protest in Geneva, Rousseau wrote his *Letter to Christophe de Beaumont*, a long reply to the condemnation of *Émile* by the archbishop of Paris. "Neither the burning nor the decrees will ever make me change my language," he wrote. "The theologians, in ordering me to be humble, will never make me be false and the philosophers, by taxing me with hypocrisy, will never make me profess unbelief." The *Letter* was published in March 1763 in Holland and sold 500 copies in one day in Geneva. When its reprinting was prohibited, Rousseau expected the citizens of Geneva to rally to his defense. When they did not, Rousseau renounced his citizenship.

In 1764, Rousseau published *Letters from the Mountain*, a defense of *Émile* and *The Social Contract* that included an attack on the Geneva council and constitution. When his house was stoned, he moved to St. Pierre, an island in the Lake of Bienne in Berne. In 1765, he was expelled from Berne and went to England at the invitation of the Scottish philosopher David Hume.

In Rome in 1766, *Émile*, *The Social Contract* and *Letter to Christophe de Beaumont* were placed on the Index of Forbidden Books. The Spanish Index also prohibited all of Rousseau's writings. Despite its banning, *Émile* was widely read and was extremely influential in its time and in forming modern views of education and childrearing.

One of Rousseau's publishers, François Grasset of Lausanne, recounted to Rousseau in 1765 the response he observed to the suppression of *Émile* in Spain. "I am sure you will be very surprised, my honoured compatriot," he wrote, "when I tell you that I saw your *Émile*, in quarto form, publicly consigned to the flames in Madrid. It took place in the principal Dominican church one Sunday, after High Mass, in the presence of a whole crowd of gaping imbeciles. The immediate consequence was that a number of Spanish grandees and foreign ambassadors began trying to get hold of a copy regardless of cost, arranging for it to be sent them by post." The censorship of *Émile* serving only to increase its fame, it became an underground bestseller throughout Europe.

A quarrel with Hume brought Rousseau back to France in 1767. After wandering through the provinces, he settled in 1770 in Paris, where he lived in a garret and copied music, undisturbed by the authorities. There he worked on his famous autobiographical *CONFESSIONS*, which was not published until after his death in 1778.

Both *Émile* and *The Social Contract* remained on the Index of Forbidden Books through its last edition compiled in 1948 and published until 1966. *Julie, or the New Héloïse* was also placed on the Index in 1806. In 1929, *Confessions* was banned by the United States Customs Department as being injurious to public morals. Rousseau's writing was also banned in the U.S.S.R. in 1935–36.

FURTHER READINGS

Collinson, Diané. *Fifty Major Philosophers: A Reference Guide*. London: Routledge, 1988.

Green, Jonathon. *The Encyclopedia of Censorship*. New York: Facts On File, 1990.

Haight, Anne Lyon. *Banned Books: 387 BC to 1978 AD*. Updated and enlarged by Chandler B. Grannis. New York: R. R. Bowker, 1978.

Hornstein, Lillian Herlands, ed. *The Readers' Companion to World Literature*. New York: New American Library, 1956.

Mason, John Hope. *The Indispensable Rousseau*. London: Quartet Books, 1979.

Scott-Kakures, Dion, Susan Castegnetto, Hugh Benson, William Taschek and Paul Hurley. *History of Philosophy*. New York: HarperCollins, 1993.

ENCYCLOPÉDIE

Editors: Denis Diderot and Jean le Rond d'Alembert
Original date and place of publication: 1751–72, France
Literary form: Encyclopedia

SUMMARY

The *Encyclopédie*, a 28-volume encyclopedia of arts and sciences published between 1751 and 1772, epitomized the rational and tolerant spirit of the 18th-century Enlightenment and was instrumental in creating the climate of ideas that culminated in the French revolution of 1789. The *Encyclopédie* was the monumental life's work of its primary editor, French philosopher, critic and dramatist Denis Diderot. Diderot's aim in producing the *Encyclopédie* was to "change the general way of thinking" by bringing together the thought of all the outstanding writers and thinkers of the time, collecting in one huge work the summary of all human knowledge as seen from a modern perspective.

Originally planned as a translation from English of Ephraim Chambers's 1728 *Cyclopaedia*, Diderot and mathematician Jean le Rond d'Alembert decided to launch an entirely new work when disagreements caused the first project to be abandoned. In 1751, Diderot and d'Alembert produced a *Preliminary Discourse* signed by d'Alembert, presenting the philosophical foundations of the project and expressing confidence in human abilities to transform the conditions of material and intellectual life. It traced the sciences and arts to their origins and classified them according to the faculties of memory, reason or imagination. It also outlined the history of intellectual progress and scientific development since the Renaissance, discussing the contributions of René Descartes, Isaac Newton and John Locke, as well as those of contemporaries Voltaire and Montesquieu.

Later that year the first folio volume of the *Encyclopédie* appeared, with contributions by the most brilliant writers of the time. Diderot's article "Political Authority" set the rational and democratic tone of the work: "No man has received from nature the right to give orders to others. . . . Power deriving from the consent of the peoples subject to it necessarily presupposes conditions that render the wielding of it legitimate, useful to society, advantageous to the state, and restricted within certain fixed limits."

Diderot's essay "Natural Right," which appeared in the fifth volume published in 1755, exemplified the philosophical bias of the project. He defended a universal natural law based on human needs and experience, rather than the doctrine of traditional innate or God-given law. "We must in all things, make use of our reason, because man is not merely an animal, but an animal with the power of reason. . . . Everything that you conceive, every course of action you consider, will be good, great, noble, sublime if it is in accordance with the general and common interest."

Despite struggles with government censors, seven folio volumes appeared at the rate of one a year until 1757 and included contributions by such luminaries as Voltaire, Montesquieu and Rousseau. In 1759, the *Encyclopédie* was officially suppressed. After d'Alembert resigned as editor, Diderot carried on the project clandestinely, publishing the last ten volumes of text in 1765 in the provinces and in 1766 in Paris. Eleven volumes of plates illustrating the industrial arts also appeared under his direction in 1772.

The *Encyclopédie* was immediately successful. Its intellectual and political impact was enormous. It promulgated the work of Bacon, Descartes, Hobbes, Locke, Berkeley, Spinoza, Bayle and Leibnitz in philosophy and the scientific advances of Copernicus, Kepler, Galileo and Newton. It implicitly advocated social change in its preference for ideas derived from experience and the senses, its glorification of the arts, sciences and industry, its stress on rationalism and scientific determinism and its attacks on legal, juridical and clerical abuses. It championed the principles of religious tolerance, democratic government and equality, supporting the philosophic doctrine that the dissemination of knowledge would lead to human emancipation.

CENSORSHIP HISTORY

In an entry in the *Encyclopédie* expounding on the meaning of the word *pardonner*, to pardon, Diderot took the opportunity to defend his work against defamation. "Some men, who produced a silly work which imbecile editors botched further," he wrote, referring to the Jesuit encyclopedia, the *Dictionnaire de Trévoux*, "have never been able to pardon us for having planned a better one. These enemies to all good have subjected us to every kind of persecution. We have seen our honor, our fortune, our liberty, our life endangered within a few months' time."

Indeed, the rational secular emphasis of the *Encyclopédie* made government officials uneasy and aroused the hostility of the Jesuits, who attacked the work as irreligious and used their influence to have it suppressed. The opening skirmish of the battle to censor the *Encyclopédie* took place after the publication of the first two volumes in 1752. Among the articles in the second volume was "Certitude," written by Jean Martin de Prades, a theology student at the Sorbonne. The thesis submitted by De Prades for his Sorbonne degree was denounced for heresy by the Parlement of Paris. It was rumored that Diderot had a hand in the thesis, which, in fact, included whole paragraphs taken from the *Preliminary Discourse*. The Sorbonne revoked De Prades's degree and ordered his arrest. He fled to Prussia, but the fallout from the De Prades affair landed squarely on the *Encyclopédie*.

De Prades's contribution was denounced to the king as evidence of the atheistic underpinnings of the project. Jesuit critics also took the editors to task for an article claiming that most men honor literature as they do religion, "as something they can neither know nor practice nor love." On January 31,

1752, the archbishop of Paris condemned the *Encyclopédie* for its subtle attack on religion.

In February the first two volumes were condemned by order of the king's council for their tendency to "destroy the royal authority, set up the spirit of independence and revolt, and under obscure and equivocal language, to raise the foundations of error, of corruptions of morals, of irreligion, and of unbelief." The council forbade further sale or publication and ordered seizure of the volumes.

The publisher, André-François Le Breton, and his associates, Antoine-Claude Briasson, Michel-Antoine David and Laurent Durand, appealed to the council with the support of Chretién-Guillaume de Lamoignon de Malesherbes, the liberal director of the book trade and powerful protector of the *Encyclopédie*. Malesherbes arranged the granting of a "tacit permission" for the publication of further volumes and, to placate the clergy, agreed that future volumes would be reviewed by three theologians. In 1754, Louis XV, influenced by anti-Jesuit sentiment within his court, granted a personal privilege for continuation of the work.

As publication of the volumes proceeded, the number of subscribers rose far beyond the number anticipated by the publishers to 4,255 by 1757. That year brought the second attempt to ban the *Encyclopédie*. In the wake of an assassination attempt against Louis XV, the crown issued a declaration in April 1757 reviving an old law that condemned to death authors, publishers and sellers of books that attacked religion and the state.

The seventh volume of the *Encyclopédie* included an article by d'Alembert on the Calvinist stronghold of Geneva, in which he compared French Catholicism unfavorably with Genevan Protestantism and represented the Calvinist clergy as denying the divinity of Christ. The article offended both Protestants and Catholics. Seizing their opportunity, the opponents of the project pressed again for its suppression. In July 1758, Claude-Adrien Helvétius's book DE L'ESPRIT was condemned by religious and civil authorities as atheistic and subversive. The anti-Encyclopédists charged that Helvétius's book, whose skeptical views were associated with those of the philosophes, was intimately connected with the *Encyclopédie*. The two books were viewed as representing a conspiracy to destroy religion and undermine the state.

The furor over the seventh volume led the king to revoke the license to publish in 1759 and a decree of his council outlawed the *Encyclopédie*. "The advantages to be derived from a work of this sort, in respect to progress in the arts and sciences, can never compensate for the irreparable damage that results from it in regard to morality and religion," the decree stated. The publishers were forbidden to sell the volumes that had already appeared or print any new ones.

On March 5, 1759, the Vatican placed the first seven volumes of the *Encyclopédie* on the Index of Forbidden Books on the grounds that the teaching and propositions contained in it were false and pernicious, tending to the destruction of morality, the promotion of godlessness and the undermining of religion. Later that year, Pope Clement XII warned all Catholics who owned the volumes to have them burned by a priest or face excommunication.

D'Alembert had resigned as editor in 1758, but Diderot and his printers continued their work in secret. Urged to give up the project and flee the country for his own safety, Diderot wrote to Voltaire that "to abandon the work is to turn one's back on the breach, and do what the rascals who persecute us desire."

The king's council further required that the publishers issue refunds to subscribers to close accounts. The edict put the publishers at risk of financial insolvency. But through the intervention of Malesherbes, the government allowed the publishers to apply the money to the production of a new book that was, in fact, the plates of the *Encyclopédie* under a different title.

The new book received a privilege in September 1759, and the publishers were able to proceed to print the last ten volumes of text. These volumes appeared all at once in 1765 and 1766 under a false imprint, Chez Samuel Faulche & Compagnie, Neufchastel. The Jesuits, the enemies of the *Encyclopédie*, had been expelled from France in 1764, and powerful figures at court and in the government quietly used their influence to allow distribution of the volumes. The government, recognizing the fait accompli, did not take further action against Diderot.

The *Encyclopédie* became the best-known work of its time and the most formidable instrument for diffusion of the progressive ideas of the Enlightenment. Its 28 volumes were reprinted in Switzerland, Italy, Germany and Russia, and numerous approved and pirated editions appeared in France—43 in all over a 25-year period. Many of the later printings were inexpensive quarto and octavo editions that reached ordinary readers everywhere in Europe. In all, about 25,000 copies of the *Encyclopédie* were circulated in Europe before 1789, at least 11,500 of them in France.

In 1804, the entire work was placed on the Index of Forbidden Books, where it remained until the last edition of the Index was published in 1966. It was not an official act of church or state, however, that was most effective in censoring the *Encyclopédie*. In 1764 after the last 10 volumes of text had already been set in type, Diderot discovered that his printer, Le Breton, had secretly deleted text and altered many articles containing liberal opinions. He had, for example, removed from Diderot's article on the Saracens the following passage: "It is a general observation that religion declines as philosophy grows. You may reach what conclusions you like either against the usefulness of philosophy or the truth of religion; but I can tell you that the more philosophers there are in Constantinople, the fewer pilgrims there will be to Mecca." The mutilated articles also included those in which Diderot had eulogized the skeptical philosophy of the 17th-century philosopher, Pierre Bayle, author of the controversial HISTORICAL AND CRITICAL DICTIONARY.

Diderot was enraged by Le Breton's betrayal. "You have driven a dagger into my heart," Diderot wrote to Le Breton. "I shall bear the wound until I die." For almost 200 years, the expurgated text was the only one available, until a volume turned up containing Le Breton's corrections of the proof and was acquired by an American collector.

FURTHER READINGS

Darnton, Robert. *The Business of Enlightenment: A Publishing History of the Encyclopédie 1775–1800*. Cambridge, Mass.: Belknap Press of Harvard University Press, 1979.

Diderot, Denis. *Diderot's Selected Writings*. Ed. and intro. by Lester G. Crocker. Trans. by Derek Coltman. New York: Macmillan Company, 1966.

Durant, Will, and Ariel Durant. *The Age of Voltaire*. New York: Simon and Schuster, 1965.

Garraty, John A., and Peter Gay. *The Columbia History of the World*. New York: Harper & Row, 1972.

Gay, Peter. *The Enlightenment: An Interpretation. The Rise of Modern Paganism*. New York: W. W. Norton & Co., 1995.

Green, Jonathon. *The Encyclopedia of Censorship*. New York: Facts On File, 1990.

Haight, Anne Lyon. *Banned Books: 387 BC to 1978 AD*. Updated and enlarged by Chandler B. Grannis. New York: R. R. Bowker, 1978.

Hornstein, Lillian Herlands, ed. *The Readers' Companion to World Literature*. New York: New American Library. 1956.

Reill, Peter Hanns, and Ellen Judy Wilson, eds. *Encyclopedia of the Enlightenment*. New York: Facts On File, 1996.

AN ESSAY CONCERNING HUMAN UNDERSTANDING

Author: John Locke
Original date and place of publication: 1690, England
Literary form: Philosophical treatise

SUMMARY

The English philosopher John Locke, the intellectual ruler of the 18th century, was the founder of the school of philosophy known as British empiricism. Educated at Oxford, he lectured there in Greek, rhetoric and philosophy. His familiarity with scientific practice gained through study of medicine had a strong influence on his philosophy. He became a physician and advisor to the first earl of Shaftesbury and in 1675 went to France, where he became acquainted with French leaders in science and philosophy. In 1679, he retired to Oxford.

Suspected of radicalism by the British government, Locke fled to Holland in 1683. During his six years in Holland, he completed *An Essay Concerning*

Human Understanding, one of the most important works in modern philosophy. First published in 1690, it was reissued in expanded editions in 1694, 1700 and 1706.

Through this essay, Locke became known in England and on the Continent as the leading philosopher of freedom. It was the most widely read philosophical book of Locke's generation, written in a lucid style and without technical philosophical terminology. Locke "created metaphysics almost as Newton had created physics," wrote Jean d'Alembert in 1751 in the *Preliminary Discourse* to the great monument to Enlightenment thought, the ENCYCLOPÉDIE.

Locke saw the philosopher's primary task as clarification, "to be employed as an under-labourer in clearing the ground a little, and removing some of the rubbish that lies in the way to knowledge." His contribution was to present philosophy as a discipline based on empirical observation and common sense judgments, rather than an esoteric study. He established the connection between philosophy and scientific thought by explaining in a manner that was consistent with 17th-century science how knowledge was acquired.

In the opening "Epistle to the Reader," Locke describes how the *Essay* developed as the fruit of a casual discussion with a few friends: "After we had awhile puzzled ourselves, without coming any nearer a resolution of those doubts which perplexed us, it came into my thoughts that we took a wrong course, and that before we set ourselves upon inquiries of that nature, it was necessary to examine our own abilities, and see what objects our understandings were, or were not, fitted to deal with."

Locke wrote down some "hasty and undigested thoughts on a subject he had never before considered" to bring to the next meeting of his friends. These first notes led to an extensive critical inquiry "into the origins, certainty and extent of human knowledge together with the grounds and degrees of belief, opinion and assent" that was to absorb 20 years of study and writing.

In the *Essay*, Locke examines the nature of knowledge and the basis for judging truth. By observing the natural world, he traces beliefs and states of mind to their psychological origins. He sets out to show that human understanding is too limited to allow comprehensive knowledge of the universe. For Locke, if we insist on certainty we will lose our bearings in the world. "[I]t becomes the Modesty of Philosophy" for us not to speak too confidently where we lack grounds of knowledge and to content ourselves with faith and probability.

He begins by refuting Plato's doctrine of "innate ideas," maintaining, instead, that all knowledge is of empiric origin. The mind at birth is a tabula rasa, a "white paper, void of all characters, without any ideas," Locke believed. Experience in the form of sensations and reflections provides raw materials that the mind analyzes and organizes in complex ways. Because all knowledge is ultimately derived from experience, language—the means by which knowledge is transmitted—has meaning only within the context of experience.

For Locke, even the idea of God is not innate. It can be discovered by a rational mind reflecting on the works of creation. Locke criticizes the innateness doctrine as esoteric and open to exploitation by those in positions of authority who claim to be guardians of hidden truths. "Vague and insignificant forms of speech, and abuse of language, have so long passed for mysteries of science . . .," Locke writes, "that it will not be easy to persuade either those who speak or those who hear them that they are but the covers of ignorance, and hindrance of true knowledge." Reason must judge the authenticity of religious revelation. To accept an irrational belief as revelation "must overturn all the principles and foundations of knowledge."

Locke's abandonment of the innateness doctrine opened the way for three influential concepts: that knowledge is cumulative and progressive; the necessity of communication; and curiosity about cultural variety. As Voltaire wrote of Locke, "Aided everywhere by the torch of physics, he dares at times to affirm, but he also dares to doubt. Instead of collecting in one sweeping definition what we do not know, he explores by degrees what we desire to know."

CENSORSHIP HISTORY

Locke's *Essay* was widely read in England and on the Continent, where most of his works became known in French translations. His rejection of innate ideas immediately involved him in controversy with theologians who saw his argument as a threat to religious belief and the maintenance of church discipline. It was, however, another aspect of the *Essay*—Locke's comment on "thinking matter"—that became its single most disputed issue.

Locke's statement that one "possibly shall never be able to know, whether any material Being thinks, or no" caused great controversy, particularly in France, where Voltaire quoted it in LETTERS CONCERNING THE ENGLISH NATION and declared it a central concept in Locke's thinking. This remark and Locke's belief that "all the great ends of Morality and Religion, are well enough secured, without philosophical Proofs of the Soul's Immateriality" were held to support materialism and atheism.

These passages became a subject of intense debate between Locke and the bishop of Worcester, Edward Stillingfleet. The bishop read the essay when it first appeared in 1690 and had not seen it as having any dangerous consequences for the doctrines of the Church of England. But with the publication in 1696 of the radical deist John Toland's CHRISTIANITY NOT MYSTERIOUS, a widely banned book positing reason as the only test of faith, Locke came under attack.

Although Toland's rationalistic approach to theology went far beyond anything Locke advocated or believed, Toland adopted Locke's theory of knowledge from the *Essay*. Stillingfleet prefaced a 1696 critique of Toland with a condemnation of Locke. Some of the issues raised by Locke's debate with Stillingfleet appeared in 1699 as material added by Locke to the fourth edition of the *Essay*.

In *The Reasonableness of Christianity*, published in 1695, Locke maintained that knowledge must be supplemented by religious faith. He dismissed the doctrine of Original Sin as unsupported by the Bible and contrary both to reason and to the idea of a benevolent God. He was accused of being anti-Trinitarian and Socinian, a heresy that rejected the divinity of the Holy Trinity.

In 1701 in London, the Latin version of *Essay* was prohibited at Oxford with the instructions "that no tutors were to read with their students" this investigation into the basis of knowledge. In 1700, the Catholic church placed the French translation of *An Essay Concerning Human Understanding* on the Index of Forbidden Books. It remained listed until 1966. *Essay* was singled out as condemned directly by the pope in a solemn manner, a designation shared by only 144 of the 4,126 works listed on the modern Index, and the only distinguished book in that category. Despite the censorship of *An Essay on Human Understanding*, Locke's book exerted a profound influence on its time and in the history of philosophy.

FURTHER READINGS

Chappell, Vere, ed. *The Cambridge Companion to Locke*. Cambridge: Cambridge University Press, 1994.

Collinson, Diané. *Fifty Major Philosophers: A Reference Guide*. London: Routledge, 1988.

Green, Jonathon. *The Encyclopedia of Censorship*. New York: Facts On File, 1990.

Scott-Kakures, Dion, Susan Castegnetto, Hugh Benson, William Taschek and Paul Hurley. *History of Philosophy*. New York: HarperCollins, 1993.

ESSAYS

Author: Michel de Montaigne
Original date and place of publication: 1580, France
Literary form: Essays

SUMMARY

Michel de Montaigne was the originator of the personal essay as a literary form and the inventor of a new form of autobiography. In his *essais*, or "trials," he set out to test his judgment on a wide range of subjects of interest to him, revealing his inner life and personality. Written over a period of 20 years, beginning in 1571 when Montaigne was 38 until his death in 1592, the 94 essays trace the evolution of Montaigne's thinking as he added to and changed his earlier writings. Books one and two were published in 1580. Revised and enlarged editions of the first two books appeared with book three in 1588; a final complete edition was published posthumously in 1595.

The earliest essays, which began as notes on Montaigne's reading, are mainly compilations of anecdotes with brief commentary. Over the years the essays became longer and more personal. His most influential philosophical essay was the book-length "Apology for Raymond Sebond," composed in 1576. Montaigne's skepticism, summed up in his famous motto "*Que Scay-je?*" (What do I know?), is revealed in this essay, a sustained argument on the impotence and vanity of presumptuous human reason. In the later essays his self-portrait emerges as the central theme.

Essays opens with Montaigne's preface, "To the Reader," in which he sets the conversational, personal and modest tone that is characteristic of his writing: "This book was written in good faith, reader. It warns you from the outset that in it I have set myself no goal but a domestic and private one. I have had no thought of serving either you or my own glory. . . . If I had written to seek the world's favor, I should have bedecked myself better, and should have presented myself in a studied posture. I want to be seen here in my simple, natural, ordinary fashion, without straining or artifice; for it is myself that I portray."

Drawing on his own recollections, conversations with neighbors and friends, readings in classical literature and the narratives of historians and ethnographers, the essays range over a vast array of subjects, from cannibalism to education, politics, friendship, nature and death. Montaigne reveals himself as intellectually curious, tolerant, skeptical and unafraid to contradict himself. His aim is to provide an unvarnished picture of his experience and attitudes, for if a man does not know himself, what does he know?

"My sole aim is to reveal myself," he writes, "and I may be different tomorrow if some new lesson changes me. . . . Contradictions of opinion, therefore, neither offend nor estrange me; they only arouse and exercise my mind."

Through his quest for self-knowledge, Montaigne is led to recognize common human traits and values. In his last essay, "On Experience," he concludes, "It is an absolute perfection and virtually divine to know how to enjoy our being rightfully. We seek other conditions because we do not understand the use of our own, and go outside of ourselves because we do not know what it is like inside. . . . The most beautiful lives, to my mind, are those that conform to the common human pattern, with order, but without miracle and without eccentricity."

CENSORSHIP HISTORY

The first attempt to censor the *Essays* took place in 1580–81, shortly after the first publication of books one and two, when Montaigne traveled to Germany, Switzerland and Italy. Upon his entry into Rome, as Montaigne recounted in his *Travel Journal*, his baggage was thoroughly examined by customs. Although he had passed through Germany and "was of an inquiring nature," he carried no forbidden books. Nevertheless, all the books he had, including a copy of the *Essays*, were confiscated for examination. They included a prayer book (suspect only because it was published in Paris, rather than Rome) and "also the books of certain German doctors of theology against the heretics, because in combatting them, they made mention of their errors."

Though Montaigne had been cordially received by Pope Gregory XIII, he was later summoned to the Vatican's Holy Office and advised that some passages in his *Essays* should be changed or deleted in future editions. The papal censor, theology professor Sisto Fabri, who did not read French, discussed with Montaigne various errors that had been identified upon the report of a French friar. The censor objected to the overuse of the word "fortune"; the defense of the fourth-century Roman Emperor Julian, who abandoned Christianity; the praise of heretical poets; the idea that one who prays should be free from evil impulses; the critical comments on torture ("All that is beyond plain death seems to me pure cruelty"); and the recommendation that children should be fit to do either good or evil so that they may do good through free choice. Though Fabri was "content with the excuses I offered," Montaigne commented, "on each objection that his Frenchman had left him he referred it to my conscience to redress what I thought was in bad taste."

Montaigne responded that these were his opinions, which he did not feel were erroneous, and suggested that perhaps the censor had improperly understood his thoughts. He did promise, however, to consider some revisions. Ultimately, he made none of the recommended revisions in the essays.

In 1595, an unauthorized, expurgated edition was published in Lyons by Simon Goulart. Produced for Calvinist consumption, a number of chapters were suppressed and passages critical of Protestants were omitted. In its complete edition, as edited by Montaigne's literary executor Marie de Gournay and published in 1595, *Essays* remained a bestseller in France into the mid-17th century and was reprinted every two or three years. The book was considered a classic and Montaigne a standard author.

Though Montaigne's writing had been forbidden by the Spanish Inquisition in 1640, it was not until 84 years after Montaigne's death, when the *Essays* had been circulating for close to a century, that it was condemned by the Vatican. In 1676, it was placed on the Index of Forbidden Books with the specification "in whatever language they may be printed." It remained on the Index for almost 300 years.

Montaigne was a faithful Catholic, but he felt that the spheres of faith and reason should be separate. He believed that when faith and reason are contradictory, faith must prevail in religious matters. Not even the most important church dogmas, such as the existence of God and the immortality of the soul, can be proven. They must, rather, be accepted on faith. Theology and philosophy were thus separated, and modern scientific discoveries, such as the new astronomy combatted by the church, could be accepted as a matter of reason without challenging religious doctrine.

"No proposition astounds me, no belief offends me," Montaigne wrote, "however much opposed it may be to my own." Montaigne's skepticism, tolerance and mistrust of dogmatic systems of belief reflected an open-minded humanistic spirit. This attitude was still possible in Montaigne's day while the liberal philosophy of Renaissance humanism prevailed. But as the Counter-Reformation gained strength and church traditions were secured against the innovations of Protestant theology, Montaigne's views on the separation of faith and reason were attacked as the heresy of "fideism." The placement of the *Essays* on the Index in 1676 is thought to be the result of criticisms by theologians influenced by the rationalism of Descartes, which declared that faith could appeal to reason.

FURTHER READINGS

Boase, Alan M. *The Fortunes of Montaigne: A History of the Essays in France, 1580–1669.* New York: Octagon Books, 1970.

Frame, Donald M., trans. and intro. *The Complete Works of Montaigne*. Stanford: Stanford University Press, 1967.

———, trans. and intro. *The Complete Essays of Montaigne*. Stanford: Stanford University Press, 1958.

Montaigne, Michel de. *Essays*. Ed. and intro. by J. M. Cohen. Middlesex, England: Penguin Books, 1958.

Tetel, Marcel. *Montaigne: Updated Edition*. Boston: Twayne Publishers, 1990.

Toulmin, Stephen. *Cosmopolis: The Hidden Agenda of Modernity*. Chicago: University of Chicago Press, 1990.

ETHICS

Author: Baruch (Benedict) Spinoza
Original date and place of publication: 1677, Holland
Literary form: Philosophical treatise

SUMMARY

The Dutch rationalist philosopher Baruch Spinoza was born in Amsterdam to Portuguese Jewish parents who had fled the Spanish Inquisition. A scholar of Hebrew, he questioned many traditional tenets of Judaism as conflicting with reason and natural science. For his heretical thinking, he was excommunicated from the Jewish community in 1656 at the age of 24. He subsequently made his living as a lens grinder and devoted himself to his philosophical writings, discussing Descartes's new philosophy with a group of secular Christians. His most important and difficult masterpiece, *Ethics*, was completed in 1665 but not published until after his death in 1677.

Of the rationalist philosophers of the period, Spinoza's ideas have the most in common with modern, secular conceptions of the cosmos. According to Spinoza, all that exists is of this world. The order of the world cannot be explained by appeal to the acts of a transcendent God. The fundamental presupposition of his method is that the structure of the cosmos can be set out in geometrical fashion and understood by appeal to self-evident claims bound by logical relations. Mathematics, which deals not in final causes, but in the essence and properties of forms, offers a standard of truth.

In all of his writing, Spinoza advocated, in opposition to traditional theology, a purely naturalistic and scientific study of all aspects of human thought and behavior free of emotional and moral attitudes, which are reflections of subjective desires and fears. All problems, whether metaphysical, moral or scientific, can be formulated and solved as if they were geometrical theorems. Thus he wrote *Ethics* in the geometrical manner, as a succession of definitions and propositions with supporting proofs.

The definitions and propositions set out in the first part of *Ethics* can be properly understood only in relation to the mutually supporting propositions that follow. Spinoza introduces definitions for his notions of substance, cause, attribute, freedom and necessity, successively explaining each in terms of the others. With the aid of these logically connected notions he defines what he means by God or Nature.

It is Spinoza's fundamental argument in *Ethics* that there can only be a single substance, God or Nature (*Deus sive Natura*), which necessarily exists and is the cause of itself. All other aspects of reality must be explained as attributes of this unique, infinite and all-inclusive substance. "Hence it follows that God alone is a free cause. For God alone exists from the mere necessity of his own nature." God is not the creator of nature beyond himself. Rather, God *is*, nature in its fullness.

Everything that exists has its place in the system of causes in nature, Spinoza believed. Every human choice, attitude or feeling is the necessary effect of causes in the infinite chain of causes. Nature has no fixed aim in view and all final causes are merely human fabrications.

Spinoza was a determinist. He believed that all actions are determined by past experience and the laws of nature. He was also a relativist, in that he believed that things are not inherently good or bad, but take on such properties in relation to circumstances.

CENSORSHIP HISTORY

Spinoza's reputation as a dangerous skeptic and heretic was firmly established upon his excommunication from the Jewish community of Amsterdam in 1656. Because of the prominence of his family, his lapse from orthodoxy caused a scandal that was viewed as a threat to the survival of the community. Jews were not yet citizens in Holland, and their leaders feared that the spread of intellectual dissent in their midst would alarm the Dutch, who were already sheltering many religious sects and schisms within their borders.

Spinoza found biblical doctrine incompatible with natural science and logic. He was uncomfortable with the notion of miracles, found the description of God in the Torah unacceptable to his reason and regarded its laws as arbitrary. He considered the Bible to have been written by humans and did not accept it as the "word of God." He also questioned whether the Jews were uniquely God's chosen people.

On July 17, 1656, the ruling council of the community announced that, having endeavored for some time without success to deter Baruch de Espinoza [as he was known in the Jewish community] from his evil ways, it was "resolved that the said Espinoza be put in *herem* (ban) and banished from the nation of Israel. . . . We warn that none may contact him orally or in writing, nor do him any favor, nor stay under the same roof with him, nor read any paper he made or wrote."

When *Ethics* was completed in 1665, in view of Spinoza's growing notoriety and criticism of his philosophy as atheistic and subversive it was clear that its publication, even anonymously, would be too dangerous while he was alive. In 1668, Adrian Coerbach, a doctor of medicine of Amsterdam, was charged with having accepted and defended opinions of Spinoza. Coerbach was sentenced to prison for 10 years and banished from Holland for another ten years.

When Spinoza's THEOLOGICAL-POLITICAL TREATISE, a defense of freedom of opinion that laid the foundations for a rational interpretation of the Jewish and Christian religions, was published in 1670, it brought Spinoza fame. It also aroused hostility because of its skepticism about religious doctrine. Although it was published anonymously under a fictitious imprint, Spinoza was known to be the author.

This treatise was the only one that Spinoza was able to publish during his lifetime, except for a 1663 exposition on Descartes's philosophy that included an introduction explaining that the work did not represent his own views. Spinoza spent the last years of his life on the *Political Treatise*, which he intended as a more popular exposition of the principles of tolerance in a rational society.

After Spinoza's death in 1677 his friends published his writing in a single volume, *Opera posthuma* by B. D. S., including *Ethics*, *Political Treatise* and several other works. *Ethics* was widely condemned as atheistic and morally subversive. Spinoza's pantheism—his identification of God with Nature—and his determinism were viewed as particularly offensive.

A series of bans against Spinoza's work in Holland ensued under the authority of the prince of Orange, states of Holland, synods of the church, local magistrates, university authorities and the burgomaster of Leiden. A total of 50 edicts or judgments against reading or circulating Spinoza's works were issued through 1680. In 1679 the Catholic church placed all of his writing on the Index of Forbidden Books. The church denounced his *Theological-Political Treatise* as a book "forged in hell by a renegade Jew and the devil."

His work remained on the Index under the most severe category of *opera omnia*, or all works condemned, through the last edition of the Index in the 20th century.

For about 100 years after his death, Spinoza's name was linked with immorality, and his philosophy was largely neglected. Only at the end of the 18th century, when Goethe aroused interest in him, was his work studied seriously again.

FURTHER READINGS

Gerber, Jane S. *The Jews of Spain: A History of the Sephardic Experience*. New York: Free Press, 1992.

Hampshire, Stuart. *Spinoza: An Introduction to His Philosophical Thought*. London: Penguin Books, 1988.

———, ed. *The Age of Reason: The 17th Century Philosophers*. New York: New American Library, 1956.

Putnam, George Haven. *The Censorship of the Church of Rome*. Vol. 2. New York: G. P. Putnam's Sons, 1906–07.

Scott-Kakures, Dion, Susan Castegnetto, Hugh Benson, William Taschek and Paul Hurley. *History of Philosophy*. New York: HarperCollins, 1993.

THE FABLE OF THE BEES

Author: Bernard Mandeville
Original date and place of publication: 1714, 1723, 1728, England
Literary form: Satirical essays

SUMMARY

The Fable of the Bees was one of the most controversial and widely read books of early 18th-century England. Its author, Bernard Mandeville, was a Dutch physician who had moved to London, where he practiced medicine and wrote on ethical subjects.

In 1705, he published a satirical poem, "The Grumbling Hive: Or, Knaves Turn'd Honest." It was reprinted in 1714 along with an essay, "An Enquiry into the Origins of Moral Virtue," and a series of remarks elaborating upon ideas expressed in the poem. The new volume was called *The Fable of the Bees: Or, Private Vices, Publick Benefits.*

A moral fable about the symbiotic relationship between vice and national greatness, Mandeville's satire mixed verse with prose, including parables, fables and anecdotes. Portraying England as a flourishing beehive, he proposed that the prosperity of the hive depended on the evil behavior of its members. The unknowing cooperation of individuals working for their own interests resulted in the satisfaction of society's needs. "Thus every Part was full of Vice, Yet the whole Mass a Paradise."

Mandeville declared that vice, rather than virtue, was the foundation of the emerging capitalist society. Examining virtuous actions taken out of self-interest, he contended that in reality they were only "counterfeited" virtues. The "most hateful qualities of its citizens"—pride, self-interest and the desire for material goods—represented, in fact, the very basis of the economic well-being of society. Economic prosperity was best maintained when there was least interference by government or charitable organizations.

Commission of crime kept the legal profession employed. The vices of vanity and luxury in the rich, for example, benefitted the poor by providing employment for them, creating wants that kept merchants and manufacturers in business. Prostitution was inevitable and socially useful. "Religion is one thing and Trade is another," Mandeville declared. Economics and morality were not natural allies. "The moment Evil ceases, the Society must be spoiled." Therefore, a nation of atheists would probably be healthier, more prosperous and more powerful than a society of believers.

In a stinging attack on clerical hypocrisy, he also indicted "reverend Divines of all Sects," who lecture on the spiritual benefits of self-denial and then demand for themselves "convenient Houses, handsome Furniture, good Fires in Winter, pleasant Gardens in Summer, neat Clothes and Money enough to bring up their Children. . . ."

Despite its bold ideas, *The Fable of the Bees* attracted little attention until 1723, when Mandeville published a new and enlarged edition of the book, adding two lengthy essays: "A Search into the Nature of Society" and "An Essay on Charity and Charity-Schools."

"A Search into the Nature of Society" provided additional illustrations of the social and economic utility of vice, attacking the optimistic philosophy of the third earl of Shaftesbury. It was Mandeville's charity-school essay, however, that became notorious.

In 1699, the Society for Promoting Christian Knowledge had organized a movement to establish charity schools for the poor in every parish in Britain. Several hundred such schools were founded, supported by the clergy and the British public. Dedicated to moral improvement of the poor, the schools provided instruction in Bible reading, the catechism and mathematics. In an attack on the schools, Mandeville contended that to lavish charity on the poor was to remove their incentive to work and foster unrealistic ambitions and desires. Defining charity as "that Virtue by which part of that sincere Love we have for our selves is transferr'd pure and unmix'd to others," Mandeville claimed that no action was genuinely charitable unless it was untainted by any selfish desire. Pity was not a virtue, since it derived from a self-indulgent wish to spare ourselves unpleasant sights and feelings. "Thousands give Money to Beggars from the same Motive as they pay their Corn-cutter, to walk easy," he wrote.

CENSORSHIP HISTORY

In a 1714 preface to *The Fable of the Bees*, Mandeville remarked: "If you ask me, why I have done all this . . . and what Good these Notions will produce? Truly, besides the Reader's Diversion, I believe, none at all. . . ." Rather than a mere diversion for Mandeville's readers, however, *The Fable of the Bees* became the subject of one of the most heated controversies of the time.

After 1723, *The Fable* was the target of attacks in the press, pulpits and courts that were to last through most of the century. "Vice and Luxury have found a champion and a Defendor, which they never did before," one critic wrote. In the view of one anonymous 18th-century poet, whose sentiments were typical of public reaction to the volume, Mandeville was the anti-Christ. "And if GOD-MAN Vice to abolish came/ Who Vice commends, MAN-DEVIL be his name."

By implying that religion was damaging to social welfare, the book seemed to advocate atheism and immorality. In 1723, Mandeville's book was the subject of a presentment by the grand jury of Middlesex, in which the book was declared a public nuisance and the author accused of a blasphemy so "diabolical" that it had "a direct Tendency to the Subversion of all Religion and Civil Government." The jury indicated concern that the continued publication of Mandeville's "flagrant Impieties" would provoke divine retribution, particularly his recommendations that vice was necessary to public welfare.

Mandeville's case never came to trial, however, because he was befriended by a former lord chancellor, the earl of Macclesfield. Also, it is assumed that because Mandeville intended his book only for people of "knowledge and education" who could afford the price of five shillings, the book was felt to be a lesser threat to public order.

Undeterred by the grand jury's findings, Mandeville immediately published a six-penny pamphlet containing the grand jury's presentment against the 1723 edition, the text of an attack on the book from the *London Journal* and his own "Vindication" of the Book. The pamphlet's contents were added to a new edition of *The Fable*, published in 1724.

During the next five years, 10 different books were published attacking *The Fable*. In 1728, the work was again presented to the grand jury of Middlesex. The grand jury alleged that Mandeville had undermined the authority of the Bible and advocated "a Freedom of thinking and acting whatever Men please." His book was "atheistical" and had "many blasphemous passages." The grand jury also complained about the new edition's inclusion of the earlier grand jury's condemnation of *The Fable*.

In late 1728, Mandeville issued yet another edition, doubling the book's size with the inclusion of part two, a series of six dialogues in which two characters, Cleomenes and Horatio, debate Mandeville's philosophy.

Attacks on *The Fable* persisted after Mandeville's death in 1733. In 1740, it was translated into French and in 1761 into German. A storm of criticism greeted the book on the Continent. In France it was ordered to be burned by the common hangman. The Catholic church also placed the book on the Index of Forbidden Books, where it remained through the last edition of the Index published until 1966.

Described by one critic as "the wickedest cleverest book in the English language," *The Fable of the Bees* today is regarded as a masterpiece of the great English age of satire. Historians also recognize Mandeville's significant contribution to social philosophy and economic theory as a precursor of Adam Smith's 18th-century doctrine of laissez-faire economics and as an influence on the 19th-century philosophy of utilitarianism, the theory that the rightness of an action is determined by its consequences.

FURTHER READINGS

Cook, Richard I. *Bernard Mandeville*. New York: Twayne Publishers, 1974.

Levy, Leonard W. *Blasphemy: Verbal Offense Against the Sacred, from Moses to Salman Rushdie*. New York: Alfred A. Knopf, 1993.

Mandeville, Bernard. *The Fable of the Bees*. Intro. by Philip Harth. London: Penguin Books, 1970.

THE GUIDE OF THE PERPLEXED

Author: Moses Maimonides
Original date and place of publication: 1197, Egypt
Literary form: Philosophical text

SUMMARY

Maimonides (Moses ben Maimon), the most important Jewish medieval philosopher, was born in Córdoba, Spain, where his father was a judge and rabbi. When Córdoba fell in 1148 to the Almohads, a fundamentalist Islamic regime from North Africa, Maimonides and his family were forced as Jews to flee Spain. They moved to Morocco, then to Palestine, and eventually settled in Egypt. Maimonides became a physician in the court of Saladin and attained wide recognition as a jurist, a philosopher and the leader of Egypt's Jewish community.

Maimonides's writings include works on law, logic, medicine and theology. His greatest legal study, the *Mishnah Torah*, an attempt to organize all of Jewish law into a single code, is regarded as one of the most important Jewish works ever written. In his principal philosophical work, *The Guide of the Perplexed*, written in 1197 in Arabic and translated in 1204 into Hebrew, Maimonides sought to reconcile Judaism with the teachings of Aristotle, explaining in a logical way all that could be known about metaphysical problems. He was considered among the most distinguished philosophers of the Islamic world to apply the methodology of Aristotle to difficult conceptual issues.

The Guide was written not for average readers, but for select contemporaries who had studied classical science and philosophy, as well as Jewish scholarship. It was addressed to a pupil of Maimonides who found it difficult to reconcile the letter of Jewish law with the discoveries of natural science and Aristotelian philosophy. The purpose of *The Guide* was, Maimonides wrote, "to give indications to a religious man for whom the validity of our Law has become established in his soul and has become actual in his belief." His aim was to guide such "perplexed" individuals to a deeper insight into philosophical truths without compromising their religious commitments.

Maimonides criticized the lack of logical rigor in the arguments of theologians addressing metaphysical problems. He viewed the world as a complex but comprehensible system of necessary laws. Exploring questions of the immortality of the soul, the basis of morality, the creation of the world, the nature of prophecy and the concept of God, Maimonides contended that Judaism and its traditions could be presented as a rational system. Yet the perplexity of the believer could not be resolved by reason alone.

Basic to Maimonides's thought in *The Guide* was the gap between our limited perspective as human beings and that of God, whose apprehension is unlimited and perfect. He was skeptical of attempted dissolutions of this gap by theologians and philosophers, but searched nevertheless for bridges to span the great divide. Maimonides claimed: "He, however, who has achieved demonstration, to the extent that it is possible, of everything that may be demonstrated; and who has ascertained in divine matters, to the extent that that is possible, everything that may be ascertained; and who has come close to certainty in those matters in which one can only come close to it—has come to be with the ruler in the inner part of the habitation."

Maimonides believed that the requirements of religion are both intellectual and moral. Believers should not simply pursue religious rituals and regulations without attempting to investigate and understand their purposes and, ultimately, the divine purpose implicit in the structure of the world. "If however, you pray merely by moving your lips while facing a wall," Maimonides wrote, "and at the same time think about your buying and selling, or if you read the Torah with your tongue while your heart is set upon the building of your habitation and does not consider what you read . . . you should not think that you have achieved the end." Maimonides concluded that we must be content to speculate about the nature of what lies beyond our experience and limit ourselves to deriving conclusions from propositions that can be established only as possible, rather than as actual.

CENSORSHIP HISTORY

Maimonides was recognized as a leading figure in Jewish thought as well as one of the most radical philosophers of the Islamic world. *The Guide of the Perplexed* also exerted profound influence on Christian thinkers. It had been translated into Latin and was well known to medieval Scholastics. However, soon after his death in 1204, *The Guide of the Perplexed* sparked furious controversy. Orthodox Jewish opponents objected to Maimonides's sympathy for Aristotelian thought, which was considered fundamentally incompatible with Hebrew tradition. They stressed the incompatibility of being both a believer and a philosopher, contending that the religion proscribed theoretical inquiry. Teaching infected by Greek philosophy and attempts to reconcile Scripture and secular rationality were condemned as heresy.

In 1232, in Montpellier, France, the learned Talmudist Solomon ben Abraham led an attack on *The Guide* and obtained the support of the rabbis of France and some of the important scholars of Spain. The work was banned from Jewish homes under penalty of excommunication. The rabbis of France approached the Catholic Dominican friars, known for an unexcelled record in "burning your heretics," and appealed to them for help in destroying the study of philosophy among Jews. If the church would burn the books of Maimonides, it would deliver "a warning to the Jews to keep away from them." The monks obligingly confiscated copies of *The Guide* and in 1233 burned them as heretical works. Maimonides is thought to be the first Jewish scholar to have his works officially burned. Three hundred years later *The Guide* was again condemned by the Yeshiva of Lublin, Poland. The work still faced bans as late as the 19th century.

FURTHER READINGS

Aronsfeld, C. C. "Book Burning in Jewish History." *Index on Censorship* 11.1 (February 1982): 18.

Gerber, Jane S. *The Jews of Spain: A History of the Sephardic Experience*. New York: Macmillan, 1992.

Green, Jonathon. *The Encyclopedia of Censorship*. New York: Facts On File, 1990.

Leaman, Oliver. *Moses Maimonides*. Cairo: American University in Cairo Press, 1993.

THE HIDDEN FACE OF EVE: WOMEN IN THE ARAB WORLD

Author: Nawal El Saadawi

Original date and place of publication: 1977, Lebanon; 1980, United States

Original publisher: al-Mu'assassat, Lebanon; Zed Books, United States

Literary form: Sociological text

SUMMARY

A medical doctor, sociologist, novelist and author of nonfiction essays and books on Arab women's issues, Nawal El Saadawi is one of the most widely translated Egyptian writers and an outspoken feminist. In this personal and often disturbing account, the author exposes the hidden abuses of girls and women in the Muslim world and the ideologies she holds responsible for their oppressed condition.

Covering a wide range of topics, from female genital mutilation and sexual abuse of girls, to prostitution, sexual relationships, marriage and divorce, El Saadawi advances the thesis that the problems of Arab women stem not from the substance and values of Islam, but rather from an economic and political system based on male domination. One of the primary weapons used to keep back the revolt of women against patriarchy and its values is the misuse of the doctrines of Islam, the exploitation of religion for social and political ends.

The oppression of women in any society is an expression of an economic structure built on landownership, systems of inheritance and parenthood and the patriarchal family as a social unit, El Saadawi contends. Arab cultures are not exceptional in having transformed women into commodities. In the very essence of Islam, the status of women is no worse than it is in Judaism or Christianity.

El Saadawi recounts her own genital mutilation at the age of six, a prevalent custom for Egyptian girls when she was growing up. "Society had made me feel, since the day that I opened my eyes on life, that I was a girl, and that the word *bint* (girl) when pronounced by anyone is almost always accompanied by a frown." Recalling her experiences as a doctor working in rural areas of Egypt, she analyzes the psychological and physical damage of genital mutilation, which is aimed at denying sexual pleasure to women in order to insure their virginity before marriage and chastity throughout.

Society, as represented by its dominant classes and male structure, El Saadawi contends, realized at an early stage the power of female sexual desire. Unless women were controlled and subjugated, they would not submit to moral, legal and religious constraints, in particular those related to monogamy. An illicit intimacy with another man could lead to confusion in succession and inheritance, since there was no guarantee that another man's child would not step into the line of descendants.

El Saadawi also discusses another taboo subject, sexual molestation of girls by male family members. She cites a study she conducted in 1973, involving 160 Egyptian girls and women from different social classes, including educated and uneducated families. One of her findings showed that sexual molestation of female children by men was a common occurrence. The increasing number of men unable to marry for economic reasons, the segregation of the sexes, the lack of sexual outlets for men, the convenient proximity of female family members or young domestic servants and the low status of women are all contributing factors to the problem.

El Saadawi systematically analyzes other abuses against women, including marriage customs and laws that transform women into merchandise to be bought in exchange for dowry and sold for the price of alimony; laws that punish a woman for committing adultery; prohibitions on abortion in most Arab countries that result in maternal deaths from illegal abortions; and marriage regulations giving the husband the right to refuse his wife permission to leave the house to work or travel.

Looking back into Egyptian history, she finds in the predominance of the female goddesses of Pharaonic Egypt a reflection of the high status of women before the advent of the systems characterized by the patriarchal family, land ownership and division into social classes. In Islamic history, she points to one of Muhammad's wives, Aisha, as an example of a liberated woman known for her strong will, eloquence and intelligence. Aisha did not hesitate to oppose or contradict the Prophet; she fought in several wars and battles, and was actively involved in politics and cultural and literary activities. The complete emancipation of women, whether in the Arab countries or elsewhere, El Saadawi says, can only occur when humanity does away with class society and exploitation and when the structures and values of the patriarchal system have been erased.

CENSORSHIP HISTORY

Nawal El Saadawi has long been a thorn in the side of Egyptian religious and political authorities, whom she has angered by her unyielding demands for women's rights, daring writings on gender and sexuality and questioning of the religious and secular foundations of patriarchal authority.

She was the first feminist in the Arab world to publicly confront issues such as female genital mutilation, prostitution, incest and sexual abuse of Arab girls and women. Her first study of Arab women's problems and their struggle for liberation, *Women and Sex*, published in Egypt in 1972, was a bestseller, but it offended religious and government leaders. As a direct result of the publication of the book, she was dismissed from her post as director general of health education in the Ministry of Health. She also lost her job as editor of the journal *Health*, and was removed as assistant general secretary of the Medical Association. Her publisher was ordered to recall all copies of *Women and Sex* and put them in storage.

The 1977 publication of *The Hidden Face of Eve* in Arabic and its subsequent translation into several languages brought her international attention but also further harassment in Egypt. During the presidency of Anwar Sadat from 1970 until 1981, despite the absence of official censorship, emergency laws allowed the prime minister to withhold printing permits for publications. When a permit was denied for *The Hidden Face of Eve*, El Saadawi had it published in Beirut, Lebanon. The book was prohibited from entry to many Arab countries, including Egypt, where Egyptian customs and excise authorities barred it under the Importing of Foreign Goods Act. "Islamicists considered its critical examination of the links between the Middle East's three social taboos—religion, sex and the ruling establishment—blasphemous," El Saadawi wrote. "A disobedient woman writer is doubly punished," she contended, "since she has violated the norm of her fundamental obligation to home, husband and children."

When the Center for New Ideas in Tehran, Iran, translated the book into Farsi in 1980, Islamic extremists among followers of the Ayatollah Khomeini burned the book and its publishing house. Despite the bannings, the book, smuggled from Lebanon and sold surreptitiously, has been widely read in Egypt and in many of the other Arab countries where it is prohibited.

El Saadawi's writings and her left-wing political views—she opposed the 1979 Camp David peace treaty between Egypt and Israel—led to her arrest and imprisonment in 1981 under the Sadat regime. Along with many other Egyptian intellectuals, she was jailed for three months for alleged "crimes against the state" and released after Sadat's assassination.

Only in the early 1980s was she able to publish a book in Egypt, though she remained blacklisted from Egyptian television and radio. After her release from prison she founded the Arab Women's Solidarity Association, an international Arab women's network to support women's rights and secularism. In July 1991, the Egyptian government under President Hosni Mubarak banned the Egyptian branch of the association and also closed down its feminist magazine.

El Saadawi has been the target of numerous death threats by Muslim fundamentalists. Sheik Mohammed al-Ghazzali, a well-known faculty member at al-Azhar University, Egypt's state-funded religious establishment, has called her "an animal." In June 1992, the government posted armed guards outside her home to protect her. "I never trusted them," says El Saadawi. "I did not believe that those in power were so concerned about my life. I also knew that political currents which were concealed behind the screen of religion killed intellectuals and writers in the name of God. . . . These religio-political currents were part of Egypt's ruling system, part of the network of power and authority. . . ." In 1993, she left Egypt, fearing for her life, and moved to the United States, where she is a visiting university professor.

FURTHER READINGS

El Saadawi, Nawal. "Defying Submission." *Index on Censorship* 19.9 (October 1980): 16.

———. *The Hidden Face of Eve: Women in the Arab World.* Preface by Nawal El Saadawi. Trans. by Sherif Hetata. London: Zed Books, 1980.

———. *The Hidden Face of Eve: Women in the Arab World.* Foreword by Irene L. Gendzier. Boston: Beacon Press, 1982.

Malti-Douglas, Fedwa, and Allen Douglas. "Reflections of a Feminist." In *Opening the Gates: A Century of Arab Feminist Writing.* Ed. by Margot Badran and Miriam Cooke, 394–404. Bloomington: Indiana University Press, 1990.

HISTORICAL AND CRITICAL DICTIONARY

Author: Pierre Bayle
Original date and place of publication: 1697, Holland
Literary form: Dictionary

SUMMARY

Bayle's *Historical and Critical Dictionary* was among the most frequently printed and widely used books of the 18th century. In its innovative form, rationalism, skepticism and subtle irony, it paved the way for such classic works of the Enlightenment as the ENCYCLOPÉDIE and Voltaire's PHILOSOPHICAL DICTIONARY.

Originally a Protestant, the French philosopher and historian Pierre Bayle converted to Catholicism but later returned to the Calvinist faith. A victim of the French monarchy's policy of persecution and banishment of Protestants, he was exiled in 1681 to Holland, where he spent most of the rest of his life.

Bayle established a reputation in Europe as a notable advocate of religious toleration and freedom of thought. His first important work, *Miscellaneous Thoughts on the Comet* (1682), which challenged the prevailing belief that comets were harbingers of evil, introduced the skeptical views found in his *Dictionary*—that tradition and authority are suspect, that morality exists independently of religion and that superstition should be combatted. In *What Wholly Catholic France under the Reign of Louis XIV Really Is* (1686), he protested the 1685 revocation of the Edict of Nantes, which renewed persecution of French Protestants. *A Philosophic Commentary on Christ's Words, "Compel Them to Come In"* (1686–87) argued against using a literal interpretation of the Bible to justify forcible conversion of heretics.

Bayle's greatest work was his *Historical and Critical Dictionary*, published in four folio volumes in 1697. A compendium of historical biographies listing important figures of classical and religious history, it included comprehensive marginal notes and commentary by Bayle appended to each article that referred to errors and omissions in the work of the author's literary predecessors. While the articles themselves seemed orthodox, the notes, often longer than the articles themselves, were subversive of religious orthodoxy and provided a mine of information for alert and inquiring readers. Using obscure quotations in Latin and Greek, cross-references and ironic and humorous digressions, Bayle challenged accepted religious beliefs and exposed conflicting interpretations of historical events.

Only theologians would find his approach dangerous, Bayle wrote in one of his *Dictionary* entries, "for it is not clear why it should seem so to the natural scientist or to the statesman. . . . We need not allow ourselves to be discouraged by the argument that the human mind is too limited to discover anything about the truths of nature, the causes that produce heat, cold, the tides. . . . We can be content to gather data from experiments and seek probable hypotheses."

In Bayle's view, the theological controversies of his time were pointless. If the truths of religion were essentially nonrational, they could not be resolved by argument. Faith is outside the realm of reason and human reason is better adapted for detecting errors than for discovering positive truth, Bayle believed. He contended further that religious convictions are unnecessary to lead a moral life and that it is possible for a society to be moral and virtuous even if its people do not believe in immortality or even in God.

For the 18th-century philosophes, Bayle was a guiding spirit and his *Dictionary* a seminal influence. The English historian Edward Gibbon—author of THE HISTORY OF THE DECLINE AND FALL OF THE ROMAN EMPIRE—acknowledged that Bayle's "vast repository of facts and opinions" had taught him respect for the facts and the subversive possibilities of historical accuracy. Voltaire described it as the first dictionary that taught men how to think, and he placed Bayle in the ranks of intellectual architects of the critical mentality.

CENSORSHIP HISTORY

After its first publication in 1697, Bayle's *Dictionary* was soon expanded and translated into English and German. The four folio volumes of the *Dictionary* went through nine editions in France in less than 50 years and, despite the large and unwieldy format and expensive price of the original folio editions, it was owned by more educated people in Europe than any other book of its time. No personal library was considered complete without it.

Bayle's views on religious tolerance expressed in his 1696 *Philosophic Commentary* had been denounced by both Catholic and Protestant clergy. A similar reaction greeted the *Dictionary*. In response to criticisms by Protestant theologians, Bayle promised to modify his text in the second edition and remove several items they found offensive. But, with the exception of a few titles, the future editions remained unaltered.

A half-century later, the attacks on Bayle's *Dictionary* increased as religious and civil authorities moved to combat the influence of Enlightenment thinking. Widely circulated both in unabridged additions and in extracts and summaries, such as *The Essential Bayle*, the *Dictionary* was seen to cast doubt on some of the most widely accepted principles of morality and religion. The influential Jesuit publication *Journal de Trévoux*, which devoted a lengthy analysis to the *Dictionary*, declared that Bayle had been a writer of extraordinary talents who had chosen to abuse those talents and become a "great skeptic."

In 1754, the *Dictionary* was publicly burned in France and in 1757 the Vatican placed all of Bayle's writing on the Index of Forbidden Books in its most severe category, *opera omnia*, or all works condemned. Bayle was still on the Index in its last edition, compiled in 1948 and in effect until 1966.

In 1764, it was discovered that text from articles in the *Encyclopédie* that praised and restated the philosophy of Bayle and criticized his clerical prosecutors had been secretly deleted by its printer, who feared repercussions from the government authorities. For almost 200 years, the expurgated text of the *Encyclopédie*, minus the full commentary on Bayle, was the only one available.

FURTHER READINGS

Dunham, Barrows. *Heroes and Heretics: A Political History of Western Thought*. New York: Alfred A. Knopf, 1964.

Gay, Peter. *The Enlightenment: An Interpretation. The Rise of Modern Paganism*. New York: W. W. Norton & Co., 1995.

Hazard, Paul. *European Thought in the Eighteenth Century: From Montesquieu to Lessing*. Cleveland: World Publishing Co., 1973.

Hollier, Denis. *A New History of French Literature*. Cambridge, Mass.: Harvard University Press, 1989.

Kilcullen, John. *Sincerity and Truth: Essays on Arnauld, Bayle and Toleration*. Oxford: Clarendon Press, 1988.

HISTORY OF THE CONFLICT BETWEEN RELIGION AND SCIENCE

Author: John William Draper
Original date and place of publication: 1874, United States
Literary form: Historical and philosophical text

SUMMARY

John William Draper's *History of the Conflict Between Religion and Science* was written as an introduction to the history of science for a mass reading audience. Draper, a scientist and historian, sought to justify the importance of scientific thought at a time when the Catholic church was expanding its political power and taking a strong stance against scientific thinking, particularly new theories of human evolution. Draper maintained that science brought about advancement and that this was a more practical and useful idea than the retreat from modernity advocated by the Catholic church. He believed that science promoted tolerance and intelligence, while religion engendered hatred for nonbelievers and submission to one way of thinking.

John William Draper was born in England and graduated from the newly built University of London in 1831. Unlike the older universities at Oxford and Cambridge, this university stressed practical education over a religion-based liberal arts curriculum. London's strong science program led Draper to pursue a course of study in chemistry. On receiving his degree, he emigrated to Virginia, where he performed chemistry experiments in a makeshift laboratory on his family's farm. He attended the University of Pennsylvania medical school, then returned to Virginia to teach at Hampden-Sydney College. In 1839, he moved to New York to teach at New York University's medical school. During this time he worked on experiments in photography, alongside Samuel F. B. Morse, the inventor of the telegraph.

While Draper was teaching physiology to medical students in New York, Charles Darwin was writing ON THE ORIGIN OF SPECIES in England. Darwin's theories of evolution sparked great debate in the mid–19th century scientific community. Draper became fascinated with the application of Darwin's theories of natural selection to human behavior. In pursuing this quest, Draper drifted from physical science to social science. He wrote books on the U. S. Civil War and the intellectual history of Europe and discussed these events as scientific processes, applying evolutionary theory to intellectual, political and military leaders' motives and actions.

Draper's histories, which first appeared in 1861, were designed to appeal to a popular audience. He published essays in *Harper's Magazine*, a well-known monthly, and served as an American spokesman for the general advancement of science. Unlike some scientists who avoided the glare of publicity in favor of the solitary lab, Draper relished his role as a science popularizer. As scientific thinking became more widely accepted, he became a more outspoken critic of antiscientific forces in intellectual life, especially religious authorities who continued to preach a literal interpretation of Scripture.

History of the Conflict Between Religion and Science, which appeared in 1874, asserted that science was justifiably winning the conflict. By this time, Draper's reputation had spread throughout Europe, as his book was translated into French, Spanish, German, Dutch, Russian, Italian, Portuguese, Polish and Serbian. It was the bestselling volume in the popular science series in which it was published.

Draper believed that Pope Pius IX's increased power and hostility to modern times, papal meddling in French and German politics and the pope's insistence on a literal interpretation of Genesis had led to an unfortunate split between intellectuals and Christians. He also believed that science, which he broadly defined as freedom of conscience and willingness to question authority, was inevitably growing stronger despite the church's objections.

Throughout his book, Draper contrasts the history of religion with the history of science. He begins by looking at Greek, Persian, Roman and Egyptian science and how early science developed alongside religion, until the Spanish Inquisition and subsequent reactionary Vatican decrees punished medieval scientists and nonbelievers, pushing scientific thought out of Europe. Draper then traces the histories of several general conflicts between religion and science and finds that scientific explanations win over religious beliefs in each case. Draper ends his book by analyzing the Catholic church and the scientific method in relation to modern civilization, warning that the church's expansion of power and antimodernism are a threat to civilization and progress.

CENSORSHIP HISTORY

Scientists and other readers who were sympathetic to Draper's optimistic view of science bought his book in great numbers around the world. Some reviewers wondered why he seemed to equate Christianity with Catholicism, especially since evangelical Protestant churches in the United States and England had also spoken against theories of creation that contradicted a literal reading of the first chapter of Genesis. Liberal clergymen writing in religious magazines found fault with Draper's history. Pointing to the great civilizations of Europe, they asserted that Christianity was not an impediment to human progress.

One minister criticized Draper's universal faith in progress, claiming that Draper's blind devotion to the scientific method could lead to a breakdown of traditional ways of life and erosion of moral standards. Religious and secular critics questioned whether the overpopulation, pollution and mechanization of modern cities, fed by advances in science and technology, constituted the utopia claimed by Draper.

An even more damning criticism came from the Catholic church. When Vatican officials read a Spanish edition of *History of the Conflict Between Religion and Science*, in September 1876 they placed it on the Index of Forbidden Books. It was the first American work to be listed, and one of only four that appeared on the Index. Two years after its initial publication, Draper had been given, in the words of a Draper biographer, "an honor which its author has shared with Galileo, with Copernicus, with Kepler, with Locke, and with Mill." He had joined the company of some of the greatest minds in science and philosophy whose works offended the Roman Catholic church.

Unlike Galileo or Copernicus, however, Draper suffered no personal punishment for offending the Catholic hierarchy. Instead, the book's sudden notoriety led many to buy the book who might not otherwise have been interested in the history of science. Draper faced no legal consequences for writing his book, even in predominantly Catholic countries. Its appearance on the Index meant little to Draper, as he was not Catholic and had no regard for what the pope thought of his work. Nor did he feel any need to apologize for or revise his book. On the contrary, he considered the continuing existence of the Index of Forbidden Books as just the sort of papal anti-modernity and power grabbing that he had railed against in his writings.

History of the Conflict Between Religion and Science remained in print for nearly 60 years, through more than 50 printings, and Draper became a popular public speaker. After his book was placed on the Index, he became president of the American Chemical Society and addressed a national gathering of Unitarian ministers on the topic of evolution. He also became a celebrated professor at New York University, where he continued his teaching and research duties until a few months before his death at age 70.

Draper today is known as one of the most prominent American scientists of the mid–19th century and an important historian and popularizer of the theory of evolution.

FURTHER READINGS

Barker, George F. *Memoir of John William Draper, 1811–1882* (reprint ed.). New York: Garland Publishing, 1974.

Draper, John William. *History of the Conflict Between Religion and Science* (reprint ed.). Westmead, Farnbrough, Hants., England: Gregg International Publishers Limited, 1970.

Fleming, Donald. *John William Draper and the Religion of Science*. Philadelphia: University of Pennsylvania Press, 1950.

THE HISTORY OF THE DECLINE AND FALL OF THE ROMAN EMPIRE

Author: Edward Gibbon
Original place and date of publication: 1776–88, England
Literary form: History

SUMMARY

Edward Gibbon's epic and magisterial six-volume history of the Roman empire from A.D. 180 to 1453 is one of the most widely read historical works of modern times. His history begins in the reign of Trajan, when the empire of Rome "comprehended the fairest part of the earth, and the most civilised portion of mankind" and ends with the fall of Constantinople, when the empire lay in ruins. It was among the ruins of ancient Rome on a visit in 1764 that Gibbon conceived the work which was to occupy nearly 20 years of his life.

Gibbon believed that the propagation of the Gospel and the triumph of Christianity were inseparably connected to the decline of the Roman monarchy. Gibbon was raised as a Protestant and converted to Catholicism as a student at Oxford. Expelled from Oxford because of his conversion, he was sent by his family to Lausanne, Switzerland, where he reconverted to Protestantism under the care of a Calvinistic minister. He became, nevertheless, a skeptic, indifferent to religious dogma and guided by the principles of the French Enlightenment.

Influenced by the ideas of French political thinker Montesquieu, Gibbon's methodology was to weigh historical evidence impartially, unencumbered by religious prejudice. He examined religions as social phenomena, rather than as received doctrine, and was opposed to superstition and fanaticism, which he saw as destructive of human liberty.

The two chapters of Gibbon's 71-chapter history that offered "a candid but rational inquiry into the progress and establishment of Christianity" became notorious. In chapter 15, "The Progress of the Christian Religion, and the Sentiments, Manners, Numbers, and the Condition of the Primitive Christians" and Chapter 16 "The Conduct of the Roman Government towards the Christians, from the Reign of Nero to that of Constantine (180–313 A.D.)," Gibbon set out to explore what he described as the "secondary causes" of the rapid growth of the Christian church.

"While that great body [the Roman empire] was invaded by open violence, or undermined by slow decay," he wrote, "a pure and humble religion gently insinuated itself into the minds of man, grew up in silence and obscurity, derived new vigour from opposition, and finally erected the triumphant banner of the Cross on the ruins of the Capitol."

Gibbon defines the duty of the theologian as "describing Religion as she descended from Heaven, arrayed in her native purity." A more melancholy duty, however, is imposed on the historian, "who must discover the inevitable mixture of error and corruption which she contracted in a long residence upon earth, among a weak and degenerate race of beings."

How did the Christian faith establish so remarkable a victory over the established religions of the earth? Gibbon asks. While allowing that the primary cause of the success of Christianity might be the convincing evidence of the doctrine itself and the "ruling providence of its great Author," Gibbon outlines five secondary reasons: Christian zeal, purified of the narrow and unsocial spirit that had deterred Gentiles from embracing the law of Moses; the promise of eternal happiness after death to those who adopted the faith; the miraculous powers ascribed to the church; the pure and austere morals of the Christians; and the unity and discipline of the Christian republic, which gradually formed an independent state in the heart of the Roman empire.

In his discussion of miracles, Gibbon uses the term "superstition" to describe how the church, from the time of apostles and their first disciples, claimed an uninterrupted succession of miraculous powers—the gifts of tongues and of vision and prophecy, the power to expel demons and the ability to heal the sick and raise the dead.

He portrays the early church hierarchy, particularly the bishops, as using executive and arbitrary power "to attack, with united vigour, the original rights of their clergy and people. . . . The prelates of the third century imperceptibly changed the language of exhortation into that of command, scattered the seeds of future usurpations, and supplied by Scripture allegories and declamatory rhetoric, their deficiency of force and of reason."

In chapter 16, Gibbon analyzes the treatment of Christians by the Roman empire, stating that the worst of the Roman emperors were no less repressive than modern sovereigns who have employed violence and terror against the religious opinions of their subjects. "We shall conclude this chapter by a melancholy truth which obtrudes itself on the reluctant mind"; Gibbon writes, "that, even admitting, without hesitation or inquiry, all that history has recorded, or devotion has feigned, on the subject of martyrdoms, it must still be acknowledged that the Christians, in the course of their intestine discussions, have inflicted far greater severities on each other than they had experienced from the zeal of infidels."

The church of Rome, he continues, "defended by violence the empire which she had acquired by fraud; a system of peace and benevolence was soon disgraced by the proscriptions, wars, massacres, and the institution of the holy office." The number of Protestants who were executed in a single province and a single reign, Gibbon contends, far exceeded that of the primitive martyrs who died at the hands of the Roman empire over three centuries of its rule.

CENSORSHIP HISTORY

The first volume of Gibbon's history, published in 1776, was immediately successful and highly praised for its learning and literary style. Gibbon wrote in his memoirs: "The first impression was exhausted in a few days; a second and third edition scarcely adequate to the demand. My book was on every table. . . ."

His comments on the early Christians, however, particularly his discussion of institutionalized Christianity as an alien and divisive element in Roman society that contributed to the empire's downfall, offended the Catholic church and pious believers. Gibbon was assailed by criticism. Nevertheless, he continued his work on the history, commenting on the reception to chapters 15 and 16, "I adhered to the wise resolution of trusting myself and my writings to the cauldron of the public. . . ."

He replied to his theological critics in 1779 with "A Vindication of Some Passages in the Fifteenth and Sixteenth Chapters" and worked on the second and third volumes, which appeared in 1781. In 1783, the book's Italian edition was placed by the Catholic church on the Index of Forbidden Books, as being in contradiction to official church history. It remained on the Index through the last edition of the Index compiled in 1948 and in effect until 1966.

Writing in his memoirs, Gibbon declared: "Had I believed that the majority of English readers were so fondly attached even to the name and shadow of Christianity, had I foreseen that the pious and the timid and the prudent would feel or affect to feel such exquisite sensibility, I might perhaps have softened the two invidious chapters, which would create many enemies, and conciliate few friends."

FURTHER READING

Gibbon, Edward. *Memoirs of My Life*. Ed. and intro. by Betty Radice. London: Penguin Books, 1984.

INFALLIBLE? AN INQUIRY

Author: Hans Küng
Original date and place of publication: 1970, Germany; 1971, United States
Original publisher: Benzinger Verlag, Germany; Doubleday & Company, United States
Literary form: Theological analysis

SUMMARY

To err is human. To err is also ecclesiastical and papal, contends Catholic theologian Hans Küng, a professor at the University of Tübingen in Germany. Küng's rejection of the doctrine of papal infallibility, as expressed in *Infallible? An Inquiry*, embroiled him in conflict with Vatican authorities.

Infallibility is defined by the Roman Catholic church as exemption from the possibility of error, bestowed on the church by the Holy Spirit. Infallibility is vested in the pope when he speaks as the head of the church on matters of faith and morals. Definitive pronouncements resulting from an ecumenical council, when ratified by the pope, are also held to be infallible. In *Infallible? An Inquiry*, Küng examines papal encyclicals and statements, conciliar pronouncements, Scripture and church history, and concludes that there is no such thing as an infallible proposition. No church teaching is automatically free from error, because the church is composed of human beings. God alone is a priori free from error in detail and in every case.

Küng believes the dogma of papal infallibility should be discarded, as it has been disproved by historical and biblical research. He suggests that it be replaced by the notion of "indefectibility"—the perpetuity of the whole church in the truth of God's word despite the possible errors of any of its parts. In the long run, he believes, in spite of errors by the teaching authority of the church, the truth of the message of God in Jesus Christ will prevail.

Küng contends that the Second Vatican Council (1962–65), for which he served as a theological consultant, despite its efforts to renew the church by broadening ecumenical understanding and opening out toward the modern world, did not go far enough in reforming church structures. The ecclesiastical teaching office is still conceived by the pope and the hierarchy in a preconciliar, authoritarian way.

"The conception of continuity, authority, infallibility of the Church and the Church's teaching has led the Catholic Church into a dangerous tight corner," Küng writes in *Infallible*. He lists numerous and indisputable past errors of the ecclesiastical teaching office, now largely recognized by the church, including the condemnation of Galileo and the excommunication of the Greek church. "A close scrutiny of the Index of Forbidden Books would be particularly revealing in this respect," he adds, "yet the teaching office found it difficult to admit these errors frankly and honestly."

Küng raises doubts about the authority of Pope Paul VI's 1968 encyclical on birth control, *Humanae Vitae*, which reaffirmed the church's traditional prohibition of contraception. In this encyclical, Küng contends, the ecclesiastical teaching office counts for more than the gospel of Christ and papal tradition is placed above Scripture. Jesus himself did not found a church, Küng says, but rather his life and death set in motion a movement which over the course of time took on increasingly institutional forms.

Küng calls for a new age of leadership, one in which "the pope exists for the Church and not the Church for the pope," in which the pope's primacy is not one of ruling, but of service. Küng writes that he remains for all his criticism a convinced Catholic theologian. But because he is deeply bound to his church, he claims the right and the duty in full awareness of his own human inadequacy and fallibility to raise a protest.

CENSORSHIP HISTORY

When *Infallible? An Inquiry* first appeared in 1970, on the centennial of the First Vatican Council's enunciation of the doctrine of papal infallibility, it sparked immediate controversy and an international debate that was unprecedented in more recent theology. The assertion of infallibility of the teaching office in the Catholic church has long been unacceptable to non-Catholic theologians. But Küng was the first major Catholic theologian to question dramatically and forcefully the most basic concept of church authority. The divergence on this issue by a theologian as distinguished as Küng represented the extent to which the doctrine had become questionable.

In his preface to *Infallible? An Inquiry*, Küng wrote: "It is true that the Index has been abolished and another name given to the Roman Inquisition. But there are still inquisitional processes against troublesome theologians. . . ." Küng himself became subject to such processes for his dissident views. In obvious reaction to Küng's ideas, the Vatican's Congregation for the Doctrine of the Faith issued on June 24, 1973, a "Declaration Against Certain Errors of the Present Day," which reiterated Catholic teaching on the infallibility of the church and the pope and declared that the pope and bishops are indeed guaranteed immunity from error when they define doctrine.

Küng's bestselling 1974 book, *On Being a Christian*, an effort to make the traditional articles of faith intelligible to modern believers, raised further doubts within the hierarchy about his orthodoxy. In 1975 the Vatican admonished Küng not to advocate two theses drawn from his 1967 book *The Church* and from *Infallible? An Inquiry*: that in case of necessity, the Eucharist might be consecrated by an unordained person and that propositions defined by the church might be erroneous. In addition, church authorities instituted an official process to examine the orthodoxy of his views. They requested repeatedly that he come to Rome for discussions. Küng called for due process, demanded the right to see the full dossier on his case before submitting to any inquiry and asked to choose his own defense counsel. In 1968, 1,360 theologians had signed a statement calling for such due process for theologicans in cases where authorities in Rome objected to their teachings. Claiming he would not receive a fair trial, Küng refused to come to Rome.

When Pope John Paul II succeeded Paul VI in 1978, he moved to confront dissident theologians. On December 18, 1979, the Congregation for the Doctrine of the Faith withdrew Küng's *missio canonica*, barring him from teaching "in the name of the Church." The Congregation accused him of "causing confusion" among the faithful by casting doubt in his writing and teachings on the dogma of papal infallibility and questioning the doctrine of Christ's divinity. Küng was informed that he could no longer be considered a Catholic theologian. He was forbidden to teach Catholic doctrine and Catholic institutions were prohibited from employing him.

Küng remained a Catholic priest, however, as well as a tenured professor at the University of Tübingen, a position protected by German law. He is professor of ecumenical theology and director of the Institute for Ecumenical Research and has continued to write and publish.

FURTHER READINGS

Bokenkotter, Thomas S. *A Concise History of the Catholic Church*. Garden City, N.Y.: Doubleday and Co., 1977.

Küng, Hans. *Infallible? An Unresolved Inquiry*. Preface by Herbert Haag. New York: Continuum, 1994.

AN INQUIRY CONCERNING HUMAN UNDERSTANDING

Author: David Hume
Original date and place of publication: 1748, England
Literary form: Philosophical treatise

SUMMARY

The Scottish philosopher and historian David Hume was among the most influential philosophers of the 18th-century Age of Enlightenment. Hume's profoundly skeptical empiricist philosophy, based on the principle that "nothing is in the mind that was not first in the senses," challenged many of the claims and conclusions of the rationalist philosophers of the 17th century. His method was to employ experience and observation to analyze human nature and the human understanding. "There is no question of importance whose decision is not compriz'd in the science of man," Hume believed.

Hume was educated in Edinburgh and lived in France from 1734 to 1737, where he completed his first philosophical work, *A Treatise of Human Nature*. The first two volumes of the *Treatise*, an empirical investigation of how human beings perceive the world, were published anonymously in 1739. To Hume's disappointment, the *Treatise* failed to make an impression and, as he later wrote, "fell dead-born from the press, without reaching such distinction as even to excite a murmur among the zealots." A third volume, an examination of morals, politics and criticism, published the following year, also attracted little notice.

Hume believed that the abstract style of the *Treatise* was a barrier to attracting a larger readership. He rewrote portions of it and in 1741 published anonymously a volume of *Essays, Moral and Political*. In 1748, a third, enlarged edition of these essays appeared under the title *Philosophical Essays Concerning Human Understanding*. This was the first volume Hume published under his own name. Another edition was published in 1751 with a new title, *An Inquiry Concerning Human Understanding*. The *Inquiry*, like the previous versions of the essays, restated sections of Hume's *Treatise* in a more accessible form.

In the *Inquiry*, Hume recommends that the experimental, inductive method of the natural sciences should be applied to the study of humanity. The process must begin with empirical data, the observation of psychological processes and behavior, in order to establish principles and causes. Hume doubts the value of unsupported generalizations and a priori propositions that form the basis for much philosophical and religious thought and suggests a new methodology for arriving at conclusions about knowledge and truth.

There are two approaches to the science of human nature, Hume observes. Philosophers who view man "chiefly as born for action" may work to stimulate people to choose virtuous conduct by displaying the beauties of virtue. Alternatively, if philosophers regard human beings as rational, rather than active, their aim may be to increase understanding rather than to improve conduct. The first type of philosophy, in Hume's view, is "easy and obvious" and thus preferred by most people; the second is "accurate and abstruse," but necessary if the first type of philosophy is to be based on any sure foundation.

In two sections of the *Inquiry*, Hume added new material on the application of his philosophy to religious thought. Before publishing the *Treatise* in 1737, he had omitted an essay doubting the reliability of reports of miracles, which he knew would be considered antireligious and feared would detract from consideration of the significance of his work. "I am at present castrating my work, that is, cutting off its nobler parts," he wrote. He decided that publishing it at that time "would give too much offense, even as the world is disposed at present."

A decade later, he included the essay as section 10: "Of Miracles" in the *Inquiry*. He also added a critical examination in dialogue form of the philosophical arguments for God's existence in section 11: "Of a Particular Providence and of a Future State." This section introduced many of the arguments later developed more fully in his final work, published posthumously more than 30 years later, DIALOGUES CONCERNING NATURAL RELIGION.

In "Of Miracles," Hume states that "a miracle can never be proved so as to be the foundation of a system of religion." He describes the concept of miracles as a violation of the law of nature and asserts that the testimony offered in support of miracles is never totally reliable and always inferior to the testimony of the senses. "The knavery and folly of men are such common phenomena," he writes, "that I should rather believe the most extraordinary events to arise from their concurrence, than admit of so signal a violation of the laws of nature."

Hume treats religious belief as a hypothesis, "a particular method of accounting for a visible phenomena of the universe," from which we can deduce only facts that we already know. He is dubious about religious authority, preferring to put faith in beliefs and values people have developed in the course of their own experiences.

"So that upon the whole, we may conclude," he states in one of the most controversial passages of the *Inquiry*, "that the *Christian Religion* not only was at first attended with miracles, but even at this day cannot be believed by any reasonable person without one."

In his celebrated conclusion to the *Inquiry*, Hume writes: "If we take in our hand any volume; of divinity or school metaphysics, for instance; let us ask, *Does it contain any abstract reasoning concerning quantity or number?* No. *Does it contain any experimental reasoning concerning matter of fact and existence?* No. Commit it then to the flames: For it can contain nothing but sophistry and illusion."

CENSORSHIP HISTORY

Hume's thoughts on religion expressed in the *Inquiry* were the most controversial of the writings published during his lifetime. His skeptical outlook offended not only religious orthodoxy, but also the deist critics of organized religion, who held that the reality of God could be established through the use of reason. Hume believed that religion was an impediment to morality, because it encouraged people to act for motives other than love of virtue for its own sake. He saw religious belief as a source of anxiety, as well as persecution, intolerance and civil strife.

Hume's friends warned him that publication of the *Inquiry* would cause a scandal. But he vowed to proceed, writing to a colleague, "In the first place, I think I am too deep engaged to think of a retreat. In the second place, I see not what bad consequences follow, in the present age, from the character of an infidel." Hume felt that progress in learning and liberty indicated that the time was right for consideration of his ideas. "Most people, in this island, have divested themselves of all superstitious reverence to names and authority," he wrote in an essay first published in 1742. "The Clergy have entirely lost their credit: Their pretensions and doctrines have been ridiculed; and even religion can scarcely support itself in the world."

In the 1748 edition of this essay, Hume changed the phrase "entirely lost their credit" to "much lost," for it became clear that, despite the increasingly receptive climate among the public for the skeptical ideas of the Enlightenment, his comments on religion went far beyond what was considered acceptable.

Hume was rejected for appointments at the universities of Edinburgh and Glasgow primarily because of the *Inquiry*. The furor over sections 10 and 11 of the *Inquiry* caused him in 1755 to suppress two essays on the topics of suicide and immortality from a volume of "Five Dissertations" that had already been printed in preparation for publication. The essays were not published until 25 years later, and then anonymously in French translation.

In 1756, Hume's opponents tried to have him formally excommunicated by the General Assembly of the Church of Scotland. But with the help of Hume's friends in the church's moderate party, the resolution was defeated. In 1761, the Vatican placed a French version of *A Treatise of Human Understanding* on the Index of Forbidden Books.

Many attacks on Hume's views on religion were published in the years following publication of the *Inquiry*. George Campbell's book, *A Dissertation on Miracles: Containing an Examination of the Principles advanced by David Hume, Esq: In an Essay on Miracles*, published in Edinburgh in 1762, was typical. "The *Essay on Miracles* deserves to be consider'd as one of the most dangerous attacks that have been made on our religion," the author proclaimed. "The danger results not solely from the merit of THE PIECE; it results much more from that of THE AUTHOR. . . . What a pity it is that this reputation should have been sullied by attempts to undermine the foundations of *natural religion*, and of *reveal'd!*" In 1770, a satirical critique of Hume by James Beattie, *An Essay on the Nature and Immutability of Truth: in Opposition to Sophistry and Scepticism*, was widely read and appeared in five editions from its first publication to the time of Hume's death.

The most significant result of the reception to the *Inquiry* was Hume's decision not to publish during his lifetime his greatest work on the philosophy of religion. *Dialogues Concerning Natural Religion*, completed in draft form in 1751, did not appear until 1779, three years after his death. In 1827, Hume's *History of England* and all his philosophical works were placed on the Index of Forbidden Books. They remained forbidden to Catholics through the last edition of the Index compiled in 1948 and in effect until 1966.

FURTHER READINGS

Collinson, Diané. *Fifty Major Philosophers: A Reference Guide*. London: Routledge, 1988.
Copleston, Frederick. *A History of Philosophy*. Vol. 5, *Modern Philosophy: The British Philosophers from Hobbes to Hume*. New York: Doubleday, 1994.
Gay, Peter. *The Enlightenment: An Interpretation. The Rise of Modern Paganism*. New York: W. W. Norton & Co., 1995.
Hume, David. *An Inquiry Concerning Human Understanding*. Ed. and intro. by Charles W. Hendel. Indianapolis, Ind.: Bobbs-Merrill Co., 1979.
——— *On Human Nature and the Understanding*. Ed. and intro. by Anthony Flew. New York: Macmillan Publishing Co., 1975.
Penelhum, Terence. *David Hume: An Introduction to His Philosophical System*. West Lafayette, Ind.: Purdue University Press, 1992.
Price, John V. *David Hume*. New York: Twayne Publishers, 1968.
Scott-Kakures, Dion, Susan Castegnetto, Hugh Benson, William Taschek and Paul Hurley. *History of Philosophy*. New York: HarperCollins, 1993.

INSTITUTES OF THE CHRISTIAN RELIGION

Author: John Calvin
Original date and place of publication: 1536–59, Switzerland
Literary form: Theological treatise

SUMMARY

Institutes of the Christian Religion, by John Calvin, the French Protestant theologian of the Reformation, was the first systematic, comprehensive and logical exposition of reform belief. As both a defense of the reform movement and a handbook for Christian instruction, its influence was profound. Completed in Basel, Switzerland, in 1536 and extensively revised and supplemented in later editions, it was originally written in Latin. In 1541, it was published in French in Calvin's own translation. The first theological treatise in French prose, its lucid and direct style was a major influence in the evolution of the French language from its medieval to its modern form.

In its first edition, the *Institutes* was a relatively small book in six chapters, designed to be carried in the pocket. The first four chapters, on the Ten Commandments, faith, the Lord's Prayer and the sacraments, followed the order of Martin Luther's catechism. The last two chapters, which discussed the rejection of the Catholic sacraments, Christian liberty and church and civil government, were more polemical in tone in their arguments on behalf of Reformation thought.

The second edition, which appeared in 1539, was three times larger than the first, more systematic and coherent and departed from the form of a catechism in favor of a formal exposition of theology. The final edition (1559) filled four volumes and fully systematized the theological thinking of the time, including discussions of ancient philosophy, the church fathers, the Scholastics and the contemporary Roman Catholic church.

In the significant introductory sentence of the *Institutes*, Calvin wrote: "All our wisdom, in so far as it really deserves the name wisdom and is sure and religious, comprises basically two things—the knowledge of God and the knowledge of ourselves." To know ourselves we can observe our own actions and motives. But to know God we must read the Scriptures, where the only true knowledge of God can be found. Calvin placed primary emphasis on study of the Bible and held it as the only authority in matters of belief and observance.

In the *Institutes*, Calvin rejected papal authority. Man is directly responsible to God and must claim salvation directly, guided only by his own conscience and the teachings of the Bible. Denying the Catholic church's stand that salvation could be merited by good works, Calvin, in agreement with Luther, asserted that it was dependent on faith alone. But Calvin went further, asserting that God has predestined those to be saved. Only the elect, the chosen of God, can achieve salvation.

"In actual fact, the covenant of life is not preached equally among all men," he wrote, "and among those to whom it is preached it does not gain the same acceptance either constantly or in equal degree. . . . As Scripture, then, clearly shows, we say that God once established by His eternal and unchangeable plan those whom He long before determined once and for all to receive into salvation, and those whom, on the other hand, he would devote to destruction."

Calvin believed that man was subject to two kinds of government, the civil law and the rule of God, and that civil government had the duty to establish religion. The state should be subordinate to the church. He approved of "a civil administration that aims to prevent the true religion which is constituted in God's law from being openly and with public sacrilege violated and defiled with impunity. . . ." He would not "allow men to make laws according to their own decision concerning religion and the worship of God."

Indeed, freedom of religion was not allowed under Calvinist administration in Geneva, as was demonstrated in a notorious manner by the execution of the young Spanish theologian Michael Servetus, author of CHRISTIANITY RESTORED. Servetus was arrested under Calvin's orders for heresy and blasphemy and burned at the stake in 1553.

Calvin regarded the church of Rome as no longer the church of God. The gospel was absent under the papacy, he believed, and the sacraments had been twisted into a form and meaning that contradicted their true character. "We had to leave them in order to come to Christ," he said of the Catholic church.

CENSORSHIP HISTORY

The new Protestant faith as promulgated by Calvin was equated by King Francis I of France with violence and lawlessness. Fearing that he might be arrested for his association with reformers, Calvin fled France for Basel in 1534, where he published *Institutes* two years later. Its entire first edition sold out within a year. Some copies were printed under the pseudonym Alcuin to divert the censors and circulated to Roman Catholic countries.

The persecution that had driven Calvin and many others away from France in 1534, and eventually to Geneva, continued sporadically in the years that followed. Francis's successor, Henri II, upon his accession in 1547, set up special courts to deal with heresy charges against evangelical Christians. After two years, heresy trials were once again taken over by the ecclesiastical courts. But when the church courts were seen as too lenient, the trials were transferred to the civil courts by the Edict of Chateaubriand. A reign of terror against Calvinists ensued.

Calvin and his followers, who had established a local government in Geneva that implemented his doctrines, sent help to the fledgling French congregations by smuggling ministers and books by Calvin into France. One result of the thriving movement of Calvinist books into France from Geneva was that printing became the major industry in Geneva and the sale of books the major export. Despite repression of Calvinism, in 1559 there were as many as 50 churches in France organized according to Calvin's thought.

In England in 1555, Queen Mary issued a proclamation requiring "that no manner of persons presume to bring into this realm any manuscripts, books, papers . . . in the name of Martin Luther, John Calvin . . . or any like books containing false doctrine against the Catholic faith." After 1558 and the accession of the Protestant Queen Elizabeth, Calvin's influence in England became substantial through the widespread circulation of his commentaries, sermons and *Institutes*, translated into English in 1561.

In the first Index of Forbidden Books published by Pope Paul IV in 1559, the writings of Calvin were condemned as heretical, along with those of Martin Luther, in the Index's Class I, the category of authors whose works were totally banned. The revised Index issued by the Council of Trent in 1564, which was effective in Belgium, Bavaria, Portugal, Italy and France, confirmed the banning of the works of Luther and Calvin. In the last Index issued by the church in 1948 and in effect until 1966, Calvin's *Institutes of the Christian Religion* was not specifically listed, but was considered as banned according to the church's canon law forbidding the reading of books "which propound or defend heresy or schism."

FURTHER READINGS

Burman, Edward. *The Inquisition: Hammer of Heresy*. New York: Dorset Press, 1992.

Parker, T. H. L. *John Calvin*. Batavia, Ill.: Lion Publishing Corporation, 1975.

Simon, Edith. *The Reformation*. New York: Time-Life Books, 1966.

Wilcox, Donald J. *In Search of God and Self: Renaissance and Reformation Thought*. Boston: Houghton Mifflin Company, 1975.

INTRODUCTION TO THEOLOGY

Author: Peter Abelard
Original date and place of publication: 1120, France
Literary form: Theological treatise

SUMMARY

The French theologian, poet and teacher Peter Abelard is best known for his tragic love affair with Héloïse, his pupil, and for the love letters he wrote to her after he entered a monastery and she became a nun. Abelard also exercised considerable influence on the intellectual life of his times as a philosopher and teacher.

Abelard reported that his love for dialectical disputation of philosophical issues led him to reject a military career and "wander about the various provinces like the peripatetics wherever I heard the pursuit of this art was vigorous." He opened his own school in Paris and attracted large numbers of students drawn by his reputation as a brilliant teacher. He became a Benedictine monk at the monastery of Saint Denis in 1120.

As a Scholastic philosopher, Abelard shifted the theological argument from reliance on authority to analysis by logic and reason, emphasizing the critical method and applying the method of Aristotle's dialectic to faith and dogma. In discussing a thesis, he put forward the views of opposing authorities and suggested the principles that might be useful in deciding a question, leaving the solution of the problem to the reader. The basic approach of Scholasticism was to use reason to deepen the understanding of what was believed on faith, ultimately giving a rational content to faith.

His first theological work, *Introduction to Theology*, was written for his students, Abelard explained in his autobiography, "because they asked for a human and philosophical basis, and preferred something they could understand to mere words. Talk alone is of no use, they said, if it is not accompanied by understanding. . . . Besides, the Lord Himself criticized the blind leading the blind."

In *Introduction to Theology*, Abelard recommended training in logic and the use of logical methods in theology. Reason must be able to understand what is accepted on authority. But reason should not supersede faith. Acceptance of dogma is an act of free will rewarded in the future life by ultimate knowledge of the grounds of faith.

The most important philosophical problem of the 12th century was the question of the relationship between the concepts of the universal and the particular. There were two approaches to the question: realism, which held that universals exist independently of the human mind and particular things, and nominalism, which proposed that the prior notion of an object does not have an independent existence. Abelard taught a doctrine of moderate realism, in opposition both to realism and extreme nominalism. He recognized the universal as a symbol to which human beings have attached significance, based on the similarity perceived in different objects.

In *Introduction to Theology*, he put forth a view of the Trinity in opposition to nominalism, which tended to make three Gods of the Trinity. His analysis was regarded by other theologians as verging on the third-century heresy of monarchianism, or Sabellianism, which challenged the doctrine of the essential Trinity by holding that God was one indivisible substance with three fundamental activities or modes that appeared successively as the Father, Son and Holy Spirit.

Abelard's analysis of Atonement, the doctrine that Christ by his suffering and death on the cross satisfied God for the sins of man, was that Jesus' sacrifice was unnecessary for the forgiveness of sins, as God had forgiven sin before Christ came. He also rejected Saint Augustine's doctrine of Original Sin, holding that mankind does not share in the guilt of Adam's sin. His most influential work was his treatise *Sic et non*, in which he compared passages in the writings of the church fathers and exposed their contradictions.

CENSORSHIP HISTORY

Abelard did not wish to place dialectics above theology, but rather, through its use, to understand revelation. His use of dialectics and his emphasis on the powers of reason revolutionized the traditional method of teaching theology. It also brought him into conflict with Abbot Bernard of Clairvaux, the most powerful theologian in Western Europe, declared a saint after his death by the Catholic church.

Bernard, a protector of tradition, polemicized against those, like Abelard, "who call themselves philosophers" and are no better than "slaves to curiosity and pride." Abelard's belief in the application of logic to faith conflicted with the mysticism of Bernard. Bernard believed that it was not man's concern to explore God's majesty, but rather to be eager to know God's will. Abelard's opinions on the Trinity, Atonement, free will and Original Sin were also regarded as subversive to the faith.

The conflict between Bernard and Abelard exemplified the differences between monasticism and the new Scholastic theology. The monks were not concerned with explaining dogma and drawing conclusions by means of dialectic, but rather with prayer and meditation, the seeking of salvation and the unity of man with God. Scholasticism was characterized by speculation, analysis and abstraction and a desire to expand the range of understanding.

In 1121, Abelard was called before the Council of Soissons and charged with heresy for his teachings on the Trinity. *Introduction to Theology* was condemned and burned and he was imprisoned for a short time in the convent of Saint Médard before he was allowed to return to Saint Denis. Abelard viewed the council's actions as contrary to ecclesiastic law, as he had not been allowed to speak in his own defense.

Abelard resumed teaching in Paris in 1136. His popularity and skill as a lecturer led Bernard to regard his continuing influence as dangerous. Referring to Abelard as "an infernal dragon and the precursor of the anti-Christ," Bernard asked the bishops of France to restrain him. Abelard was charged with heresy by the Council of Sens in 1140. Among the charges against him was the claim that he said "the Father has perfect power, the Son a certain amount, and the Holy Ghost none at all."

In the "Profession of Faith" which Abelard wrote to defend himself against the charges of Sens, he replied that "Such words are more diabolical than heretical. I am in full conformity with justice in detesting them, abhorring them, condemning them as I would condemn anyone who wrote them. If perchance they can be found in my writings, then I admit I am indeed a favorer of heresy."

The verdict of the convocation was to ban all of his writings as heretical. Abelard left for Rome to appeal directly to Pope Innocent II, unaware that Bernard had already persuaded the pope to support the council. En route in Cluny, France, he learned that the pope had confirmed the judgment of Sens and supervised the burning of his works, along with those of Abelard's pupil, the Italian monk Arnold of Brescia. The pope also ordered Abelard confined to a monastery, forbade him to continue writing and excommunicated all his followers.

Abelard submitted to the pope's judgment as a dutiful son of the church. In a letter to Héloise he said, "I do not wish to be an Aristotle by separating myself from Christ, since there is no other name under heaven by which I can be saved." Peter the Venerable, the abbot of Cluny, convinced Abelard to seek reconciliation with Bernard, who was able to persuade the pope to mitigate the condemnation.

Abelard did not preach again, but remained at the monastery of Cluny, where he died in 1142. Although Abelard reconciled with the church, he remained confident that his theology was in conformity with church doctrine. In his last, unfinished work, *The Dialogue between a Jew, a Philosopher and a Christian*, he proudly referred to his *Introduction to Theology* as an admirable work.

Arnold of Brescia, however, continued to preach Abelard's teachings and his own views opposing the church's possession of temporal property. He was exiled by the pope and in 1145 was summoned to Rome to do penitence. There Arnold became a leader in the movement on behalf of democratic rights and headed a republican city-state that forced the pope into temporary exile. He was eventually tried by the Roman Curia and executed as a political rebel by secular authorities at the pope's request.

In the first Index of Forbidden Books in 1559 and in the Tridentine Index of 1564, all of Abelard's writings were prohibited as heretical. Modern editions of the Index, however, did not include Abelard's works.

FURTHER READINGS

Christie-Murray, David. *A History of Heresy*. Oxford: Oxford University Press, 1976.

Dunham, Barrows. *Heroes and Heretics: A Political History of Western Thought*. New York: Alfred A. Knopf, 1964.

Grane, Leif. *Peter Abelard: Philosophy and Christianity in the Middle Ages*. Trans. by Frederick and Christine Crowley. New York: Harcourt, Brace & World, 1970.

Haight, Anne Lyon. *Banned Books: 387 BC to 1978 AD*. Updated and enlarged by Chandler B. Grannis. New York: R. R. Bowker, 1978.

Thilly, Frank. *The History of Philosophy*. Rev. by Ledger Wood. New York: Holt, Rinehart and Winston, 1957.

Wippel, John F., and Alan B. Wolter. *Medieval Philosophy: From St. Augustine to Nicholas of Cusa*. New York: Free Press, 1969.

AN INTRODUCTION TO THE PRINCIPLES OF MORALS AND LEGISLATION

Author: Jeremy Bentham
Original date and place of publication: 1789, England
Literary form: Philosophical treatise

SUMMARY

The English jurist, philosopher and political theorist Jeremy Bentham is known as the founder of utilitarianism, or, as he called it, "the greatest happiness principle." Bentham was an intellectual prodigy who entered Oxford at the age of 12. Though trained as a lawyer, he devoted himself instead to the scientific analysis of morals and legislation and efforts to correct abuses and faults of legal and political systems.

His greatest and best-known philosophical work was *An Introduction to the Principles of Morals and Legislation*, which won him recognition throughout the Western world when it was published in 1789. Bentham was influenced by the work of the French philosopher Claude Adrien Helvétius, who in DE L'ESPRIT posited self-interest as the motive for all action.

Bentham also held that the greatest happiness of the greatest number is the fundamental principle of morality. Pleasure, which can be intellectual, moral, social and physical, is synonymous with happiness. The aim of legislation is to increase total happiness in any way possible.

An Introduction to the Principles of Morals and Legislation is a scientific attempt to assess the moral content of human action by focusing on its results and consequences. It includes an exposition of Bentham's ethical positions and an analysis of the aspects of psychology relevant to legislative policy. It begins with a definition of his principle of utility: "Nature has placed mankind under the governance of two sovereign masters, *pain* and *pleasure*. It is for them alone to point out what we ought to do, as well as to determine what we shall do. On one hand the standard of right and wrong, on the other the chain of causes and effects, are fastened to their throne."

Bentham proposes that every action should be judged right or wrong according to its tendency to promote or damage the happiness of the community, or the happiness of those affected by the action. He explains his theory of morals as emerging from the observable facts of human nature, from feelings and experience, without recourse to religious or mysterious concepts. He divides motives into three general categories: social, dissocial and self-regarding. "The motives, whereof the influence is at once most powerful, most constant, and most extensive, are the motives of physical desire, the love of wealth, the love of ease, the love of life, and the fear of pain: all of them self-regarding motives."

He also defines four sanctions of sources of pain and pleasure: physical, political, moral and religious. In 1814, he added a fifth, the sanction of sympathy. He devises methods to measure and judge the relative value of pleasure or pain, allowing society to determine how to react when confronted with situations requiring moral decision making. He concludes his analysis with a discussion of punishment and the proper role that law and jurisprudence should play in its determination and implementation.

Bentham devoted much of his life to the work of reforming jurisprudence and legislation in accordance with the principles outlined in the *Introduction*. He and his followers promoted democracy and self-government and sponsored such measures as health control, insurance, poor laws and humanitarian prison reform. Legal codes drawn up by Bentham were adopted in whole or part by France, Germany, Greece, Spain, Portugal, India, Australia, Canada and other countries of Europe and South America, as well as by several U.S. states.

CENSORSHIP HISTORY

The tenor of Bentham's philosophy was frankly secular. In his writings on ethics and legislation he denied the existence of any divinely implanted moral consciousness or norms. He maintained that human knowledge was either positive or inferential and that inferential knowledge, such as that drawn from religious teachings, was inherently uncertain. He believed that religious sanctions, embodied in the fear of punishment after death, were largely ineffective as a means of deterring people from misconduct. He felt also that religion produced repression, unhappiness and dissension in society among the adherents of different faiths and sects.

In his first published work on religion, *Church of Englandism* in 1818, Bentham made similar references to the church's reliance on authority and obfuscation in propagating its doctrines. Much of Bentham's writing on religion remained unpublished in manuscript form. His most radical attack on religion in general, *Analysis of the Influence of Natural Religion on the Temporal Happiness of Mankind*, appeared in 1822 under a pseudonym.

Some of the most vehement opposition to Bentham's ideas came from the clergy of both the Church of England and the Roman Catholic church. José Vidal, a Dominican theologian at the University of Valencia, argued in response to Bentham in 1827 that, since the Creator had endowed mankind with free will, it was not true that man had been placed under the "governance" of pain and pleasure. If this principle were accepted, the notion of individual responsibility for actions would be eliminated.

In the 1830s and 1840s, Benthamism came under attack in England by leaders of the Tractarian or Oxford movement, a religious movement of Anglican clergymen at Oxford University aimed at renewal of the Church of England by revival of certain Roman Catholic doctrines and rituals.

Between 1819 and 1835, four works of Bentham were placed by the Catholic church on the Index of Forbidden Books: *Introduction to the Principles of Morals and Legislation*, *The Rationale of Judicial Evidence*, *Deontology* and *Three Tracts Relevant to Spanish and Portuguese Affairs*. In the 1897 Index of Pope Leo XIII, these works were confirmed as prohibited reading for Catholics. They remained on the Index through its last edition published until 1966.

FURTHER READINGS

Bentham, Jeremy. *The Principles of Morals and Legislation*. Buffalo: Prometheus Books, 1988.

Collinson, Diané. *Fifty Major Philosophers: A Reference Guide*. London: Routledge, 1988.

Dinwiddy, John. *Bentham*. Oxford: Oxford University Press, 1989.

INTRODUCTORY LECTURES ON PSYCHOANALYSIS

Author: Sigmund Freud
Original date and place of publication: 1933, Germany; 1935, United States
Original publisher: Kiepenheuer, Germany; Liveright, United States
Literary form: Psychological text

SUMMARY

Introductory Lectures on Psychoanalysis is probably Freud's most widely read book. As the title suggests, it is a compilation of his lectures on aspects of the psychoanalytic theory he had been developing for over 20 years. Originally, Freud delivered these lectures to students at the University of Vienna, where he was an assistant professor. His work in the academy was secondary, however, to his career as an analyst in private practice. Still, the demands of teaching university students forced Freud to condense his ideas and make them comprehensible to a wide audience. Thanks to this lecture format, *Introductory Lectures* is among the easiest of Freud's works to understand.

The 1933 edition of *Introductory Lectures* brings together Freud's 1915–17 Vienna lectures with new talks delivered in 1933. Freud believed that these two series comprised his whole psychoanalytic thought. The 1917 *Introductory Lectures* discusses parapraxes (more commonly known as Freudian slips), dream analysis and neuroses. The 1933 work revises and refines Freud's earlier ideas, especially the analysis of dreams. Freud also adds a look at the creation of femininity and the development of a scientific Weltanschauung, or world view.

Freud's discussion of parapraxes is his first line of argument in presenting his theory. He uses slips of the tongue and other blunders to show the power of the unconscious mind. Dream analysis became one of the most popular applications of Freud to everyday life. Freud came under fire for treating dream interpretation as a science, because astrologers, fortunetellers and other pseudoscientists had been analyzing dreams for centuries. Freud viewed dreams, like parapraxes, as useful avenues for psychoanalysis. As everyday occurrences without apparent purposes, they offered insight into the workings of the subconscious mind. Equally important was the way the patient described dreams. Rather than asking the patient to interpret the dreams, Freud believed that the psychoanalyst, due to rigorous training, was best equipped to unlock the symbols and fears hidden in dreams.

The final chapter of his first *Introductory Lectures* concerns neuroses, the mental disorders and compulsive behaviors that interfere with a person's everyday life. In his lectures on neurosis, Freud discusses such now-famous concepts as the Oedipal complex, the libido and narcissism. He concludes the chapter with a discussion of anxiety and the "talking cure": months, or even years, of analytic therapy, sharing the implications of the patient's verbal slip-ups, dreams, compulsions and fears.

The second part of the *Introductory Lectures*, written in 1933, addresses criticism of Freudian methods. Freud discusses arguments with other psychoanalysts and tackles subjects that critics noted he omitted from his earlier works, especially the psychoanalysis of women. While his theories of women's psychosexual makeup have been widely criticized, his idea that some of his female patients' neuroses could be traced to "penis envy" was popularized and detracted from women's efforts to win social equality.

The final chapter of the *Introductory Lectures* concerns the development of a Weltanschauung, or worldview. Freud believed that psychoanalytic theory contributed to a scientific Weltanschauung that was rapidly displacing religious cosmologies. He saw this process as inevitable and desirable, as advancements in science brought order to the otherwise indeterminate workings of the mind. He asserted that religious belief was the main source of resistance to his ideas, especially as most religions were reluctant to acknowledge his thinking on issues of sexuality.

While Freud is interested in the ways that religion provides an ethos and an explanation for the universe, he ultimately finds that the same mental conflicts are at work in religion that operate in the mind of a neurotic patient. He sees religious explanations for the creation of the world as a child's view of his father: the father is idealized and the religious person's faith and dependence are like a child's dependence on a parent.

CENSORSHIP HISTORY

Religious leaders were among the loudest of Freud's detractors. In earlier works, Freud referred to religion as a neurosis, finding similarities between the rituals of organized faiths and the compulsive behaviors of neurotic patients. By 1933, Freud had written *Totem and Taboo*, where he examined anthropologists' research on remote pagan cultures and compared their views to modern Christianity, and *The Future of an Illusion*, where he most forcefully made his case that religion was a kind of mass neurosis.

Although for more than 20 years Freud had argued that religion could be analyzed like a human neurosis, it was not until 1934 that Catholic church authorities took notice of psychoanalysis and censored psychoanalytic works. Offending the Catholic church at this time was problematic, as the church's power in Freud's native Austria counterbalanced the nationalistic impulses of Nazism. In 1934, Pope Pius XI forced an Italian psychoanalytical journal to stop publishing, and he released a statement in which he expressed his disagreement with Freud's ideas, especially regarding religious belief.

Freud feared that the church would clamp down on his profession altogether. In a letter to a friend, Freud wrote, "One cannot publish this formula (psychoanalytic theory) without running the risk of the Catholic authorities forbidding the practice of analysis." This would mean more than mere censorship. By the mid-1930s, psychoanalysts had just begun to gain international respectability among scientists and the general public and the church's ban would be a huge setback for the whole discipline.

In response to his fear of a backlash against psychoanalysis, Freud delayed publishing *Moses and Monotheism*, a book on his analysis of the story of Moses and the birth of Judaism, until 1939, after he had left Austria and the Nazi menace and was safely in England. Freud's books were among the 25,000 volumes by Jewish authors burned by the Nazis in Germany in May 1933. "Against the soul-destroying glorification of the instinctual life, for the nobility of the soul! I consign to the flames the writings of the school of Sigmund Freud," read the declaration announced at the book burning.

The Catholic church viewed *Introductory Lectures on Psychoanalysis* as especially dangerous because of its widespread popularity. Written in an easygoing style and translated into 16 languages, it used examples from everyday life to explain Freud's complex theories. Freud's idea that sexual activity was natural, though a breeding ground for neuroses, was interpreted as advocating free sexuality and following one's impulses. Traditional moralists looked at Freud as just another manifestation of the moral decay brought on by Darwinism and scientific rationality in general.

Freud was not specifically mentioned in the last edition of the Index of Forbidden Books compiled in 1948. However, his writings were considered off-limits to Catholics according to canon law, a general prohibition of works that by their nature were considered dangerous to faith or morals. In *What Is the Index?*, a guide for American Catholics published in 1952, readers were advised according to canon law provisions against reading Freud's *Origins and Development of Psychoanalysis* as part of a national Great Books program.

Although the first translation of Freud's writings was into Russian and, after the 1917 Bolshevik revolution, the Soviet government recognized psychoanalysis as a science and awarded its practitioners state funds, Freud's works were banned from bookstores and libraries under Stalin in 1930 as bourgeois ideology. They circulated only in bootleg editions until the mid-1980s.

FURTHER READINGS

Clark, Ronald W. *Freud: The Man and the Cause*. London: Jonathan Cape and Weidenfeld and Nelson, 1980.

Costigan, Giovanni. *Sigmund Freud: A Short Biography*. New York: Macmillan Company, 1965.

Freud, Sigmund. *The Complete Introductory Lectures on Psychoanalysis*. Ed. and trans. by James Strachey. New York: W. W. Norton, 1966.

Gay, Peter. *Freud: A Life for Our Times*. New York: W. W. Norton and Company, 1988.

Ritvo, Lucille B. *Darwin's Influence on Freud: A Tale of Two Sciences*. New Haven: Yale University Press, 1990.

Stanley, Alessandra. "Freud in Russia: Return of the Repressed." *The New York Times*. (December 11, 1996): 1, 10.

THE KORAN

Original date and place of publication: Seventh century A.D., Arabia
Literary form: Religious text

SUMMARY

The Koran, or *Qur'an* (recitation), is the earliest and the finest work of classical Arabic prose and the sacred book of Islam. Muslims believe that it was revealed by God to the Prophet Muhammad, transmitted over time by the angel Gabriel, beginning in A.D. 619 until the Prophet's death in A.D. 632. To Muslims, the Koran is an unalterable reproduction of original scriptures that are preserved in heaven. Originally committed to memory and recited by Muhammad's followers, the Koranic revelations were written down during the Prophet's lifetime on palm leaves, stones, bones and bark. The verses of the Koran were collected by the caliph Umar and the canonical text was established in A.D. 651–52 under the caliph Uthman by Arabic editors following the instructions of the Prophet's secretary.

The Koranic revelations are divided into 114 *suras*, or chapters, each beginning with the phrase, "In the Name of Allah, the Compassionate, the Merciful." Excepting the brief first chapter that is included in Muslim daily prayers, the *suras* are arranged generally by length, with the longest first and the shortest last. The longest *suras* relate to the period of Muhammad's role as head of the community in Medina. The shorter ones, embodying mostly his ethical teachings, were revealed earlier during his prophethood in Mecca.

The Koran preaches the oneness of God; God's omnipotence and omniscience are infinite. He is the creator of heaven and earth, of life and death. The Koran also emphasizes God's divine mercy and compassion. As his omnipotence is tempered with justice, he is forgiving to the sinner who repents. In the Koran, God speaks directly in the first person and makes known his laws. The Koran provides the basic rules of conduct fundamental to the Muslim way of life. Believers must acknowledge and apply both beliefs and acts in order to establish their faith as Muslims. The religion took on the title of Islam because Allah decreed in the Koran: "Lo the religion with Allah is *al-Islam* (the Surrender) to His will and guidance."

Duties in Islam are incumbent on all the faithful, regardless of status in society. "Verily there is no preference for any of you except by what ye enjoy in good health and your deeds of righteousness," says the Koran. The most important duties for the believer, known as the Five Pillars of Islam, are the profession of faith in Allah and his apostle, daily prayer at appointed hours, almsgiving, fasting in the month of Ramadan, and, if possible, the pilgrimage to Mecca. "Lo! Those who believe and do good works and establish worship and pay the poor-due, their reward is with their Lord and there shall no fear come upon them, neither shall they grieve," the Koran says.

For Muslims, the Koran is the living word of God, "the Scripture whereof there is no doubt," and, as such, contains not only eternal Truth but also the most perfect representation of literary style.

CENSORSHIP HISTORY

An early translation of the Koran into Latin was made around 1141 by Peter the Venerable, the abbot of Cluny. During the period of the medieval Crusades, Christian hostility toward Arabs and their religion mounted. The church fathers regarded Islam as a heresy, Muslims as infidels and the Muhammad as a "renegade bishop, an imposter" who rebelled against the central mission of Christ. By 1215, the church had introduced legislation severely restricting Muslims in Christendom.

The Arabic text of the Koran was not published in Europe until 1530, in Venice. The pope ordered the burning of this edition. Latin translations of the Koran were prohibited by the Spanish Inquisition, a ban that remained in effect until 1790.

In 1541 a printer in Basel, Switzerland—Johannes Oporinus—began printing Robert of Ketton's 12th-century Latin translation of the Koran. City authorities confiscated the entire edition. Martin Luther argued that the edition should be released because knowledge of the Koran would work to "the glory of Christ, the best of Christianity, the disadvantages of the Moslems, and the vexation of the Devil." The edition was allowed to appear in 1542 with prefaces by both Luther and Protestant reformer Melanchthon.

The first English edition of the Koran and a new Latin translation were produced in the 17th century. The Koran had still not been printed in the Islamic world. It could be reproduced only in the original handwritten format used by the Prophet's disciples. In the late 17th century, a Turkish printer in Istanbul, Ibrahim Müteferrika, secured the sultan's permission to set up the first printing press in a Muslim country. In 1727, despite protests by calligraphers, he was granted an imperial edict to print books. But the printing of the Koran itself was still expressly forbidden. It was not until 1874 that the Turkish government gave permission to print the Koran, but only in Arabic. In modern times an English translation was tolerated. In the rest of the Muslim world, printing of the Koran was still prohibited.

The first printed edition of the Koran in Egypt appeared in 1833 under Muhammad Ali Pasha, credited with having laid the foundations of modern Egypt. His Bulaq Press became the first and most distinguished publisher in the Arab world. But on his deathbed religious leaders persuaded his successor, Abbas Pasha, to lock up all printed copies and ban their circulation. Only under Said Pasha, who ruled from 1854 to 1863, were they released.

The first official printed version of the Koran was published by the Egyptian government in 1925. But this version and other late 20th-century editions of the Koran published in other Muslim countries were reproduced in block printing or lithography, considered closer to handwritten script, rather than movable type. Although Islamic law prohibits only the liturgical use of the Koran in a language other than Arabic, some Muslim theologians today believe that it is a sacrilege to translate the Koran because Allah declared to Muhammad, "We have revealed unto thee an Arabic Koran." But despite such objections, unauthorized translations have been made into 43 different languages.

In 1995, *Bacaan*, a Malay translation of the Koran by Othman Ali, published in Singapore, was banned by the government of Malaysia. The banning was part of an official policy aimed at outlawing "deviant" Islamic sects. *Bacaan* was labeled as "deviational" because it offered an interpretation that differed from the official government-approved version and did not include the original text in Arabic.

Modern government censorship of the Koran has been recorded in socialist countries. In 1926 in the Soviet Union, government directives to libraries stated that religiously dogmatic books such as the Gospels, the

Koran and the Talmud could remain only in large libraries, accessible to students of history, but had to be removed from the smaller ones. Such restrictions were lifted after a *modus vivendi* was worked out between Muslims and the state during World War II.

In China during the Cultural Revolution of the 1960s and 1970s, study of the Koran was forbidden and its reading in mosques prohibited. The Koran had been printed in China since the 19th century and translated into Chinese since the 1920s. The Communist government had published an authorized Chinese translation in 1952.

In 1986 in Ethiopia, under the socialist military government, it was reported that copies of the Koran were destroyed or confiscated by the army, Koranic schools and mosques were closed or razed, Muslims were prohibited from praying and some were ordered to convert to Christianity and burn the Koran. Ethiopia's ruling military council, the Derg, feared that a resurgence of Islamic fundamentalism would provide moral and financial aid to Muslims who opposed the Marxist-Leninist revolution.

The Koran is today the most influential book in the world after the Bible and is, with the Bible, the most widely read of sacred texts. More portions of it are committed to memory than those of any other similar body of sacred writings.

FURTHER READINGS

Boorstein, Daniel J. *The Discoverers: A History of Man's Search to Know His World and Himself*. New York: Random House, 1983.

Dawood, N. J., trans. and intro. *The Koran*. Baltimore, Md.: Penguin Books, 1968.

Farah, Caesar E. *Islam: Belief and Observances*. New York: Barron's Educational Services, 1987.

Lippman, Thomas W. *Understanding Islam: An Introduction to the Muslim World*. New York: Penguin Books USA, 1990.

Nugent, Philippa. "Of Such Is Reputation Made." *Index on Censorship* 25.2 (March/April 1996): 160.

LAJJA (SHAME)

Author: Taslima Nasrin
Original date and place of publication: 1993, Bangladesh; 1994, India
Original publisher: Ananda Publishers Pvt. Ltd., Bangladesh; Penguin Books, India
Literary form: Novel

SUMMARY

Taslima Nasrin, a physician, poet, novelist and journalist, is an outspoken feminist from Bangladesh and the author of 21 books. *Lajja* (Shame) is a documentary novel about the plight of a Hindu family in Bangladesh persecuted by Muslim fundamentalists during an outbreak of anti-Hindu violence in 1992. On December 6, 1992, Hindu extremists demolished the Babri Masjid, a 16th-century mosque in Ayodha, India. The incident set off weeks of mob violence in India during which more than 1,200 people were killed. In Bangladesh, Hindus were terrorized and Hindu temples, shops and homes were ransacked and burned in retaliation. Hindus are a minority in Bangladesh, which has an Islamic constitution.

The novel traces the events of 13 days in the life of a fictional family, the Duttas—Sudhamoy Dutta, a physician, his wife, Kironmoyee, and their grown children, Suranjan and Maya—in the aftermath of the razing of the Babri mosque. It also reflects Hindu complaints of persistent violation of their rights.

Many Hindu friends of the Dutta family crossed the border into India to settle with relatives, particularly after a 1990 wave of anti-Hindu violence. But Sudhamoy, now an invalid, had long ago moved from the countryside to the capital, Dhaka, after being forced from his house and land. He chooses to stay, though his wife wants to flee to India.

Sudhamoy, an atheist who fought for the independence of Bangladesh from Pakistan, believes with a naive mix of optimism and idealism that his country will not let him down. His son, Suranjan, rebels against the prospect of having to flee his home as they had in 1990 when the family took shelter in the home of Muslim friends.

"After independence the reactionaries who had been against the very spirit of independence had gained power," Suranjan thinks, "changed the face of the constitution and revived the evils of communalism and unbending fundamentalism that had been rejected during the war of independence." Unlawfully and unconstitutionally, Suranjan recalls, Islam became the national religion of Bangladesh.

Suranjan catalogs the hundreds of violent incidents representing the heavy toll that communalism—chauvinism and prejudice based on religious identity—and religious fundamentalism have taken in Bangladesh over the years. He remembers the looting and burning in Hindu communities in October 1990. Women were abducted and raped, people were beaten and thrown out of their houses and property was confiscated. Suranjan is critical of the failure of the government to protect Hindus.

"Why don't we work to free all State policies, social norms and education policies from the infiltration of religion?" he asks. "If we want the introduction of secularism, it does not necessarily mean that the Gita must be recited as often as the Quran is on radio and TV. What we must insist on is the banning of religion from all State activities. In schools, colleges and universities all religious functions, prayers, the teachings of religious texts and the glorifying of lives of religious personae, should be banned."

The terror finally reaches the Dutta family when a group of seven young men invade the house and abduct 21-year-old Maya. Suranjan and his Muslim friend, Haider, search the streets of Dhaka for Maya but can find no sign of her. Maya is never found and is presumed dead. In the end Suranjan and his family decide to flee to India, their lives and their hopes for their country in ruins. "There was absolutely no one to depend upon," Nasrin writes. "He was an alien in his own country."

CENSORSHIP HISTORY

Taslima Nasrin is an uncompromising critic of patriarchal religious traditions that she sees as oppressive to women, and an outspoken advocate of women's social, political and sexual liberation. In her crusading syndicated newspaper columns, which have been collected and published in two books, she protested religious intolerance and increasing incidents of violence against women by local *salish*, or Islamic village councils, as well as the failure of the government to take adequate measures to stop them. According to Amnesty International, *salish* have sentenced women to death by stoning, burning or flogging for violating the councils' interpretation of Islamic law.

The newspaper columns, Nasrin's bold use of sexual imagery in her poetry, her self-declared atheism and her iconoclastic lifestyle aroused the fury of fundamentalist clerics. By early 1992, angry mobs began attacking bookstores that sold her works. They also assaulted Nasrin at a book fair and destroyed a stall displaying her books. That year, en route to a literary conference in India, her passport was confiscated by the Bangladeshi government, ostensibly because she listed her employment as a journalist rather than a doctor. (In addition to being a writer, Nasrin is also a gynecologist and at the time was employed by the ministry of health.)

Lajja (Shame) was published in Bangladesh in the Bengali language in February 1993, three months after the razing of the Babri mosque in India that touched off a wave of violence against Hindus in Bangladesh. Nasrin states in a preface to the English-language edition of the novel that she wrote the book in seven days soon after the demolition of the mosque because "I detest fundamentalism and communalism. . . . The riots that took place in 1992 in Bangladesh are the responsibility of us all, and we are to blame. *Lajja* is a document of our collective defeat."

During the first six months after its publication, the novel sold 60,000 copies in Bangladesh. Though panned by some critics as a didactic political tract, it was a commercial success in both Bangladesh and neighboring Bengali-speaking Calcutta. Pirated copies of the novel were widely circulated in India by militant Hindus. In 1994, the novel was published in English in New Delhi. (It was published in the United States in October 1997.)

After protests by Muslim fundamentalists in Bangladesh, in July 1993 the Bangladeshi government banned *Lajja* on the grounds that it had "created misunderstanding among communities." On September 24, 1993, Nasrin opened her daily newspaper and saw a prominently displayed notice calling for her death. A *fatwa*, or death decree, had been issued by a *mullah*, or

Muslim cleric, of the Council of Soldiers of Islam, a militant group based in Sylhet, Bangladesh. It called for her execution for blasphemy and conspiracy against Islam.

The group offered a $1,250 bounty for her death. In the following weeks, additional bounties were promised. Thousands of Muslim fundamentalists attended mass rallies and marched through the streets of Dhaka, hanging and burning Nasrin in effigy. Nasrin was only able to obtain police protection after suing the government, which, in response to international pressure, posted two police officers outside her home.

The International PEN Women Writers' Committee organized a campaign on Nasrin's behalf, enlisting the support of human rights and women's organizations around the world. It called on Bangladesh's government to protect Nasrin, prosecute those who sought her death, lift the ban on her book and restore her passport. The governments of Sweden, Norway, the United States, France and Germany lodged official protests. Sweden and Norway ultimately threatened to cut off all economic assistance.

Almost overnight, Nasrin, who was unknown outside Bangladesh and India, became a symbol in the Western world of freedom of expression and women's rights. The government of Bangladesh returned Nasrin's passport, but no arrests were made, even though making a death threat and offering a reward for it is a crime in Bangladesh.

At the time, Bangladesh was governed by the Bangladesh Nationalist Party under Prime Minister Begum Khaleda Zia, the widow of President Ziaur Rahman, an army general assassinated in 1981. Prime Minister Zia was elected with the support of the Muslim party, Jamaat-e-Islami, which held 20 seats in Parliament. Critics of the government contended that she capitulated to fundamentalist demands in the Nasrin case to preserve her electoral coalition.

In April 1994, after the return of her passport, Nasrin traveled to France, where she spoke at a meeting marking International Press Freedom Day. Returning to Bangladesh through India, she gave an interview to the English-language daily, the *Calcutta Statesman*, which quoted her as saying, "the Koran should be revised thoroughly." In an open letter to the Bangladeshi and Indian press, Nasrin denied making the reported remarks, but in her denial she wrote that "the Koran, the Vedas, the Bible and all such religious texts" were "out of place and out of time."

In Bangladesh, fundamentalists took to the streets by the tens of thousands in daily demonstrations calling for her death. The offices of newspapers that showed sympathy for her were attacked; bookstores carrying her books were ransacked; and religious groups pressed the government for her arrest. On June 4, 1994, the Bangladeshi government brought charges against her under a rarely used 19th-century statute dating from the era of British colonialism that proscribes statements or writings "intended to outrage the religious feeling of any class by insulting its religion or religious believers." The crime carries a maximum penalty of two years in prison.

When a warrant was issued for her arrest, Nasrin left her apartment and went underground. In an interview given just before going into hiding, Nasrin explained, "So many injustices are carried out here in the name of Allah. I cannot stop writing against all these simply to save my own skin. . . . The Quran can no longer serve as the basis of our law. . . . It stands in the way of progress and in the way of women's emancipation. . . . The problem is the intolerance of the fundamentalists. I fight with my pen, and they want to fight with a sword. I say what I think and they want to kill me. I will never let them intimidate me."

On August 3, after protracted negotiations among her legal advisors, Western ambassadors and the government of Bangladesh, Nasrin was granted bail and ordered to appear for trial at a later, unspecified date. She fled to Stockholm, Sweden, and remains in exile in Europe.

"The mullahs who would murder me will kill everything progressive in Bangladesh if they are allowed to prevail," Nasrin wrote in her preface to *Lajja*. "It is my duty to try to protect my beautiful country from them and I call on all those who share my values to help me defend my rights. . . . I am convinced that the only way the fundamentalist forces can be stopped is if all of us who are secular and humanistic join together and fight their malignant influence. I, for one, will not be silenced."

FURTHER READINGS

Crossette, Barbara. "A Cry for Tolerance Brings New Hatred Down on a Writer." *The New York Times* (July 3, 1994): 7.

Riaz, Ali. "Taslima Nasrin: Breaking the Structured Silence." *Bulletin of Concerned Asian Scholars* 27.1 (January–March 1995): 21–27.

Tax, Meredith. "Taslima Nasrin: A Background Paper." *Bulletin of Concerned Asian Scholars* 25.4 (October–December 1993): 72–74.

Weaver, Mary Anne. "A Fugitive from Justice." *The New Yorker* (September 12, 1994): 47–60.

Whyatt, Sara. "Taslima Nasrin." *Index on Censorship* 23.4–5 (September/October 1994): 202–207.

THE LAST TEMPTATION OF CHRIST

Author: Nikos Kazantzakis
Original date and place of publication: 1953, Greece; 1960, United States
Original publisher: Athenai, Greece; Simon & Schuster, United States
Literary form: Novel

SUMMARY

The Last Temptation of Christ by the Greek novelist, poet, dramatist and translator Nikos Kazantzakis, best known for his novel *Zorba the Greek*, retells the life story of Jesus of Nazareth, imagining the human events of the gospel accounts in a vivid mosaic colored by extravagant imagery. Kazantzakis's Jesus is not the self-assured son of God following a preordained path, but a Christ of weakness, whose struggles mirror those of human beings who face fear, pain, temptation and death. Though Jesus is often confused about the path he should choose, as the story proceeds his sense of mission becomes clear. When he dies it is as a hero who has willed his own destiny.

Though the story follows the gospel narrative, its setting and atmosphere derive from the peasant life of Kazantzakis's native Crete. The novel was written in the rich, metaphor-laden vocabulary of demotic Greek, the everyday language of modern Greece.

In the 33 chapters of *The Last Temptation of Christ*, corresponding to the number of years in Jesus' life, Kazantzakis portrays what he describes as "the incessant, merciless battle between the spirit and the flesh," a central concern explored in his novels and philosophical writings. Jesus is tempted by evil, feels its attractiveness and even succumbs to it, for only in this way can his ultimate rejection of temptation have meaning.

The novel opens with the scene of a young man in the throes of a nightmare, dreaming that hordes are searching for him as their Savior. Jesus of Nazareth, the village carpenter, has been gripped since childhood by strange portents and has felt the hand of God clawing at his scalp. He shrinks from these signs and visions, hoping that, if he sins, God will leave him alone.

Jesus has loved Mary Magdalene, the daughter of the village rabbi, since childhood. He had wished to marry her, but had been mercilessly forced by God to reject her. She has become a prostitute in order to forget Jesus. Overwhelmed by remorse, Jesus seeks refuge in a desert monastery. A reluctant Messiah, he cries out to God, "I love good food, wine, laughter. I want to marry, to have children. . . . Leave me alone . . . I want Magdalene, even if she's a prostitute. I want you to detest me, to go and find someone else; I want to be rid of you! . . . I shall make crosses all my life, so that the Messiah you choose can be crucified."

During his stay in the desert, Jesus finds the courage and determination to embark upon his public ministry. The central chapters of the novel trace the familiar episodes of the Gospel, leading to the moment of the Crucifixion, where the last temptation comes to Jesus in his delirium on the cross in the form of a dream of erotic bliss and of a worldly life. His guardian angel had snatched him away from the Crucifixion. He had taken the smooth, easy road of men and had at last married Magdalene. Upon Magdalene's death he married Martha and Mary, the sisters of Lazarus, and fathered children. Now, as an old man, he sits on the threshold of his house and recalls the longings of his youth and his joy to have escaped the privations and tortures of the cross.

He comes face to face with his former disciples, led by Judas, who accuses him of being a traitor, a deserter and a coward. "Your place was on the cross," he says. "That's where the God of Israel put you to fight. But you got cold feet and the moment death lifted its head, you couldn't get away fast enough." Jesus suddenly remembers where he is and why he feels pain. A wild joy takes possession of him. Though temptation had captured him for a split second and led him astray, he had stood his ground honorably to the end. The joys of marriage and children were lies, illusions sent by the devil. He has not betrayed his disciples, who are alive and thriving, proclaiming his gospel. "Everything had turned out as it should, glory be to God."

CENSORSHIP HISTORY

Kazantzakis's unorthodox portrait of Jesus was recommended by critics as a powerful and important novel, an extraordinary and original work of art, which in the deepest sense celebrates the spiritual struggles of humankind. It was widely acknowledged, however, that, from an orthodox point of view, his interpretation might be considered as heretical or blasphemous.

Kazantzakis's primary motive in writing *The Last Temptation of Christ* was not, however, to disagree with the church. He wanted, rather, to lift Christ out of the church altogether, to portray Jesus as a figure for a new age, in terms which could be understood in the 20th century. In a 1951 letter, Kazantzakis explained his intentions: "It's a laborious, sacred creative endeavor to reincarnate the essence of Christ, setting aside the dross—falsehoods and pettiness which all the churches and all the cassocked representatives of Christianity have heaped up on His figure, thereby distorting it."

"That part of Christ's nature which was profoundly human helps us to understand him and love Him and pursue his passion as if it were our own," Kazantzakis wrote in the prologue of the novel. "If he had not within him this warm human element, he would never be able to touch our hearts with such assurance and tenderness; he would not be able to become a model for our lives. . . . This book was written because I wanted to offer a supreme model to the man who struggles; I wanted to show him that he must not fear pain, temptation or death—because all three can be conquered, all three have already been conquered."

Kazantzakis was excommunicated in 1954 from the Eastern Orthodox church as a result of the publication in Greece of *The Last Temptation of Christ*. Kazantzakis wrote, "The Orthodox Church of America convened and damned *The Last Temptation* as extremely indecent, atheistic and treasonable, after admitting they hadn't read it. . . ." Kazantzakis wrote to Orthodox church leaders, quoting the third-century Christian thinker Tertullian: "At Thy Tribunal, Lord, I make my appeal," adding, "You have execrated me, Holy Fathers; I bless you. I pray that your conscience may be as clear as mine and that you may be as moral and as religious as I am."

The same year the novel was also placed on the Catholic church's Index of Forbidden Books. Kazantzakis commented, "I've always been amazed at the narrow-mindedness and narrow-heartedness of human beings. Here is a book that I wrote in a state of deep religious exaltation, with a fervent love of Christ; and now the Pope has no understanding of it at all. . . ."

The furor over the novel, however, had the result of increasing sales of the book. "I have ended up by becoming famous in Greece," Kazantzakis wrote in 1955. "All the newspapers, except two, have declared themselves on my side, and from all over Greece telegrams are being sent in protest over the priests' wanting to seize my books. . . . And the books are sold out the moment they are printed and certain booksellers buy up a number of copies and sell them at very high black market rates. What a disgrace! How medieval!"

Ultimately the Greek Orthodox church was forced to halt its anti-Kazantzakis campaign. Princess Marie Bonaparte read the book and recommended it to the queen of Greece. The queen "kept the Greek Orthodox church from making itself ridiculous," wrote Helen Kazantzakis in her biography of her husband.

In 1962–65 in Long Beach, California, the novel, in the company of Jessica Mitford's *The American Way of Death* and poetry by Langston Hughes, was the target of a three-year campaign by a right-wing group aimed at removing it from the public library. The campaign was unsuccessful.

A 1988 film of the novel directed by Martin Scorsese caused worldwide controversy and was banned in several countries mainly because of the sequence drawn from the novel in which a delirious Jesus on the Cross imagined that he had loved, married and fathered children. Scorsese and the director of the Venice Film Festival were prosecuted for blasphemy in Rome, but were acquitted. In the U.S., the film was criticized by Roman Catholic authorities as blasphemous. Three Republican congressmen introduced a resolution to force the withdrawal of the film. The Dallas, Texas, city council passed a resolution condemning it. A national video rental chain, Blockbuster Video, announced that it would not carry the film. In Escambia County, Florida, the board of county commissioners voted for an ordinance to prohibit the showing of the movie in the county at risk of 60 days in jail or a $500 fine or both. U.S. District Court Judge Roger Vinson issued a restraining order against the ban as an unconstitutional violation of the First Amendment.

Director Scorsese's response to the film censorship echoed that of Kazantzakis 34 years earlier. "My film was made with deep religious feeling. . . . It is more than just another film project for me. I believe it is a religious film about suffering and the struggle to find God." In December 1988, the novel was banned in Singapore as a result of pressure from fundamentalist Christians related to the controversy over the film.

FURTHER READINGS

Heins, Marjorie. *Sex, Sin, and Blasphemy: A Guide to America's Culture Wars*. New York: New Press, 1993.

Kanzantzakis, Helen. *Kazantzakis: A Biography Based on His Letters*. Trans. by Amy Mims. New York: Simon & Schuster, 1968.

Kazantzakis, Nikos. *The Last Temptation of Christ*. Trans. and afterword by P. A. Bien. New York: Simon & Schuster, 1960.

Levy, Leonard. *Blasphemy: Verbal Offense Against the Sacred, from Moses to Salman Rushdie*. New York: Alfred A. Knopf, 1993.

Thompson, David, and Ian Christie, eds. *Scorsese on Scorsese*. London: Faber and Faber, 1989.

LETTER ON THE BLIND

Author: Denis Diderot
Original date and place of publication: 1749, France
Literary form: Philosophical essay

SUMMARY

The versatile French writer and reformer Denis Diderot, who was responsible for the production of the ENCYCLOPÉDIE, the greatest single work of the French Enlightenment, was also the author of essays, works of dramatic and art criticism, novels and plays. Among his most notable philosophical writings is his first mature work, *Letter on the Blind, for the Use of Those Who See*, an essay containing the most complete statement of his materialism.

Published in 1749, *Letter on the Blind* presented an original analysis of the impact of the senses on moral and metaphysical ideas. The *Letter* began with an account of Diderot's visit to a blind widower. He was struck by the man's sense of order, the keenness of his surviving senses and the differences in his values accountable to his blindness. His sense of beauty was confined to tactile qualities. He had no shame in nudity and considered theft a major crime, since he was so helpless against it. Diderot concluded that the ideas of right and wrong are derived from sensory experience. "I have never doubted that the state of our organs and of our senses has a great influence on our metaphysics and our ethics," Diderot explained, "and that our most purely intellectual ideas, if I may express it thus, are very much dependent on the structure of our body. . . ."

In *Letter on the Blind*, Diderot investigated the psychology of the blind, the effect of the absence of one sense on the human view of morality and the universe, and the blind person's reaction to proofs of God and the origin and formation of ideas. Far in advance of his time, Diderot also envisioned the possibility of teaching the blind to read by the sense of touch. The Braille system of reading was not invented by French professor Louis Braille until the 19th century.

Taking issue with the idea that the nature's marvels are an argument for God's existence, he used as an example the case of a blind man who has never seen such marvels and declares, " 'For these things are proofs only to those who can see, like you. If you desire me to believe in God, then you must make me touch and feel him. . . . And even if the physical mechanism of animals is as perfect as you claim—and I am certainly willing to believe it, for you are an honest man and incapable of any attempt to deceive me—what has that to do with a sovereignly intelligent being?' "

Diderot was particularly critical of the tendency to regard everything that is beyond human comprehension as a miracle or "the work of God." "Can we not reason with a little less pride and a little more philosophy?" he asked. "If nature presents us with a knot that is difficult to untie, then let us leave it as it is; let us not insist in cutting it there and then and on employing for the task the hand of a being who thereupon becomes a knot even more difficult to untie than the first."

CENSORSHIP HISTORY

In 1746, Diderot published his first original work, *Philosophic Thoughts*, an attack on Christianity and a defense of deism, combining cosmological speculations with moral considerations. The volume was highly successful and sold in several editions. The boldness of Diderot's thoughts on religion in the essay attracted vocal criticism. The book was burned by order of the Parlement of Paris and, from that time on, Diderot was subject to investigation by the authorities. "A very bright young fellow, but extremely dangerous," was the description of him found in police records. In 1747, in a surprise visit to his apartment the police found another antireligious manuscript, *Skeptic's Stroll*, which was not published until 1830.

When *Letter on the Blind* appeared in 1749, its philosophical speculation was considered a flagrant challenge to government authorities. Its conclusion that human spiritual and moral concepts depend on the senses rather than on the received doctrine of the church, was viewed as an attack on orthodox religious ideas. On July 24, 1749, Diderot's home was searched by the police, who confiscated a few copies of *Letter on the Blind* and boxes of material he was preparing for the *Encyclopédie*. Diderot was arrested and imprisoned in the dungeon of Vincennes, a few miles east of Paris. After a month in solitary confinement, he was persuaded under threat of life in prison to admit his guilt in a formal confession. He acknowledged his authorship of three books that were "intemperances of intellect which escaped me," and promised never again to write on religion.

He was then transferred to a neighboring chateau and given freedom to walk in the park and write. On November 3, 1749, after 102 days in confinement, he was released. Diderot did not abide by his promise to hew to orthodoxy. His next great project was the *Encyclopédie*, the epitome of Enlightenment rationalism.

FURTHER READINGS

Diderot, Denis. *Diderot's Selected Writings*. Ed. and intro. by Lester G. Crocker. Trans. by Derek Coltman. New York: Macmillan Company, 1966.

Durant, Will, and Ariel Durant. *The Age of Voltaire*. New York: Simon and Schuster, 1965.

Garraty, John A., and Peter Gay. *The Columbia History of the World*. New York: Harper & Row, 1972.

Green, Jonathon. *The Encyclopedia of Censorship*. New York: Facts On File, 1990.

Haight, Anne Lyon. *Banned Books: 387 BC to 1978 AD*. Updated and enlarged by Chandler B. Grannis. New York: R. R. Bowker, 1978.

Reill, Peter Hanns, and Ellen Judy Wilson. *Encyclopedia of the Enlightenment*. New York: Facts On File, 1996.

LETTERS CONCERNING THE ENGLISH NATION

Author: Voltaire (François Marie Arouet)
Original date and place of publication: 1733, London
Literary form: Essays

SUMMARY

The French philosopher and author François Marie Arouet, known as Voltaire, personified the 18th-century Enlightenment and did more to popularize the new science and philosophy of rationalism and empiricism than any other thinker of his age. Voltaire was an implacable enemy of intolerance and despotism and a foe of institutional Christianity, particularly the Catholic church. His polemical genius made him the most admired and feared writer of his age.

At a young age Voltaire began a battle with institutional authority and censorship that continued throughout his long life. In 1717, at age 23, he spent 11 months in the Bastille under suspicion of writing satirical verses insulting to the regent Philippe II of Orléans. In 1726, he was imprisoned again when a young nobleman, the Chevalier de Rohan-Chabot, took offense at a joke by Voltaire at his expense. He had Voltaire beaten and then, through the influence of Rohan-Chabot's powerful family, sent to the Bastille. Voltaire was released after two weeks only upon his promise to leave France for England.

During the three years Voltaire spent in exile in England, he was impressed by the greater freedom of thought and influenced by the scientific discoveries of Isaac Newton and the philosophy of Francis Bacon and John Locke. Bacon's and Locke's application of the scientific method to philosophy, based on empirical observation and common sense judgment, appealed to Voltaire.

He returned to France full of enthusiasm for England's more tolerant form of government and the intellectual movement that fostered confidence in human reason and a rational and scientific approach to religious, social, economic and political issues. The chief literary fruit of this sojourn was *Letters Concerning the English Nation*, also known by the title *Philosophical Letters*. His *Letters*, called "the first bomb hurled against the old regime," launched the interest in English philosophy and science that was to characterize the literature of the Enlightenment on the Continent.

In 24 letters to a friend in France, Voltaire discussed the English Parliament, constitution, commerce and other issues, such as the benefits of inoculation against disease and motivations for suicide, criticizing by comparison French institutions. France had a single monarch, a single church and a feudal economy. In England the monarchy was constitutional, commerce thrived and almost all religions were acceptable. "The English are the only people on earth who have been able to prescribe limits to the powers of kings by resisting them," he wrote, "and who, by a series of struggles, have at length established that wise and happy form of government where the prince is all-powerful to do good, and at the same time is restrained from committing evil; where the nobles are great without insolence or lordly power, and the people share in the government without confusion."

Voltaire praised England's progress in extending religious tolerance: "An Englishman, like a free man, goes to heaven by the path he prefers." He celebrated Newton, Bacon and Locke in glowing terms. Instead of those who promote brute force and violence, a man such as Newton should be revered and admired, he declared, "who sways our minds by the prevalence of reason and the native force of truth" and "who by the vigor of his mind is able to penetrate into the hidden secrets of nature's vast frame of the universe."

He commended Bacon as the father of experimental philosophy and Locke as the genius who, in his modest way, had done for the human mind what Newton had done for nature. "Mr. Locke has laid open to man the anatomy of his own soul, just as some learned anatomist would have done that of the body," he declared. "Everything contributes to prove that the English are greater philosophers, and possessed of more courage than we. It will require some time before a true spirit of reason and a particular boldness of sentiment will be able to make their way over the Straits of Dover."

CENSORSHIP HISTORY

Before publishing the *Letters*, Voltaire attempted to negotiate with Abbé de Rothelin, a confidante of Cardinal Fleury, the state censor. Voltaire was told that he might receive permission to publish the book, except for those passages commenting on Locke's philosophy. Locke was held by the church to support materialism and atheism and the French translation of his AN ESSAY CONCERNING HUMAN UNDERSTANDING had been listed in 1700 on the

Index of Forbidden Books. Rather than accepting the censor's suggestions, he decided to publish the *Letters* in London in English.

The English edition appeared in 1733. Voltaire negotiated the book's underground publication in France through a printer in the city of Rouen, Claude-François Jore, who was willing to issue it without a privilege, or official permit. Before any book could be published in France, the king had to grant permission, usually given upon recommendation of a censor who testified that the book contained nothing contrary to religion, public order or sound morality. Even after publication with a privilege, the censor's verdict could be superseded by the police, other government officials, the Sorbonne or ecclesiastical authorities. Thousands of books appeared without the privilege. In some cases a tacit permission could be received from the censor allowing a book's publication without fear of prosecution.

Voltaire warned Jore not to circulate the book right away, but in 1734, several clandestine copies reached Paris. News of the London and Rouen editions attracted the interest of the underground printers of Paris, and a pirate publisher printed a large edition without Voltaire's knowledge.

Everywhere in France clandestine printing presses, sometimes secretly protected by the police, reproduced smuggled copies or printed original manuscripts. Along the French frontier, relay stores were established for forbidden books destined to be smuggled into the capital. The public was eager to buy forbidden books such as Voltaire's and there was a lucrative underground trade.

A French parliamentary decree on June 10, 1734, declared the book "scandalous and against religion" and "likely to inspire the most dangerous license toward religion and the civil peace." It ordered the burning of the book by the public executioner and the prosecution of its author. Several printers were sent to the Bastille for the publication of the *Letters*. Voltaire took refuge at the home of Madame de Châtelet at Cirey, near the frontier of Lorraine, from where he could slip out of the country, if necessary, to escape arrest. He remained there for 10 years. Though the book's sale was forbidden in France, it was distributed underground and widely read. Its notoriety served only to increase its fame and influence.

Two years later, however, the government, recognizing a fait accompli, agreed to rescind the order for Voltaire's arrest if he would disavow authorship of the book. Voltaire agreed to these conditions as part of the game of cat and mouse he played with the censors. "They say I must retract," he wrote to the Duchess d'Aguillon. "Very willingly I will declare that Pascal is always right; . . . that all priests are gentle and disinterested; . . . that monks are neither proud nor given to intrigue nor stinking; that the Holy Inquisition is the triumph of humanity and tolerance." Voltaire's order of arrest was withdrawn with the proviso that he remain at a respectful distance from Paris.

In 1752, the *Letters* was placed on the Catholic church's Index of Forbidden Books, where it remained through the last 20th-century edition of the

Index published until 1966. Between 1758 and 1800 practically all of Voltaire's books were placed on the Index. A total of 38 were individually listed, including PHILOSOPHICAL DICTIONARY. The Spanish Index also prohibited all of his writings.

FURTHER READINGS

Bachman, Albert. *Censorship in France from 1715–1750: Voltaire's Opposition*. New York: Burt Franklin, 1971.

Durant, Will, and Ariel Durant. *The Age of Voltaire*. New York: Simon and Schuster, 1965.

Gay, Peter. *The Enlightenment: An Interpretation. The Rise of Modern Paganism*. New York: W. W. Norton & Company, 1995.

Haight, Anne Lyon. *Banned Books: 387 BC to 1978 AD*. Updated and enlarged by Chandler B. Grannis. New York: R. R. Bowker, 1978.

Redman, Ben Ray, ed. and intro. *The Portable Voltaire*. New York: Penguin Books, 1977.

LEVIATHAN

Author: Thomas Hobbes
Original date and place of publication: 1651, England
Literary form: Political philosophy

SUMMARY

The greatest work of the English philosopher Thomas Hobbes was *Leviathan or the Matter, Forme, and Power of a Commonwealth Ecclesiastical and Civil*. Published in 1651, it represented Hobbes's contribution to what he called "a science of politics," a body of knowledge on how human beings live in society that would offer solutions to the problems of government.

Hobbes was deeply concerned about social anarchy, "the dissolute condition of masterless men," resulting from the English Civil War, the execution of King Charles I and religious disputes. In *Leviathan*, he proposed a system of rules for society, a political structure and authority that would end such anarchy.

He believed that the Commonwealth, which he called Leviathan, is created as a result of a social contract. Man in the state of nature is a selfish animal motivated by appetites, desires and fears, "a perpetual and restless desire of power after power, that ceaseth only in death." Human life is "solitary, poor, nasty, brutish, and short." The passions that incline human beings to live peacefully are "fear of death; desire of such things as are necessary to commodious living; and a hope by their industry to obtain them."

For self-preservation and to obtain peace and order, people agree to relinquish their freedom, submitting to the authority of the state. For "where there is no common power, there is no law; where no law, no justice." In his

Commonwealth, order is secured by the sovereign, who is responsible for the administration of both civil and ecclesiastical law. The sovereign is the "supreme pastor," who is the best interpreter of God's will and whose authority supersedes that of the Catholic church and the pope.

Although his recommendation of absolutism as the price for obtaining peace in society was unexceptional, the method he used to arrive at his political theory was innovative. Hobbes was inspired by recent developments in physical sciences and mathematics to apply the deductive reasoning of geometry and physics to analysis of the organization and conduct of society.

Just as Galileo used the deductive method to study the physical universe, Hobbes applied it to the study of human activities. "Reasoning from authority of books . . .," he wrote, "is not knowledge, but faith." Only the use of logic, proceeding from a basic premise and moving step by step to conclusions, as opposed to speculation and opinion, could produce incontrovertible conclusions about the organization and conduct of political society.

CENSORSHIP HISTORY

The frank materialism of *Leviathan* offended many of Hobbes's contemporaries. He was regarded as an atheist and blasphemer for viewing human beings as no more than bits of matter in motion whose motivations were crude and animalistic, for his skeptical attitude toward Christianity and his advocacy of state control over the church. *Leviathan* was regarded as one of the most damaging and systematic attacks ever made upon revealed religion. The book had been published during Oliver Cromwell's reign as lord protector of England. After the restoration of the monarchy and militant Anglicanism, Hobbes came under attack in Parliament.

In October 1666, as a solution to eliminate the influence of blasphemers such as Hobbes, the House of Commons discussed the revival of the 15th-century writ that sentenced heretics to burning. The great fire that had devastated London that year and the plague of the previous year were seen as evidence of divine wrath for Hobbes's sins. The House of Commons established a committee to which it submitted for consideration a bill "touching such books as tend to atheism, blasphemy, and profaneness, or against the essence and attributes of God, and in particular . . . the book of Mr. Hobbes called the Leviathan." The bill failed to pass in Parliament.

Hobbes was the last eminent writer to fear the application of the writ against heretics. Parliament permanently abolished it in 1677. However, Hobbes was forbidden from publishing his philosophical opinions thereafter and turned to the writing of history. *Leviathan*, along with the works of the Dutch philosopher, Spinoza, was also widely condemned throughout Holland during the period 1650 to 1680.

In 1703, the Catholic church in Rome placed *Leviathan* on the Index of Forbidden Books. In 1709, 30 years after his death, Hobbes's complete works were included on the Index. They remained listed through the last edition of the Index published until 1966.

FURTHER READINGS

Collinson, Diané. *Fifty Major Philosophers: A Reference Guide*. London: Routledge, 1988.

Curtis, Michael, ed. and intro. *The Great Political Theories*. Vol. 1. New York: Avon Books, 1981.

Jordan, W. K. *The Development of Religious Toleration in England*. Vol. 4. Gloucester, Mass.: Peter Smith, 1965.

Levy, Leonard W. *Blasphemy: Verbal Offense Against the Sacred, from Moses to Salman Rushdie*. New York: Alfred A. Knopf, 1993.

Putnam, George Haven. *The Censorship of the Church of Rome*. Vol. 1. New York: G. P. Putnam's Sons, 1906–07.

THE LIFE OF JESUS

Author: Ernest Renan
Original date and place of publication: 1863, France
Literary form: History

SUMMARY

Ernest Renan was a French historian, philologist, critic and essayist who studied religion from a historical, rather than a theological, perspective. Although educated for the priesthood, he rejected orthodox Catholicism and turned to faith in science. His historical studies of the Old and New testaments, explaining their origins in their geographic, social and political environments, popularized the use of scientific and historical methods in biblical study.

The first volume in Renan's series of religious histories was *The Life of Jesus*. Renan had traveled to Syria in 1860–61 to direct the first large-scale archeological expedition ever conducted there. During this scientific mission he went to Galilee, visiting Jerusalem, Hebron and Samaria. Tracing Jesus' footsteps, he was deeply moved and resolved to devote himself to a work on the life of Jesus that would make the Savior more real historically.

In his introduction, Renan described his plans for four books on the origins of Christianity. "On the whole, I admit as authentic the four canonical Gospels. All, in my opinion, date from the first century, and the authors are, generally speaking, those to whom they are attributed; but their historic value is very diverse." The duty of the historian, Renan wrote, is to explain supernatural accounts, rather than accepting them.

When Renan first conceived the idea of a history of the origins of Christianity, he had intended to write a history of doctrines. "But I have learned since that history is not a simple game of abstractions; that men are more than doctrines." To write the history of a religion, Renan contended, it is necessary first to have believed it and, in the second place, to believe it no longer, "for absolute faith is incompatible with sincere history."

Jesus cannot belong solely to those who call themselves his disciples, as he is the common honor of all who share a common humanity, Renan wrote. "His glory does not consist in being relegated out of history; we render him a truer worship in showing that all history is incomprehensible without him."

Renan began his biography of Jesus thus: "At that time there lived a superior personage, who, by his bold originality, and by the love which he was able to inspire, became the object and fixed the starting-point of the future faith of humanity." He described Jesus' birth in humble circumstances in Nazareth and his upbringing and education in the tradition and culture of Judaism. The perusal of the books of the Old Testament made a great impression upon Jesus. He never attached much importance to the political events of his time and probably knew little about them. Jesus never once gave utterance to the sacreligious idea that he was God, Renan claimed. He did, however, believe himself to be the Son of God and in direct communication with God.

Renan described Jesus as a sweet, amiable and gentle character, a perfect idealist with a dream of a great social revolution, in which rank would be overturned and all worldly authority would be humiliated. Renan denied the supernatural nature of the miracles Jesus is said to have performed, asserting that a miracle, understood as the specific intervention of superhuman power in the operation of nature, is an impossibility.

Jesus is miraculous only in the sense that he is governed by a fresh and powerful religious instinct. In the opinion of Jesus' contemporaries, two means of proof—miracles and the accomplishment of prophecies—could verify a supernatural mission. Jesus, and especially his disciples, employed these two processes of demonstration in perfect good faith, as miracles were regarded as the indispensable mark of the divine and the sign of the prophetic vocation.

Almost all the miracles Jesus thought he performed appear to have been those of healing, particularly exorcism or the expulsion of demons, Renan explained. Scientific medicine was unknown to the Jews of Palestine at the time. The presence of a superior man, treating the diseased with gentleness and assuring them of their recovery, was often viewed as a decisive remedy. "Healing was considered a moral act; Jesus, who felt his moral power, would believe himself specially gifted to heal." Jesus was not a founder of dogmas or a maker of creeds; he infused into the world a new spirit of perfect idealism. The faith, enthusiasm and constancy of the first Christian generation is inexplicable, Renan claimed, unless Jesus was a man of surpassing greatness.

According to Renan, the transformation of a great religious leader into a God is a recurring pattern of religious history. Jesus' death on the cross gave further impetus to his deification, a process already begun during his lifetime. Jesus' character condensed all that is good and elevated in human nature, Renan believed. Jesus was not sinless, however, and he conquered the same passions that all human beings combat. "But whatever may be the unexpected phenonemona of the future," Renan concluded, "Jesus will not be surpassed. His worship will constantly renew its youth, the tale of his life will cause ceaseless tears . . . all the ages will proclaim that, among the sons of men, there is none born who is greater than Jesus."

CENSORSHIP HISTORY

When *The Life of Jesus* was published in France in 1863 it caused a sensation. The success of the biography, the first to use modern historical methods to recount the life of Jesus, was immediate and unprecedented for a scholarly work on a religious subject. "It was one of the world-shaking books of a world-shaking epoch," Renan's English-language translator declared. "Like Macauley's *History of England*, it lay on every library table, and was the subject of universal discussion."

Only five months after its first publication, it had gone through 11 editions, and 60,000 copies had been sold. In the next year, it was translated into all the major European languages, and Renan became one of the best-known writers of his time. In 1864, Renan published a low-cost edition for the poor under the title *Jesus*, which was also a bestseller.

While *The Life of Jesus* elevated Renan's literary reputation, it also plunged him into controversy. He firmly believed that his critical approach restored greater dignity to Jesus by humanizing him. Renan's intention was to preserve the religious spirit while dispelling superstitions and historical inaccuracies, which he felt were opposed to science and common sense. "If the Gospels are like other books," he wrote in the preface to the 13th edition of *The Life of Jesus*, "I am right in treating them in the same manner as the student of Greek, Arabian or Hindu lore treats its legendary documents which he studies. Criticism knows no infallible texts; its first principle is to admit the possibilities of error in the text which it examines."

However, Renan's rationalistic and skeptical perspective, his denial of the divinity of Christ and his attempts to explain in purely human terms such fundamental tenets of Christianity as the Resurrection of Jesus scandalized the devout. The year before the publication of *The Life of Jesus*, he had realized his great ambition to succeed a former professor in the chair of Hebrew, Chaldaic and Syriac languages at the Collège de France. In earlier essays he had introduced his theory that the life of Jesus represented an extraordinary historical event, rather than a supernatural one, which human reason could explain in psychological terms. In the course of his inaugural lecture, he made clear his philosophical position of denial of Jesus' divinity. Quickly, anti- and pro-clerical student factions created noisy disturbances centered around his views. Soon afterward *The Life of Jesus* came off the press.

In the atmosphere of controversy surrounding the publication of the book, Renan was expelled from his professorship in 1864, becoming a central figure in debates on the moral and political issues of academic freedom. In exile from academia, he was appointed assistant director of manuscripts in the imperial library. With the advent of the Third Republic (1870–1940), marking the end of imperial rule, Renan regained his academic position. In 1876, *The Life of Jesus* was republished in revised form as part of an eight-volume work, *History of the Origins of Christianity* (1876–1881). Renan was elected to the French Academy and in 1883 appointed director of the Collège de France. Until his death in 1892 and for decades after, he was regarded as among the most influential literary figures of his age, particularly on the development of modern views of religious history.

Beginning in the 1860s, the Catholic church and the French government became engaged in a bitter struggle. Pope Pius IX condemned the liberal trends that reflected modern scientific thinking in his 1864 encyclical, *Quanta Cura*, and in 1870 defined papal infallibility as a dogma. The French state, on the other hand, was moving toward the complete secularization of government and education, a movement that gained momentum under the Third Republic and culminated in the official separation of church and state in the Separation Law of 1905. It was in this context that, in 1897, *The Life of Jesus* was placed on the Index of Forbidden Books along with 19 other works by Renan.

Despite its condemnation by the Catholic church, many more editions of the book appeared in France and other countries. Though the furor over *The Life of Jesus* had long since subsided by the 1920s, Renan's work remained on the Index through its last edition compiled in 1948 and in effect until 1966. Once regarded as one of the most controversial authors in the Western world, Renan is not widely read today and *The Life of Jesus*, despite its impressive blend of scholarship and art, has been superseded by more modern works.

FURTHER READINGS

Chadbourne, Richard M. *Ernest Renan*. New York: Twayne Publishers, 1968.

———. *Ernest Renan as an Essayist*. Ithaca, N.Y.: Cornell University Press, 1957.

Putnam, George Haven. *The Censorship of the Church of Rome*. Vol. 2. New York: G. P. Putnam's Sons, 1906–07.

Renan, Ernest. *The Life of Jesus*. Intro. by John Haynes Holmes. New York: Modern Library, 1955.

MEDITATIONS ON FIRST PHILOSOPHY

Author: René Descartes
Original date and place of publication: 1641, France
Literary form: Philosophical essays

SUMMARY

The 17th-century French philosopher and scientist René Descartes is the founder of modern philosophy and mathematics. His *Meditations on First Philosophy* contains the most thorough exposition and defense of his philosophical ideas.

In six meditations, Descartes attempted to apply the scientific method to philosophical concepts, approaching philosophy through analysis of experience rather than assertion of faith. He began his meditations with a letter addressed to the Sacred Faculty of Theology of Paris. "I have always thought that the two questions, of God and of the soul, were the principal questions among those that should be demonstrated by [rational] philosophy rather than theology," he wrote. "For although it may suffice us faithful ones to believe by faith that there is a God and that the human soul does not perish with the body, certainly it does not seem possible ever to persuade those without faith to accept any religion, nor even perhaps any moral virtue, unless they can first be shown these two things by means of natural reason."

In his first meditation, Descartes introduced the concept of universal doubt, examining the principles underlying his opinions. He intended to base his theories only on what could be proven to be true and began his search for truth by doubting everything he had been taught. Doubt delivers the mind from prejudices and makes available a method of accustoming the mind to independence from the senses, he believed. Though the senses sometimes mislead, there are some ideas that cannot reasonably be doubted.

The first certainty is that I am thinking about these matters, Descartes declared. And if I am thinking, I must exist. And, as Descartes wrote in DISCOURSE ON METHOD, his earlier essay on the scientific method, "*Cogito ergo sum.*" (I think, therefore I am).

From the certainty of the existence of a thinking being, Descartes moved to consider the existence of God. He asserted that in order for an idea to contain a particular objective reality, it must obtain from some cause, a first idea or archetype. If there is something that could not have come from himself, it must come from an infinite, omniscient entity that created all things. Descartes could not conceive of an infinite substance unless the idea had been placed in him by some substance which was, in fact, infinite. Therefore, he must conclude that God exists.

The existence of God leads to the reality of perception of the physical world. God could not deceive the thinking mind by illusory perceptions because it is impossible for God to deceive, as in all fraud and deception there is some kind of imperfection. Therefore, man cannot err if volition is restricted to the boundaries of knowledge. Everything that we perceive clearly and distinctly is wholly true. Though we should not rashly admit everything that the senses seem to teach us, neither should we doubt them in general.

Descartes describes the physical world as mechanistic and entirely divorced from the mind, the only connection between the two being by intervention of God. In Descartes's concept of dualism, mind and body exist independently, even though they happen to coincide here on earth. There is no doubt that what nature teaches contains some truth. Yet human life is often subject to error in particular matters. God made human beings perfect in their potential, rather than in actuality. They must use their perceptions wisely by restricting the will only to accept clear and distinct perceptions.

CENSORSHIP HISTORY

See DISCOURSE ON METHOD.

FURTHER READINGS

Descartes, René. *Meditations on First Philosophy*. Trans. and intro. by Laurence J. Lafleur. New York: Bobbs-Merrill Co., 1960.

Green Jonathon. *The Encyclopedia of Censorship*. New York: Facts On File, 1990.

Jolley, Nicholas, "The Reception of Descartes' Philosophy." In *The Cambridge Companion to Descartes*. Ed. by John Cottingham, 393–423. Cambridge: Cambridge University Press, 1992.

THE MERITORIOUS PRICE OF OUR REDEMPTION

Author: William Pynchon
Original date and place of publication: 1650, England
Literary form: Religious text

SUMMARY

The Meritorious Price of Our Redemption was the first work to be burned publicly in North America. Its author, William Pynchon, was a prominent British merchant and colonizer of the Connecticut River valley in western Massachusetts. After sailing to New England with John Winthrop in 1630, he founded the city of Roxbury, Massachusetts. History does not record exactly why Pynchon left the Boston area for the sparsely populated western edge of the Massachusetts Bay Colony. Historians speculate that he moved for economic reasons: Demand for beaver pelts was increasing and there was a huge beaver population in the Connecticut River valley. He also may have been motivated to move by his disagreements with the growing Puritan orthodoxy in the Boston area. Whatever his reasons, Pynchon moved to Springfield in 1636 and immediately became one of the town's most powerful citizens.

Until 1650, it appears that Pynchon was content running his fur-trading business and serving as a local magistrate. He first appeared in Massachusetts court records as the judge in an early witchcraft case, which he dismissed for lack of evidence. Witchcraft cases were just beginning to appear in Massachusetts in the late 1640s, and if it were for this case alone, he would have remained a footnote to legal history. However, Pynchon's spare-time writings were the subject of Massachusetts' first case of public book-burning.

In *The Meritorious Price Of Our Redemption*, Pynchon set out to refute the Calvinist idea that Christ had suffered for mankind's sins. It seemed illogical to Pynchon that God would have punished Christ with the eternal damnation that would have been the result of dying for all the sins of mankind. Rather, Pynchon believed, Christ achieved a perfect atonement for all Christians' misdeeds. Through his obedience of the divine plan for him, he avoided undergoing the punishments of hell. If Christ had suffered these torments, then God would have punished him twice.

As Pynchon pointed out, "I never heard that any Tyrant did require [the payment of] full price for their Galley-slaves, and to bear their punishment of their curse and slavery in their stead. . . . [Calvinist doctrine] makes God the Father more rigid in the price of our Redemption than ever a Turkish Tyrant was. . . ." In Pynchon's opinion, theologians who maintained that Christ did suffer in hell were portraying God as a merciless tyrant.

The Meritorious Price of Our Redemption also questioned the era's thinking about who killed Jesus. Most theologians blamed the crucifixion on Roman soldiers, but Pynchon was convinced that the Jews had persuaded the Romans to kill Jesus. Pynchon's anti-Semitism reappeared in *The Jewes Synagogue: or a Treatise Concerning the ancient Orders and manner of Worship used by the Jewes in their Synagogue-Assemblies*, published in 1652. Pynchon's toleration for free thought was in fact quite narrow, not extending beyond more rights for Presbyterians.

Pynchon was no defender of broad definitions of religious liberty or freedom of conscience, as was fellow wilderness-dweller Roger Williams. Pynchon believed that only Presbyterians should have been allowed to vote for office in Massachusetts along with the majority Congregationalists. He shared this belief with a dissident group called the Remonstrants, but did not share the Remonstrants' desire to see a British-appointed governor of the Massachusetts Bay Colony. While Pynchon believed that "a world of good hath been done by ministers that haue no certaine forme of discipline," he feared the radical movements that had come to power during the English Civil War, and subscribed to mainstream Presbyterianism.

Toward the end of his life, Pynchon returned to England, where he bought a large estate on the Thames and continued to produce theological tracts, though none brought him as much attention as *The Meritorious Price of Our Redemption*. He was buried in an Anglican churchyard, apparently proof that he rejoined the Church of England shortly before his death.

CENSORSHIP HISTORY

The Meritorious Price of Our Redemption was published in England in June 1650 and quickly found its way to Boston. Pynchon's book was a literary sensation in England. British readers took great interest in the religious feuds of their day and were particularly interested to hear how interdenominational battles were fought in the colonies. Pynchon satisfied this demand by signing his book "William Pinchon, Gentleman, in New England."

Once Pynchon's book reached Boston that October, local religious and civil authorities were furious. By including his place of residence, Pynchon implied that his opinions were representative of other respectable New Englanders. If Parliament thought that a majority of Massachusetts landholders held such unorthodox views, colonial leaders feared that they might well be tempted to cut off financial support for the colony. The document also confused colonial leaders, as Pynchon had been a respectable landholder, town founder and fur merchant for nearly 20 years. No one had suspected that he held such unorthodox, and possibly blasphemous views.

On October 15, 1650, Boston's general court, the judicial body charged with approving new books, decided that *The Meritorious Price of Our Redemption* was "erronious and daingerous" and ordered an Anglican theologian to prepare a response to it. The court summoned Pynchon to appear before its next session to answer its questions and declared that the book would be burned in the Boston market the next day.

In all likelihood, Pynchon had never intended to offend the authorities. It seems more likely that he had merely committed to paper the ideas he had held for several decades and provoked an unforeseen rebuke from Boston. He appeared in court on May 7, 1651, and over the course of the next two weeks he made a partial apology and retraction of the statements that inflamed the general court. Pynchon spent his days conversing with theologians, explaining his justification for his ideas while listening to the elders' objections. Finally, Pynchon admitted that he had not "spoken in my booke so fully of the prize and merrit of Christs sufferings as I should have done." He never did recant his statement that Christ could not have been sentenced to suffer in hell, however.

On May 13, 1651, Pynchon was allowed to return to Springfield, for the purpose of writing a book that would correct the objectionable ideas in *The Meritorious Price of Our Redemption*. The general court asked Pynchon to have the book ready for its October meeting. Pynchon did not appear at the October session. But the judges ruled that he should be given more time to finish his book, in order to fully repent for his offenses, and so that he had a chance to read the official rebuttal to *The Meritorious Price of Our Redemption.* If Pynchon did not show up at the May 1652 session, the court decided, he would be fined £100 and would be subject to other penalties.

In late 1651, the court received letters from prominent Englishmen asking that it treat Pynchon lightly because he had not intended to create controversy by publishing his book. The members of the general court responded politely but firmly. Pynchon's book had lent credence to false images of New England religious life and the book's blasphemous passages had to be burned and recanted. The court informed Pynchon's English supporters that his sentence would be carried out, though the court agreed that Pynchon had been an important New England leader.

Pynchon had returned to England by April of 1652. He never published a refutation of his own work; rather, he responded with a counterattack on the Boston Puritans. In his British theological writings he continued to insist that Christ could not have suffered torment in hell, and generally argued fine doctrinal points with Massachusetts clergy. While his writings caused some controversy in England, the official censor approved them for printing, and Pynchon never again had his books publicly burned.

Unlike other religious dissenters of this period, Pynchon had not arrived at his ideas through involvement with a radical dissenting sect. Rather, he evidently formulated them while living in the wilderness of early Springfield, Massachusetts. Pynchon was no young hothead when he wrote *The Meritorious Price of Our Redemption*: He was a well-connected, well-respected entrepreneur and colonist. For these reasons he escaped the harsher punishments heaped on Roger Williams for his publication of THE BLOUDY TENENT OF PERSECUTION and William Penn for THE SANDY FOUNDATION SHAKEN.

FURTHER READINGS

Armytage, Frances, and Juliette Tomlinson. *The Pynchons of Springfield: Founders and Colonizers* (1636–1702). Springfield, Mass.: Connecticut Valley Historical Museum, 1969.

Burt, Henry M. *The First Century of the History of Springfield: The Official Records from 1636 to 1736.* Springfield, Mass.: (self-published), 1898.

McIntyre, Ruth A. *William Pynchon: Merchant and Colonizer*. Springfield, Mass.: Connecticut Valley Historical Museum, 1961.

Smith, Joseph H., ed. *Colonial Justice in Western Massachusetts (1639–1702): The Pynchon Court Record.* Cambridge: Harvard University Press, 1961.

THE METAPHYSICS

Author: Aristotle
Original date and place of publication: Fourth century B.C.
Literary form: Philosophical treatise

SUMMARY

Aristotle, one of the greatest of the ancient Greek philosophers, was born in Macedonia in 384 B.C. and studied for 20 years under Plato at the academy in Athens. In 335 B.C., he founded his own school, the Lyceum, which attracted large numbers of scholars. Though much of his writing was lost, almost 50 works survived, mainly in the form of notes or summaries of his lectures made by his students and edited in the first century B.C. Aristotle's work included almost every field of study known in his time: biology, physics, politics, ethics, economics, grammar, rhetoric, poetry, metaphysics and theology. He created the study of logic, the science of reasoning, which he regarded as the necessary tool of any inquiry.

The Metaphysics is a collection of lectures written at different dates during the late development of his thought. Their subject is what he called first philosophy, the study of the first causes of things. Aristotle considered first philosophy to be the discerning of the self-evident changeless first principles that form the basis of all knowledge, the true nature of reality. "All men by nature desire to know," *The Metaphysics* begins. But there are different degrees of knowledge. "Sense perception is common to all and therefore easy and no mark of wisdom," Aristotle declares. The highest wisdom is the pursuit of knowledge for its own sake, the science of first principles or first causes. Though metaphysics is the most abstract science, the most removed from the senses, it is the most exact.

All things, whether they are changing or unchanging, quantitative or nonquantitative, fall within the purview of first philosophy. The universe, which is constantly moving and changing, can best be understood through the doctrine of the four causes: the material cause (the substance of which the thing is made), the formal cause (its design), the efficient cause (its maker or builder) and the final cause (its purpose or function).

Aristotle depicts a hierarchy of existence, a ladder of nature proceeding from formless matter at the bottom to pure form, which is the Unmoved Mover, at the top. There is one unchangeable perfect being, which causes motion while remaining itself unmoved. This Prime Mover, or God, energizes the whole, so that each thing strives to attain its complete or perfect form. Thus study of first philosophy culminates in theology, or the study of God.

Differing with Plato, Aristotle believed that a form, with the exception of the Prime Mover, has no separate and independent existence, but rather is immanent in matter. Instead of inhabiting separate worlds of their own, forms exist materially in the individual things they determine.

CENSORSHIP HISTORY

In the ninth century, Arab and Jewish scholars reintroduced Aristotle to the West. His works became the basis of medieval Scholasticism, particularly through the writing of Saint Thomas Aquinas. During the 12th and 13th centuries, Aristotle's writings, accompanied by the work of the masterful Arabic commentators Avicenna and Averroës, profoundly influenced European thought, dominating the intellectual life of the University of Paris, the Christian world's center of learning.

For the first time, Christian thinkers were confronted with a completely rationalistic interpretation of human experience and a powerful metaphysical system that analyzed the world without reference to the tenets of Christian orthodoxy. The interpretation of Aristotle by Averroës in his COMMENTARIES, which was thought to imply rejection of the reality of individual intellect, denial of personal immortality and the eternal and non-created nature of the universe, was viewed as opposing Christian doctrine.

In 1210, the bishops of the Provincial Council of Paris forbade the public or private teaching of the natural philosophy and metaphysics of Aristotle. The ban, which applied to instruction at the arts faculty of the University of Paris, was imposed under penalty of excommunication and confirmed in 1215 by the papal legate, Robert de Curzon. In 1231, Pope Gregory IX prohibited the reading of the works of Aristotle until they had been purged of heresy, and he appointed a commission of theologians to correct them. The prohibition was extended to Toulouse in 1245 by Pope Innocent IV.

The bans on Aristotle were impossible to enforce and were gradually lifted. During the same period, study of Aristotle was widespread at Oxford and at the theological faculty of the University of Paris, where his writings were not forbidden. Between 1241 and 1247, Roger Bacon lectured on Aristotle at the arts faculty of the University of Paris, and by mid-century all the known works of Aristotle and the commentaries on them were part of the curriculum of the university. By the mid-14th century, the Legates of Urban V required that all candidates for the Licentiate of Arts at Paris prove their familiarity with Aristotle's works.

FURTHER READINGS

Bokenkotter, Thomas. *A Concise History of the Catholic Church*. New York: Doubleday & Company, 1977.

Copleston, Frederick. *A History of Philosophy*. Vol. 1, *Greece and Rome, Part II*. New York: Doubleday & Company, Inc., 1962.

———. *A History of Philosophy*. Vol. 2, *Medieval Philosophy*. New York: Doubleday, 1993.

Wippel, John F., and Alan B. Wolter, eds. *Medieval Philosophy: From St. Augustine to Nicholas of Cusa*. New York: Free Press, 1969.

THE NEW ASTRONOMY

Author: Johannes Kepler
Original date and place of publication: 1609, Germany
Literary form: Scientific treatise

SUMMARY

The brilliant German mathematician and astronomer Johannes Kepler developed the first significant improvement of the astronomical theories of the 16th-century astronomer Nicholas Copernicus. Kepler was convinced of the truth of the Copernican heliocentric hypothesis—that the earth and the planets revolve around the sun. His aim, he explained in 1605, was "to show that the celestial machine is to be likened not to a divine organism, but rather to a clockwork." Relying on the astronomical calculations of Mars' orbit by Danish astronomer Tycho Brahe, which were much more accurate than any earlier work, Kepler found that the positions of the planets differed from those calculated in Copernican theory.

In the Copernican theory of planetary motion, as in the geocentric Ptolemaic theory that had dominated astronomy since the second century A.D., planetary orbits were described as perfect circles. Many complex circular motions had to be combined to reproduce variations in the planets' movements. After attempting to combine circular motions in a way that would generate the observed planetary paths, it occurred to Kepler that the planets might move in oval, or elliptical, paths.

In *The New Astronomy* (1609), considered one of the most important books on astronomy ever published, Kepler stated the first of his three laws of planetary motion: that the planets move in elliptical orbits. While Copernicus took the revolutionary step of describing a change in the relations of the heavenly bodies, he had not altered the view of their movements as circles or the circular shape of the whole system. Kepler was the first to abandon the Aristotelian circular perfection of celestial movements.

In *Harmonies of the World* (1619), Kepler stated his second and third laws: that the speeds of the planets in their orbits are greatest when nearest the sun, and that there is a mathematical proportion between the square of the time it takes a planet to travel around the sun and the cube of its distance from the sun. The modern era in astronomy is commonly dated from the discovery of what became known as Kepler's laws. Kepler's laws paved the way for the development of celestial mechanics and the development by the English physicist Sir Isaac Newton of the law of universal gravitation.

CENSORSHIP HISTORY

In 1616, the Copernican system was denounced as dangerous to the faith and Galileo was summoned to Rome and warned by Pope Paul V not to "hold, teach or defend" Copernican theories. In 1619, the Vatican prohibited Kepler's *The New Astronomy* and his textbook of Copernican astronomy, *The Epitome of Copernican Astronomy* (1618), under a general prohibition covering all books teaching the heliocentric theory. According to the papal bull accompanying these bans, to teach or even to read the works of Copernicus or Kepler was forbidden.

Kepler was informed by a colleague that, in fact, his *Epitome*, a low-cost textbook prepared for students with an easily understood analysis, could be read in Italy, but not by those for whom it was intended. Only learned people and those with scientific training, who had received special permission, could legally have access to the book.

In a 1619 "Memorandum to Foreign Booksellers, Especially in Italy," regarding the publication of *Harmonies of the World*, Kepler wrote: "The greater the freedom of thought the more will faith be awakened in the sincerity of those who are devoted to scientific research. . . . You booksellers, if it is true, will act according to law and order if, considering the judgment, you will not openly offer copies of my book for sale. But you must realize that you have to serve philosophy and the good writers. . . . Therefore, please sell the book only to the highest clergy, the most important philosophers, the experienced mathematicians, to whom I, personally, as the advocate of Copernicus have no other approach. These men may decide whether one should make these immeasurable beauties of the divine works known to the common people or rather diminish their glory and suppress them by censures."

Kepler was undeterred by the censorship of his work. As Albert Einstein later wrote of Kepler: "Neither by poverty, nor by incomprehension of the contemporaries who ruled over the conditions of his life and work, did he allow himself to be discouraged. In addition, he dealt with a field of knowledge that immediately endangered the adherent of religious truth. He belonged, nevertheless, to those few who cannot do otherwise than openly acknowledge their convictions on every subject." After 1619, Kepler published eight additional treatises before his death in 1630.

The Index of Forbidden Books of 1664 confirmed the condemnation of the works of Copernicus, Kepler and Galileo and any other writings affirming the movement of the earth and the stability of the sun. This prohibition remained in effect up to the Index of Benedict XIV in 1753, which omitted the general prohibition.

It was not until 1824, however, when Canon Settele, a professor of astronomy in Rome, published a work on modern scientific theories, that the church finally announced its acceptance of "the general opinion of modern astronomers" and granted formal permission for the printing in Rome of books reflecting the theories of Copernicus, Kepler and Galileo. In the next Index of Forbidden Books, published in 1835, the names of Copernicus, Kepler and Galileo were finally omitted.

FURTHER READINGS

Baumgardt, Carola. *Johannes Kepler: Life and Letters*. Intro. by Albert Einstein. New York: Philosophical Library, 1951.

Boorstein, Daniel J. *The Discoverers: A History of Man's Search to Know His World and Himself*. New York: Random House, 1983.

Garraty, John A., and Peter Gay. *The Columbia History of the World*. New York: Harper & Row, 1972.
Green, Jonathon. *The Encyclopedia of Censorship*. New York: Facts On File, 1990.

THE NEW TESTAMENT

Translator: William Tyndale
Original date and place of publication: 1526, Germany
Literary form: Religious text

SUMMARY

The English Protestant reformer and linguist William Tyndale was the first person to translate the Bible into English from the original Greek and Hebrew and the first to print the Bible in English. Many scholars consider his influence on English literature comparable to Shakespeare's.

In 1524, when Tyndale, an Oxford graduate and Catholic priest, resolved to translate the Bible, England was the only European country without a printed vernacular version. The 1408 synod of Canterbury had forbidden translation into English of any portion of the Scriptures by an unauthorized individual. Only the fifth-century Latin Vulgate edition of the Bible translated by Saint Jerome was considered acceptable.

Translation of the Bible into the vernacular remained illegal in England for fear that anarchy and schism would be brought about by the spread of Lutheranism. Lutheran books had been publicly burned in Cambridge and London in 1520. Martin Luther's doctrine of *sola scriptura*, the Bible alone, which emphasized the ability of believers to read and understand the Bible themselves without church intervention, was considered to defy church authority. Scripture could be interpreted only by the infallible pope and the hierarchy.

Tyndale could find no religious authority in London who would support his work. "And so in London I abode for almost a year, and marked the course of the world. . .," he later wrote, "and saw things whereof I defer to speak at this time and understood at the last not only that there was no room in my lord of London's palace to translate the New Testament, but also that there was no place to do it in all England, as experience doth now openly declare."

In 1524, Tyndale left England for Germany. The following year in Cologne, he began printing his translation of the New Testament from the Greek. The printing had reached Matthew 22 when it had to be suspended. His translation was violently opposed by the clergy, who, fearing Lutheranism, saw it as "pernicious merchandise." When the Cologne authorities moved to arrest him and his assistant and impound their work, they fled to Worms, where publication of the 700 pages of the New Testament was completed clandestinely and anonymously at the press of Peter Schoeffer in

1526. Six thousand copies of Tyndale's New Testament were smuggled into England the following year and widely distributed. For the first time, all 27 books of the New Testament were available in clearly printed portable form in a language that every reader could understand.

The primary source for Tyndale's New Testament was the original Greek, although he drew from both the Latin Vulgate and Martin Luther's German translation. Because he believed that the word of God should speak directly to the reader in an understandable way, his first aim was clarity, to write in everyday spoken English. "If God spare my life, ere many years, I will cause a boy that driveth a plough shall know more of the Scripture than thou dost," he told a learned man before leaving England.

His ability to write in simple, direct and rhythmic prose and, as his contemporary biographer David Daniell says, "to create unforgettable words, phrases, paragraphs and chapters, and to do so in a way that . . . is still, even today, direct and living" had an indelible impact on both the language of the Bible and English prose.

"Am I my brother's keeper?" "Blessed are the pure of heart; for they shall see God." "No man can serve two masters." "Ask and it shall be given to you." "There were shepherds abiding in the fields." These and hundreds of proverbial phrases such as "the signs of the times," "the spirit is willing" and "fight the good fight" come from Tyndale's New Testament.

Tyndale's 1534 revision of the New Testament, published in Antwerp under his own name, was carried forward into later Renaissance Bibles and formed the basis of the Authorized or King James Version of the Bible published in 1611.

Living in concealment in the Low Countries, Tyndale also translated the first half of the Old Testament from the original Hebrew. His masterly translation of the Pentateuch appeared in 1530, beginning with Genesis: "In the beginning God created heaven and earth. . . . Then God said: let there be light and there was light." The Book of Jonah was completed in 1536. Tyndale's Old Testament books were published in pocket volumes and smuggled into England. His Old Testament was also adopted in large part into the King James Version of the Bible.

CENSORSHIP HISTORY

Tyndale's 1526 edition of the New Testament was immediately denounced by church dignitaries in England. In the summer of 1526, the English bishops met and agreed that "untrue translations" should be burned, "with further sharp corrections and punishment against the keepers and readers of the same." The English ambassador to the Low Countries was instructed by Catholic Cardinal Thomas Wolsey, who controlled domestic and foreign policy for Henry VIII, to act against printers or booksellers involved in the production and distribution of the English New Testament. Tyndale's New

Testament was the first printed book to be banned in England. Wolsey ordered Tyndale to be seized at Worms, but Tyndale found refuge with Phillip of Hess at Marburg.

Although Henry VIII was to break with Rome in the early 1530s, he had no sympathy with Protestant views and saw Tyndale's New Testament as Lutheran in its influence. Tyndale had translated the Greek word *ekklesia*, for example, as "the congregation," which is the body of Christ, rather than "the church." The English bishops saw this as among the heretical aspects of the translation, in that the word *congregation* implied equality of the gathering of believers. They believed that this idea was Lutheran and denied the church's authority. Copies of the books were publicly burned at Saint Paul's Cathedral in 1526. In May 1527, church authorities ordered all copies to be bought up and destroyed. But despite the ban, reprints continued to be distributed, many imported clandestinely from the Low Countries.

Tyndale, in hiding in Antwerp, continued to publish polemics from abroad in defense of the principles of the English reformation, including *The Obedience of a Christian Man* and *The Parable of the Wicked Mammon* in 1528, an exposition of the New Testament teaching that faith is more important than works. When *Wicked Mammon* began to circulate in England, the church, viewing it as containing Lutheran heresies, moved to suppress it. Those who were found with it were arrested and severely punished. *Wicked Mammon*, like the New Testament translation, was widely read, nevertheless, and continued to be influential, even years later when it was still prohibited.

The English ambassador to the Low Countries was instructed to demand that the regent extradite Tyndale and his assistant William Roye to England, but they could not be found. In 1530, Tyndale further enraged King Henry VIII by publishing *The Practice of Prelates*, which condemned the king's divorce. In May 1535, Tyndale, working in Antwerp on his translation of the Old Testament, was arrested as the result of a plot masterminded by English authorities. He was imprisoned in Vilvoorde Castle near Brussels, charged with Lutheran heresy and disagreeing with the Holy Roman Emperor. Tyndale was put on trial, formally condemned as a heretic, degraded from the priesthood and handed over to the secular authorities for punishment. In early October 1536, he was strangled at the stake and his dead body burned with copies of his Bible translation. His last words were: "Lord, open the king of England's eyes."

At the time of Tyndale's death, about 50,000 copies of his Bible translations in seven editions were in circulation in England. A small portion of Tyndale's translation was included in a complete English Bible published illegally in Germany by his colleague Miles Coverdale. In 1537, Matthew's Bible appeared in England under the pseudonym of John Matthew. Its editor, John Rogers, was a Catholic priest who converted to Protestantism, and a friend of Tyndale's. Two-thirds of Matthew's Bible printed Tyndale's translations unchanged.

Matthew's Bible was the first Bible in English to be licensed by the government. Despite its inclusion of Tyndale's translations, it was approved by Henry VIII. His break with the Catholic church had been completed by the Act of Supremacy in 1534, which established the Church of England. Tyndale's and Coverdale's translations were also included in Henry VIII's Great Bible of 1539, which was declared the official Bible of the Church of England.

In 1546, the Catholic church's Council of Trent said that the Latin Vulgate of Saint Jerome was the sole canonical text of the Bible. Catholics were forbidden to read any translation such as Tyndale's without special permission of the pope or the Inquisition. This restriction remained in effect until the late 18th century.

During the reign of the Catholic Queen Mary I in England from 1553 to 1558, the ban on Protestant Bibles was reinstated. In 1555, a royal proclamation commanded "that no manner of persons presume to bring into this realm any manuscripts, books, papers . . . in the name of Martin Luther, John Calvin, Miles Coverdale, Erasmus, Tyndale . . . or any like books containing false doctrines against the Catholic faith."

The committee assembled in 1604 by King James I to prepare the Authorized Version of the Bible—often acclaimed as the greatest work ever produced by a committee and ranked in English literature with the work of Shakespeare—used as its basis Tyndale's work. Nine-tenths of the Authorized Version's New Testament is Tyndale's. Many of its finest passages were taken unchanged, though unacknowledged, from Tyndale's translations.

The tragedy of Tyndale's execution at the age of 42 is compounded by the knowledge that he was cut down before having completed his life's work. Tyndale was unable to go on to translate the poetic books and prophecies of the Old Testament or revise again his New Testament translation. As his biographer, Daniell, laments, it is as though Shakespeare had died halfway through his life, before his greatest tragedies had been written.

FURTHER READINGS

Daniell, David. *Let There Be Light: William Tyndale and the Making of the English Bible.* London: British Library, 1994.

———. *William Tyndale. A Biography.* New Haven: Yale University Press, 1994.

Haight, Anne Lyon. *Banned Books: 387 BC to 1978 AD.* Updated and enlarged by Chandler B. Grannis. New York: R. R. Bowker, 1978.

NINETY-FIVE THESES

Author: Martin Luther
Original date and place of publication: 1517, Switzerland
Literary form: Theological tract

SUMMARY

Martin Luther, a German monk of the Augustinian order, was the founder of the Protestant Reformation in Europe. He was a doctor of divinity and town preacher of Wittenberg, where he taught theology at the university. A visit to Rome had convinced him of the decadence and corruption of the Catholic pope and clergy. In 1516, he began to question the efficacy of indulgences in a series of sermons.

In 16th-century Roman Catholic doctrine, the pope could transfer superfluous merit accumulated by Christ, the Virgin Mary or the saints to an individual sinner in order to remit temporal penalties for sin later to be suffered in purgatory. Such transfers of indulgences could benefit both the living and the dead. Luther's evangelical emphasis on the complete forgiveness of sins and reconciliation with God through God's grace alone led him to question the doctrine of indulgences and the pervasive ecclesiastical practice of selling them.

The following year, Tetzel, a Dominican monk, hawked indulgences to pay a debt that Albert of Brandenburg had incurred to purchase the Bishopric of Mainz and to help pay for the new basilica of Saint Peter in Rome. Luther resolved to voice his pastoral concern about the spiritual dangers of indulgences as an obstacle to the preaching of true repentance and interior conversion.

On October 15, 1517, Luther challenged his academic colleagues to debate the subject. Luther issued his challenge in the traditional manner—by posting a placard written in Latin on the door of the Castle Church in Wittenberg. Luther's notice contained his 95 theses on indulgences. To his surprise, the theses were circulated in Latin and German throughout Germany and within a few weeks to much of Europe, unleashing a storm of controversy that was to lead to the Protestant Reformation.

In his *Ninety-Five Theses or Disputation on the Power and Efficacy of Indulgences*, Luther argued that the pope could remit only those penalties he had imposed himself, and denied the pope's authority to remit sin. Luther rejected the idea that the saints had superfluous merits or that merit could be stored up for later use by others.

The pope has no control over the souls in purgatory, Luther asserted. "They preach only human doctrines who say that as soon as the money clinks into the money chest, the soul flies out of purgatory." If the pope does have such power, Luther asked, "why does not the pope empty purgatory for the sake of holy love and the dire need of all the souls that are there if he redeems an infinite number of souls for the sake of miserable money with which to build a church?"

He branded indulgences as harmful because they gave believers a false sense of security. By implying that the payment of money could appease the wrath of God, the sale of indulgences impeded salvation by diverting charity and inducing complacency. "Christians should be taught that he who gives to the poor is better than he who receives a pardon. He who spends his money for indulgences instead of relieving want receives not the indulgence of the pope but the indignation of God." Those who believe that their salvation is assured because they have indulgence letters will face eternal damnation, "together with their teachers," who preach unchristian doctrine.

Luther objected to the church's intent to raise money for a basilica by sale of indulgences. "Why does not the pope, whose wealth is today greater than the wealth of the richest Crassus, build this one basilica of St. Peter with his own money rather than with the money of poor believers?" Luther asked. Luther believed that to repress by force the objections of the laity to the sale of indulgences, rather than resolving them reasonably, "is to expose the church and the pope to the ridicule of their enemies and to make Christians unhappy."

Luther's theses were directed toward church reform. He did not see them as an attack on the pope's authority or as the beginnings of a schism. But the church's response to Luther's proposals pushed him toward a more radical stance that led ultimately to a break with Rome and the founding of a new church.

CENSORSHIP HISTORY

At first Pope Leo X did not take serious notice of Luther's theses, viewing them instead as a reflection of the rivalry between Luther's Augustinian order and the Dominicans, who were Luther's most vociferous critics. But the theses, rapidly distributed in Germany, found active support among the peasantry and civil authorities, who objected to Rome's siphoning of local funds. The hierarchy became convinced that the abuses of indulgences should be corrected and Luther silenced.

In 1518, the pope asked Hieronymus, bishop of Ascoli, to investigate Luther's case. Luther was summoned to Rome to answer charges of heresy and contumacy, or insubordination. Frederick III of Saxony stepped in to demand that Luther's hearing be held on German soil. When the hearing before the papal legate was transferred to Augsburg, where the imperial diet (the legislative assembly) was unsympathetic to papal claims, Luther refused to retract any of his theses. In a debate in Leipzig in 1519 with the German professor Johannes Eck, Luther argued that because the authority of the pope was of human origin, rather than rooted in divine right, he could be resisted when his edicts contravened the scriptures.

Johannes Froben of Basel had published the *Ninety-Five Theses* in an edition with Luther's sermons. In February 1519, Froben reported that only ten copies were left and that no book from his presses had ever sold out so quickly. Taking full advantage of the new potential of the printing press, the book had been distributed not only in Germany, but in France, Spain, Switzerland, Belgium, England and even in Rome. The same year the theological faculties of the Universities of Louvain and Cologne ordered copies of the theses to be burned for heresy.

The pope appointed commissions to study Luther's writings. On June 15, 1520, the pope proclaimed in a papal bull, *Exsurge Domine*, "Rise up O Lord and judge thy cause. A wild boar has invaded thy vineyard." The bull pronounced 41 errors of Luther as "heretical, or scandalous, or false, or offensive to pious ears, or seductive of simple minds, or repugnant to Catholic truth, respectively." In his preface the pope wrote, "Our pastoral office can no longer tolerate the pestiferous virus of the following forty-one errors. . . . The books of Martin Luther which contain these errors are to be examined and burned. . . . Now therefore we give Martin sixty days in which to submit." It was forbidden to print, distribute, read, possess or quote any of Luther's books, tracts or sermons.

Then in August, October and November of 1520, Luther published three revolutionary tracts that dramatically raised the stakes of his disagreement with the church: ADDRESS TO THE CHRISTIAN NOBILITY OF THE GERMAN NATION, which attacked the claim of papal authority over secular rulers; THE BABYLONIAN CAPTIVITY OF THE CHURCH, which rejected the priesthood and the sacraments; and *The Freedom of Christian Man*, which reiterated his doctrine of justification by faith alone. The first edition of 4,000 copies of the *Address* sold out within a week. Riding the crest of a wave of public support, Luther in his sermons, debates and writings proposed a radical alternative to the Catholic church.

On October 10, the papal bull reached Luther in Germany. Luther wrote a stinging reply to the bull: *Against the Execrable Bull of Antichrist*. "They say that some articles are heretical, some erroneous, some scandalous, some offensive," Luther wrote. "The implication is that those which are heretical are not erroneous, those which are erroneous are not scandalous, and those which are scandalous are not offensive." Calling on the pope to "renounce your diabolical blasphemy and audacious impiety" he concluded, "It is better that I should die a thousand times than that I should retract one syllable of the condemned articles."

Luther's books were burned in Louvain and Liège during October, and the following month in Cologne and Mainz. On December 10, 1520, Luther and his followers publicly burned the papal bull at Wittenberg, along with copies of canon law and the papal constitutions. "Since they have burned my books, I burn theirs," Luther said. In January 1521 the pope issued a new bull, *Decet Romanum Pontificum*, which affirmed the excommunication of Luther and his followers and the burning of his works.

Luther's enormous popularity, bolstered by his appeal to German nationalist objections to Roman intervention in their affairs, saved him from the fate of other heretics. Elector Frederick III of Saxony, Luther's temporal ruler, refused to give him over for trial to Rome. The only power in Europe capable of suppressing Luther was the Holy Roman Emperor Charles V, a devout Catholic determined to root out the heresy.

On April 18, 1521, Luther was called before the Diet of Worms. Before the emperor and the assembled princes of the empire he refused to recant or disown his writings. "Should I recant at this point," he said, "I would open the door to more tyranny and impiety, and it will be all the worse should it appear that I had done so at the instance of the Holy Roman Empire." He continued, "Unless I am convicted by Scripture and plain reason—I do not accept the authority of popes and councils, for they have contradicted each other—my conscience is captive to the Word of God."

On May 26, 1521, Charles V decreed in the Edict of Worms that Luther was "a limb cut off from the Church of God, an obstinate schismatic and manifest heretic. . . . no one is to harbor him. His followers are also to be condemned. His books are to be eradicated from the memory of man." The edict included a Law of Printing, which prohibited printing, sale, possession, reading or copying Luther's work or any future works he might produce.

Though the emperor had persuaded most of the princes of Germany to sign the condemnation, few strongly supported it. Though the edict called for Luther's arrest, his friends were able to harbor him at the castle in Wartburg of Elector Frederick III of Saxony. There he translated the New Testament into German and began a 10-year project to translate the entire Bible. He returned to Wittenberg in March 1522 at considerable risk to his life and spent the rest of his life spreading his new gospel.

Censorship of Luther's writing was pervasive throughout Europe. His works and those of his disciples were destroyed and banned in England, France, Spain and the Netherlands. In 1524 the Diet of Nürnberg declared that "each prince in his own territory should enforce the Edict of Worms in so far as he might be able." As the edict implied, it could not be enforced in most of northern Germany. Cities in southern Germany and elsewhere in northern Europe joined the Lutheran reform. "Lutheran books are for sale in the marketplace immediately beneath the edicts of the Emperor and the Pope who declare them to be prohibited," a contemporary commented.

In 1555, Charles V signed the Peace of Augsburg, giving up further attempts to impose Catholicism on the Protestant princes. The peace allowed each prince to choose the religion of his state and declared that people could not be prevented from migrating to another region to practice their own religion. Lutheranism had taken hold.

Luther's works remained on the Vatican's Index of Forbidden Books until 1930, when they were omitted from the list. They were still prohibited, however, according to the church's canon law barring Catholics under penalty of mortal sin from reading books "which propound or defend heresy or schism."

FURTHER READINGS

Bainton, Roland H. *Here I Stand: The Life of Martin Luther*. New York: Penguin Group, 1995.

Bokenkotter, Thomas S. *A Concise History of the Catholic Church*. Garden City, N.Y.: Doubleday and Co., 1977.

Christie-Murray, David. *A History of Heresy*. Oxford: Oxford University Press, 1989.

Haight, Anne Lyon. *Banned Books: 387 BC to 1978 AD*. Updated and enlarged by Chandler B. Grannis. New York: R. R. Bowker, 1978.

Putnam, George Haven. *The Censorship of the Church of Rome*. Vol. 1. New York: G. P. Putnam's Sons, 1906–07.

Spitz, Lewis W., ed. *The Protestant Reformation*. Englewood Cliffs, N.J.: Prentice-Hall, 1966.

Wilcox, Donald J. *In Search of God and Self: Renaissance and Reformation Thought*. Boston: Houghton Mifflin Company, 1975.

OF THE VANITIE AND UNCERTAINTIE OF ARTES AND SCIENCES

Author: Henricus Cornelius Agrippa
Original date and place of publication: 1530, Belgium
Literary form: Theological treatise

SUMMARY

Of the Vanitie and Uncertaintie of Artes and Sciences is the most significant work of German scholar Henricus Cornelius Agrippa, best known for his earlier writings on the occult sciences. His treatise on magic, *De occulta philosophia*, written in 1510 but not published until two decades later, studied occult traditions found in long-neglected ancient writings. Agrippa contended that the metaphysical Hermetic writings on magic, astrology and alchemy and the esoteric system of Scripture interpretation found in the writings of the Cabala provided new insights into the meaning of Biblical texts. His aim in *De occulta* was to redeem the sacred tradition of magic, purging it of dangerous and superstitious elements.

Of the Vanitie and Uncertaintie of Artes and Sciences (*De incertitudine et vanitate scientarum declamatio inuectiua*), a satire on the state of religion, morals and society, appeared to disavow his own earlier studies on the occult. He attacked the occult sciences and their authorities, appealing to the Bible and the grace of God as the only real source of truth. He stressed the superiority of the Christian gospel to human learning, denying the power of reason to know reality.

Of the Vanitie was also a bitter denunciation of ecclesiastical abuses in contemporary society—the corruption of monks, the intrusion of pagan customs into worship and the worldliness and immorality of the papacy. Agrippa was particularly critical of the papacy as having excessive power over the clergy, the faithful and temporal affairs that are outside the spiritual realm. Though he regarded the basic power and authority of the pope as legitimate, because it came from God, Agrippa recognized papal jurisdiction only when it did not conflict with Scripture.

He regarded the claim that the pope can release souls from purgatory as heretical and implied that the pope could err. Yet he believed it was dangerous and unwise to oppose the pope, at the risk of martyrdom as a heretic, "just as Jerome Savanarola, theologian of the Order of Preachers and also a prophetic man, was formerly burned at Florence."

Agrippa also argued that the path to God and the ultimate good of man was found neither in pursuit of knowledge nor by participating in external acts of worship. "Those carnal and external ceremonies are unable to profit men with God, to whom nothing is acceptable except faith in Jesus Christ, with ardent imitation of Him in charity, and firm hope of salvation and reward. . . . The path to God and the ultimate good of man is not found in knowledge, but in a good life."

CENSORSHIP HISTORY

Agrippa was a Catholic who was allied with the humanists and reformers in Germany, France and Italy who pressed for changes in what they regarded as a corrupt church. Though he was hostile to the Catholic conservatives who dominated the theology faculty of the Sorbonne in Paris, he was not fully associated with the Protestant reformers who moved to break away from the Catholic church. Nevertheless, the view that Agrippa was a covert supporter of the Protestant Reformation appeared in many attacks on his writings.

Of the Vanitie was published in Latin in Antwerp, Belgium, by imperial license, and in Paris and Cologne in 1530. The following year book one of *De occulta* appeared in the same cities. In 1531, the theological faculty of the University of Louvain denounced and banned *Of the Vanitie* as scandalous, impious, and heretical. Agrippa, instead of recanting the charges against him, wrote two defenses, a *Querela* attacking the "theosophists" who charged him, and an *Apologia*, in which he refuted them point by point. "I have replied to the Louvain slanders modestly, of course, but not without salt and vinegar and even mustard," he wrote.

That same year the theology faculty of the Sorbonne prohibited the French edition, which it changed with favoring Lutheran doctrine and being "against the worship of images, temples, feasts, and ceremonies of the church and . . . also blasphemous against the writers of the holy canon; and so must be publicly burned. . . ."

In 1532, publication of the second part of *De occulta* was underway in Cologne, but the Dominican inquisitor of Ulm denounced Agrippa's books as suspect of heresy and unfit to be printed. The city council forced the printer to suspend work and impounded the completed parts. Agrippa wrote a defense of his book in a long letter to the city council denouncing the theology faculty at Cologne for having impeded publication of the book. In 1533, the attention of the Inquisition in Rome was drawn to *De occulta* and book one was banned on charges of magic and conjury.

Of the Vanitie was reprinted and translated in many editions in the 16th and 17th centuries. It was an important source for the skeptical thought of Michel de Montaigne's ESSAYS. Montaigne drew from Agrippa's work extensive passages of his influential philosophical essay, "Apology for Raymond Sebond," composed in 1576, in which he argued against the impotence and vanity of presumptuous human reason.

FURTHER READING

Nauert, Charles G., Jr. *Agrippa and the Crisis of Renaissance Thought*. Urbana, Ill.: University of Illinois Press, 1965.

OLIVER TWIST

Author: Charles Dickens
Original date and place of publication: 1838, England
Literary form: Novel

SUMMARY

The publication of *Oliver Twist*, Dickens's second novel, the story of an orphan who falls into the hands of a group of thieves in the slums of London, firmly established the literary eminence of its 25-year-old author. Within a few years Dickens was the most popular and widely read writer of his time. Beginning in 1837, *Oliver Twist* appeared in monthly installments in a London magazine. The following year it was published in three volumes in book form. *Oliver Twist* offers the first glimpse of the genius of Dickens that would reach full flower in his later novels. It is among the most powerful works of fiction portraying the misery of daily life for the urban poor and the uncaring bureaucracies that sustain an oppressive system.

When Dickens was 12, his father was taken to debtors' prison. While the rest of the family accompanied his father to the workhouse, Dickens was sent to paste labels on bottles in a blacking factory. This experience left him with a bitter and passionate opposition to child labor and inhumane treatment of the poor and is reflected in the biting sarcasm that animates the early chapters of *Oliver Twist*.

When Oliver's destitute mother, found lying in the street, dies giving birth to him in a nearby workhouse, the infant becomes the ward of the local parish overseers. He is dispatched to a parish institution where he and other orphans are brought up under cruel conditions, "without the inconvenience of too much food or too much clothing."

At age nine Oliver is returned by the parish to the workhouse by Mr. Bumble, the unctuous parish beadle. The workhouse boys are fed three meals of thin gruel a day, with an onion twice a week and half a roll on Sunday. "Please, sir, I want some more," Oliver says. In punishment for the "impious and profane offence of asking for more," Oliver is ordered into instant solitary confinement.

He is then apprenticed by Mr. Bumble to the undertaker, Mr. Sowerberry, where he lives and works in mean circumstances. After fighting with his bullying coworker Noah, Oliver is beaten and runs away to London. There he unwittingly falls into the hands of Fagin, the nefarious leader of a gang of thieves, whose other chief members are the burglar Bill Sikes, Sikes's companion Nancy, and the pickpocket known as the Artful Dodger. When the Dodger picks the pocket of an elderly gentleman, Oliver is caught and brought to the police magistrate. Injured and ill, Oliver is rescued by the benevolent Mr. Brownlow, who takes him into his household. But Nancy finds Oliver and brings him back to the gang. When Oliver is made to accompany Bill Sikes on a burgling expedition and is shot and wounded, he comes into the hands of Mrs. Maylie and her protegee, Rose, who treat him kindly.

A sinister person named Monks, who is known to Fagin, appears to have a special interest in Oliver. Nancy, who overhears a conversation between Fagin and Monks, goes to Rose and reveals to her that Monks is Oliver's older half brother, knows the secret of Oliver's parentage and wishes all proof of it destroyed. When Nancy's betrayal is discovered by the gang, she is brutally murdered by Sikes.

While trying to escape capture by a mob, Sikes accidentally hangs himself. Fagin is arrested and sentenced to execution. Monks confesses that he pursued Oliver's ruin so that he could retain the whole of his late father's property. Upon the death of his mother, Oliver was to have inherited the estate, as long as he had in his minority never stained the good name of his family. Fagin had received a reward from Monks for turning Oliver into a thief. It turns out that Rose is the sister of Oliver's late mother. In the end Oliver is adopted by Mr. Brownlow. Mr. Bumble ends his career as a pauper in the very same workhouse over which he formerly ruled.

In Dickens's preface to the third edition of the novel, he wrote, "I wished to show, in little Oliver, the principle of Good surviving through every adverse circumstance and triumphing at last." All ends happily in *Oliver Twist*, yet the haunting memory of the evils that beset Oliver in the poorhouses and streets of London remains.

CENSORSHIP HISTORY

"The walls and ceiling of the room were perfectly black with age and dirt. . . . Some sausages were cooking; and standing over them, with a toasting fork in this hand, was a very old shriveled Jew, whose villainous-looking and repulsive face was obscured by a quantity of matted red hair." The sinister and evil Fagin is introduced to readers of *Oliver Twist* with an archetypal anti-Semitic image dating back many centuries in Western culture, that of the Satanic and fiendish Jew. Dickens's caricature of Fagin has been the object of protest and debate since the time of the novel's publication.

The character of Fagin, referred to as "the Jew" hundreds of times throughout the novel, is shaped according to a traditional pattern commonly employed to portray Jews in literature and on the stage in the 19th century. Fagin's red hair and beard were commonly associated with ancient images of the devil. He has a hooked nose, shuffling gait, a long gabardine coat and broad-brimmed hat and is a dishonest dealer in second-hand clothes and trinkets. Fagin is portrayed, like Satan, as serpent-like, gliding stealthily along, "creeping beneath the shelter of the walls and doorways . . . like some loathsome reptile, engendered in the slime and darkness through which he moved. . . ."

Though literary critics believe that Dickens did not intend to defame or injure Jews in his creation of the character of Fagin, Dickens was a product of the anti-Semitic culture of his time. Reflected in laws, public discourse, literature and popular entertainment, prejudice against Jews was a part of the early Victorian heritage. In the 1830s, Jews were barred from owning stores within the city of London, could not work as attorneys, receive a university degree or sit in Parliament. Because they were confined to certain occupations, the majority of England's 20,000 to 30,000 Jews made their living by buying and selling old clothes, peddling and moneylending.

In a letter to a Jewish woman who had protested the stereotypical treatment of Fagin, Dickens wrote, "Fagin is a Jew because it unfortunately was true, of the time to which the story refers, that class of criminal almost invariably was a Jew." The 1830 trial of Ikey Solomons, a Jewish fence, who, like Fagin, dealt in stolen jewelry, clothing and fabrics, had been extensively publicized and was one of the influences on Dickens's portrayal of Fagin.

The years 1830 to 1860 saw a rise in the status of Jews in England. Legal barriers and commercial restrictions were removed, Jews were elected to posts in local and national government and many became socially prominent. Social attitudes also changed, reflected in Dickens's increased awareness of and sensitivity to anti-Semitism in the years that followed the initial publication of *Oliver Twist*. "I know of no reason the Jews can have for regarding me as inimical to them," Dickens wrote in 1854.

In 1867–68, a new edition of Dickens's works was published. Dickens revised the text of *Oliver Twist*, making hundreds of changes, most in relation to Fagin. He eliminated the majority of the references to Fagin as "the Jew," either cutting them or replacing them with "Fagin" or "he." Nevertheless, "Fagin remains 'the Jew,' " literary critic Irving Howe commented, "and whoever wants to confront this novel honestly must confront the substratum of feeling that becomes visible through Dickens's obsessive repetition of 'the Jew.' " A critical reading of the novel can lead to a better understanding of the anti-Semitic stereotypes that were part of the popular culture of early 19th-century England. "There is nothing to 'do' [about Fagin]," wrote Howe, "but confront the historical realities of our culture, and all that it has thrown up from its unsavory depths."

In 1949, a group of Jewish parents in Brooklyn, New York, protested that the assignment of *Oliver Twist* in senior high school literature classes violated the rights of their children to receive an education free of religious bias. Citing the characterization of Fagin in *Oliver Twist* and Shylock in Shakespeare's play *The Merchant of Venice*, they sued the New York City Board of Education. They asked that both texts be banned from New York City public schools "because they tend to engender hatred of the Jew as a person and as a race."

In *Rosenberg v. Board of Education of City of New York*, the Kings County Supreme Court decided that the two works should not be banned from New York City schools, libraries or classrooms, declaring that the Board of Education "acted in good faith without malice or prejudice and in the best interests of the school system entrusted to their care and control, and, therefore, that no substantial reason exists which compels the suppression of the two books under consideration."

In denying the plaintiffs' bid to ban the books, the presiding judge stated, "Except where a book has been maliciously written for the apparent purpose of fomenting a bigoted and intolerant hatred against a particular racial or religious group, public interest in a free and democratic society does not warrant or encourage the suppression of any book at the whim of any unduly sensitive person or group of person, merely because a character described in such book as belonging to a particular race or religion is portrayed in a derogatory or offensive manner." Removal of the books "will contribute nothing toward the diminution of anti-religious feeling," the court said.

FURTHER READINGS

Dickens, Charles. *Oliver Twist*. Intro. by Irving Howe. New York: Bantam Books, 1982.

Doyle, Robert P. *Banned Books 1996 Resource Guide*. Chicago: American Library Association, 1996.

Kaplan, Fred, ed. *Oliver Twist: A Norton Critical Edition*. New York: W. W. Norton & Co., 1993.

Veidmanis, Gladys. "Reflections on 'the Shylock Problem.' " In *Censored Books: Critical Viewpoints*. Ed. by Nicholas J. Karolides, Lee Burress and John M. Kean, 370–78. Metuchen, N.J.: Scarecrow Press, 1993.

ON CIVIL LORDSHIP

Author: John Wycliff
Oriqinal date and place of publication: 1376, England
Literary form: Theological treatise

SUMMARY

The religious scholar and reformer John Wycliff, who studied and taught theology at Oxford, was the most eminent English heretic to challenge the Catholic church before the 16th-century Protestant Reformation. In his Latin treatise, *On Civil Lordship*, read to his students at Oxford in 1376, in his sermons in English in Oxford and London and through the preaching of the itinerant "poor priests" who spread his views, he attacked orthodox church doctrines. He claimed that the Scriptures rather than the church were the supreme authority on matters of faith.

Going beyond criticism of the abuses of the church hierarchy, Wycliff came to the radical conclusion that the church was incapable of reforming itself and must be brought under secular supervision by the king, as God's vicar on earth.

He transferred salvation from the agency of the church to the individual. "For each man that shall be damned shall be damned by his own guilt," he wrote, "and each man that is saved shall be saved by his own merit." He believed that the popes of the period were Antichrists and that the pope and the hierarchy, having abdicated their rights to lead the church by their displays of greed, cruelty and lust for power, should not be obeyed. Power within the church should be a function of grace rather than of entitlement.

Anticipating fundamental convictions of the Protestant Reformation, Wycliff opposed the sale of indulgences, image worship, auricular confession and the cult of saints, relics and pilgrimages. He also refused to acknowledge the doctrine of transubstantiation, by which the bread and wine of the Eucharist are held to be transformed into the Body and Blood of Christ. He developed the doctrine of the priesthood of all elected believers, proposing that in certain circumstances laymen could conduct the sacrament of the Eucharist. He also advocated the translation of the Bible into English, on the theory that Christians could read and understand Scripture without intervention by the clergy. The first translation of the Latin Vulgate Bible into English was carried out by his followers.

CENSORSHIP HISTORY

The church hierarchy viewed Wycliff's deviations from orthodoxy as a serious danger. For the first time, a learned church scholar of brilliant intellect had questioned the church's authority and, further, had endeavored to spread his heretical ideas among ordinary people.

In 1377, Pope Gregory XI issued five bulls attacking Wycliff's doctrines as expressed in *On Civil Lordship*, condemning him for "heretical pravity, tending to weaken and overthrow the status of the whole church, and even the secular government." Gregory XI commanded Wycliff's prosecution by secular authorities as a heretic. Despite the hostility of the archbishop of Canterbury and the bishop of London, Wycliff was protected by John of Gaunt, the duke of Lancaster, one of the most influential nobles in England and a supporter of Wycliff's movement.

In 1381, a council at Oxford pronounced eight of Wycliff's theses as unorthodox and 14 as heretical and prohibited him from further lecturing or preaching. The following year a council at Blackfriars repeated the condemnation, and in 1383 his disciples, known as the Lollards, were barred from Oxford. Though he was condemned as a heretic and the Lollards were persecuted, Wycliff was not disturbed in his retirement and died peacefully in his rectory in 1384.

By 1386, the spread of Lollardy provoked Parliament to outlaw heretical writings and to make their teaching a crime, punishable by forfeiture of properties and imprisonment. In 1401 under the orthodox Henry IV, burning at the stake became the legal penalty for heresy. Parliament passed the act known as *De Haeretico Comburendo* ("On the Desirability of Burning Heretics"). The Act recommended that convicted heretics be burned in a prominent place so "that such punishment may strike fear to the minds of others." Wycliff's writings were further proscribed in 1408 by the Convocation of Canterbury. Lollards were ruthlessly persecuted, hanged or burned at the stake, and the heresy was extirpated from England.

The marriage of Richard II to Anne of Bohemia in 1382 opened a channel for the transmission of Wycliff's ideas when many Bohemians visited England during the excitement caused by Wycliff's controversies. These Bohemians carried his writings back to Prague, where they found fertile ground through the efforts of Wycliff's disciple, John Hus. Church and secular authorities moved to stem the heresy. In 1403, 45 articles extracted from Wycliff's writing were formally condemned by the university of Prague.

A papal bull ordering the surrender of Wycliff's works was carried out in 1409 under the instructions of Archbishop Sbynko of Prague. Two hundred volumes of Wycliff's writings were burned in the palace courtyard. In 1413, the Council of Rome pronounced an authoritative condemnation of Wycliff. Two years later a church council at Constance, Germany, proclaimed Wycliff a hesiarch, or arch-heretic, condemning him on 260 different counts, and ordered his bones exhumed and removed from sacred ground. Wycliff's bones were burned and his ashes thrown into a running stream. John Hus, whose treatise DE ECCLESIA reflected Wycliff's heresies, was burned at the stake upon order of the council on July 6, 1415.

FURTHER READINGS

Christie-Murray, David. *A History of Heresy*. Oxford: Oxford University Press, 1989.

Dunham, Barrows. *Heroes and Heretics*. New York: Alfred A. Knopf, 1964.

Green, Jonathon. *The Encyclopedia of Censorship*. New York: Facts On File, 1990.

Haight, Anne Lyon. *Banned Books: 387 BC to 1978 AD*. Updated and enlarged by Chandler B. Grannis. New York: R. R. Bowker, 1978.

Lea, Henry Charles. *History of the Inquisition of the Middle Ages*. Vol. 2. New York: Russell & Russell, 1955.

Levy, Leonard W. *Blasphemy: Verbal Offense Against the Sacred, from Moses to Salman Rushdie*. New York: Alfred A. Knopf, 1993.

ON JUSTICE IN THE REVOLUTION AND IN THE CHURCH

Author: Pierre-Joseph Proudhon
Original date and place of publication: 1858, France
Literary form: Political theory

SUMMARY

The French social theorist, anarchist philosopher and reformer Pierre-Joseph Proudhon achieved notoriety with a series of incendiary pamphlets and books in which he condemned the abuses of private property and the absolutism of church and state. In Proudhon's first notable work, *What Is Property?*—described by Karl Marx as "the first decisive, vigorous, and scientific examination of property"—Proudhon claimed that property was not a natural right and that its attributes of profit, rent and interest represented exploitation of labor and a denial of the fundamental principles of justice and equality. Workers had the right to own the products of their labor, as well as houses, land for subsistence and the tools of trade, Proudhon maintained, but the means of production should be held in common. His answer to the question, "What is property?"—"Property is theft"—became the most famous revolutionary phrase of the 19th century.

The key to Proudhon's revolutionary thought was his hostility to the state. He proposed to replace government by a system of voluntary contracts, or associations between free individuals. According to his theory of "mutualism," small, loosely federated groups would bargain with one another over economic and political matters within the framework of a consensus on fundamental principles. Proudhon rejected the use of force to impose any system, however, hoping that ethical progress would eventually make government unnecessary. He believed that the victory of the proletariat, which was to be brought about gradually through the establishment of a system of free credit, would inaugurate a just order of mutuality and cooperation.

Though he is most often remembered today for his claim that property is theft, Proudhon was an uncommonly prolific writer, with 20,000 published pages of writing to his credit and nearly 2,000 more pages left in unpublished manuscripts. Among his most important books were *System of Economic Contradictions; or the Philosophy of Poverty*, published in 1846, and his three-volume masterwork, *On Justice in the Revolution and in the Church*, published in 1858 and enlarged and revised in 1860.

From his early years, Proudhon, as an anarchic individualist, was hostile to conventional organized religion. Under the rule of Emperor Napoleon III, who expanded his powers after an 1852 coup d'etat, Proudhon became more intensely anticlerical, convinced that the Catholic clergy were allied with the government to suppress liberty and that the church was a reactionary force. In *On Justice*, Proudhon describes justice as "the central star which governs society . . . the principal and regulator of all transactions." The Catholic church and the state, as absolutist institutions, are the enemies of justice, as the balance between interests of the individual and those of the community is upset by centralization of government and authority.

Proudhon recognizes no external authority as the appropriate source of societal norms. The rules guiding society must stem from the internal, rational faculties of individuals. Justice is "*Logos*," he writes, "the common soul of humanity, incarnate in each one of us." Proudhon repudiates any absolute and inflexible system of thought based on a priori reasoning as a negation of morality. Because the church is inaccessible to rational faculties, is based on dogmatic ideas and suppresses individuality, it is immoral. The Christian doctrines of the fall of man, Original Sin and the authority of revelation are stultifying to conscience and therefore to justice. Proudhon sees the annihilation of the individual conscience as "the fatal stumbling block of every church and every religion."

Proudhon rejects the absolute idea of God as all-powerful and infinite. He neither affirms nor denies the existence of God, but believes that theology should be supplanted by secular philosophy and that the religious spirit, or transcendental justice, should be replaced by a human sense of justice, or immanent justice. Religion's ultimate weapon is intimidation, Proudhon asserts. By means of its "dogmas, its mysteries, its sacraments, its discipline, its terror, its promises," religion frightens the socially inferior into staying in their place. The moral sense can only develop by "the cessation of myth, by the return of the soul to itself . . . [and by] the end of the reign of God." For progress to occur, individual reason must succeed myth, miracles and mystery.

CENSORSHIP HISTORY

Proudhon found it difficult to find a publisher for his first important pamphlet, *What Is Property?*, because it was a provocative work by an unknown author. It was published, unannounced and unadvertised, only after he agreed to cover the cost of the printing and to sell copies to his friends and acquaintances at his own risk. He escaped public prosecution recommended by the law officers of the crown when the minister of justice, impressed with the quality of Proudhon's mind, sent the book to the Academy of Moral Sciences for evaluation. The academy asked one of its distinguished fellows, the economist Adolfe Blanqui, brother of the militant communist Auguste Blanqui, to report on the book. He recommended to the academy that, despite some inflammatory language, its scientific and scholarly character was undeniable and worthy of respect and it should not be banned.

The government's tolerance did not extend, however, to Proudhon's next revolutionary pamphlet, *Warning to the Proprietors*, published in 1842. His printer was raided by the police, who confiscated 500 copies of the pamphlet by order of the public prosecutor in Besançon, France. Proudhon was summoned to appear before the Doubs assize court to answer to nine charges. The public prosecutor contracted the list of charges to four: attack on the constitutional right of property, incitement of hatred of government, incitement to hatred of several classes of citizens and offense to religion. Proudhon was acquitted of all charges when the jury returning the verdict admitted that his ideas were too difficult to understand. "It is impossible to be sure that he is guilty and we cannot condemn at random," the jury stated.

In 1848, Proudhon founded a newspaper, *Representative of the People*, to propagate his ideas. When it was suppressed by the government, he started another newspaper, *The People*. He was charged with sedition for denouncing the newly elected President Louis-Napoleon Bonaparte (later to become Emperor Napoleon III) for "conspiring to enslave the people," and escaped to Belgium.

He returned secretly to France to liquidate the people's bank he had founded and continued to edit his newspaper in hiding. He was finally caught and spent three years in prison, where he continued to write. He founded *The Voice of the People*, which was repeatedly suspended and finally prohibited.

When *On Justice in the Revolution and in the Church* appeared in April 1858 under the Catholic empire of Napoleon III and the Empress Eugenie, it immediately became a bestseller, selling in thousands of copies within a few days. In November 1857, while the book was in press, its printer and publisher had been visited by the police commissioner of the interior ministry's press licensing department, who demanded to know the contents of the book Proudhon was about to publish. The publisher did not cooperate and, as there was no statute allowing for prepublication censorship, publication went forward.

Within five days of its publication, however, the government ordered its seizure and the remaining stock was confiscated. Proudhon was put on trial and charged with offenses against church and state. His derogatory criticism of the Catholic church and its authoritarian position in French society was perceived as an outrage against public and religious morality and a threat to the status quo. Proudhon was convicted and received the maximum sentence—a fine of 4,000 francs and three years in prison.

Proudhon appealed his conviction but, while awaiting the appeals court's decision, took refuge in Brussels, where his book was printed. The appeals court confirmed his sentence and he was later informed that in the future no work of his would be allowed into France. Proudhon remained in exile in Belgium for four years. When the French government extended an amnesty in 1859 to all those convicted under the press laws, only one person was excluded by name—Proudhon. However, he was later pardoned by the emperor and returned to France in 1862, three years before his death. Because of his prosecution for *On Justice*, he met with great difficulty finding French firms to publish his subsequent books. Though two publishers offered to guarantee him large sums if he would moderate his writing to avoid further prosecution, he refused despite his poverty.

During Proudhon's lifetime, the Catholic church placed all of his writing on the Index of Forbidden Books in the most severe category of *opera omnia*, or all works condemned; his works remained proscribed through the last edition of the Index.

In the 1860s, groups of French working-class men began to found mutual credit and other cooperative movements based on Proudhon's ideas. The great mass of Proudhon's writing was an influential legacy to later political theorists in many countries, notably the syndicalists and anarchic socialists in the later 19th century in France, Italy and Spain.

FURTHER READINGS

Hall, Constance Margaret. *The Sociology of Pierre Joseph Proudhon (1809–65)*. New York: Philosophical Library, 1971.

Hoffman, Robert L. *The Social and Political Theory of P.-J. Proudhon*. Urbana, Ill.: University of Illinois Press, 1972.

Hyams, Edward. *Pierre-Joseph Proudhon: His Revolutionary Life, Mind and Works*. New York: Taplinger Publishing Company, 1979.

ON MONARCHY

Author: Dante Alighieri
Original date and place of publication: 1310–13, Italy
Literary form: Political treatise

SUMMARY

The Florentine poet Dante Alighieri—author of *The Divine Comedy*, among the greatest of literary classics—argued in *On Monarchy*, his treatise on political philosophy, against papal claims of control over secular authority. Dante claimed that the emperor ruled by divine right, just as the pope did, and that the emperor was supreme in secular matters, while the pope oversaw the spiritual realm.

Dante saw the emperor and the pope as dual guardians of the welfare of society, each dependent on God for their separate powers. He challenged the papal analogy that spiritual power is the sun and secular power the moon, receiving its light from the sun and thus subordinate to it. He believed that lack of cooperation between the two leaders prevented the achievement of peace and justice in his time, in which politics was dominated by the struggle for domination between the empire and the papacy.

The cause of conflict was the papacy's claim to temporal power, which it justified by a document known as the Donation of Constantine, later proven to be an eighth-century forgery. The document maintained that in the year 312, when Emperor Constantine I shifted the seat of his empire to Constantinople, he transferred to Pope Sylvester I, the bishop of Rome, political dominion over Italy and the Western empire. The papacy's desire for temporal power, Dante believed, was based on spurious premises and weakened both civil government and the church's mission of spiritual guidance.

Two warring political parties, the Guelphs and Ghibellines, had arisen in Italy in the 12th century, their party lines originally drawn over the dispute between the papacy and the emperor. The Guelph party had split into two factions, the White and the Black. Dante was a passionate supporter of the White Guelphs and the return of imperial rule to Italy. After the victory of the Black Guelphs, assisted by Pope Boniface VIII, Dante was dispossessed and banished from Florence in 1302, sentenced to be burned alive if he ever returned. In exile he served various princes but supported Emperor Henry VII as the potential savior of Italy.

Dante's position in the conflict is reflected in *On Monarchy*. For the well-being of the world, he believed, a single temporal government should rule. The betterment of mankind depends upon the unity of the will of its members. This is impossible unless there is one will that dominates all others. "But the human race is most one when all are united together, a state which is manifestly impossible unless humanity as a whole becomes subject to one Prince and consequently comes most into accordance with that divine intention which we showed is the good, nay, the best disposition of mankind."

If the church had received power from God, it would have been by divine or natural law, he wrote. God does not approve anything contrary to nature's intentions. "It is indisputable that nature gave not this law to the Church. . . . In the bosom of the two Testaments, wherein is embodied every divine law, I am unable to discover any command for the early or later priesthood to have care or solicitude in temporal things." Because he knew that his argument would be offensive to religious leaders, he supported his position with quotations from the Old and New testaments, Aristotle and the church fathers. Church traditions, he argued, while worthy of respect, were subordinate to the Scriptures.

CENSORSHIP HISTORY

Dante, as an orthodox Catholic, accepted church dogma without reservation. Although he criticized individual popes, particularly his bitter enemy Boniface VIII, an exponent of the political supremacy of the papacy who exiled him from Florence, Dante revered the office of the pope as vicar of Christ. The church, though, had declared as dogma that the authority of kings derived from the pope, rather than directly from God. Dante was aware that his position that the Roman prince ruled by divine right would generate controversy. In Book Three of *On Monarchy*, he writes: "Since the truth about it can scarcely be brought to light without putting certain people to shame, it may give rise to anger against me. . . . But I take courage from the words of Daniel, quoted above, assuring us that the defenders of the truth are shielded by divine power. . . ."

In 1329, *On Monarchy* was publicly burned in the marketplace of Bologna on the order of Pope John XXII, who condemned the book. The pope, in the throes of a struggle with Holy Roman Emperor Louis IV, whose throne the pope claimed, feared the influence of Dante's work. More than two centuries later, *On Monarchy* was still anathema to the papacy on the same grounds. The 16th-century papacy was concerned with the threat to its temporal power and independence posed by domination of Italy by Holy Roman Emperor Charles V. *On Monarchy* was among the books that Pope Paul IV placed on the church's first Index of Forbidden Books in 1559. The Tridentine Index of 1564, which consolidated and expanded the earlier Index, ordered the excision of the passages in *On Monarchy* that argued that imperial authority derives from God rather than from the pope. The Spanish Inquisition placed *On Monarchy* on its Index of Forbidden Books in 1558 and 1612.

Although in his epic masterpiece, *The Divine Comedy*, Dante had placed corrupt popes in the eighth circle of hell and engaged in bitter invective against Pope Boniface VIII, *The Divine Comedy* was not prohibited in Italy. The Inquisition in Portugal and Spain, however, found such sentiment in *The Divine Comedy* to be offensive. In 1581, authorities in Lisbon called in all copies for expurgation and the Spanish Index of 1612 eliminated three short passages from the poem.

On Monarchy remained on the Roman Index for 400 years, until it was finally removed in the 19th century. In 1921, Pope Benedict XV issued an encyclical in praise of Dante's works.

FURTHER READINGS

Burman, Edward. *The Inquisition: Hammer of Heresy*. New York: Dorset Press, 1992.

Curtis, Michael, ed. and intro. *The Great Political Theories*. Vol. 1. New York: Avon Books, 1981.

Dante. *On Monarchy and Three Political Letters.* Trans. and intro. by Donald Nicholl. London: Weidenfeld and Nicholson, 1954.

Putnam, George Haven. *The Censorship of the Church of Rome.* Vol. 1. New York: G. P. Putnam's Sons, 1906–07.

ON THE INFINITE UNIVERSE AND WORLDS

Author: Giordano Bruno
Original date and place of publication: 1584, France
Literary form: Philosophical treatise

SUMMARY

The Italian philosopher Giordano Bruno entered the Dominican order at a young age and was expelled in 1576 at the age of 28 when he was charged with heresy. He traveled throughout Europe for 15 years, one step ahead of the censors, teaching at Toulouse, Paris, Oxford, Wittenberg and Frankfurt. In *On the Infinite Universe and Worlds*, his major metaphysical work, published in 1584, he refuted the traditional cosmology of Aristotle and its limited conceptions of the universe. Instead, Bruno asserted that the physical universe is infinite and includes an indefinite number of worlds, each with its own sun and planets. He pictured the world as composed of individual, irreducible elements of being, called monads, governed by fixed laws of relationship.

Bruno's philosophy prefigured modern cosmic theory. He accepted Copernicus's hypothesis that the sun, rather than the earth, is the center of our world. But he went further than Copernicus in arguing that the sun is simply one star among others. All judgments about position are relative, since there are as many possible modes of viewing the world as there are possible positions. Therefore, no one star or planet can be called the center of the universe. Human beings cannot conclude that they are unique, because the presence of life, even that of rational beings, may not be confined to earth. There is no absolute truth and there are no limits to the progress of knowledge.

The infinite universe is the product of a pantheistic infinite divine power or cause whose work is manifest in human beings and in all of nature. "The Divine one extols his own glory and sets forth the greatness of his sway, not in one sun, but in uncountable suns; not in one earth, but in words without end."

Because God's power is infinite, his creation must also be infinite. The agent would be imperfect if his works did not fulfill his power. Bruno believed that understanding of the universe as the manifestation of God would free the human spirit. "[It] opens the senses, contents the soul, enlarges the mind and brings true blessed news to man. . . . For deeply considering the Being and substance in which we are fixed, we find that there is no such thing as death, not for us alone, but for the true substance."

CENSORSHIP HISTORY

"I wish the world to possess the glorious fruits of my labor," Bruno wrote in *On the Infinite Universe and Worlds*, "to awaken the soul and open the understanding of those who are deprived of that light, which, most assuredly, is not mine own invention. Should I be in error, I do not believe I willfully go wrong."

In the view of his contemporaries, Bruno had indeed gone wrong. His assault on Aristotelian views of the universe and his construction of a "new philosophy" challenged the Scholasticism that dominated the universities. It ran counter to the beliefs held by all the ecclesiastical institutions, whether Catholic, Lutheran or Calvinist. His speculation about an endless number of celestial worlds was viewed as heretical pantheism.

In 1577, the Inquisition in Naples initiated proceedings against him and Bruno fled Italy. In 1592, he rashly returned and, denounced by a Venetian nobleman, was delivered to the Inquisition in Venice. He was imprisoned and tried on charges of blasphemy, immoral conduct and heresy. On May 26, 1592, the Holy Tribunal met to consider his case. Bruno told the judges: "I have ever expounded philosophically and according to the principles of Nature and by its light . . . although I may have set forth much suspicious matter occasioned by my own natural light . . . never have I taught anything directly contrary to the Catholic religion. . . ." When asked whether he believed that the Father, Son and Holy Spirit were one in essence but distinct persons, he admitted "I have never been able to grasp the three being really Persons and have doubted it. . . ." Bruno offered to submit to all church doctrines, but he refused to abjure his philosophy.

Bruno remained in prison for months awaiting the decision of the Venetian Inquisition. Because he was regarded as a "hesiarch," an originator and leader of heresy, the chief inquisitor at the Holy Office in Rome demanded that he be delivered there for trial. He was extradicted to Rome and on February 27, 1593, was imprisoned for seven years. He was allowed neither books nor writing material, and his only visitors were officials of the Inquisition and priests sent to urge him to repent. In 1559, several cardinals interrogated him regarding heresies extracted from his books. At a final interrogation he declared he would recant nothing. In January 1660, at a meeting presided over by the pope, it was decreed that he would be burned at the stake for "many various heretical and unsound opinions." He was executed in Rome on February 17, 1600.

On August 7, 1603, all of Bruno's writings were placed on the Index of Forbidden Books, where they remained through the last edition of the Index, in effect until 1966. Cardinal Robert Bellarmino, who had overseen Bruno's trial and punishment, was declared a saint by the Catholic church in 1930. Bruno's works had never been popular in England or on the Continent and were scarce in Catholic countries because of their suppression. John Toland, the 17th-century English deist and author of CHRISTIANITY NOT MYSTERIOUS, recognized Bruno as a forerunner of the freethinkers of his own era; Toland translated part of *The Infinite Universe and Worlds* and wrote an account of the book. Bruno's philosophy also had an important influence on the philosophers Spinoza and Leibnitz.

FURTHER READINGS

Boulting, William. *Giordano Bruno: His Life, Thought and Martyrdom*. New York: Books for Libraries Press, 1972.

Copleston, Frederick. *A History of Philosophy*. Vol. 3, *Late Medieval and Renaissance Philosophy*. New York: Doubleday, 1993.

George, Leonard. *Crimes of Perception: An Encyclopedia of Heresies and Heretics*. New York: Paragon House, 1995.

Green, Jonathon. *The Encyclopedia of Censorship*. New York: Facts On File, 1990.

Jaspers, Karl. *The Great Philosophers*. Vol. 3. New York: Harcourt Brace & Company, 1993.

Levy, Leonard W. *Blasphemy: Verbal Offense Against the Sacred, from Moses to Salman Rushdie*. New York: Alfred A. Knopf, 1993.

ON THE LAW OF WAR AND PEACE

Author: Hugo Grotius
Original date and place of publication: 1625, France
Literary form: Legal treatise

SUMMARY

The Dutch statesman, jurist and theologian Hugo Grotius (Huig de Groot) was the most renowned man of letters of 17th-century Holland and is regarded as the father of modern international law. *On the Law of War and Peace* is the first definitive text on the subject.

Grotius was a civil servant who studied law at Orleans and Leiden. He became a leader of the bar at The Hague, then Dutch ambassador to England and later chief magistrate of Rotterdam. He was a political ally of Johann van Oldenbarneveldt, the chief policymaker of the United Provinces, of which Holland was a prominent member. Oldenbarneveldt was a leader of the Remonstrants, or Dutch Arminians, a dissenting Protestant sect opposed to strict Calvinism.

Doctrinal disputes between the Calvinists and the Remonstrants led to a constitutional crisis. The local government of Holland, led by Maurice (Maurits) of Nassau, prince of Orange and commanding general of the Dutch army, who was obliged by oath to uphold the tenets of Calvinism, came into conflict with the central government of the United Provinces led by Oldenbarneveldt. Maurice of Nassau, determined to crush the Remonstrants, ousted Oldenbarneveldt in a coup d'etat and in 1618 convoked the Synod of Dort to condemn the Remonstrants' doctrine. Oldenbarneveldt was arrested, convicted of treason and executed. Grotius, as a supporter of Oldenbarneveldt and a Remonstrants leader, was sentenced to life imprisonment in the castle of Loevestein.

In 1621, he succeeded in a daring escape from prison, hidden in a large chest of books, and fled to Paris. He was warmly received in France, where he published several important books on politics, law and religion. These included *Defense of the Lawful Government of Holland* (1622), which was banned in the Netherlands; *On the Law of War and Peace* (*De jure belli ac pacis*) (1625); and *On the Truth of the Christian Religion* (1627), a Christian epic written in simple verse, which was translated into 12 languages and spread Grotius's fame worldwide. He later returned to Rotterdam, but was forced into exile again and went to Sweden. From 1635 to 1645 he represented Sweden at the French court. In addition to his writing on law, Grotius also published major works of theological and biblical criticism.

Grotius's theory of international law, as expressed in his influential treatise *On the Law of War and Peace*, was based on natural law common to all men and nations. Natural law, he believed, prescribed rules of conduct both for nations and individuals that were reasonable, universal and binding. "Natural law," he wrote in a famous passage, "is so unalterable that God himself cannot change it." Assuming that God did not exist, he proposed in another controversial passage, the rules of natural law would retain their validity. The primary rule of natural law is that whatever is necessary is lawful.

The treatise defined the legal obligations of human societies and recommended procedures for enforcing rules and punishing violations. Grotius drew the specifics of his proposed international law from both the Bible and the Roman classics. The central tenet of his legal theory was that a nation may use armed force against another only in defense of rights or property or to punish criminal acts, and if no tribunal had been authorized to settle the dispute. His legal provisions were directed toward making conditions of warfare more humane by inducing respect for noncombatants and their property.

His own experience of imprisonment and exile led Grotius to criticize the tendency within Protestantism to adopt rigid doctrinal systems and to secure or maintain dominance by force. He saw these practices as destructive of the spiritual nature of religion and particularly dangerous when enforced by the power of the state. Inflexible church structures had provoked nations to war and impeded unity of Christians based on common acceptance of fundamental truths.

In *On the Law of War and Peace*, he proposed a policy of toleration. Religion may not be imposed on individuals or nations through coercion. "From the kind of evidence on which Christianity rests," he wrote, "it is plain that no force should be used with nations to promote its acceptance." Christ taught that only reason and persuasion, rather than force, could be used to disseminate the Gospel. Grotius warned against the disastrous results of "the zealous attachment of every one to his own tenets; an evil which Galen says is more difficult to be eradicated than any constitutional disease."

CENSORSHIP HISTORY

The first of Grotius's books to be censored was *Defense of the Lawful Government of Holland* (1622), written after his escape from Loevestein castle to defend both his innocence and the concepts of religious tolerance and to protest the illegality of the procedures that condemned him to prison. When Dutch authorities discovered that the book was being printed in Amsterdam, they seized the manuscript at the printer's house. Published instead in 1622 in another city in the Netherlands and in Paris, the book was widely read in Holland.

In November 1622, the States-General of the Netherlands declared the book to be notorious, seditious and scandalous libel. It was declared illegal to print, distribute, possess, read, give to others or otherwise handle the book. In response to a request from Grotius, Louis XIII of France replied to the decree of the States-General in 1623 by taking Grotius under his special protection and forbidding persons "of every quality, nation, or condition" from harming him. Grotius contended that, since the book's publication in France was authorized by the king, the Dutch decree was an infringement of the laws of France.

The publication history of Grotius's masterpiece, *On the Law of War and Peace*, was unaffected by the political censorship of his *Defense*. *On the Law of War and Peace* became a definitive work on international law that maintained its influence for centuries after its publication. Grotius's work was read and debated by the educated people of Europe, particularly in the Netherlands, Germany, England and France. By the late 18th century, the book had appeared in 77 editions in its original Latin, as well as in Dutch, French, German, English and Spanish. Enlightenment philosophes, such as Edward Gibbon and Montesquieu, expressed their admiration for his thinking. It was consulted by generations of statesmen and diplomats, including the founding fathers of the American nation.

Although Grotius was a Christian who championed the doctrine of freedom of the will against the Calvinist belief in predestination and who wrote influential annotations on the Old and New testaments, he considered all church systems as detrimental to both religious and civil life. He felt that the clergy should be restrained by civil authority because, if unchecked, they would seek to exercise religious tyranny and interfere in temporal affairs. Though his hypothetical construction of a natural law without God was not meant to cast doubt on God's existence, his natural law existed outside scriptural revelation or the teachings of Christianity.

In his last major ecclesiastical treatise, *A Vote for Peace in the Church*, published in 1642, Grotius wrote a justification for the ecumenical unity of Protestantism and Catholicism. He proposed that both branches of Christianity be reunited under the Roman pope, with reduced ecclesiastical powers. Calvinist writers bitterly attacked him, and the rumor spread that Grotius had secretly become a Catholic. The Vatican sent a Jesuit theologian to meet with Grotius, who decided that Grotius was "not sufficiently Catholic." This view of Grotius led the Spanish Inquisition to place all of Grotius's main works, including *On the Law of War and Peace*, on the Spanish Index of Forbidden Books.

It took the Catholic church in Rome another century to decide that his writings were dangerous enough to warrant condemnation. When the church moved in the 18th century to do battle with the rationalist and anticlerical philosophy of the Enlightenment, Grotius's writings on theology were placed on the Roman Index of Forbidden Books in 1757. The church placed his books in the most severe category of *opera omnia*, or all works condemned. They remained on the Index through its last edition published until 1966.

FURTHER READINGS

Durnbauld, Edward. *The Life and Legal Writings of Hugo Grotius*. Norman, Okla.: University of Oklahoma Press, 1969.

Gay, Peter. *The Enlightenment: An Interpretation. The Rise of Modern Paganism*. New York: W. W. Norton & Co., 1966.

Gellinek, Christian. *Hugo Grotius*. Boston: Twayne Publishers, 1983.

Jordan, W. K. *The Development of Religious Toleration in England*, Vol. 2. Gloucester, Mass.: Peter Smith, 1965.

ON THE ORIGIN OF SPECIES

Author: Charles Darwin
Original date and place of publication: 1859, England
Literary form: Scientific text

SUMMARY

The British naturalist Charles Darwin published his groundbreaking work, *On the Origin of Species*, 22 years after he initially wrote it, in response to competition from other scientists who were preparing to publish similar ideas. In this book, Darwin outlines the observations he made while sailing around South America on the H.M.S. *Beagle* from 1831 to 1836.

Darwin believed in "descent with modification," that generations of organisms changed over time and those that best withstood climatic and other changes were most likely to survive and multiply. Darwin stated that these changes occurred through natural selection, controlled by the organisms themselves, over millions of years. *On the Origin of Species* discussed these broad concepts through specific examples of evolution in pigeons and ants, as well as in discussion of embryology and morphology. Though his theory was based on careful measurements and observations, Darwin understood that it would be seen as radically at odds with prevailing ideas about the design of nature. Attempting to head off criticism, Darwin acknowledged that "nothing at first may be more difficult to believe than that the more complex organs and instincts should have been perfected . . . by the accumulation of innumerable slight variations, each good for the individual possessor."

Most readers of Darwin's book had been taught that God created the world according to an orderly plan, placing humans on earth with dominion over nature. Darwin's ideas provided much less certainty than traditional, biblical-based explanations of nature. Popular impressions of Darwinism, however, differed from Darwin's actual writings. Social scientists summed up his concept of descent with modification through natural selection as "survival of the fittest" and used this term to explain relations between social classes. To so-called social Darwinists, wealthier, more powerful people deserved to hold on to their advantages because they were the "fittest" human beings. Under social Darwinism, any aid to the disadvantaged became an unnatural act, needlessly prolonging the lives and traits of the "unfit." Social Darwinists shortened Darwin's ideas by using the term "evolution" and added a belief that evolution always resulted in progress.

Darwin never intended this linear approach to the study of nature. He was most interested in the mutations that occurred over generations of organisms, whether the mutations resulted in progress or not. Further, Darwin never wished to explore his theories in the realm of human behavior and social organization. When he discussed his ideas in relation to humans, he focused on the development of organs and systems in the body, not in society.

Darwin was part of a movement in science toward reliance on empirical data. He was a contemporary of scientists like John William Draper, author of HISTORY OF THE CONFLICT BETWEEN RELIGION AND SCIENCE, who questioned religious-based models for scientific observation. While Darwin was careful not to attack religion directly, as Draper did, his quiet, measured arguments did not include any mention of a divine power ordering the universe.

CENSORSHIP HISTORY

Historians of science believe that one of the reasons why Darwin delayed publishing his work for so long was his fear that his ideas were too radical for the time and would be greeted with hostility. Seeing himself as a scientist, he refused to comment on the wider importance of his ideas. Near the end of his life, after publishing several other works in which he affirmed his belief in natural selection, he continued to think only in terms of advancing science and hoped that his quiet example would win people to his ideas.

On the Origin of Species by means of Natural Selection, or the Preservation of Favoured Races in the Struggle for Life was published on November 24, 1859, in an edition of only 1,250 copies by the reluctant John Murray, who did not anticipate much interest in the book. The first edition was sold out on the day of publication and a second edition of 3,000 copies soon after. The book appeared in six editions through 1872. An American edition appeared in May 1860 and was greeted with widespread controversy.

"Sixteen thousand copies have now (1876) been sold in England," Darwin wrote in his autobiography, "and considering how stiff a book it is, it is a large sale. It has been translated into almost every European tongue. . . ." He counted more than 265 reviews and numerous essays. Darwin's ideas gained wide currency in academic scientific circles almost immediately and became the foundations of modern evolution theory.

However, the publication of *On the Origin of Species* also unleashed one of the most dramatic controversies of the Victorian era. Darwin was accused of "dethroning God," as one critic put it, by challenging the literal interpretation of the book of Genesis. Clergy railed against him from pulpits all over Britain. His book was barred from Trinity College at Cambridge, even though Darwin was a graduate. Darwin, referring to occasions when he was "contemptuously criticised," declared that "I could not employ my life better than in adding a little to natural science. This I have done to the best of my abilities, and critics may say what they like, but they cannot destroy this conviction."

Unlike ZOONOMIA, a scientific treatise written by Darwin's grandfather, Erasmus Darwin, which was banned by the Catholic church because it expressed a theory of evolution, *On the Origin of Species* was never placed on the Index of Forbidden Books.

A resurgence of opposition to Darwinism began in the 1920s in the United States. By the early 20th century, American high school science textbooks had begun to incorporate Darwinian evolution in discussing human origins and biology. In 1919, the World Christian Fundamentals Association (WCFA) was founded to oppose teaching of evolution in American public schools. Local school boards and state boards of education in areas with large fundamentalist Christian populations were pressured to reject the new textbooks and legislatures around the country were lobbied to pass antievolution resolutions. More than 20 state legislatures considered such measures.

In 1925, in the most famous example of antievolutionary sentiment, Tennessee passed a law prohibiting teachers from teaching the theory of evolution in state-supported schools. A combination of factors compelled the Tennessee state legislature to pass such a sweeping measure. The 1920s were an era of pleasure-seeking in popular culture, especially among teenagers; at the same time, fundamentalist religion and nativism were on the increase as a reaction to these "modern" ideas. Fundamentalist Christians feared that a materialistic philosophy such as natural selection would send a damaging, nihilistic message to schoolchildren. They believed that schools would produce more orderly students if they taught the biblical account of creation, with a God designing nature according to a set plan. Local leaders in the small town of Dayton, Tennessee, welcomed the chance to put their town on the map in the context of this battle.

John T. Scopes, a science teacher in Dayton, volunteered to be the test case for Tennessee's antievolution law. Representing the state was William Jennings Bryan, a populist leader and three-time Democratic presidential candidate who had served as Woodrow Wilson's secretary of state and was popular among fundamentalists for his biblically-inspired rhetoric and his devotion to maintaining traditional, rural ways of life. Clarence Darrow, a noted defense lawyer and avowed agnostic, defended Scopes, arguing that academic freedom was being violated and that the legislation violated the separation of church and state. Members of the American Civil Liberties Union, at that time a new organization devoted to defending free speech, also contributed to Scopes's side.

The Scopes "monkey trial," as it became known, was an event of national importance during the summer of 1925. Newspapers from around the country sent correspondents to Dayton to cover the proceedings and Dayton merchants sold souvenirs of the trial, including stuffed monkeys to represent the idea that Darwin claimed humans were descended from apes. Reporters from big-city newspapers reported on the trial with amusement, while fundamentalist observers saw the proceedings as a crucial battle against the forces of modernism.

Both sides claimed victory. Scopes was found guilty of violating Tennessee's statute prohibiting the teaching of evolution. As a state employee, the judge ruled, Scopes could not disobey state laws. His backers were also pleased, as the decision gave them the chance to appeal the matter to a higher court, where the case for evolution and freedom of expression could get even more publicity. The Scopes case, however, was thrown out on a technicality. In the original case the judge, rather than the jury, had fined Scopes $100. This procedural error reversed the verdict that found Scopes guilty.

Antievolution efforts did not end with the conclusion of the Scopes trial. The Tennessee antievolution law remained on the books until 1967 and grassroots fundamentalists in the United States launched efforts to remove Darwin's ideas from public school textbooks. In 1968, the U.S. Supreme Court considered a case similar to Scopes's. Susan Epperson, a high school biology teacher, challenged the constitutionality of the Arkansas Anti-Evolution Statute of 1928, which provided that teachers who used a textbook that included Darwin's theory of evolution could lose their jobs. The Supreme Court ruled that the law was unconstitutional and conflicted with the First and Fourteenth Amendments. Government power could not be used to advance religious beliefs.

Having been defeated in the courts, antievolutionists shifted their focus to requiring instruction in "creationism" as an alternative to evolutionary theories. They defined creationism as the theory that all life forms came into existence instantaneously through the action of a single intelligent creator. In the early 1980s, Arkansas and Louisiana state boards of education required the teaching of both creationism and evolution in public schools. These laws were ruled unconstitutional in 1987 by the U.S. Supreme Court in *Edwards v. Aguillard* as advocating a religious doctrine and violating the establishment clause of the First Amendment. However, battles about the teaching of evolution still rage on, especially at the local school board level.

In 1935, *On the Origin of Species* was prohibited in Yugoslavia and in 1937 it was banned under the right-wing Metaxas regime in Greece. But unlike other cases of book censorship, the book was generally not removed from bookstore or library shelves in the United States. It was, rather, the ideas expressed in the book that were censored.

FURTHER READINGS

Boorstein, Daniel J. *The Discoverers: A History of Man's Search to Know His World and Himself.* New York: Random House, 1983.

Delatorre, Joan. *What Johnny Shouldn't Read: Textbook Censors in America*. New Haven: Yale University Press, 1992.

Demac, Donna A. *Liberty Denied: The Current Rise of Censorship in America*. New York: PEN American Center, 1988.

Gould, Stephen Jay. *Ever Since Darwin: Reflections on Natural History*. New York: W. W. Norton and Company, 1977.

Larson, Edward J. *Trial and Error. The American Controversy Over Creation and Evolution*. New York: Oxford University Press, 1985.

Numbers, Ronald L., ed. *Creation-Evolution Debates*. New York: Garland Publishing, 1955.

Rogers, Donald J. *Banned! Book Censorship in the Schools*. New York: Julian Messner, 1988.

ON THE REVOLUTION OF HEAVENLY SPHERES

Author: Nicholas Copernicus
Original date and place of publication: 1543, Germany
Literary form: Scientific treatise

SUMMARY

The celebrated Polish astronomer Nicholas Copernicus was the first to propose the heliocentric theory—that the planets, including the earth, move in orbits around the sun. The geocentric Ptolemaic theory of the universe, which had held sway since antiquity and was considered authoritative in philosophy, science and church teaching, placed the earth at the center of the universe, with the sun and planets moving around it.

Copernicus developed his revolutionary theory from a study of ancient astronomical records. He understood that it was the turning of the earth on its axis that gave the impression that the sun was moving. By liberating astronomy from the geocentric viewpoint, Copernicus laid the foundations of modern astronomy, paving the way for the work of Johannes Kepler, Galileo and Sir Isaac Newton.

Copernicus was a cathedral canon in the city of Frauenburg, East Prussia, and had studied canon law, mathematics and medicine. He developed his heliocentric theory as an avocation. His friends and disciples, including a Catholic cardinal and a bishop, urged him to have it published. "They insisted," Copernicus wrote, "that, though my theory of the Earth's movement might at first seem strange, yet it would appear admirable and acceptable when the publication of my elucidatory comments would dispel the mists of paradox."

A brief popular account of his theory was circulated in manuscript from 1530. In 1540 Copernicus granted permission to one of his disciples, Georg Joachim, known as Rheticus, to publish an initial report about his ideas. When the demand for Rheticus's report required a second edition in 1541, and hearing no objections from the church, Copernicus began preparing for publication the manuscript of his great work, *On the Revolution of Heavenly Spheres*. Copernicus asked Rheticus to supervise its publication. When Rheticus was unable to complete the task, he entrusted it to an acquaintance, Andreas Osiander, a militant Lutheran theologian. Copernicus was on his deathbed when *On the Revolution of Heavenly Spheres* was published in 1543.

The book, dedicated to Pope Paul III, contained a lengthy unsigned preface stating that the heliocentric theory was not an account of the actual physical organization of the heavens, but rather a mere hypothesis, a convenient device for simplifying astronomical calculations. "For these hypotheses need not be true nor even probable," the preface claimed.

Later it was discovered that this introduction had not been written by Copernicus at all. In the cause of Lutheran orthodoxy, Osiander had suppressed Copernicus's introduction and substituted one he had written himself. The German mathematician Johannes Kepler uncovered Osiander's deception and defended the integrity of Copernican theories. "He thought that his hypotheses were true," Kepler wrote, "no less than did those ancient astronomers. . . . He did not merely think so, but he proves they are true. . . ."

CENSORSHIP HISTORY

During Copernicus's lifetime and for a half-century after his death, *On the Revolution of Heavenly Spheres* was not opposed by Catholic church authorities. Although Copernicus was attacked by Martin Luther, who referred to him as "an upstart astrologer" who "wishes to reverse the entire science of astronomy," Copernicus's book, read at some of the best Catholic universities, was not seen as a threat to prevailing scientific and religious concepts.

The early 17th-century astronomical writings of Johannes Kepler and Galileo, which demonstrated, proved and popularized Copernican theory, led the church to see it as a challenge to orthodoxy. In 1616, *On the Revolution of Heavenly Spheres* was placed on the Index of Forbidden Books. Particular objection was raised to passages representing the heliocentric hypothesis as a certainty. Johannes Kepler's writings on Copernican theory, including THE NEW ASTRONOMY, were also placed on the Index and Galileo was warned not to teach or write on the heliocentric theory.

In 1633 Galileo was put on trial by the Inquisition for heresy for his defense of Copernican theories in DIALOGUE CONCERNING THE TWO CHIEF WORLD SYSTEMS. The *Dialogue* was formally condemned and banned along with all of Galileo's works and in 1644 the Index of Forbidden Books confirmed the condemnation of the works of Copernicus and Galileo.

It was not until the 18th century that the index of Benedict XIV in 1753 omitted the general prohibition against Copernican theory. Finally, in 1835, the names of Copernicus, Galileo and Kepler were removed. On October 31, 1992, more than four centuries after the publication of *On the Revolution of Heavenly Spheres*, Pope John Paul II formally rehabilitated Galileo and his defense of Copernicus's heliocentric theory.

FURTHER READINGS

Boorstein, Daniel J. *The Discoverers: A History of Man's Search to Know His World and Himself*. New York: Random House, 1983.

Garraty, John A., and Peter Gay. *The Columbia History of the World*. New York: Harper & Row, 1972.

Green, Jonathon. *The Encyclopedia of Censorship*. New York: Facts On File, 1990.

OPUS MAIUS

Author: Roger Bacon
Original date and place of publication: 1268, England
Literary form: Philosophical treatise

SUMMARY

The 13th-century English scientist and philosopher Roger Bacon, known as "Doctor Mirabilis," was a Franciscan friar who came under suspicion of heresy for advocating the experimental method in science. Bacon had an extensive knowledge of the sciences, was an accomplished Greek scholar and knew Hebrew and Aramaic. Among his accomplishments in practical science were the invention of spectacles and a unique understanding of how a telescope might be constructed. He was the first European to describe in detail the manufacture of gunpowder and to suggest that it would be possible in the future to have boats, coaches and flying machines powered by the sun's energy.

Bacon studied in Paris, where he was among the first scholars to lecture on Aristotle's natural philosophy and metaphysics. He wrote several works on Aristotelian thought and on Aristotle's Arab commentators. In 1247, disenchanted with the rise of Scholasticism in Paris, he returned to Oxford, where he called for a return to the study of the Scriptures and the biblical languages. He devoted the next 10 years to the study of science and languages and to scientific experimentation. In 1257, the Franciscan order sent Bacon back to Paris, where he was confined for 10 years. He was forbidden to write for publication because it was believed that he experimented with the "black arts" of magic and had adopted mystical interpretations of history. Bacon's interest in alchemy may have led his contemporaries to suspect him of dabbling in magic.

Bacon was critical of methods of contemporary academic learning and conceived a plan to reform science to better place it at the disposal of theology. At the request of his friend, Pope Clement IV, who had met Bacon when Clement was a church cardinal, he outlined his ideas in three Latin works, completed in 1268. *Opus Maius*, his great encyclopedic work, included discussion of grammar, logic, mathematics, physics and modern philosophy. *Opus Secundum* and *Opus Tertium*, which summarized and expanded the content of the first opus, followed shortly after.

In *Opus Maius*, Bacon expressed his distinctive philosophic ideas. The work is divided into seven parts: the causes of error, philosophy as an aid to theology, the study of languages, mathematics, optics, experimental science and moral philosophy. Bacon asserts that all wisdom stems from God through three channels of revelation: the Scriptures, the works of nature and the interior illumination of the soul achieved in seven stages of internal experience. Knowledge of foreign languages, mathematics and the moral and spiritual disciplines are needed to decipher these revelations. But the truth can be found only by appeal to experience or the use of the deductive scientific method. Reason may guide the mind to a right conclusion, but it is only confirmation by experience that removes doubt.

Bacon began *Opus Maius* by stating that the chief causes of error and failure to attain truth are "submission to faulty and unworthy authority, influence of custom, popular prejudice, and concealment of our own ignorance accompanied by an ostentatious display of our knowledge." Where these impediments hold sway, "no reason influences, no right decides, no law binds, religion has no place, nature's mandate fails, the complexion of things is changed, their order is confounded, vice prevails, virtue is extinguished, falsehood reigns, truth is hissed off the scene."

Bacon asserted that although all truth is contained in the Scriptures, both canon law and philosophy are needed to lead man to the knowledge and service of God. Philosophy and the use of reason cannot be condemned, because reason is of God. Pagan philosophy—that is, the philosophy of the ancient Greeks—should be consulted in an intelligent manner and should neither be ignorantly rejected nor blindly followed.

He emphasized the importance of study of languages, in order to understand both the Scriptures and the Greek and Arab philosophers, and of mathematics, which he saw as the "door and key" of other sciences. In the concluding section of *Opus Maius*, Bacon said that all other human sciences are subordinate to moral philosophy, which is closely related to theology, as it instructs people about their relations with God, their fellow human beings and themselves. God is the illuminating active intellect.

CENSORSHIP HISTORY

Bacon's thought blended traditional medieval ideas with a scientific outlook that was foreign to the thinking of the majority of contemporary theologians and philosophers. He fought for years to have the teaching of science recognized as part of the university curriculum. Although it is commonly assumed that *Opus Maius* was sent to Bacon's protector, Pope Clement IV, the pope died in 1268, the year of its publication, and it is not known for certain if he received it or how he reacted to it. The death of Pope Clement put an end to Bacon's plans to expand scientific study. For the rest of his life Bacon remained unpopular with his fellow intellectuals.

Bacon's Franciscan order regarded the ideas expressed in *Opus Maius* as heresy. In 1277, he wrote another work, the *Speculum Astronomiae*, in which he defended his ideas on astronomy against charges of determinism and asserted that the influence and movements of the heavenly bodies affected earthly and human events. According to a 14th-century work, the *Chronicle of the Twenty-four Generals*, in 1278 Bacon was accused of "certain suspect novelties" by Jerome de Ascoli, general of the Franciscan order, who later became Pope Nicholas IV, and sent to prison. He may have spent as many as 14 years behind bars, though some reports say that he was imprisoned for only two years. It is known that when he died in 1292 he was in the process of writing a new work, a compendium of theological studies.

FURTHER READINGS

Boorstein, Daniel J. *The Discoverers: A History of Man's Search to Know His World and Himself*. New York: Random House, 1983.

Copleston, Frederick. *A History of Philosophy*. Vol. 2, *Medieval Philosophy*. New York: Doubleday, 1994.

Green, Jonathon. *The Encyclopedia of Censorship*. New York: Facts On File, 1990.

Haight, Anne Lyon. *Banned Books: 387 BC to 1978 AD*. Updated and enlarged by Chandler B. Grannis. New York: R. R. Bowker, 1978.
Manguel, Alberto. *A History of Reading*. New York: Viking, 1996.
Wippel, John F., and Alan B. Wolter, eds. *Medieval Philosophy: From St. Augustine to Nicholas of Cusa*. New York: Free Press, 1969.

PENGUIN ISLAND

Author: Anatole France (Jacques Anatole Thibault)
Original date and place of publication: 1908, France; 1909, United States
Original publisher: Calmann-Lévy, France; Dodd, Mead & Co., United States
Literary form: Novel

SUMMARY

Anatole France was one of the most popular and influential French authors in his lifetime. In *Penguin Island* he presents a satirical history of France, telling the story of the Penguins from mythological prehistory through the present and into the future. Throughout *Penguin Island* the author attacks the hypocrisies of organized religion and the French Socialist party of the early 20th century.

In the first section of the novel, France indulges his interest in myths and religion of the Middle Ages by creating a detailed Penguin world that alludes to and spoofs early French history. The Penguins at the start of the novel are actual birds, but after a monk baptizes them and a conference of saints agrees to give them souls, they take on human form and behavior. The Penguins' humble beginnings and Anatole France's description of Penguin Island as an area south of Brittany poke fun at nationalist myths about early France and French prejudices against Bretons. The Penguins' transformation into humans also reflects the author's interest in human evolution.

The present-day section of *Penguin Island* focuses largely on an allegory of the Dreyfus affair, which rocked France at the turn of the century. Alfred Dreyfus, a French Jew, was wrongly accused of stealing from the French army and was sent to Devils Island penal colony off the coast of French Guiana. Leftist intellectuals such as Anatole France took up Dreyfus's case and persuaded the French government to grant him another trial, in which Dreyfus was cleared of wrongdoing.

Penguin Island's Pyrot, accused of stealing 80,000 bales of hay, is a stand-in for Dreyfus. The Penguin Socialists initially take Pyrot's side in the controversy, but their pacifism compels them to oppose Pyrot, following an argument that "if Pyrot is a good soldier, then his duties consist of shooting the people." The socialist debate over supporting or opposing Pyrot mirrored the debate within French Socialist party circles about Dreyfus.

In the final section of his novel, Anatole France depicts a grim future for Penguinia. He is skeptical of progress defined solely by the accumulation of wealth, demonstrating his socialist conviction that capitalism inevitably leads to concentration of wealth among a few people and that charity, art and scholarship will suffer as a result. This last chapter begins and ends with the same paragraph, showing Anatole France's belief that a decline of civilization is inevitable and would occur time and again, as fallen capitalist societies are rebuilt in the same image.

CENSORSHIP HISTORY

Penguin Island touched off controversy among Anatole France's socialist colleagues as well as among religious groups. The Dreyfus case had split the French Socialist party, as some members doubted Dreyfus's innocence and attempted to speak for all socialists against him. By 1908, the socialists who had opposed Dreyfus wanted to patch up their differences and saw France's satire as prolonging the conflict. Some thought the author's vision of the future was nihilistic, as they espoused a belief in a perfect, socialist future, rather than Anatole France's flawed capitalist one.

Religious readers disliked his mixture of pagan and Christian allusions in the early history of the Penguins. With this tactic, Anatole France implied that the two beliefs were interchangeable. He pointed out churchgoers' fondness for lavish displays of wealth in the name of religious piety. He made a connection between holy pilgrimage sites and vacation spots for the wealthy. Further, the book's references to the Dreyfus case were found offensive by the church, in view of the church's position against Dreyfus and the strongly anticlerical elements within the pro-Dreyfus movement.

In 1922 in Rome, the Index of Forbidden Books placed its most stringent prohibition on Anatole France's writing by designating *opera omnia*, or all of his works, as condemned. France remained on the Index through its last edition revised in 1948 and in effect until 1966. Despite these criticisms and the church's censorship, France's work sold weil in his homeland and around the world. He was awarded the Nobel Prize in literature in 1921. While his works are seldom read today, 100 years ago he was widely admired as an independent-thinking skeptic whose books enjoyed popular and critical success.

FURTHER READINGS

Dargan, Edwin Preston. *Anatole France*. New York: Oxford University Press, 1937.

Jefferson, Carter. *Anatole France: The Politics of Skepticism*. New Brunswick, N.J.: Rutgers University Press, 1965.

THE PERSIAN LETTERS

Author: Charles-Louis de Secondat, baron de la Brède et de Montesquieu
Original date and place of publication: 1721, Holland
Literary form: Novel

SUMMARY

In his epistolary novel *The Persian Letters*, the French political philosopher Montesquieu satirized and criticized French institutions through the imaginary correspondence of Persians traveling in Paris and Venice. The letters, commenting with wit and irony on contemporary events and issues, included pungent observations of politics, religion, government, law, agriculture, economics and philosophy. Many of the perspectives Montesquieu attributed to the Persian travelers were drawn from his own experiences when, in 1709, he moved from the French provinces to the world of Parisian high society.

The first edition, published anonymously in 1721, contained 150 letters exchanged during a nine-year period between two engaging Persian travelers, Usbek and Rica, and their friends, servants and wives in Persia. Their accounts of life in Persia were gleaned by Montesquieu from a contemporary translation of *The Thousand and One Nights* and from travelers' writings. Montesquieu revised *The Persian Letters* several times; the final edition, published as part of his complete works three years after his death, had expanded Rica and Usbek's correspondence to 161 letters.

The Persian Letters was a comedy of Parisian manners, but it also addressed serious issues of political and religious abuses in 18th-century France in an irreverent and entertaining style. Among the targets of Montesquieu's satire were royal absolutism and the Catholic church, particularly the pope, the Jesuit order and the church's suppression of dissent. "I see here people who dispute endlessly about religion," Usbek writes from Venice, "but who at the same time apparently compete to see who can least observe it. These people are not better Christians than others; they are not even better citizens."

Discussing the Jesuits, Usbek observes, "These dervishes make three vows, of obedience, poverty, and chastity. It is said that the first is the best observed; as for the second, I assure you it is certainly not; I leave it to you to judge the third." The "dervishes" hold in their hands most of the state's wealth, Usbek continues, "and they are an avaricious lot, always taking and never giving, constantly hoarding their revenue so as to acquire capital."

Usbek describes to his correspondent the "magician" called the pope: "Sometimes he makes the prince believe that three is only one, or that the bread he eats is not bread, or that the wine drunk is not wine, and a thousand similar things." Those who publicize a novel proposition are at first called heretics, writes Rica. "But no one is a heretic unless he wishes to be, for he needs only to split the difference and to offer some subtle distinction to his accusers, and no matter what the distinction is, or whether it is intelligible or not, it renders a man pure as snow and worthy of being called orthodox." This is the case in France and Germany, but "I have heard in Spain and Portugal that there are dervishes who do not understand a joke, and who have a man burned as if he were straw."

Transposing the situation to Persia, Montesquieu criticized the revocation of the Edict of Nantes by Louis XIV in 1685, which denied religious freedom to the Protestant minority in France. Usbek concludes that a strong state should have several religions since "those who practice the tolerated religion are usually more useful to the state than those in the majority religion" and that war and conflict come from the intolerance engendered by a single dominant religion.

Beyond the particular social criticisms that Montesquieu expressed through the observations of his Persian travelers, his fundamental purpose was to explore the idea of cultural relativity. "How can you be a Persian?" an incredulous Frenchman asks Rica in one of the most memorable sentences in the novel. Montesquieu makes this question a tool for cultural inquiry. Using the empirical and inductive method of the early Enlightenment, Montesquieu sought to understand how ideas and institutions varied and to discover amid diversity the absolutes in human society.

CENSORSHIP HISTORY

In 1720, Montesquieu brought a completed manuscript of *The Persian Letters* to Pierre-Nicholas Desmolets, a priest, librarian and literary critic, to seek his opinion on whether it should be published. As a priest, Desmolets argued that the book's publication would show disrespect for religion and disregard for the obligations of Montesquieu's aristocratic social position. He predicted it would cause a scandal. But as a critic, he said that if Montesquieu disregarded his advice and published the book, it could not fail "to sell like bread."

Montesquieu did not take Desmolet's advice. Published anonymously in Amsterdam with the imprint of a fictitious Cologne publisher, *The Persian Letters* was smuggled into France early in 1721. The publisher applied for a "tacit permission" to distribute the book in France, but the censor neither granted nor denied the request. Although the book was allowed into the country without danger of prosecution, it was not listed in the catalogs of French booksellers until some 10 years later.

As Desmolet had warned, *The Persian Letters* caused a sensation and, in some political and religious circles, a scandal. During its first year of publication it sold out in multiple printings and attracted widespread notice throughout Europe. Although Montesquieu did not formally acknowledge his authorship of *The Persian Letters* until years later, it was widely known that he had written it and he became instantly famous. A new edition was published annually for the next eight years, and there were many unsuccessful imitations. In "Some Reflections on *The Persian Letters*," a commentary added to the 1754 edition, Montesquieu wrote that "*The Persian Letters* had such a prodigious sale when they first appeared that publishers made every effort to obtain sequels. They buttonholed everyone they met. 'Sir,' they would say, 'write me some more *Persian Letters*.' "

Despite the book's success, clerical disapproval of the book was responsible for a delay of seven years in Montesquieu's acceptance to the prestigious French Academy. According to Montesquieu's son, Montesquieu himself met with the prime minister, Cardinal Fleury, who opposed his election to the academy. Fleury's primary objection was to *The Persian Letters*; he had never read the work, but what he had heard about it through an abstract given to him "made the hair on his head stand up."

Montesquieu replied that he neither admitted nor denied being the author and that he preferred to give up a seat in the academy rather than disavow the book. He challenged Fleury to read the entire book. The cardinal did so, and subsequently withdrew his opposition. Montesquieu was finally admitted to the academy in 1728. Despite the cardinal's approval, *The Persian Letters* and Montesquieu's masterpiece of political theory, THE SPIRIT OF LAWS, were listed by the Catholic church in 1752 on the Index of Forbidden Books, where they remained through the last edition of the Index compiled in 1948 and in effect until 1966.

Commenting on the criticisms of the book, Montesquieu wrote in "Some Reflections on *The Persian Letters*": "Some people have found certain remarks excessively bold, but they are advised to regard the nature of the work itself. . . . Far from intending to touch upon any principle of our religion, he did not even suspect himself of imprudence. The remarks in question are always found joined to sentiments of surprise and astonishment, never to a sense of inquiry, and much less to one of criticism. . . . Certainly the nature and the design of *The Persian Letters* are so obvious that they can deceive only those who wish to deceive themselves." Despite the church's ban, *The Persian Letters* remained popular throughout the rest of the century.

FURTHER READINGS

Conroy, Peter V., Jr. *Montesquieu Revisited*. New York: Twayne Publishers, 1992.

Haight, Anne Lyon. *Banned Books: 387 BC to 1978 AD*. Updated and enlarged by Chandler B. Grannis. New York: R. R. Bowker, 1978.

Montesquieu. *The Persian Letters*. Trans. and intro. by George R. Healy. Indianapolis: Bobbs-Merrill Company, 1964.

Shklar, Judith N. *Montesquieu*. Oxford: Oxford University Press, 1987.

PHILOSOPHICAL DICTIONARY

Author: Voltaire (François Marie Arouet)
Original date and place of publication: 1764, France
Literary form: Essays

SUMMARY

Voltaire, perhaps the most famous individual of the 18th century and among the greatest of its writers, was the chief standard-bearer of the Enlightenment. In the name of rationalism and tolerance, he declared war on dogmatic religion, especially Catholicism and its traditions. As a deist, Voltaire affirmed his personal belief in God but rejected the doctrines of institutionalized religion. In a 1762 letter to Jean d'Alembert, an editor of the famous ENCYCLOPÉDIE, to which Voltaire was a contributor, he attacked persecution, torture and other abuses of religious freedom carried out by the church with the phrase, "*Écrasez l'infâme*" (Stamp out the infamous thing). Voltaire's denunciation of Christianity became his most repeated watchword and the militant battle cry of the Enlightenment.

Theological religion is "the source of all imaginable follies and discords; it is the mother of fanaticism and civil discord; it is the enemy of mankind," Voltaire wrote in his *Philosophical Dictionary*. A series of alphabetical essays on a variety of subjects, the *Dictionary* is regarded as Voltaire's anti-Christian *summa*. It collected short articles on a wide range of subjects, including religion, government, war, friendship, beauty and love. The articles were written with the elegant irony, clarity and uncompromising frankness characteristic of Voltaire's style. First published in a pocket edition in 1764, it was gradually enlarged to six volumes, becoming a compendium of Voltaire's philosophical writings.

In a sentence that at first glance seemed innocuous, Voltaire gave his readers a taste of the iconoclastic nature of the book in the opening entry in the *Dictionary*'s first edition. "Abraham is one of the names famous in Asia Minor and in Arabia," he wrote, "like Toth among the Egyptians, the first Zoroaster in Persia, Hercules in Greece, Orpheus in Thrace, Odin among the northern nations, and so many others whose fame is greater than the authenticity of their history." Voltaire had in a matter-of-fact manner ranked the biblical personage of Abraham among pagan or mythological figures whose historical origins were doubtful. Voltaire's skeptical approach to the Bible was to inquire into the veracity of the events of Scripture and, if he determined that a particular event really occurred, to ask whether it was good and conformed to the idea of justice.

Jesus taught no metaphysical dogma at all, Voltaire claimed. "He abandoned to the Franciscans and the Dominicans, who were to come 1,200 years after him, the trouble of arguing whether his mother had been conceived in original sin. . . . He instituted neither monks nor inquisitors. He commanded nothing of what we see today." In the article "Religion," Voltaire analyzed the qualities that in his view determined the "least bad" religion. He asked whether it might be the simplest, the one that taught morality and very little dogma and "that which did not order one to believe in things that are impossible, contradictory, injurious to divinity, and pernicious to mankind, and which dared not menace with eternal punishment anyone possessing common sense?"

Voltaire reserved his most scathing and impassioned comments for what he described as religious fanaticism leading to persecution and injustice, which he viewed as a thousand times worse than atheism. As the most detestable example of the disease of fanaticism, he cited the massacre of St. Bartholomew's Day, when French Catholics butchered 70,000 French Protestants on August 24, 1572, and subsequent days. "There is no other remedy for this epidemic illness than the spirit of free thought, which, spreading little by little, finally softens men's customs, and prevents the renewal of the disease."

In "Torture," an article added to the 1769 edition, he commented on the case of the Chevalier de Barre, a promising young man in Abbeville, France, who, according to Voltaire, was convicted of blasphemy for singing impious songs and passing a procession of Capuchin monks without removing his hat. He was tortured and burned to death in 1766. Barre's personal copy of the first edition of the *Philosophical Dictionary* went to the flames with him. "Foreign nations judge France by her theatre, her novels, her charming verse, the girls of her opera, whose morals are very agreeable. . . ," Voltaire declared. "They do not know that there is no nation more cruel at bottom than the French."

In "Japanese Catechism" Voltaire asked, "If there are a dozen caterers, each of whom has a different recipe, must we on that account cut each other's throats instead of dining? On the contrary every man will eat well in his fashion with the cook who pleases him best." The *Philosophical Dictionary* is full of such bons mots on the subject of tolerance. From "Freedom of Thought": "It's shameful to put one's mind into the hands of those whom you wouldn't entrust with your money. Dare to think for yourself."

CENSORSHIP HISTORY

"The greatest misfortune of a writer is not perhaps to be the object of his colleagues' jealousy, the victim of intrigue, to be despised by the powerful of this world—it is to be judged by fools," wrote Voltaire in the *Philosophical Dictionary*, predicting the reception of censors to his book. "Fools sometimes go far, especially when ineptitude is added to fanaticism, and vengefulness to ineptitude."

Voltaire's "alphabetic abomination" was immediately condemned by religious and civil authorities throughout Europe. It was banned and burned in

France, Geneva, the Netherlands and Rome. When Geneva's public prosecutor, Jean Robert Tronchin, was asked in 1764 by the city council to give his opinion of the book, he described it as indecent, scandalous and destructive of revelation, a contagious poison and "a deplorable monument of the extent to which intelligence and erudition can be abused." One of the prosecutor's most vehement and puzzling objections was that Voltaire quoted passages from the Bible which "taken literally would be unworthy of Divine Majesty."

Comparing his *Dictionary* with the monumental ENCYCLOPÉDIE, Voltaire wrote, "Twenty folio volumes will never make a revolution. It is the little portable volumes of thirty *sous* that are to be feared." Indeed, Voltaire's alphabetical essays became enormously popular and influential and, despite their banning, were published clandestinely in numerous editions, some prepared under Voltaire's supervision, but more often pirated by underground printers. On numerous occasions Voltaire felt obliged to deny that he had written the book. In the absence of proof to the contrary, he was able to avoid prosecution.

Because Voltaire had planned the *Dictionary* as a deliberately revolutionary book, in which he would express liberal ideas in accessible form, its banning did not come as a surprise; nor did its placement on the Catholic church's Index of Forbidden Books, ultimately in the company of 37 other works by Voltaire, including LETTERS CONCERNING THE ENGLISH NATION.

The Catholic church's antipathy to Voltaire was again demonstrated in 1938 when Alfred Noyes, a British Catholic writer, was denounced to the Vatican for having written a biography of Voltaire that was regarded as sympathetic. The second edition of *Voltaire*, which had earlier received favorable reviews in both the Catholic and Anglican press in England, was about to be published when an anonymous letter writer reported it to the Vatican.

According to Noyes, the purpose of his book was to show that atheists and skeptics were unaware of the support Voltaire had given to the central principles and beliefs of religious faith. The Supreme Congress of the Holy See issued a temporary suspension of the book. As a Catholic, Noyes was compelled to consider the church's views of the book or face excommunication. The archbishop of Westminster—British Cardinal Arthur Hinsley—wrote to Rome to inquire about the Vatican's specific objections; in response, the matter was referred back to him for settlement. In April 1939, Hinsley issued a public letter that was prominently published on major newspapers and in the Catholic press, stating that the competent authorities desired no alteration in the text of the book. Noyes, by agreement with the church, wrote a new preface, clarifying his thoughts on Voltaire, and there was no further objection to the biography.

FURTHER READINGS

Bachman, Albert. *Censorship in France from 1715–1750: Voltaire's Opposition*. New York: Burt Franklin, 1971.

Gay, Peter. *The Enlightenment: An Interpretation. The Rise of Modern Paganism*. New York: W. W. Norton & Company, 1995.
Noyes, Alfred. *Two Worlds for Memory*. Philadelphia: J. B. Lippincott Co., 1953.
Voltaire. *Philosophical Dictionary*. Ed., trans. and intro. by Theodore Besterman. New York: Penguin Books, 1972.

THE POLITICAL HISTORY OF THE DEVIL

Author: Daniel Defoe
Original date and place of publication: 1726, England
Literary form: Religious history

SUMMARY

The English writer Daniel Defoe, author of more than 500 works of journalism and pamphlets, including the censored THE SHORTEST WAY WITH THE DISSENTERS, and novels such as *Robinson Crusoe* and *Moll Flanders*, devoted three long books during the prolific last decade of his life to supernatural matters. *The Political History of the Devil* and *A System of Magick; or, A History of the Black Art* in 1726 and *An Essay on the History and Reality of Apparitions* in 1727 reflected Defoe's lifelong interest in the occult, in common with many intellectuals of his time. Though these books have puzzled modern readers, they were of great interest during the 1720s in plague-ridden London, when superstition, folklore and magic proliferated. Even clergymen who wrote books combatting superstition admitted the possibility of the appearance in the world of devils, apparitions and omens.

Defoe's aim in these books was to separate legitimate consideration of the supernatural from superstition. In *The Political History of the Devil*, Defoe, blending the serious and the comic, explores the evidence for the actions and influence of Satan in the world. He ridicules faith in wizards, witches and astrologers, but affirms that those who believe in God cannot deny the existence of Satan. The devil, as a spirit, however, lacks the power to take human form and interfere with the natural order of things. Satan's power lies, rather, in his influence on human inclinations and passions, in "mischief, seducing and deluding mankind, and drawing him in to be a rebel like himself."

The devil cannot be used as an excuse: "Bad as he is, the Devil may be abus'd,/Be falsely charged; and causelessly accus'd,/When men Unwilling to be blam'd alone,/Shift off those Crimes on Him which are their own." Defoe dismisses as profane and ridiculous popular belief that the devil is a person or that hell is a physical location. Hell is, rather, "Absence from . . . all Beatitude," despair and lack of hope, redemption or recovery. This "devilish spirit," he writes, "forms a hell within us, and . . . imperceptibly . . . transforms us into devils." Hell is a state of mind and the "devilish spirit" is evil as visibly manifest in history through human actors. The power of the devil is limited. "He can only bark, but cannot bite."

CENSORSHIP HISTORY

Though they are little read today, all three of Defoe's books on the supernatural were popular in the early 18th century. *The Political History of the Devil* went into a second edition in 1727 and before Defoe's death was translated into French and German. *The Political History of the Devil*, the only one of the three to be censored by the Catholic church, was placed on the Index of Forbidden Books in 1743. In the book, Defoe refers to the church's Inquisition as the "perfection of devilism," and imputes the presence of evil in the actions of the church hierarchy. "[T]yranny of the worst sort crept into the pontificate," he wrote, "errors of all sort into the profession, and they proceeded from one thing to another, till the very popes . . . professed openly to confederate with the Devil, and to carry on a personal and private correspondence with him."

Though Defoe's novels have faced various bans for obscenity and *Robinson Crusoe* was placed on the Spanish Index of Forbidden Books in 1720, *The Political History of the Devil*, among the most obscure of Defoe's hundreds of works, stands out as the only one to be placed on the Roman Index. Its presence on the Index was reconfirmed by Pope Leo XIII in 1897, and it remained forbidden reading for Catholics through the last edition compiled in 1948 and in effect until 1966. Defoe's book again emerged from obscurity when a quotation from it was selected by Salman Rushdie as the epigraph of the most censored book of the 20th century, THE SATANIC VERSES.

FURTHER READINGS

Backscheider, Paula R. *Daniel Defoe: His Life*. Baltimore: Johns Hopkins University Press, 1989.

Earle, Peter. *The World of Defoe*. New York: Atheneum, 1977.

Levy, Leonard W. *Blasphemy: Verbal Offense Against the Sacred, from Moses to Salman Rushdie*. New York: Alfred A. Knopf, 1993.

Richetti, John J. *Daniel Defoe*. Boston: Twayne Publishers, 1987.

POPOL VUH

Original date and place of composition: ca. 1000–1550, Guatemala
Literary form: Religious text

SUMMARY

The Popol Vuh, the sacred book of the Quiché Maya, is the most important text in the native languages of the Americas and the greatest Mesoamerican mythological work. It is considered to be among the world's masterpieces of religious writing. Blending myth, legend and history, it recounts the cosmology, migratory tradition and history of the Quiché Mayas of Guatemala's highlands. The Quichés, who number over a half million today, live in the same land and among the same landmarks whose ancient history is described in the Popol Vuh or "Council Book," consulted by the lords of Quiché when they sat in Council.

The narrative in part one of the Popol Vuh begins in the primeval darkness before creation, in an empty world of only sky and sea and the gods who live in the waters. The Heart of Sky (a tripartite being also called Hurricane) and the Sovereign Plumed Serpent, who resides in the primordial sea, resolve to create the world. They say "Earth" and it suddenly comes into being, rising like a cloud or a mist. The gods begin their efforts to create human beings. On the first try they create beings who can only squawk, chatter and howl. Because they cannot speak properly to worship their gods, they are condemned to be killed for food. Their descendants are the birds and animals.

A second experiment creates a being of mud that dissolves into nothing, incapable of speaking or worshipping. Before their third attempt, the younger gods consult the elderly divinities—the matchmaker, Xpiyacoc, and the midwife, Xmucane, both daykeepers or diviners who can interpret the auguries of the calendar cycle. They approve the creation of human beings made of wood. Because the wooden manikins are empty-headed, with no memory of their creators, Heart of Sky brings a great flood down upon them. They are crushed and destroyed and their only descendants are the monkeys of the forests.

Before telling of the fourth attempt to create human beings, the narrators recount in parts two and three the three-part cycle of the exploits of the hero twins. First Hunahpu and Xbalanque, the twin grandsons of Xpiyacoc and Xmucane, in a series of adventures, vanquish Seven Macaw (the Big Dipper) and his offspring Zipacna and Earthquake.

Then the story flashes back to an earlier story of the exploits in Xibalba, the underworld, of another set of twins—One Hunahpu and Seven Hunahpu, the father and uncle of Hunahpu and Xbalanque and the sons of Xpiyacoc and Xmucane. They are summoned to the underworld and fail a series of tests and traps set by their hosts. They are sacrificed in Xibalba by the lords of death.

The final segment relates the adventures in the underworld of the first set of hero twins, Hunahpu and Xbalanque. They are successful in escaping from the traps that had caused the demise of their father and uncle and plan a way to die that will allow them to come back to life. The twins then ascend from Xibalba into the heavens to become the sun and the moon.

The stage is now set for the fourth creation. In part four, as the sun, moon and stars are about to rise, Xpiyacoc and Xmucane find yellow and white corn in a mountain. Xmucane grinds it together nine times. Mixed with water, the corn provides the material for the first human beings: Jaguar Quitze, Jaguar Night, Mahucutah and True Jaguar, the first mother-fathers of the Quiché people. But as the new men are too perfect, the gods worry that their creations will compete with them in greatness. The gods weaken the men's eyes so that they can see only nearby things clearly, limiting their powers of knowing and understanding. Then the gods make a wife for each new man and the leading Quiché lineages descend from these pairs. Finally, after much sacrifice and prayer, the sun appears for the first time. "There were countless peoples, but there was just one dawn for all tribes."

The creation myth recounted in the Popol Vuh is an actual map of the sky that replays creation in the pattern of its yearly movements. The actions of the gods, the heroes and their enemies correspond to the movements of the sun, moon, planets and stars. Creation is not a single act but a process through which the essence of divinity continually creates and maintains life. The Popol Vuh concludes in part five with a lengthy migration story that recounts episodes comprising the mythological and actual history of the Quiché people and their Mayan neighbors. It lists the names of 14 generations of the rulers of Quiché up to the time when this version of the Popol Vuh was written. In the 12th generation, the names of Three Deer and Nine Dog are followed by two sentences. "And they were ruling when Tonatiuh (Pedro de Alvarado) arrived. They were hanged by the Castilian people."

CENSORSHIP HISTORY

The Popol Vuh was originally written in Mayan hieroglyphics by Quiché Maya nobles during the Postclassic period (A.D. 1000 to 1500) and was in use by the Quiché at the time of the Spanish conquest in the 16th century. Illustrations on painted pottery and inscriptions carved on stone monuments indicate that the myths and legends told in the Popol Vuh are much older, dating at least to the Classic period (A.D. 250 to 900), the time of the highest flourishing of Mayan art and culture.

After 1523, when the Spanish conquistador Pedro de Alvarado was sent by Hernán Cortés to subdue the Mayan peoples of Guatemala, thousands of hieroglyphic books were burned by Spanish missionaries. The original Popol Vuh is assumed to have been among them. Hieroglyphic books were regarded as superstitious works of the devil. Their destruction was a part of a sustained campaign to eradicate Mayan religion and culture and impose European Catholicism.

In the 1550s, a text of the Popol Vuh was secretly rewritten in the Roman alphabet in the town of Santa Cruz del Quiché, Guatemala, by descendants of the lordly lineages who once ruled the Quiché Kingdom. Its anonymous authors had been taught by missionaries to write their language in the alphabet. In 1701–03 the book was translated into Spanish by a Dominican friar, Francisco Ximénez, the parish priest of the nearby town of Chichicastenango, who was shown the document and recognized its importance. He also made what is now the only copy of the Quiché Maya text.

The original Popol Vuh would have been fully illustrated, a folding screen manuscript painted on bark paper thinly coated with lime plaster. It would have included astrological tables and ritual almanacs used for divination, similar to the pages of the only four Mayan hieroglyphic books or fragments, called codices, that survived the depredations of the Spanish conquest. Three codices from Yucatan, Mexico, were taken to Europe in colonial times and bear the names of the cities where they were found in museums or libraries: the Dresden, Paris and Madrid codices. A fourth fragment, known as the Grolier Codex, now in Mexico City, was found in a cave in Chiapas, Mexico, in 1971. The Popol Vuh of the 16th century presented an expanded version of the original hieroglyphic book, telling the full story behind the charts and pictures.

According to the writers of the alphabetic version, the hieroglyphic codex was among the most precious possessions of the Quiché rulers because "they knew whether war would occur; everything they saw was clear to them. Whether there would be death or whether there would be famine. . . . [T]hey knew it for certain, since there was a place to see it, there was a book." The "Council Book" allowed the Quiché lords to recover the vision lost by the first four humans.

The highly praised first unabridged English-language translation of the Popol Vuh by Dennis Tedlock, published in 1985, incorporates the insight of a contemporary Quiché Maya daykeeper and head of his patrilineage, Andrés Xiloj. It is engaging and readable, despite the complexity of the mythology it contains, and has brought the Popol Vuh to a larger audience.

FURTHER READINGS

Freidel, David, Linda Schele and Joy Parker. *Maya Cosmos: Three Thousand Years on the Shaman's Path*. New York: William Morrow and Company, 1993.

Gallenkamp, Charles. *Maya: The Riddle and Discovery of a Lost Civilization*. New York: David McKay and Company, 1976.

Markman, Roberta, and Peter Markman. *The Flayed God: The Mythology of Mesoamerica*. New York: HarperCollins, 1992.

Stuart, Gene S., and George E. Stuart. *Lost Kingdoms of the Maya*. Washington, D.C.: National Geographic Society, 1993.

Tedlock, Dennis, trans. *Popol Vuh: The Definitive Edition of the Mayan Book of the Dawn of Life and the Glories of Gods and Kings*. New York: Simon & Schuster, 1985.

THE POWER AND THE GLORY

Author: Graham Greene
Original date and place of publication: 1940, England, United States
Original publisher: Heinemann, England; Viking, United States
Literary form: Fiction

SUMMARY

The Power and the Glory, widely regarded as Graham Greene's finest novel, tells the story of a dissolute fugitive priest pursued by a fanatical police lieutenant during an anticlerical purge in Mexico in the 1930s. In 1938, Greene visited Mexico to research a report commissioned by the Catholic church on religious persecution under the new revolutionary regime. His journey took him through the southern states of Chiapas and Tabasco, where Catholic churches had been destroyed and priests banished or executed. Greene wrote a nonfiction account of his trip, *The Lawless Roads*, and drew on his experiences for the setting and theme of *The Power and the Glory*.

The unnamed priest of the novel, sometimes known as Montez, more commonly as "the whiskey priest," is the last surviving priest in the state. He defies the government ban on administering the sacraments, moving from village to village, keeping one step ahead of the police and certain arrest on charges of treason. The whiskey priest, an alcoholic who has fathered a child by a parishioner in a tiny village, is troubled by guilt and the knowledge of his own weakness and sinfulness.

Montez's relentless pursuer, a young policeman, is an ardent and upright revolutionary who believes that only when Mexico is rid of the Catholic church and its clergy will the poor find liberation. His fervent atheism is described by Greene as a kind of mysticism. "There are mystics who are said to have experienced God directly. He was a mystic, too, and what he had experienced was vacancy—a complete certainty in the existence of a dying, cooling world, of human beings who had evolved from animals for no purpose at all."

The priest has come to the coast to board a boat that will take him to safety in the port of Vera Cruz. But a boy pleads with him to administer the last rites to his dying mother, several miles inland. Now in the interior, he is at risk of capture by the revolutionary Red Shirts, who shoot priests on sight. He finds temporary refuge in a remote banana plantation run by an Englishman, Captain Fellows.

The priest eventually makes his way to the village where his daughter, Brigida, and her mother, Maria, live. Before dawn he conducts a secret Mass for the villagers, interrupted by the arrival of the police. Maria pretends the priest is her husband and, although a hostage from the village is taken, no one informs on him.

In the company of a poor and wily mestizo, whom he fears will betray him for a reward, he travels to a town where he is able to elude his companion, but he is arrested for illegal possession of liquor and thrown into jail overnight. His fellow prisoners, who realize he is a priest, protect his identity. He is released by the police lieutenant, who does not recognize him as the priest he seeks.

On his way to safe territory in the city of Las Casas, he again encounters the Judas-like figure of the mestizo, who tells him that an American bandit has been wounded by the police and wishes to receive the last rites. Fully suspecting that he will walk into a police trap, the priest embraces his duty and accompanies the mestizo into the mountains. He is captured by the police lieutenant, tried for treason and sentenced to be shot.

He spends his last night in despair and regret at his own uselessness and failures. "The eight hard hopeless years seemed to him to be only a caricature of service: a few communions, a few confessions, and an endless bad example. He thought: If I only had one soul to offer, so that I could say, Look what I've done. . . . People had died for him, they had deserved a saint, and a tinge of bitterness spread across his mind for their sake that God hadn't thought to send them one."

Yet, while he was without sin in his early years as a priest, he was bereft of the love he has come to feel for his daughter and compassion for the poor whose squalid existence he now shares. The night after his death, a young boy who has been moved by his quiet bravery spurns the lieutenant he once admired and welcomes another fugitive priest who has come secretly to town. The corrupt whiskey priest has been vindicated, for the work of the church has gone forward, and in his flawed and wretched life he has attained a kind of saintliness.

CENSORSHIP HISTORY

The first British edition of *The Power and the Glory* in 1940 (published the same year in the United States as *The Labyrinthine Ways*) was only 3,500 copies. Published during the "phony war" period of World War II, a month before Hitler invaded the Low Countries, it was overshadowed by public crisis; despite favorable reviews and its receipt of the Hawthornden Prize for 1940, there was little public interest in Greene's story of remote Mexico. The book did not sell well during the war, but immediately after, its English publisher released a pocket edition of 18,650 copies and, in 1949, another 23,450 for a uniform edition of Greene's work. Interest in the novel was revived, especially in France, where it was published with a sympathetic introduction by the Nobel laureate François Mauriac.

Mauriac has described Greene's novels as being about "the utilization of sin by Grace." In Greene's fictional world, God's grace is often bestowed on sinners, the wretched who are close to despair. Many of his most sympathetically drawn characters, such as the whiskey priest in *The Power and the Glory*, are those in a state of doubt or unbelief.

Greene had converted to Catholicism in 1926, but preferred to be known as a writer who was a Catholic, rather than as a Catholic writer. "I always considered myself a protestant inside the Church rather than being a protestant outside," he said. In a 1948 essay, *Why Do I Write?*, Greene defended his right to be "disloyal" to the church. To preserve his artistic integrity, he wrote, he must be able to write "from the point of view of the black square as well as from the white," for if his writing merely conformed with official dogma, the result would be propaganda.

Greene recounted that the story of the drunk priest was partly inspired by his irritation at "the smug Protestant treatment of the erring priest. It always seemed to me a very superficial kind of condemnation. I wanted to show that the man's office doesn't depend on the man. A priest in giving a sacrament believes he is giving the body and blood of Christ, and it doesn't matter whether he himself is a murderer, an adulterer, a drunkard." The priest in the novel says "I can put God into a man's mouth just the same—and I can give him God's pardon. It wouldn't make any difference to that if every priest in the Church was like me."

Greene's sympathetic portrayal of the whiskey priest led two Catholic bishops in France to denounce the book to Rome on two different occasions. Fourteen years after the book's publication, it was condemned by Giuseppe Cardinal Pizzardo, of the Vatican's Holy Office, on the grounds that it was "paradoxical" and "dealt with extraordinary circumstances." In 1953, Greene was summoned by Cardinal Griffin, the archbishop of Westminster, and told of Cardinal Pizzardo's action. Griffin read Greene a letter from the Holy Office in which Pizzardo requested that changes be made in the text, "which I naturally—though I hope politely—refused to make," Greene wrote in his memoirs. He used the excuse that the copyright was in the hand of his publisher.

Griffin added that he would have preferred that Rome had condemned another of Greene's novels, *The End of the Affair*, rather than *The Power and the Glory*. "You and I receive no harm from erotic passages, but the young. . . .," he said. When the interview ended, Griffin provided a copy of his pastoral letter, which was read in the churches of his diocese during Advent of 1953. His letter condemned not only *The Power and the Glory* but also, by implication, *The Heart of the Matter* and *The End of the Affair*, both among Greene's most highly regarded novels.

"It is sadly true that a number of Catholic writers appear to have fallen into this error," the letter said. "Indeed, novels which purport to be the vehicle for Catholic doctrine frequently contain passages which by their unrestrained portrayal of immoral conduct prove a source of temptation to many of their readers. . . . The presentation of the Catholic way of life within the framework of fiction may be an admirable object but it can never be justified as a means to that end the inclusion of indecent and harmful material."

Despite this rebuke, the church took no further action against the novel. "The affair was allowed to drop into that peaceful oblivion which the Church wisely reserves for unimportant issues," Greene wrote. Though Greene did not dwell on the church's attempts to censor his writings when he recounted the incident in his memoirs and the censorship had little effect on the book's reputation or its sales, his authorized biographer, Norman Sherry, reported that Greene was deeply troubled by the incident.

In later years, Greene had an audience with Pope Paul VI in Rome. The pope told Greene that he had read *The Power and the Glory*. Greene responded that it had been condemned by the Holy Office. "Who condemned it?" the pope asked. "Cardinal Pizzardo," Greene responded. The pope repeated the name with a smile and added, "Mr. Greene, some parts of your books are certain to offend some Catholics, but you should not worry about that."

Four of Greene's books—*The Heart of the Matter*, *The End of the Affair*, *England Made Me* and *The Quiet American*—did offend Catholics on the Irish censorship board and were banned by the Eire government. In each case the ban was successfully reversed upon an appeal by his publishers. In the case of *The Heart of the Matter*, prohibited in 1948 for being "indecent in tendency," Greene remarked that the banning helped to sell copies.

FURTHER READINGS

Donaghy, Henry J., ed. *Conversations with Graham Greene*. Jackson, Miss.: University Press of Mississippi, 1992.

Greene, Graham. *A Sort of Life*. New York: Simon and Schuster, 1971.

———. *Ways of Escape*. New York: Simon and Schuster, 1980.

O'Prey, Paul. *A Reader's Guide to Graham Greene*. New York: Thames and Hudson, 1988.

Sherry, Norman. *The Life of Graham Greene*. Vol. 2, *1939–1955*. New York: Viking Penguin, 1994.

THE PRAISE OF FOLLY

Author: Desiderius Erasmus
Original date and place of publication: 1511, France
Literary form: Satirical essay

SUMMARY

The Dutch humanist Desiderius Erasmus, a proponent of reform within the Catholic church, was among the best-known and influential men of his time. Through the new technological advances of printing, his work became known throughout Europe. He produced dozens of volumes on a wide range of subjects, including scholarly editions of the writing of the church fathers and translations of classical authors, a ground-breaking translation of the Greek New Testament into Latin, numerous commentaries and homilies, moral, religious and political essays, books on education and a dictionary of proverbs.

Erasmus's original works, written in Latin, the language of the 16th-century scholar, were mainly satirical and critical. In advocating moderation and tolerance, Erasmus's writing combined erudition with sharp wit and style. *The Praise of Folly* is a light satire suggested by Sir Thomas More, at whose home in England Erasmus wrote the book while resting from an Italian journey in 1509. In the preface he declared, "We have praised folly not quite foolishly," for *The Praise of Folly* had the same serious purpose as all of his writing: to criticize abuses in the church and in society and to promote a purer spirituality in religion.

In *The Praise of Folly*, Folly is presented as a person who offers an oration of praise to herself. She claims as her own all human activity except that which is governed by reason. She exalts the life of instinct, proclaiming her superiority over wisdom. The followers of Folly are devotees of self-love and ignorance in every trade and profession. By ironically praising stupidity and corruption, Erasmus exalts the Christian humanist way of life and the values that Folly, or the fool, disdains. He targets for ridicule superstitious practices within Catholicism, castigates insincere monks, "who make a good living out of squalor and beggary," and church authorities who betray their high offices by leading unchristian lives.

Erasmus reserves his most scathing criticism for the "tortuous obscurities" of quibbling Scholastic theologians, "a remarkably supercilious and touchy lot. I might perhaps do better to pass over them in silence without stirring the mud of Camarina or grasping that noxious plant, lest they marshal their forces for an attack and force me to eat my words. If I refuse they'll denounce me as a heretic on the spot, for this is the bolt they always loose on anyone to whom they take a dislike."

Delving into theological minutiae, the theologians interpret hidden mysteries to suit themselves. Erasmus suggests that there are many more worthy questions to be considered: "Could God have taken on the form of a woman, a devil, a donkey, a gourd, or a flintstone? If so, how could a gourd have preached sermons, performed miracles, and been nailed to the cross? . . . Shall we be permitted to eat and drink after the resurrection? We're taking due precaution against hunger and thirst while there's time."

Such is the erudition and complexity displayed by the theologians, Erasmus writes, "that I fancy the apostles themselves would need the help of another Holy Spirit if they were obliged to join issue on these topics with our new breed of new theologian. . . . Who *could* understand all this unless he has frittered away 36 whole years over the physics and metaphysics of Aristotle and Scotus?" The apostles refuted the philosophers with whom they disagreed, but did so more by the example of their way of life than by syllogisms.

CENSORSHIP HISTORY

At the time of Erasmus's death in 1536, 36 Latin editions of *The Praise of Folly* had been published. It was translated into Czech, French, German, Italian and English. Published in over 600 editions over the centuries, it remains his most popular work today. Upon its appearance in 1511, it was well received by humanists, but evoked sharp criticism in clerical circles, where it was regarded as heretical. In *The Praise of Folly*, Erasmus lambastes theologians who appoint themselves as the world's censors and "demand recantation of anything which doesn't exactly square with their conclusions. . . ." This was an apt description of his satire's reception.

Though Erasmus wrote that he thought so little of the work that he was unsure it was worth publishing, "hardly anything of mine has had a more enthusiastic reception, especially among the great. A few monks only, and those the worst, took offense at its freedom; but more were offended when Listrius added notes, for before that moment it had gained from not being understood." Erasmus said that he had originally conceived the idea of writing three simultaneous declamations, in praise of Folly, Nature, and Grace. "But some people I could name proved so difficult that I changed my mind."

The theologian Maarten van Dorp of Louvain, Belgium, was among those who reproached Erasmus for his hostility toward professional theologians. Erasmus replied to Dorp in the form of an apologia addressed to all conservative theologians. "First then, to be perfectly frank," he wrote, "I am almost sorry myself that I published my Folly. That small book has earned me not a little reputation coupled with ill will. My purpose was guidance and not satire; to help, not to hurt; to show men how to become better and not to stand in their way."

Erasmus declared that anyone who claims that he was injured by his satire "betrays his own guilty conscience, or at any rate his apprehensions." Dorp was later converted to Erasmus's position, but such was not the case with other theologians. Though the pope was said to be delighted with *The Praise of Folly*, it was prohibited at the universities of Paris, Louvain, Oxford and Cambridge.

Despite bans of the book, Erasmus enjoyed great popularity and was hailed as a hero among humanists. "Every day I receive letters from learned men which set me up as the glory of Germany and call me its sun and moon," he wrote in 1515. He was given benefices, offered teaching posts and in 1515 appointed councilor to Prince Charles. By the 1520s, however, his situation had changed. "There is no party that does not hate me bitterly," he reflected.

The turning point in Erasmus's career had come with the publication in 1516 of his magnum opus, his translation into Latin of the Greek New Testament, and with the rise of Martin Luther. Already unpopular with theologians because of his sharp criticism of the profession in *The Praise of Folly*, his pursuit of biblical studies was considered meddling.

Conservative theologians challenged Erasmus's authority to translate the Bible; his version revised and corrected errors that had crept into the standard Vulgate text over the years. Although he dedicated his translation to Pope Leo X, who praised him for "exceptional service to the study of sacred theology and to the maintenance of the true faith," Erasmus was unable to quell the controversy that arose over his translation.

But it was the conflict over Martin Luther's views that brought about a definitive change in Erasmus's fortunes. In a "Brief Outline of His Life," an autobiographical sketch he composed in 1524, Erasmus explained that "[t]he sad business of Luther had brought him [Erasmus] a burden of intolerable ill will; he was torn in pieces by both sides, while aiming zealously at what was best for both." Martin Luther had looked upon Erasmus as an ally in attacking clerical abuses in the church. Eager for church reform, Erasmus at first welcomed Luther's initiatives. However, powerful Catholic friends urged him to declare himself against Luther. He refused, preferring to engage in debates with the Protestant reformers while remaining a loyal Catholic.

Erasmus eventually withdrew his support for Luther, attacking his position on predestination and free will. But conservative Catholics thought he had done too little too late. Erasmus was assailed by both sides in the dispute. The Lutherans and Calvinists called him a traitor to their cause, and Catholics, who viewed him as a Lutheran sympathizer, denounced him for heresy. In 1524, the university of the Sorbonne in Paris forbade the sale or reading of Erasmus's COLLOQUIES, a book designed to teach schoolchildren good Latin, because of "its Lutheran tendencies." In 1527, the Spanish Inquisitor General convened a conference to examine his writings. Four years later, the prestigious faculty of theology at Paris also reviewed his works and condemned a number of passages as scandalous and unorthodox.

After Erasmus's death in 1536, the onslaught continued. In 1544, his works were forbidden at the Sorbonne. *The Praise of Folly* and most of his other works were prohibited in Spain. The Index of Forbidden Books published by the Inquisition of Toulouse, France, in 1548 included the work of Erasmus along with Luther's. In 1550, all of his works were placed on the Spanish Index of Forbidden Books. In 1551, the Parlement of Paris forbade the printing or sale of his books. The following year the Louvain theologians joined their colleagues at the Sorbonne and described condemned passages from his writings as erroneous, scandalous and heretical. In 1555 Mary, Queen of Scots, forbade the reading of his works in Scotland.

The papacy in Rome, however, had not yet seen Erasmus as an enemy, having been friendly toward him during his lifetime. But as the Counter-Reformation intensified, Erasmus's work came under attack with the publication of the first Index of Forbidden Books by Pope Paul IV in 1559. Erasmus was condemned as harshly as Luther and Calvin as a major influence on the Protestant Reformation. His name was placed in the Index's Class I, the list of authors whose works were totally banned. "All of his Commentaries,

Remarks, Notes, Dialogues, Letters, Criticisms, Translations, Books and writings, including even those which contain nothing concerning religion," stated the Index, were prohibited.

Among the new features of the 1559 Index, evident in its full title, *Index Auctorum et Librorum Prohibitorum*, was the simultaneous banning of books and authors. In some cases a single book was chosen to be suppressed, but, in other cases, notably that of Erasmus, all the author's works were banned. This blanket condemnation was slightly modified by the Tridentine Index of 1564, issued by the Council of Trent. In the revised Index some of Erasmus's works were permitted in expurgated form. Others, such as *The Praise of Folly* and *Colloquies*, remained suppressed. Apart from Spain, which had its own Index, the Tridentine Index was effective in Belgium, Bavaria, Portugal, Italy and France.

Subsequent Indexes, both in Rome and Spain, maintained the bans on Erasmus. A list of his forbidden works took up 55 quarto pages in the Index of Quiroga, Spain, in 1583. The list had increased to 500 double-columned folio pages by 1640. Erasmus was consigned to the ranks of incorrigible heretics and the words *auctoris damnati* (of a condemned author) were inserted after his name on all title pages.

Erasmus's reputation recovered only when the intellectual climate changed in the 18th century, as the progressives of the Enlightenment discovered a kindred spirit in his values of reason and tolerance. Erasmus's works, nevertheless, remained on the Index of Forbidden books for four centuries, until his name was finally removed in 1930.

FURTHER READINGS

Burman, Edward. *The Inquisition: Hammer of Heresy*. New York: Dorset Press, 1992.

Erasmus, Desiderius. *The Praise of Folly*. Trans. by John Wilson. Ann Arbor: University of Michigan Press, 1958.

Rummel, Erika, ed. *The Erasmus Reader*. Toronto: University of Toronto Press, 1990.

Wilcox, Donald J. *In Search of God and Self: Renaissance and Reformation Thought*. Boston: Houghton Mifflin Company, 1975.

PRINCIPLES OF POLITICAL ECONOMY

Author: John Stuart Mill
Original date and place of publication: 1848, England
Literary form: Economics treatise

SUMMARY

The British philosopher, economist and social reformer John Stuart Mill was one of the leading intellectual figures of the 19th century. His treatise on toleration, *On Liberty*, published in 1859, celebrated the primacy of the individual and opposed repression of individual rights by church, state or the "tyranny of the majority." "Whatever crushes individuality is despotism, by whatever name it may be called, and whether it professes to be enforcing the will of God or the injunctions of men," he wrote.

In his philosophical writings, such as *System of Logic*, published in 1843, which became the standard philosophical text of the time, he maintained that knowledge was derived from experience and attacked the theory that knowledge and behavior were governed by innate ideas. His most influential contribution in philosophy was his advocacy of the moral theory of utilitarianism, espoused by his father, the philosopher James Mill, and by the political theorist Jeremy Bentham.

Utilitarianism assessed the value of human actions by evaluating their consequences in experience and the general welfare of those affected by them. The aim of the utilitarians was to test institutions in the light of reason and common sense in order to determine whether they contributed to the happiness of the greater number of people. Believing that concern for human emotions was lacking in their system, John Stuart Mill sought to temper the utilitarian doctrines of his father and Bentham with humanitarianism.

In his essay *Utilitarianism*, published in 1861, he introduced into the utilitarian calculus a principle that suggested weighing not only the quantity, but also the quality of pleasure in determining the rightness of an action. Mill's utilitarianism suggested that the right thing to do in a given situation was the action that brought about "the best state of affairs."

In *Principles of Political Economy*, an earlier work published in 1848, Mill applied his views to the study of economics, using economic theory to explain how men could affect the moral progress of society. Mill built on the classic economic theories of his predecessors Adam Smith and David Ricardo. Smith, in his 1776 *Wealth of Nations*, identified self-interest as the basic economic force. Ricardo's "iron law of wages" asserted that wages tended to stabilize at the subsistence level. In addition to self-interest, Mill introduced habit and custom as economic motives and challenged the classical economic theory of the immutability of natural law by demonstrating that wages, rent and profit could be controlled by human intervention.

Mill asserted that the province of economic law was confined to production, rather than distribution. Though man cannot change the modes and conditions under which production must take place, society can decide to distribute what has been produced as it pleases. There is no correct form of distribution, and natural law does not determine how society should share what is produced. "The things once there," Mill wrote, "mankind, individually or collectively, can do with them as they please. They can place them at the disposal of whomsoever they please, and on whatever terms. . . ." The distribution of wealth depends on the laws and customs of society and the opinions and feelings of the ruling portion of the community. Mill argued further that if economic growth caused the population to increase and if, as economist Thomas Malthus argued, population would eventually outstrip the means of subsistence, perhaps economic growth should be relinquished in order to build a better society.

In place of the wage system, Mill advocated cooperative societies in which the employees would collectively own the capital and control the managers. While maintaining the right of workers to retain what they gained by their own efforts, he suggested heavy taxation of unearned rents and inheritances. Under this system, the formation of new capital would cease, thereby preventing growth of industry and maintaining population at a more stationary level. In this static, no-growth society, he hoped that the general leisure would increase, create enhanced opportunities for educational pursuits and allow for the solution of social problems. Because a static population would require less social care, there would be a reduced need for government interference and a decreased danger that a bureaucracy would make political decisions.

CENSORSHIP HISTORY

Heated criticism of Mill's theories came from both conservatives and liberals who believed that there were much narrower limits than Mill recognized on the freedom of societies to structure their distribution. Nevertheless, *Principles of Political Economy* was an enormous success, published in seven editions during Mill's lifetime. Mill also had it printed at his own expense in an inexpensive compact edition that would be affordable to the working class. This edition sold out in five separate editions. Mill was regarded as the great economist of his day.

The Catholic church, however, generally opposed Mill's secular philosophical perspective; his utilitarianism, which denied the existence of any divinely implanted moral consciousness or norms; his empiricism, which posited experience rather than religious authority as the source of all knowledge; and his defense of the rights of the individual as being more important than the institutions of church or state.

Jeremy Bentham's utilitarian works, including AN INTRODUCTION TO THE PRINCIPLES OF MORALS AND LEGISLATION, had already been condemned by the church earlier in the century. In 1856, the Vatican placed on the Index of Forbidden Books the major works published by Mill up to that time, *System of Logic* and *Principles of Political Economy*. The prohibition of Mill's writing, as well as works such as Auguste Comte's THE COURSE OF POSITIVE PHILOSOPHY, which had influenced Mill, reflected the church's battle against the trends in philosophy and political and economic theory that reflected the modern scientific thinking of the 19th century. In 1864, Pope Pius IX issued an encyclical, *Quanta cura*, accompanied by a "Syllabus of Errors," listing erroneous modernist statements and condemning toleration and "progress, liberalism and civilization as lately introduced." The advanced thinkers of the time, according to the pope, were "evil men, who . . . endeavored by their fallacious opinions and most wicked writings to subvert the foundations of Religion and of Civil Society, to remove from our mind all virtue and justice, to deprave the hearts and minds of all." Six years later at the First Vatican Council, the church confirmed the papal denunciations of modernity and liberalism by defining papal infallibility as a doctrine.

However, the Catholic church's instructions on appropriate reading material for Catholics had little influence in England, a predominantly Protestant country. The condemnation of Mill's work by the Vatican had no discernible impact on Mill's standing as a philosopher and social theorist or on the popularity of his writings. Despite the fact that Mill's economic theories had long since been superseded, his works remained on the Index of Forbidden Books until 1966, when the Index was abolished after the reforms of the Second Vatican Council.

FURTHER READINGS

Christie-Murray, David. *A History of Heresy*. Oxford: Oxford University Press, 1976.

Heilbroner, Robert. *The Worldly Philosophers: The Lives, Times and Ideas of the Great Economic Thinkers*. New York: Simon & Schuster, 1986.

Mill, John Stuart. *Essential Works of John Stuart Mill*. Ed. and intro. by Max Lerner. New York: Bantam Books, 1971.

Scott-Kakures, Dion, Susan Castegnetto, Hugh Benson, William Taschek and Paul Hurley. *History of Philosophy*. New York: HarperCollins, 1993.

Van Hollthoon, F. L. *The Road to Utopia: A Study of John Stuart Mill's Social Thought*. Assem, Netherlands: Van Gorcum & Company, 1971.

THE PROVINCIAL LETTERS

Author: Blaise Pascal
Original date and place of publication: 1656–57, France
Literary form: Satire

SUMMARY

The French scientist, mathematician and religious philosopher Blaise Pascal was a convert to Jansenism, a reform movement within the Catholic church. Following the ideas of Cornelius Jansenius, Catholic bishop of Flanders, and of the Abbé de Saint-Cyran of France, Jansenism advocated a return to greater personal holiness and strictness in morals, stressing the corruption of human nature, the weakness of the will and the need for divine grace to convert the soul to God.

Reacting against the pessimism and dour piety of Calvinism, the prevailing form of Protestantism in France, the influential Jesuit order promoted an opposing doctrine known as Molinism. Rather than stressing human corruption and dependence on divine grace, the Jesuits held that free will and good works played the major role in effecting human salvation. Jansenism, seen as reflecting Protestant beliefs, was regarded by the church as heresy.

In 1653, Pope Innocent X declared that five propositions found in Jansenius's *Augustinius*, a commentary on the works of Saint Augustine, published posthumously in 1640, were heretical in that they emphasized predestination of salvation for the elect. Though Jansenius was loyal to the Catholic church and rejected the Calvinist doctrine of justification by faith alone, he emphasized personal religious experience and the direct contact of man with God in sudden conversion.

Jansenius's disciple, Antoine Arnauld, based at the Jansenist religious community at Port-Royal, near Paris, denied that the condemned propositions were found in Jansenius's work. He admitted the pope's right to pronounce on questions of faith, but claimed that the pope was not infallible in factual matters. Accused of Calvinism, Arnauld was condemned by the theologians of the Sorbonne, and the Jesuits moved to expel him from the university.

At the request of Jansenists, Pascal came to Arnauld's defense, writing a series of *Provincial Letters*, published individually over an 18-month period during 1656 and 1657. Using a pseudonym, Pascal assumed the character of a puzzled bystander explaining in letters to a friend the course of events at the Sorbonne.

"Sir, How wrong we were!" he wrote in his first letter. "I only had my eyes opened yesterday. Until then I thought that the arguments in the Sorbonne were about something of real importance and fraught with the gravest consequences for religion. So many meetings of a body as famous as the Faculty of Paris, at which so much has occurred that is extraordinary and unprecedented, raise expectations so high that it seems incredible that the subject should be anything but extraordinary."

Using the techniques of modern journalism, Pascal interviewed the various parties to the dispute to clarify the theological issues at stake in the debate. Quoting from Jesuit statements, he trapped the experts into contradictory statements on questions of fact and faith, demonstrating the absurdity of the Jesuit position. The 11th through 18th letters were addressed directly to Jesuit fathers. Arnauld had already been expelled from the Sorbonne, and Pascal's tone became more indignant and impassioned as he moved from a defense of Arnauld to a stinging attack on what he considered to be Jesuit hairsplitting, hypocrisy and dishonesty. "I have told you before, and I tell you again, violence and truth have no power over each other," he wrote. "You strain every effort to make people believe that your disputes are over points of faith, and it has never been more evident that your whole dispute is simply over a point of fact."

Like Arnauld, Pascal questioned the authority of the pope to decide questions of fact, asserting that his infallibility extended only to supernatural matters. "It was in vain, too," he wrote, addressing his Jesuit correspondents, "that you obtained from Rome the decree against Galileo, which condemned his opinion regarding the earth's movement. It will take more than that to prove that it keeps still, and if there were consistent observations proving that it is the earth that goes round, all the men in the world put together could not stop it from turning, or themselves turning with it."

CENSORSHIP HISTORY

The success of *The Provincial Letters* was immediate. The work was distributed clandestinely in major cities of France, translated into Latin and English and circulated throughout Europe. The clarity and wit of Pascal's style and his use of French, rather than Latin, made the theological debates accessible to a wider audience, removing them from the narrow circle of clerics.

The anti-Jesuit flavor of the *Letters* aroused a storm of criticism. Pascal was attacked for not having written in Latin, the language of theological discussion; for having used the satirical dialogue form, deemed inappropriate for religious discussion; and for having made a mockery of Jesuit theological disputes.

On February 9, 1657, the first 16 *Letters* were condemned by the Parlement of Aix. Jesuit influence at court resulted in an order by Louis XIV that the *Letters* be torn up and burned at the hands of the high executioner, "fulfillment of which is to be certified to His Majesty within the week; and that meanwhile all printers, booksellers, vendors and others, of whatever rank or station, are explicitly prohibited from printing, selling, and distributing, and even from having in their possession the said book under pain of public (exemplary) punishment."

Publication of new *Letters* ended in March 1657, as it had become too dangerous for Pascal to continue. The suppression of *The Provincial Letters*, however, did not impede the work's growing popularity. Despite police raids and arrests of publishers, the book was reprinted in France in numerous editions. Pascal stayed out of public sight, moving from place to place to avoid arrest. Though among the Jansenists at Port-Royal it was an open secret that Pascal was the author, Pascal's anonymity was officially retained until after his death. On September 6, 1657, *The Provincial Letters* was placed on the Index of Forbidden Books in Rome.

When Pascal was asked later in his life if he regretted having written *The Provincial Letters*, he replied that "far from regretting it, if I had to write them at the present time I would make them even stronger. . . . People ask why I used a pleasant, ironic and amusing style. I reply that, if I had written in a dogmatic style, only scholars would have read it, and they did not need to, because they knew as much about it as I. . . ."

The popularity and influence of *The Provincial Letters* was enduring, both as a work of polemical relevance and, later, when the religious controversies of the 17th century had long been forgotten, as a masterpiece of French classicism. *The Provincial Letters* was reprinted repeatedly in France in the first half of the 18th century as anti-Jesuit propaganda and was cited as prime evidence in the trial of Jesuits in parlement that ended with their expulsion from France in 1762. Later in the century the *Letters* became a favorite work of the writers of the Enlightenment. Both Montesquieu's PERSIAN LETTERS and Voltaire's LETTERS CONCERNING THE ENGLISH NATION were indebted to Pascal. The introduction by Voltaire, the scourge of Catholicism, to the 1776 edition of *Pensées*, Pascal's book of thoughts in defense of Christian belief, not previously regarded by the church as dangerous to the faith, caused it also to be placed on the Index in 1789. Both *The Provincial Letters* and the 1776 edition of *Pensées* remained on the Index until the 20th century.

FURTHER READINGS

Pascal, Blaise. *The Provincial Letters*. Ed. and intro. by J. Krailsheimer. Middlesex, England: Penguin Books, 1967.

Rex, Walter. *Pascal's Provincial Letters: An Introduction*. New York: Holmes & Meier Publishers, 1977.

THE RAPE OF SITA

Author: Lindsey Collen
Original date and place of publication: 1993, Mauritius; 1995, United States
Original publisher: Ledikasyon pu Travayer, Mauritius; Heinemann Educational Books, United States
Literary form: Novel

SUMMARY

The Rape of Sita, a complex and lyrical novel by the South African-born feminist writer Lindsey Collen, who lives in Mauritius, won the 1994 Commonwealth Writers Prize for the best novel from Africa. Sita, the novel's protagonist, is a political activist, trade unionist, feminist and champion of the oppressed in Mauritius. Her namesake, the goddess Sita, a model of virtue, was abducted and rescued in the Sanskrit epic, the Ramayana. The story of the contemporary Sita, told by the narrator Iqbal the Umpire, a male friend of Sita's, echoes ancient myths, folk tales and religious prophecies. Yet Sita must unearth her own past, buried not in myth and legend, but in the recesses of her memory.

On April 30, 1982, while on an overnight visit to the French colony of Reunion, in transit between Mauritius and the Seychelles, Sita loses 12 hours, time that she cannot account for. As she plumbs her memory for clues to what happened on that date—more than eight years previous—she bumps into a heavy, dense presence, like the big hole in the universe. It is anger, rage and fury. "Closely knotted into that anger was imprisonment. The hands that were hers and that wanted to perpetrate an act of murder, were trapped. She saw herself trapped, or was it locked up, or tied down physically, or handcuffed, or ball-and-chained, or paralyzed, or perhaps with a rock on her chest under water. Or being buried alive."

She has only a few clues to the mystery. First there were the missing hours. Then there was her reaction on a visit to Reunion with her husband in 1987, five years after the day of lost hours. She had become violently ill at the thought of phoning their acquaintances Rowan Tarquin, a probation officer, and his wife Noella, the only people she knows in Reunion.

On the eve of the declaration of war against Iraq in 1991, Sita is diving into her past and comes up with the buried memory of what happened to her in 1982. She had taken a plane to the Seychelles to go to a women's conference. She had called Tarquin asking if she could stay overnight on her way. At her arrival at the airport in Reunion, she learned that Tarquin and his wife had separated. Though alarmed by the news, she had gone to his apartment, where he raped her. Fearing she would never win a rape case, Sita returned home without reporting the crime. Not knowing what she should say, or how to say it, she never spoke of the rape. It was incised from her memory, yet a knot of murderous anger remained.

Why, the narrator asks, are women blamed for the violence perpetrated against them by men? "Should a woman never accept to go into the same house as a man is in on his own, even a man she knows? Should a woman never accept an invitation for a cup of tea? And what about the lift? . . . And what about the stairway? . . . Should a woman take a taxi? What should she do if she misses the last bus? . . . What time is trespass for woman? What place?"

The novel addresses not only Sita's rape, but also the social, religious and political conditions that support and condone violence against women. Sita's rape comes to symbolize all rapes, all violations, all colonizations. Addressing an open letter to "God, or god, Sir or Madam," Sita writes, "Why have you forsaken me?" God will not answer. "Wait for the silence, girls," Sita says. "For the gods if they ever spaketh in the past, hath stopped in the present."

CENSORSHIP HISTORY

On December 7, 1993, four days after *The Rape of Sita* was published in Mauritius, as its author Lindsey Collen describes, it was "plunged into a strange limbo." It was driven from circulation by Hindu fundamentalists, banned by the Mauritian government and temporarily withdrawn by the author and her publishers. "Hindu fundamentalists whipped up hysteria within 72 hours of publication," Collen wrote, "and I started to get anonymous rape and death threats." As no one had yet read the book, though 250 people had already ordered copies, Collen and her publisher withdrew it from bookstores to create an opportunity for an open debate and to decide whether or not to change the title.

Hindu fundamentalists regard the name of the Hindu deity Sita, revered as a prototype of noble womanhood and virtue, as sacred. The suggestion that she might be raped was considered blasphemous. Collen chose the name, which is common in Mauritius, to create a contrast between the story of the Hindu goddess, who was rescued by armies sent by the gods, and the contemporary Sita in the book, who is bereft of protection. Collen says she used the name of Sita to be "evocative, not provocative," and considers the book to be a defense "of women's rights and women's struggles."

A few hours after the book's withdrawal, but apparently unaware of it, Mauritian Prime Minister Aneerood Jugnauth halted the proceedings of Parliament to make a statement attacking the book and its author. Jugnauth said, "a glance at the back page of the book suffices to indicate that this publication may constitute an outrage against public and religious morality" under Section 206 of the Criminal Code. Jugnauth, referring to his own decree to ban Salman Rushdie's SATANIC VERSES, gave instructions for the police to act against Collen.

"The prime minister acted under pressure from what we call 'communal' lobbies," Collen wrote. "I am known not only as a writer, but also as a feminist. Feminists generally annoy fundamentalists of all ilk, and I have been no exception." Collen also believes the book was targeted because of her activism in the left-wing political party, Lalit.

The following day the police arrived with orders to confiscate all copies of the books and to take a statement from Collen as part of an official inquiry. Collen and her publisher informed the police that they had no legal right to confiscate the books, as the books were not exhibited for sale as required by the law. Collen refused to give a statement, kept the books and distributed them. The case was referred by the police to the director of public prosecutions.

Though *The Rape of Sita* was widely reviewed in the press in Mauritius and caused literary and social debate on a national scale, as of late 1996, the book remained banned. Those who support the banning have made it clear that they have not read the book. The book has been published in Great Britain and North America, and there was an outpouring of both international and local support in Mauritius for Collen.

FURTHER READINGS

Atwood, Margaret. *The Women's Review of Books* 12.10–11 (July 1995): 28.

Collen, Lindsey. "The Rape of Fiction." *Index on Censorship* 12.4–5 (September/October 1994): 210–212.

Moore, Celia. "Banned in Mauritius." *Ms.* (November/December 1995): 89.

Piggott, Jill. "Rage Deferred." *The Women's Review of Books* 12.10–11 (July 1995): 28.

THE RED AND THE BLACK

Author: Stendhal (Marie Henri Beyle)
Original date and place of publication: France, 1831
Literary form: Fiction

SUMMARY

Stendhal—the pseudonym of Marie Henri Beyle—was among the greatest French novelists of the 19th century. *The Red and the Black*, the story of Julien, an ambitious small-town youth who is executed for shooting his wealthy mistress, is regarded as one of the most boldly original masterworks of European fiction.

In *The Red and the Black*, Stendhal portrays a vivid tableau of French society and politics during the 1820s, the final years of the Restoration of the Bourbon monarchy. "Everywhere hypocrisy, or at least charlatanism, even among the most virtuous, even among the greatest," says Julien, echoing Stendhal's view of the times. The ultraroyalist partisans of absolute monarchy, found among the nobility, the wealthy and the clergy, had from 1815 waged a struggle to restore the ancien regime, the political state that existed before the 1789 revolution. Upon his accession to the throne in 1824, Charles X initiated antiliberal, pro-Catholic policies which, after 20 years of exile, returned the government and the army to the control of the nobility and passed measures increasing the power of the clergy. Hostility aroused by his policies culminated in the July Revolution of 1830, which ended the rule of the elder branch of the Bourbons.

The subject of the novel was also provided by a newspaper article about a young man, Antoine Berthet, who was guillotined in 1828 for an attempt to kill his former mistress, Madame Michoud, whose children he had tutored. The story of Julien Sorel closely parallels the case of Antoine Berthet. Verrières, the fictional town in which the story takes place, is much like the provincial city of Grenoble, where Berthet lived and where Stendhal spent his childhood.

Julien Sorel is an intelligent young man of peasant origins who is eager to attain a social position beyond his station in life. Under the rule of Napoleon, his most likely path to success would have been through the military. Now that the country is at peace under Bourbon rule, which has restored the political influence of the clergy, the road to advancement leads him to the Catholic church. Julien studies Latin and theology to prepare for entrance into a seminary and attains a position as a tutor for the children of Monsieur de Rênal, the wealthy mayor of Verrières.

He becomes involved in an affair with the mayor's wife, a relationship that for Julien is fueled by the thrill of conquering a woman of a higher social class, rather than by affection. When Rênal receives an anonymous letter exposing the affair, Julien leaves the household and enters the seminary at Besançon. The seminary proves, however, not to be a refuge from the provincial life of Verrières, which Julien sees as mired in greed and petty politics. The church's institution for training future leaders is a haven of hypocrisy and mediocrity, rife with political intrigue as sordid as that of the outside world. The motivation of the young seminarians is neither spiritual nor intellectual, but, rather, strictly economic.

"Almost all were the sons of peasants," Stendhal writes, "who preferred to gain their daily bread by repeating a few Latin words instead of swinging a pickax." Their religious vocation is based in the desire to have a good dinner and a warm suit of clothes in winter. "Learning counts for nothing here," Julien observes. "The church in France seems to have understood that books themselves are its real enemy. In the eyes of the church, inward submission is all. . . ."

Julien admires two of the priests at the seminary—the elderly Curé Chélan and the seminary's director, the devout Jansenist Abbé Pirard, who is finally ousted by the pro-Jesuit faction led by the vice principal. When Pirard resigns, he takes Julien with him to Paris, where he becomes private secretary to a nobleman, the Marquis de la Mole. Julien embarks on an affair with the marquis's daughter, Matilde, who is fascinated by Julien's daring and ambition. When Matilde becomes pregnant, her father reluctantly consents to her marriage to Julien and agrees to provide him with a private income and a title. But when the marquis makes inquiries about Julien in Verrières, he receives a denunciatory letter from Madame de Rênal, dictated by her confessor. After the marquis cancels the wedding plans, Julien shoots and wounds Madame de Rênal as she kneels at church attending Mass. He is immediately arrested.

Julien is put on trial but refuses to defend himself. Despite attempts by the local clergy to manipulate the jury on his behalf, he is convicted. As Julien awaits death by the guillotine, he searches for meaning, finding it only in his belated affection for Madame de Rênal. "My word, if I find the God of the Christians, it's all up with me," he thinks. "He's a despot and, as such, full of vengeful ideas; his Bible talks of nothing but frightful punishments. I never liked him; I never could believe that anyone sincerely loved him. He is merciless (and he recalled several scriptural passages). He will punish me in some abominable way . . . I have loved truth. . . . Where is it?"

CENSORSHIP HISTORY

Stendhal's literary reputation was slow to develop. His contemporaries found the detachment and psychological realism of his novels difficult to comprehend, as his work did not fit any of the literary stereotypes of the day. Some readers were scandalized by what was viewed as Stendhal's indifference to morality and his unapologetic and understanding portrayal of a character who was seen as an unscrupulous monster. "I have been ambitious, but I have no intention of blaming myself for that; I was acting in those days according to the code of the times," Julien explains from his prison cell.

Stendhal said that he wrote "for the happy few" and correctly predicted that he would not be appreciated until 50 years later. Indeed, only one edition of *The Red and the Black* was published during his lifetime. The complete absence of a religious worldview in his novels, his portrayal of the God of the Bible as a "petty despot" and his anticlericalism led the Catholic church to censor his writing. Stendhal's anticlericalism reflected the intellectual inheritance of the antireligious spirit of Voltaire. It also had its origins in his unhappy childhood education at the hands of Jesuit priests.

The church portrayed in *The Red and the Black* is torn between two factions—the Jesuits, the wily and worldly agents of international reaction and proponents of the ancien regime, and the austere Jansenists. Stendhal's bitterly critical attitude toward the Jesuits was common to many in France at the time. The Jesuits had been banished from the country in 1764, but continued to function in secret until 1814. Under the Bourbon regime their influence was restored. In *The Red and the Black*, Stendhal portrays the political manipulations of a powerful secret Jesuit society known as the Congregation (patterned after an organization of the time called the Knights of Faith), dedicated to advancing ultraroyalist views and the agenda of the Vatican to the detriment of France's sovereignty and the liberal agenda.

The Red and the Black and all of Stendhal's "love stories" were placed by the Vatican in 1864 on the Index of Forbidden Books and confirmed by the Index of Pope Leo XIII in 1897. They remained on the list through the last edition compiled in 1948 and in effect until 1966. In Russia, *The Red and the Black* was banned in 1850 by Czar Nicholas I, whose motto in a campaign to suppress liberal thought was "autocracy, orthodoxy, and nationality." In a similar campaign in Spain in 1939, the novel was purged from Spanish libraries by the dictatorship of Francisco Franco.

FURTHER READINGS

Brombert, Victor, ed. *Stendhal: A Collection of Critical Essays*. Englewood Cliffs, N.J.: Prentice-Hall, 1962.

Haight, Anne Lyon. *Banned Books: 387 BC to 1978 AD*. Updated and enlarged by Chandler B. Grannis. New York: R. R. Bowker, 1978.

Stendhal. *Red and Black: A Norton Critical Edition*. Trans. and ed. by Robert M. Adams. New York: W. W. Norton & Company, 1969.

Talbot, Emile J. *Stendhal Revisited*. New York: Twayne Publishers, 1993.

RELIGIO MEDICI

Author: Sir Thomas Browne
Original date and place of publication: 1643, England
Literary form: Religious commentary

SUMMARY

Religio Medici, "A Doctor's Faith," was written in 1635 by Thomas Browne, an Oxford-educated physician who practiced as a country doctor in Norwich, England. A confession of his religious faith and a collection of his opinions on a vast range of subjects generally connected to religion, it was not intended for publication, but was composed during his leisure time for his "private exercise and satisfaction." The manuscript had circulated among his friends for several years when a pirated edition was published without his knowledge or consent in 1642. Browne felt bound to issue a "full and intended copy" to correct errors in the unauthorized edition, and had an authorized edition published in 1643.

Browne's eclectic reflections on faith reveal a scientific, rational and skeptical thinker, but one whose temperament is essentially religious. He is unable to render his full intellectual allegiance to secularism. "For my Religion," Browne wrote, "though there be several Circumstances that might perswade the World I have none at all, (as the general scandal of my Profession, the natural course of my Studies, the general indifferency of my Behaviour and Discourse in matters of Religion, neither violently Defending one, nor with that common ardour and contention Opposing another;) yet, in despight thereof, I dare without usurpation assume the honourable Stile of a Christian."

In an informal and memorable prose style, commenting on vices and virtues, science, the Scriptures, the classics, miracles and common superstitions, Browne offered a carefully crafted balance between skepticism and belief. His firm allegiance to the Church of England, a church "whose every part so squares unto my Conscience," did not deter him from exercising his wide-ranging intellectual curiosity or tolerance of the beliefs of others.

In the famous opening sentences of the second part of *Religio Medici*, Browne told his readers "I am of a constitution so general that it consorts and sympathizeth with all things. . . . All places, all airs, make unto me one Countrey; I am in England every where, and under any Meridian." As an enlightened skeptic, Browne could not accept completely any dogma, including the dogma of skepticism. "Many things are true in Divinity, which are neither inducible by reason, nor confirmable by sense; and many things in Philosophy confirmable by sense, yet not inducible by reason."

Browne concluded *Religio Medici* with a prayer that succinctly expressed both his profession of faith and his appeal to reason: "Bless me in this life with but peace of my Conscience, command of my affections, the love of Thy self and my dearest friends, and I shall be happy enough to pity Caesar. . . . Dispose of me according to the wisdom of Thy pleasure; Thy will be done; though in my own undoing."

CENSORSHIP HISTORY

Soon after its authorized publication, *Religio Medici* became popular in England. When a Latin translation appeared in Paris and Leiden in 1644, its resounding success placed Browne among the intellectual elite of Europe. The book went through a dozen reprints during his lifetime. Browne was attacked, however, for his tolerance of "heretics and papists" in an age of bitter religious controversy and his serene exposition of a faith remote in temperament from the contending creeds of the day.

"I borrow not the rules of my Religion from Rome or Geneva, but the dictates of my own reason," Browne wrote. Though Browne professed to be free of heretical opinions, he insisted upon his right to his own views when no specific guidance was proffered by church or Scripture. He considered himself to be "of that Reformed new-cast Religion" that required "the careful and charitable hands of these times to restore it to its primitive Integrity."

The popularity of *Religio Medici* brought the book to the attention of the Vatican, which placed the Latin translation on the Index of Forbidden Books in 1645, where it remained listed through the Index's last edition published until 1966. As a skeptical, rationalist work, despite its deeply felt religious motivation, *Religio Medici* contradicted Roman Catholic doctrine. Further, because Browne professed allegiance to the Anglican church, which had broken with the Roman Catholic church in the 16th century, his ideas were not acceptable reading for Catholics.

Browne published several other books, notably *Pseudodoxia Epidemica*, known as *Vulgar Errors* (1646), and *Hydriotaphia: Urn Burial* (1658), a solemn reflection on death and immortality. He was knighted in 1671 by King Charles II. Browne is remembered today as an important figure in the literature of the baroque age.

FURTHER READINGS

Browne, Sir Thomas. *The Religio Medici and Other Writings of Sir Thomas Browne.* Intro. by C. H. Herford. New York: E. P. Dutton & Co., 1906.

Haight, Anne Lyon. *Banned Books: 387 BC to 1978 AD.* Updated and enlarged by Chandler B. Grannis. New York: R. R. Bowker, 1978.

RELIGION WITHIN THE LIMITS OF REASON ALONE

Author: Immanuel Kant
Original date and place of publication: 1793, Prussia
Literary form: Philosophical treatise

SUMMARY

The philosophical system of Immanuel Kant, one of the most important philosophers in Western culture, was designed to lay a firm foundation for the entire range of scientific, moral and aesthetic experience. In THE CRI-

TIQUE OF PURE REASON, published in 1781, Kant offered a radical new approach to fundamental issues of epistemology and metaphysics. Mediating between rationalist claims of knowledge of what lies beyond sense perception and the opposing philosophy of skepticism, which denied the possibility of any real knowledge, Kant defined the boundaries of valid thought.

Kant's philosophy of religion is principally contained in *Religion within the Limits of Reason Alone*. Kant asserts that the existence of God can neither be affirmed nor denied on theological grounds and that all proofs derived from pure reason are invalid. Religion is outside the province of reason, as the divine cannot be an object of thought and knowledge is limited to the world of phenomena.

Kant nevertheless supports the legitimacy of religious belief. Though the existence of God cannot be scientifically demonstrated, Kant's moral philosophy shows the necessity of God's existence. For Kant, religion resides "in the heart's disposition to fulfill all human duties as divine commands." Kant's conception of religion can be described as ethical theism. He argues that moral law requires that people should be rewarded in proportion to their virtue. Since this does not always occur, he infers that there must be another existence where they are rewarded. This leads him to the conclusion that there is an eternal life and a God.

For Kant, a valid religious belief can derive only from the implications of moral principles and the nature of the moral life. Morality, however, does not require the idea of a supreme being and "thus in no way needs religion for its own service . . . but in virtue of pure practical reason, it is sufficient unto itself." In contrast to religious systems that relate doing good to securing a reward, the basis of religion should be the doing of good for its own sake.

Kant divides all religions into those that are "*endeavors to win favor* (mere worship) and *moral religions*, i.e., religions of *good life-conduct*." In the first type, Kant declares, "man flatters himself by believing either that God can make him eternally happy (through remission of his sins) without his having *to become a better man*, or else, if this seems to him impossible, that God can certainly *make him a better man* without his having to do anything more than to *ask* for it. Yet since, in the eyes of a Being who sees all, to ask is no more than to *wish*, this would really involve doing nothing at all; for mere improvements to be achieved simply by a wish, every man would be good."

According to Kant, man's moral growth begins not in the improvement of his practices, but rather in the transformation of his cast of mind and in the grounding of character. Kant describes as a peculiar "delusion of religion" that man supposes that he can do anything, apart from the good actions of his life, to become acceptable to God. "Man *himself* must make or have made himself into whatever, in a moral sense, whether good or evil, he is or is to become. Either choice must be an effect of his free choice; for otherwise he could not be held responsible for it and could therefore be *morally* neither good nor evil."

CENSORSHIP HISTORY

As the Prussian state moved to prosecute the battle against the freethinkers of the 18th-century Enlightenment, censorship of printed matter was increased. A government edict allowed toleration of views divergent from Lutheranism "so long as each quietly fulfills his duties as a good citizen of the state, but keeps his particular opinion in every case to himself, and takes care not to propagate it or to convert others and cause them to err or falter in their faith."

Because Kant was a prominent author who enjoyed the confidence of the king, his earlier works of critical philosophy, such as *The Critique of Pure Reason*, not intended for the general reader, were spared censorship. In 1791, a proposal to prohibit Kant's literary activity was submitted to the king by the high ecclesiastical councillor, but was not acted upon.

In 1792, Kant's essay "On the Radical Evil in Human Nature," which was to become the first part of *Religion within the Limits of Reason Alone*, was approved by the government censor for appearance in the publication *Berlinische Monatsschrift*. But because it dealt with biblical matters, the continuation of Kant's treatise, "On the Struggle of the Good Principle with the Evil for Mastery over Mankind," was handed over for approval to a theological censor, who refused permission to publish.

Kant supplemented the two essays with two additional pieces and prepared a book, *Religion within the Limits of Reason Alone*, which he brought for approval to the theological faculty of the University of Königsberg, where he was a professor. The theologians at Königsberg regarded the book as being outside their purview to censor because it did not deal with biblical theology. Kant received, instead, an imprimatur from the philosophical faculty at the University of Jena and the book was published in 1793.

In October 1794, King Frederick William II (successor to Frederick the Great on the throne of Prussia), who was offended by the book, wrote to Kant accusing him of having "misused" his philosophy over a long period of time and of "the destruction and debasing of many principal and basic teachings of the Holy Scripture of Christianity." He warned Kant not to write or publish any similar works on religion, or "otherwise you can unfailingly expect, on continued recalcitrance, unpleasant consequences." *Religion within the Limits of Reason Alone* was banned by the Lutheran church in Prussia.

Kant wrote to the king in his own defense that his book was not directed toward the general public, but rather exclusively intended for discussion among scholars, and that, further, it could not have contained a "debasing of Christ and the Bible, for the reason that the sole theme was the evolution of pure rational religion, not the critique of historical forms of belief."

Though Kant refused to retract his opinions, he promised "thus to prevent even the least suspicion on this score . . . cheerfully to declare myself Your Royal Majesty's most faithful subject: that I will refrain entirely in the future from all public discourse concerning religion, natural or revealed, in lectures and in writing alike." Kant kept his promise to the king, but considered it binding only during the king's lifetime. After the king's death, in 1798 Kant published *The Conflict of the Faculties*, in which he discussed the relation between theology and the critical reason and made public his correspondence with the king about the censorship of *Religion within the Limits of Reason Alone*.

Kant's philosophy did not attract the attention of the Catholic church until 1827, when an Italian translation of *The Critique of Pure Reason* was published. Kant's contention that the existence of God can be neither confirmed nor denied through the use of reason caused the book to be placed on the Index of Forbidden Books, where it remained through the last edition in effect until 1966.

Religion within the Limits of Reason Alone, although it offered a more direct critique of institutionalized religion that conflicted with the church's doctrine, was never banned by the Vatican. It was, however, prohibited in the Soviet Union in 1928, along with all of Kant's writing, presumably because the metaphysical and transcendental themes of Kant's works were thought to conflict with Marxist-Leninist ideology. All of the works of "such disgraceful writers" as Kant and Goethe were also purged from the libraries of Spain under the Franco dictatorship in 1939.

FURTHER READINGS

Appelbaum, David. *The Vision of Kant*. Rockport, Mass.: Element Books, 1995.

Cassirer, Ernst. *Kant's Life and Thought*. Trans. by James Hader. Intro. by Stephan Korner. New Haven: Yale University Press, 1981.

Collinson, Diané. *Fifty Major Philosophers: A Reference Guide*. London: Routledge, 1988.

Copleston, Frederick. *A History of Philosophy*. Vol. 6, *Modern Philosophy: From the French Enlightenment to Kant*. New York: Doubleday, 1994.

Green, Jonathon. *The Encyclopedia of Censorship*. New York: Facts On File, 1990.

Kant, Immanuel. *The Philosophy of Kant: Immanuel Kant's Moral and Political Writings*. Ed. and intro. by Carl J. Friedrich. New York: Modern Library, 1993.

Popkin, Richard, and Avrum Stroll. *Philosophy Made Simple*. New York: Doubleday, 1993.

THE RIGHTS OF THE CHRISTIAN CHURCH ASSERTED

Author: Matthew Tindal
Original date and place of publication: 1706, England
Literary form: Religious treatise

SUMMARY

Matthew Tindal was one of the most prominent deists of the 18th century. A convert to Catholicism who returned to the Church of England, and a one-time law fellow at All Souls College, Oxford, Tindal sought to reconcile rationalism with religious belief. Deists held that the natural religion of reason, which sought evidence of God in his creation in the external world, was superior to any alternative form of truth and accessible to all people, regardless of their education and social standing. Biblical revelation was superfluous to natural religion.

In such works as John Toland's CHRISTIANITY NOT MYSTERIOUS (1696) and Tindal's best-known work, *Christianity as Old as the Creation* (1730), regarded as the "Bible" of deism, reason was held to be the only arbiter of religious truth. In *Christianity*, Tindal effectively expressed the deist position as a coherent theory.

While all deists subordinated revelation to reason, Tindal welcomed revelation as providing alternative popular proofs of doctrine. He viewed the gospel as a "Republication of the Religion of Nature." The teachings of Christianity and the discoveries of reason had to agree. He wrote in *Christianity*: "If Christianity is found contradictory to any thing the Light of Nature makes manifest, or should require of us to believe any thing of which we could form no Ideas, or none but contradictory ones, we should be forced so far to acknowledge is faulty and false." Only those parts of Christianity were true, he maintained, which honored God and served man.

The Rights of the Christian Church Asserted, an earlier work, published in 1706, first established Tindal's notoriety as a freethinker. In *Rights*, Tindal expressed uncompromising Erastian views of the subordination of church to state authority. Erastianism, which achieved its definitive expression in the 17th century in Thomas Hobbes's LEVIATHAN, held that civil authorities should control punitive measures and that all authority, including ecclesiastical authority, derived from the king and Parliament.

Government is based on agreement, founded on the consent of the parties governed, Tindal explained in *Rights*. If the church is a part of the organized community and the magistrate is responsible for everything affecting the public interest, his power must extend to the church and those who serve it. "There's no branch of spiritual jurisdiction which is not vested in him [the king] and . . . all the jurisdiction which the archbishop, bishops, or any other inferior ecclesiastical judges have, is derived from him," Tindal wrote. The church has no independent jurisdiction and the clergy cannot claim any rights that exempt it from state control.

"The clergy's pretending to be an independent power has been the occasion of infinite mischief to the Christian world," Tindal declared, "as it is utterly inconsistent with the happiness of human society." Those who try to extend priestly rights are binding the church in "ecclesiastical tyranny." Persecution for disagreement on questions of belief cannot be allowed.

CENSORSHIP HISTORY

In 1707, the grand jury of Middlesex, England, made a presentment against Tindal, his printer and his bookseller, characterizing *The Rights of the Christian Church Asserted* and its Erastian views as a blasphemous attack on the established church and a public nuisance. The book was proscribed by Parliament and burned by the public hangman in 1710. In response to the grand jury presentment, in 1708 Tindal published two important defenses of *Rights*, in which he proclaimed the necessity of press freedom, elevating it to the status of a natural right. "There is no freedom either in civil or ecclesiastical [affairs], but where the liberty of the press is maintain'd," he wrote. Everyone has a right to hear views "on all sides of every subject, including civil and governmental matters, even if antiministerial." Tindal's defenses of *Rights* were also banned and burned.

FURTHER READINGS

Burne, Peter. *Natural Religion and the Nature of Religion: The Legacy of Deism*. London: Routledge, 1991.

Cragg, G. R. *Reason and Authority in the Eighteenth Century*. Cambridge: Cambridge University Press, 1964.

Gay, Peter. *The Enlightenment: An Interpretation. The Rise of Modern Paganism*. New York: W. W. Norton & Company, 1995.

Levy, Leonard W. *Blasphemy: Verbal Offense Against the Sacred, from Moses to Salman Rushdie*. New York: Alfred A. Knopf, 1993.

Sullivan, Robert E. *John Toland and the Deist Controversy: A Study in Adaptations*. Cambridge, Mass.: Harvard University Press, 1982.

THE SANDY FOUNDATION SHAKEN

Author: William Penn
Original date and place of publication: 1668, England
Literary form: Religious text

SUMMARY

Among the most controversial of the religious groups of the mid-17th century was the Society of Friends, or Quakers. In addition to the visible emotion they displayed in their services, they were also notorious for allowing equality between men and women, for their plain dress and abstinence, and for their pacifism.

William Penn was not born a Quaker, but from the time he heard a Quaker preacher at the age of 13, he began to question his upbringing in the

Church of England. He studied theology at Oxford and was expelled in 1662 for religious nonconformity. After attending a French seminary, he returned to England to become a lawyer. By late 1667, he had officially joined the Society of Friends and was thrown into jail for his beliefs. One year later, following a series of arguments with the Presbyterian theologians Thomas Danson and Thomas Vincent, Penn wrote *The Sandy Foundation Shaken* as a damning critique of Presbyterianism.

The Sandy Foundation Shaken refutes Presbyterian views of the Holy Trinity. In his introduction to his blast at three Presbyterian doctrines, Penn addresses "the Unprejudiced READER," asking that the reader consider how Presbyterianism has "adulterated from the Purity both of Scripture Record, and Primitive Example." Penn contends that Presbyterians have strayed from the true word of God. He goes on to describe how prominent Presbyterian theologians visited a Quaker meeting and mocked it by pretending to pray and by condemning the members of the congregation.

In the first section of his theological argument, Penn disputes the view that one God exists in the Father, Son and Holy Ghost. Penn believed that this notion of the Trinity was too abstract. To support his argument, he refers to more than a dozen New Testament references to one God, without any mention of a Trinity. Under the heading "Refuted from Right Reason," Penn extrapolates that "if each Person [of the Trinity] be God, and that God subsist in three persons, then each Person are three Persons or Gods, and from three, they will increase to nine, and so *ad infinitum*." Penn believed the Presbyterians' ideas absurd, and he minced no words in saying so.

The second argument of the book points to a contradiction at the heart of the moralistic temper of Penn's time. Penn explains that, according to Scripture, it is impossible to satisfy God if a person has committed a sin. First, Penn notes the passages where the Bible says that God will forgive sinners. Next, he points out passages where the Bible mentions that Christ died for all mankind's sins. Clearly, this creates a paradox; people are unable to erase their debt to God because Christ has already died, thus forgiving their sins. Penn outlines nine "Consequences Irreligious and Irrational" that stem from this paradox. In concluding this second section, Penn cautions readers that he does not believe in these principles. He still holds that people should repent for their sins, for instance. But the existence of these absurdities should show people that a more "primitive" form of worship and belief, such as the Quakers practiced, is the true road to salvation.

Penn asserts further that Presbyterian doctrine allows wicked people to be forgiven by merely attending Presbyterian church services, without necessarily altering their behavior and seeking forgiveness. Penn ends this third, complex section with a direct refutation of the Presbyterian theologian Theodore Vincent's lecture "For whatsoever is Born of God, Overcometh the World." Penn concludes his treatise by foreseeing the controversy his views will arouse. Fearing misunderstanding by rival denominations eager to harass and imprison Quakers, he reaffirms the Quakers' faith in one God, in the virgin birth of Jesus Christ and in the truth of Jesus' teachings.

CENSORSHIP HISTORY

William Penn's frequent asides to the reader, cautioning against misreading his ideas as anti-Christian, did nothing to prevent his imprisonment or his book's censorship. Penn's enemies misinterpreted his work as an attack on all Protestant beliefs. In December 1668, Penn and his printer John Darby were jailed in the Tower of London on charges of blasphemy. The stated reason for their imprisonment was their failure to get permission from London's archbishop to print the book. Yet most printers and authors customarily did not consult the archbishop. Many Londoners of the time thought the real reason for their incarceration was a plan to charge them with the crime of blasphemy, which had been made a capital offense only a few months previous to the publication of *The Sandy Foundation Shaken*.

From jail, Darby petitioned the authorities, protesting his innocence. He claimed that Penn's haphazardness in transmitting the manuscripts for the book prevented him from understanding how dangerous the ideas were. Penn had sent Darby his copy in small installments and occasionally improvised passages as he stood over Darby's shoulder. Darby persuaded the court that, given the hurried way he had to print it, he was unable to comprehend Penn's message, and he was set free. It became obvious that Penn was being held in prison for blasphemy.

The archbishop of London gave Penn an ultimatum on Christmas Eve, 1668: "Recant or stay in prison until you die." Penn responded with an appeal to the idea of freedom of conscience: "My prison shall be my grave before I will budge a jot, for I owe my conscience to no mortal man." Despite the attempts of the archbishop's negotiators to convince Penn to recant, a stalemate ensued.

While Penn lingered in prison, his father, the well-connected Admiral William Penn, mulled over what to do about his 24-year-old nonconformist son. The elder Penn was an Anglican, though not a follower of the era's detailed theological disputes. His military background led him to believe that some discipline would serve his son well, so at first he did not use his connections to intervene on the younger Penn's behalf. After five months, however, the elder Penn wrote the privy council asking for his son's release. In his letter he ascribed the younger Penn's noncomformity to "a great affliction," and reassured the authorities that he had not taught his son his blasphemous ideas.

At about the same time, Penn showed some signs of moderating his views. He continued his discussions with the archbishop's emissary, though Penn wanted to show the British king and other followers of his case that he was not about to recant. Penn wrote, "The Tower is the worst argument in the world to convince me. Whoever is in the wrong, those who use force in religion can never be in the right." Through months of imprisonment on vague charges, Penn held to his belief in liberty of conscience and freedom of religion.

Having taken his stand, Penn still wanted to get out of jail. He petitioned a court secretary to set him free on the grounds that he had never received a fair trial. In addition, he wrote a follow-up to *The Sandy Foundation Shaken*, titled *Innocency with Her Open Face*. He called this new pamphlet an "Apology for the Book entitled, *The Sandy Foundation Shaken*." A Penn biographer calls Penn's strategy "the first of a series of arrangements . . . whereby conscience accommodated itself to irresistible official pressure." Penn's plan allowed both sides to claim a victory.

Innocency with Her Open Face reaffirms his cautions to the readers of *The Sandy Foundation Shaken*. Penn tried to clear his name with Londoners who had been following the controversy. After all, *The Sandy Foundation Shaken* was intended primarily to show the righteousness of Quakerism, and only secondly to attack Presbyterianism. In *Innocency with Her Open Face*, he states that he had no quarrel with the existence of a Trinity; rather, he merely disputed the Presbyterians' notions of it. By extension, Penn was reaffirming the Anglican church's ideas and trying again to discredit the Presbyterians. Penn was released from prison in 1669, after nearly eight months locked in the Tower of London. He did not stay in England long enough to see if his campaign was successful, but traveled to Ireland for business and missionary work.

At first glance, William Penn's brush with censorship looks like an obscure matter of interdenominational squabbling among British Protestants. Yet Penn continued to hold beliefs in freedom of conscience and religious tolerance and made those ideas law in the colony he founded—Pennsylvania.

FURTHER READINGS

Dunn, Mary Maples, and Richard S. Dunn, eds. *The Papers of William Penn*. Vol. 1, *1644–1679*. Philadelphia: University of Pennsylvania Press, 1981.

Dunn, Richard S., and Mary Maples Dunn, eds. *The World of William Penn*. Philadelphia: University of Pennsylvania Press, 1986.

Endy, Melvin B., Jr. *William Penn and Early Quakerism*. Princeton: Princeton University Press, 1973.

Wildes, Harry Emerson. *William Penn*. New York: Macmillan Publishing Co. 1974.

THE SATANIC VERSES

Author: Salman Rushdie

Original date and place of publication: 1988, England; 1989, United States

Original publisher: Penguin Books, England; Viking Penguin, United States

Literary form: Fiction

SUMMARY

The Satanic Verses, by the Indian-born British author Salman Rushdie, holds a unique place in the history of literary censorship. In 1989 Iran's leader, Ayatollah Ruhollah Khomeini, condemned the book for blasphemy against Islam and issued an edict calling for its author's execution. The death threat drove Rushdie into hiding, and the furor over the novel escalated to become an unprecedented event of global dimensions.

Rushdie's complex and challenging novel is a surreal and riotously inventive mixture of realism and fantasy. In a cycle of three interconnected tales set in present-day London and Bombay, an Indian village and seventh-century Arabia, it explores themes of migration and dislocation, the nature of good and evil, doubt and loss of religious faith. "It is a migrant's-eye view of the world," Rushdie explained, commenting on the intentions of his novel. "It is written from the experience of uprooting, disjuncture and metamorphosis (slow or rapid, painful or pleasurable) that is the migrant condition, and from which, I believe, can be derived a metaphor for all humanity."

The novel opens at 29,000 feet in the air as two men fall toward the sea from a hijacked jumbo jet that has blown up over the English Channel. The two—both Indian actors—mysteriously survive the explosion and wash up on an English beach. Gibreel Farishta, formerly Ismail Najmuddin, is a legendary star of Indian movies; Saladin Chamcha, formerly Salahuddin Chamchawala, is an urbane Anglofile who makes a successful living in London doing voiceovers for television commercials.

As Rushdie describes his protagonists, "*The Satanic Verses* is the story of two painfully divided selves. In the case of one, Saladin Chamcha, the division is secular and societal; he is torn, to put it plainly, between Bombay and London, between East and West. For the other, Gibreel Farishta, the division is spiritual, a rift in the soul. He has lost his faith and is strung out between his immense need to believe and his new inability to do so. The novel is 'about' their quest for wholeness."

To their surprise and puzzlement, Gibreel and Saladin find after their fall from the sky that they have undergone a metamorphosis, acquiring characteristics alien to their own personalities. Gibreel, the womanizer, develops a halo, assuming the appearance of the Archangel Gibreel (Gabriel), while the mild and proper Saladin grows horns, hooves and a tail in the image of Satan. The fantastic adventures in England and India of these two walking symbols of good and evil form the central thread of the narrative.

The second tale, told in alternating chapters, evokes the historical origins of Islam in narratives dealing with the nature and consequences of revelation and belief. It takes place in the dreams of Gibreel Farishta, in which he becomes the archangel Gibreel, and in a film based on his imaginings in which he plays the role of the archangel. The dream-film sequences, which parallel the story of the prophet Muhammad in Mecca, tell the story of

Mahound (a derogatory medieval name for Muhammad). He is a businessman turned prophet of Jahilia, the city of sand, who receives divine revelation through the intercession of the angel Gibreel and founds a religion called Submission (the literal English translation of the Arabic word *Islam*).

In the third tale, also dreamed up by Farishta, a charismatic holy woman cloaked in butterflies leads the faithful of a Muslim village in India on a pilgrimage to Mecca. As they walk toward Mecca, they perish when the waters of the Arabian sea do not part for them as expected.

The parts of the novel recounting Gibreel's painful visions, set in Mahound's city of Jahilia, are the primary focus of the controversy about the book. They allude to a legendary episode in the Prophet's life in which Muhammad added verses to the Koran that elevated to angelic status three goddesses worshipped by the polytheistic citizens of Mecca. Later, Muhammad revoked these verses, realizing that they had been transmitted to him not by Allah but by Satan posing as the angel Gabriel.

In contrast to the version of the incident recounted in Islamic history, Gibreel in his dream says that he was forced to speak the verses by "the overwhelming need of the prophet Mahound," implying that Mahound, rather than Satan, put the false verses into Gibreel's mouth for opportunistic reasons. "From my mouth," Gibreel says, "both the statement and the repudiation, verses and converses, universes and reverses, the whole thing, and we all know how my mouth got worked."

In another dream passage alluding to an incident drawn from Islamic historical accounts, a scribe called Salman alters the text of the book dictated to him by Mahound. "Mahound did not notice the alterations," the scribe says, "so there I was, actually writing the Book, or re-writing anyway, polluting the word of God with my own profane language. But, good heavens, if my poor words could not be distinguished from the Revelation by God's own Messenger, then what did that mean?" Salman notices that the angel Gibreel's revelations to Mahound are particularly well timed, "so that when the faithful were disputing Mahound's views on any subject, from the possibility of space travel to the permanence of Hell, the angel would turn up with an answer, and he always supported Mahound."

Another provocative episode from Gibreel's dreams is a cinematic fantasy about a brothel in Jahilia called The Curtain (a translation of the Arabic word *hijab*, the Muslim women's veil), where business booms after 12 prostitutes assume the names and personalities of Mahound's 12 wives. A line of men awaiting their turns circles the innermost courtyard of the brothel, "rotating around its centrally positioned Fountain of Love much as pilgrims rotated for other reasons around the ancient Black Stone."

Hearing the news of the prostitutes' assumed identities, "the clandestine excitement of the city's males was intense; yet so afraid were they of discovery, both because they would surely lose their lives if Mahound or his lieutenants ever found out that they had been involved in such irreverences, and because of their sheer desire that the new service at The Curtain be maintained, that the secret was kept from the authorities."

Rushdie prefaces the story of the brothel with a statement that proved to be prescient in view of the events that engulfed his novel: "Where there is no belief, there is no blasphemy." Only because the men of Jahilia had accepted the tenets of their new faith could they find illicit pleasure in patronizing a brothel serviced by prostitutes impersonating the wives of the prophet.

As the novel ends, Saladin Chamcha has become reintegrated into Indian society. He has completed a process of renewal and regeneration in his embrace of love and death and his return to his roots in India. Gibreel Farishta, tormented by his epic dreams and visions of doubt and skepticism, has lost his faith and failed to replace it by earthly love. Unable to escape his inner demons, he is driven mad and commits suicide.

CENSORSHIP HISTORY

The Satanic Verses was published in the United Kingdom on September 26, 1988. Rushdie's eagerly awaited fourth novel received laudatory reviews in the British press. It was hailed as "a masterpiece," "truly original" and "an exhilarating . . . extraordinary contemporary novel . . . a roller coaster ride over a vast landscape of the imagination."

Even before its publication, however, the controversy about the novel had already begun. Syed Shahabuddin and Khurshid Alam Khan, two Muslim opposition members of India's Parliament, alerted to the book's content by articles in Indian publications, launched a campaign to have it banned.

"Civilization is nothing but voluntary acceptance of restraints," Shahabuddin wrote in defense of censorship. "You may hold whatever private opinions you like but you do not enjoy an absolute right to express them in public." Expressing a view that was echoed by many opponents of the book as the controversy continued, Shahabuddin admitted that he had not read *The Satanic Verses* and did not intend to. "I do not have to wade through a filthy drain to know what filth is," he declared.

India's government, fearing civil disorder among the country's Muslim population, was the first to censor the book. On October 5, 1988, only nine days after its publication in Britain, the importation of the British edition was prohibited under a ruling of the Indian Customs Act. Muslims in India contacted Islamic organizations in Britain, urging them to take up the protest campaign. Two London publications sponsored by the Saudi Arabian government prominently featured stories denouncing the novel. At his home in London, Rushdie began to receive death threats.

The U.K. Action Committee on Islamic Affairs released a statement demanding withdrawal and destruction of the book, an apology and payment of damages to an Islamic charity. "The work, thinly disguised as a piece of literature," the statement read, "not only greatly distorts Islamic history in general, but also portrays in the worst possible colours the very characters of the Prophet Ibrahim and the Prophet Mohamed (peace upon them). It also disfigures the characters of the Prophet's companions . . . and the Prophet's holy wives and describes the Islamic creed and rituals in the most foul language."

The British-based Union of Muslim Organizations called for Rushdie's prosecution under rarely enforced British laws prohibiting blasphemy against the doctrines of the Church of England. The British government declined to consider expansion of the laws to include transgressions against the Islamic faith. On November 11, Prime Minister Margaret Thatcher announced that "there are no grounds on which the government could consider banning the book." On November 21, the grand sheik of Egypt's Al-Azhar, the mosque and university that is considered the seat of Islamic authority, called on all Islamic organizations in Britain to join in taking legal steps to prevent the book's distribution.

In the United States, where the novel had not yet appeared, its publisher, Viking Penguin, received bomb threats and thousands of menacing letters. On November 24, 1988, *The Satanic Verses* was banned in South Africa, even though it had not yet been published there. A planned visit by Rushdie was cancelled when its sponsors feared that his safety could not be guaranteed. Within weeks, the book was also banned in several countries with predominantly Muslim populations: Pakistan, Saudi Arabia, Egypt, Somalia, Bangladesh, Sudan, Malaysia, Indonesia and Qatar.

That month in England, *The Satanic Verses* received the Whitbread literary prize for best novel. In December and again in January, Muslims in Bolton, near Manchester, and in Bradford, Yorkshire, held public book burnings. A large group of demonstrators marched in London to protest the book. The Islamic Defence Council in Britain presented a petition to Penguin Books, demanding that the publisher apologize to the world Muslim community, withdraw the book, pulp the remaining copies and refrain from printing future editions.

The petition listed as insulting to Muslims the fact that Abraham was referred to in the book as "the bastard"; that the Prophet Muhammad was given the archaic medieval name of Mahound, meaning devil or false prophet; that the text states that revelations the Prophet received were well timed to suit him when "the faithful were disputing"; that the Prophet's companions were described in derogatory terms and the namesakes of his wives were depicted as prostitutes; and that the Islamic holy city of Mecca was portrayed as Jahilia, meaning ignorance or darkness.

Penguin Books refused to comply with the petitioners' demands. On January 22, 1989, Rushdie published a statement in defense of his novel. *The Satanic Verses* is not an antireligious novel, he said. "It is, however, an attempt to write about migration, its stresses and transformations, from the point of view of migrants from the Indian subcontinent to Britain. This is for me, the saddest irony of all; that after working for five years to give voice and fictional flesh to the immigrant culture of which I am myself a member, I should see my book burned, largely unread, by the people it's about, people who might find some pleasure and much recognition in its pages."

Rushdie's repeated efforts throughout the controversy to clarify the intentions and meaning of his book had little impact on the fervent opposition to it. Few of those who protested against the book had read it and, for many, the very title of the novel, which seemed to imply that the Koranic verses were written by the devil, was sacrilegious and sufficient to condemn it.

It is never stated within Gibreel Farishta's dreams that Satan wrote the sacred book. However, the passages in which Gibreel claims to have received the verses directly from Mahound, rather than from God, imply that the book was written without divine intervention. Attributing the Koran to human composition is considered blasphemous in Muslim belief.

Rushdie explained that Gibreel's blasphemous visions were intended to dramatize the struggle between faith and doubt, rather than to insult the Muslim religion. "Gibreel's most painful dreams, the ones at the center of the controversy," Rushdie wrote, "depict the birth and growth of a religion something like Islam, in a magical city of sand named Jahilia (that is 'ignorance,' the name given by Arabs to the period before Islam). Almost all of the alleged 'insults and abuse' are taken from these dream sequences. The first thing to be said about these dreams is that they are *agonizingly painful to the dreamer*. They are a 'nocturnal retribution, a punishment' for his loss of faith. . . . The first purpose of these sequences is not to vilify or 'disprove' Islam, but to portray a soul in crisis, to show how the loss of God can destroy a man's life."

The tale of the brothel was frequently cited by the novel's would-be censors as particularly offensive to Muslims. Rushdie pointed to a distinction often ignored by his critics, that the prostitutes only take the names of the prophet's wives. The real wives are "living chastely in their harem." "The purpose of the 'brothel sequence,' then," Rushdie explained, "was not to 'insult and abuse' the Prophet's wives, but to dramatize certain ideas about morality; and sexuality, too, because what happens in the brothel . . . is that the men of 'Jahilia' are enabled to act out an ancient dream of power and possession. . . . That men should be so aroused by the great ladies' whorish counterfeits says something about *them*, not the great ladies, and about the extent to which sexual relations have to do with possession."

Rushdie's use of the name "Mahound," the Satanic figure of medieval Christian mystery plays, for the Muhammad-like character of the novel, was also noted as evidence of his invidious intentions. Rushdie described his choice of the name as an example of how his novel "tries in all sorts of ways to reoccupy negative images, to repossess pejorative language." "Even leaving aside the obvious fact that my Mahound is a dream-prophet and not the historical Muhammad," Rushdie wrote, "it may be noted that on page 93 of the novel there is this passage: 'Here he is neither Mahomet nor Moehammered;

has adopted, instead, the demon tag the farangis hung around his neck. To turn insults into strengths, whigs, tories, blacks all chose to wear with pride the names that were given in scorn. . . .' "

Rushdie's view that "there are no subjects that are off limits and that includes God, includes prophets" was clearly not shared by those who urged banning of the novel. "The use of fiction was a way of creating the sort of distance from actuality that I felt would prevent offence from being taken," Rushdie declared. "I was wrong."

On February 12, 1989, during violent demonstrations against the book in Islamabad, Pakistan, six people died and 100 were injured. The next day in Srinigar, India, rioting led to the death of another person and the injury of 60. On February 14, Iran's leader, the Ayatollah Khomeini, issued a *fatwa*, or religious edict, against the book.

Khomeini's edict stated: "I inform all zealous Muslims of the world that the author of the book entitled *The Satanic Verses*—which has been compiled, printed, and published in opposition to Islam, the Prophet, and the Qur'an—and all those involved in its publication who were aware of its contents, are sentenced to death. I call on all zealous Muslims to execute them quickly, wherever they find them, so that no one else will dare to insult the Islamic sanctities. God willing, whoever is killed on this path is a martyr. In addition, anyone who has access to the author of this book, but does not possess the power to execute him, should report him to the people so that he may be punished for his actions."

The 15 Khordad Foundation, an Iranian charity, offered a reward for Rushdie's murder: 1 million dollars was promised if the assassin were non-Iranian and 200 million rials (approximately $750,000) for an Iranian. The reward was later raised by the foundation to 2.5 million dollars. During the days following Khomeini's *fatwa*, several Middle East terrorist organizations sponsored by the Iranian government publicly declared their determination to execute Rushdie. Demonstrations were held outside the British embassy in Tehran, and all books published by Viking Penguin were banned from Iran.

On February 16, Rushdie went into hiding under protection of the British government. Two days later, he issued a public statement regretting that some Muslims might have been offended by his book. "As author of *The Satanic Verses*," he said, "I recognize that Muslims in many parts of the world are genuinely distressed by the publication of my novel. I profoundly regret the distress that the publication has occasioned to sincere followers of Islam. Living as we do in a world of many faiths, this experience has served to remind us that we must all be conscious of the sensibilities of others." Khomeini responded with a statement refusing the apology and confirming the death sentence. "Even if Salman Rushdie repents and becomes the most pious man of [our] time," he declared, "it is incumbent on every Muslim to employ everything he has, his life and his wealth, to send him to hell."

On February 22, *The Satanic Verses* was published in the United States. Hundreds of threats against booksellers prompted two major bookstore chains temporarily to remove the book from a third of the nation's bookstores. On February 28, two independently owned bookstores in Berkeley, California, were firebombed.

Violent demonstrations continued to occur in India, Pakistan and Bangladesh during the month after Khomeini's edict. On February 24, 12 people died during rioting in Bombay. Nonviolent protests against the book also took place in Sudan, Turkey, Malaysia, the Philippines, Hong Kong and Japan. On March 7, Britain broke off diplomatic relations with Iran. Later that month, two moderate Muslim religious leaders in Belgium who had publicly expressed opposition to the death sentence against Rushdie were shot dead in Brussels.

In mid-March, the Organization of the Islamic Conference, while it refused to endorse the death threat, voted to call on its 46 member governments to prohibit the book. Most countries with large Muslim populations banned the sale or importation of *The Satanic Verses*. The Revolutionary Government of Zanzibar, for example, threatened a sentence of three years in prison and a fine of $2,500 for possession of the book. In Malaysia, the penalty was set at three years in prison and a fine of $7,400. In Indonesia, possession of the book was punishable by a month in prison or a fine. Turkey was the only country with a predominantly Muslim population where it remained legal. Several countries with Muslim minorities, including Papua New Guinea, Thailand, Sri Lanka, Kenya, Tanzania, Liberia and Sierra Leone, also imposed bans.

In some cases, countries with negligible Muslim populations took steps to suppress the book. In Venezuela, owning or reading it was declared a crime under penalty of 15 months' imprisonment. In Japan, the sale of the English-language edition was banned under threat of fines. The governments of Bulgaria and Poland also restricted its distribution. Many countries banned the circulation of issues of magazines, such as *Time*, *Newsweek*, *Asiaweek* and *Far Eastern Economic Review*, that had published articles about the controversy.

Despite the bannings, the book was imported and circulated clandestinely in countries where it was forbidden, such as Kuwait, Senegal, Egypt, India and even Iran, where a few copies were smuggled in and passed from hand to hand. As a result of its notoriety, *The Satanic Verses* became a bestseller in Europe and the United States. By the end of 1989, more than 1.1 million copies of hardcover English-language editions had been sold.

On June 3, 1989, the Ayatollah Khomeini died. The edict against Rushdie, however, remained in force, reaffirmed by Iranian government officials. Acts of terrorism related to protests against the book continued to occur. During 1990, five bombings targeted booksellers in England. In July 1991, in separate incidents, Hitoshi Igarashi, the Japanese translator of *The*

Satanic Verses was stabbed to death and its Italian translator, Ettore Capriolo, was seriously wounded. In October 1993, William Nygaard, its Norwegian publisher, was shot and seriously injured. Rushdie has remained in hiding under the protection of Scotland Yard. Though his public appearances have increased in number and he has been able to travel outside Britain, he is still under around-the-clock protection by British government security services.

FURTHER READINGS

Appignanesi, Lisa, and Sara Maitland, eds. *The Rushdie File*. Syracuse, N.Y.: Syracuse University Press, 1990.

Barnes, Julian. "Staying Alive." *The New Yorker* (February 21, 1994): 99–105.

For Rushdie: Essays by Arab and Muslim Writers in Defense of Free Speech. New York: George Braziller, 1994.

Harrison, James. *Salman Rushdie*. New York: Twayne Publishers, 1992.

Levy, Leonard W. *Blasphemy: Verbal Offense Against the Sacred, from Moses to Salman Rushdie*. New York: Alfred A. Knopf, 1993.

Pipes, Daniel. *The Rushdie Affair: The Novel, the Ayatollah, and the West*. New York: Carol Publishing Group, 1990.

Rushdie, Salman. *Imaginary Homelands: Essays and Criticism 1981–1991*. New York: Penguin Books, 1991.

Ruthven, Malise. *A Satanic Affair: Salman Rushdie and the Wrath of Islam*. London: Hogarth Press, 1991.

Weatherby, W. J. *Salman Rushdie: Sentenced to Death*. New York: Carroll and Graf Publishers, 1990.

A SHORT DECLARATION OF THE MISTERY OF INIQUITY

Author: Thomas Helwys
Original date and place of publication: 1612, Holland
Literary form: Theological treatise

SUMMARY

Thomas Helwys was an English Separatist who, with John Murton, founded the first permanent Baptist church in England. *A Short Declaration of the Mistery of Iniquity*, published in Holland in 1612, was the first work printed in English to advocate religious liberty for all subjects and is an outstanding contribution to the literature of toleration.

Separatists were Christians who withdrew from the Church of England because they desired freedom from church and civil authority over their religious beliefs, control of congregations by their membership and changes in ritual. Because Helwys held a prominent position in the Separatist movement, he became a target for persecution. He and the other Separatists fled to

Amsterdam. His wife, who chose to remain, was arrested and for some time was imprisoned in York Castle.

In Holland, under the leadership of John Smyth, nonconformist clergyman and early believer in adult baptism, they formed in 1608 the first English Baptist congregation. This was the first of the churches known as the General Baptists, as its members held that the Atonement of Christ is not limited only to the elect but, rather, in general to all believers. The Baptists believed that baptism as administered by the Anglican church was unlawful because infant baptism was not authorized by the Scriptures. They maintained the right of any group of Christians to baptize and to ordain their own ministers and officers.

The earliest publication by Helwys in 1611 contained the first Confession of Faith of the Church of English Baptists. It consisted of 27 brief articles asserting the equality of every church member in knowledge of spiritual and religious matters. Next he published a small volume on Baptist opposition to Calvinist doctrines of particular election and redemption.

Helwys and others broke with Smyth over doctrinal disputes. About the time of John Smyth's death in 1612, Helwys became convinced that it was wrong to flee from persecution and that he and the other Baptists should have remained in England to proclaim their message. In *A Short Declaration of the Mistery of Iniquity*, published in 1612, he wrote of the Separatist leaders, "How much better had it been that they had given their lives for that truth they profess in their own Countries." Helwys, John Murton and a handful of followers returned to London to establish their church there.

Helwys sent King James I a copy of his book, personally inscribed. "The King is a mortal man and not God," he wrote in *A Short Declaration*, and "therefore hath no power over the immortal soules of his subjects to make lawes and ordinances for them to set spritual Lords over them." No state had lawful authority to force conscience or foster religion. Church and state should be separated, as the world has long suffered from a confusion of temporal and spiritual powers. Earthly crimes should be punished by earthly penalties and spiritual errors by spiritual penalties.

Helwys lamented the "general departing from the faith and an utter desolation of all true religion" that he had observed in the Roman Catholic church, the Church of England and other Christian denominations. He attacked those Separatists who had retained as valid the baptism of the Church of England. He also indicated a deep concern about the salvation of the king. Only the king could free the truth to make its way in his kingdom without persecution.

Every individual is responsible to God for his own salvation, Helwys asserted. Erroneous opinions on religion are of no concern to the state and its established church. "For man's religion to God, is betwixt God and themselves; the King shall not answer for it, neither may the King be judge betweene God and man. Let them be heretikes, Turcks, Jewes, or whatsoever it apperteynes not to the earthly power to punish them in the least measure."

Though Helwys detested Roman Catholicism, he extended his principles of religious liberty to Catholics and believed that they should be accorded the same tolerance he requested for himself. Helwys asked "Whether there be so unjust a thing and of so great cruel tyranny under the sun as to force men's conscience in their religion to God, seeing that if they err they must pay the price of their transgression with the loss of their souls?"

Helwys pleaded to the king, "Do not when a poor soul by violence is brought before you to speak his conscience in the profession of his religion to his God—do not first implore the oath *ex officio*. Oh, most wicked course! And if he will not yield to that then imprison him close. Oh, horrible severity! . . . Let these courses be far from you, for there is no show, of grace, religion nor humanity in these courses." The right to seek truth in one's own way is the most necessary and sacred of all rights.

CENSORSHIP HISTORY

Helwys tried to forestall the charge that he was promoting sedition against the state in *A Short Declaration* by pointing out to King James that he ascribed to the doctrine of nonresistance. "If the King or any in authority under him shall exercise their power against any, they are not to resist by any way or means, although it were in their power, but rather to keep their consciences to God. . . ."

Helwys referred to the passage in the Scriptures in which Jesus rebuked those who would have called down fire upon his opponents. "Christ will have no man's life touched for his cause. . . .The King's understanding heart will easily discern this," Helwys wrote. The king's heart, however, was not understanding. He was determined to enforce his Anglican preferences in religion, and the result of Helwys's approach to him was a term in Newgate Prison. It is recorded that Helwys's colleague, John Murton, was imprisoned in 1613 and it is assumed that Helwys was behind bars that year and possibly the next. By 1616 he was dead.

The cause of religious freedom made little headway during the reign of King James. But despite the suppression of the English Baptists, they won converts. At the close of King James's reign, the first Baptist church in London counted about 150 members, and several other Baptist churches had been established in southeastern England.

Helwys's book was notable and influential as the first work in England to advocate freedom for all religions. Neither Castellio's CONCERNING HERETICS (1554) nor Acontinius's *Satan's Stratagems* (1565), pathbreaking books on toleration that were published in Latin and translated into Dutch, had appeared in English. The advocates of civil and religious liberty at the time of the mid-17th-century Commonwealth found in Helwys's writing an important storehouse of arguments in favor of religious freedom.

FURTHER READINGS

Burgess, Walter H. *John Smith, Thomas Helwys and the First Baptist Church in England.* London: James Clarke & Co., 1911.

Jordan, W. K. *The Development of Religious Toleration in England.* Vol. 2. Gloucester, Mass.: Peter Smith, 1965.

Levy, Leonard W. *Blasphemy: Verbal Offense Against the Sacred, from Moses to Salman Rushdie.* New York: Alfred A. Knopf, 1993.

THE SHORTEST WAY WITH THE DISSENTERS

Author: Daniel Defoe
Original date and place of publication: England, 1702
Literary form: Parody

SUMMARY

The English novelist and journalist Daniel Defoe was one of the most prolific writers in the English language, with more than 500 works to his credit. His work includes newspaper articles, essays, pamphlets and novels, notably *Robinson Crusoe*, MOLL FLANDERS, *Journal of the Plague Year* and *Roxana*.

A turning point in Defoe's career came in 1702 with his publication of a notorious pamphlet, *The Shortest Way with the Dissenters: Or Proposals for the Establishment of the Church*. The pamphlet was a parody of the intolerant views of High Church extremists within the Tory party, who favored the restriction of the rights of Dissenters, or non-Anglicans, who were members of other Protestant sects. These Tories supported legislation that would, in effect, disqualify Dissenters like Defoe from holding political office by ending the practice of "occasional conformity." This practice allowed non-Anglicans to receive the sacraments occasionally at an Anglican church while preserving their allegiance to their own religions.

Henry Sacheverell, a High Church preacher, urged approval of the legislation in inflammatory sermons laced with biblical metaphors. In a parody written in pitch-perfect, though exaggerated, imitation of Sacheverell, Defoe put forth a diatribe favoring total and violent repression of Dissenters. Defoe intended the anonymous pamphlet, published in December 1702, to be read as the work of a Tory zealot.

"This is the time to pull up this heretical weed of sedition that has so long disturb'd the peace of our church and poisoned the good corn," the anonymous writer declared. The Church of England could best be served "by extirpating her implacable Enemies." He proposed the "shortest way" to vanquish the Dissenters: "If one severe law were made, and punctually executed, that whoever was found at a conventicle shou'd be banish'd the nation and the preacher be hang'd, we shou'd soon see an end of the tale; they wou'd all come to church, and one age wou'd make us one again."

For the sake of future generations, the writer urged his readers to imitate Moses, "a merciful meek man, and yet with what fury did he run thro' the camp, and cut the throats of three and thirty thousand of his dear Israelites, that were fallen into idolatry; what was the reason? t'was mercy to the rest, to make these be examples, to prevent the destruction of the whole army." The pamphlet concluded, "*Now let us Crucifie the Thieves* . . . let the Obstinate be rul'd with the Rod of Iron."

Once the pamphlet was praised by anti-Dissenters, Defoe intended to admit its authorship and expose them as the intolerant fanatics he believed they were. Recalling years later his motivation in publishing it, Defoe wrote that he intended to "speak in the first person of the party, and then thereby not only speak their language, but make them acknowledge it to be theirs, which they did so openly that [it] confounded all their attempts afterwards to deny it, and to call it a scandal thrown upon them by another."

CENSORSHIP HISTORY

Though *The Shortest Way with the Dissenters* must be counted as a successful parody, it has been described as a spectacular failure as a work of irony. Defoe was undone by his great talent for impersonation and mimicry that caused almost everyone who read the pamphlet to believe it was genuine. As Defoe explained three years after its publication, to the "High Church Men the piece in its outward figure, look'd so natural, and was as like a brat of their own begetting, that like two apples, they could not know them asunder."

When it was discovered that Defoe, a prominent Dissenter, was the pamphlet's author, the High Church Tories, many of whom undoubtedly agreed with the sentiments it expressed, condemned it as "a blasphemous attack on Mother Church." The government viewed Defoe's pamphlet as seditious libel because it implied that the government's policy of religious toleration was a sham.

On January 23, 1703, the earl of Nottingham, the secretary of state, issued a warrant for Defoe's arrest. Defoe was apprehended but escaped. After a reward of £50 was offered, he was betrayed by an informer and rearrested in May 1603. A complaint lodged against him in the House of Commons charged that the pamphlet was "full of false and scandalous Reflections upon this Parliament, and tending to promote sedition." The House ordered the burning of the pamphlet by the public hangman.

In July, Defoe was tried at Old Bailey for having written a "Seditious, pernicious, and Diabolical Libel" whose purpose was "to Disunite and set at variance the Protestant Subjects of . . . the Queen, and to alarm All her

Protestant Subjects Dissenting from the Church of England with the Fear of being deprived of the Exemption. . . ." Defoe pleaded guilty, admitting that he had written and caused *The Shortest Way* to be published, but asked for mercy because his intent was not seditious. He had written the work ironically and his aim was neither to stir up Dissenters nor to encourage others to persecute them.

In spite of the intercession of the Quaker William Penn, Defoe received no mercy, rather, he was meted an unusually severe punishment. He was sentenced in July 1703 to stand three times in the pillory, pay the large fine of 200 marks (about £135 pounds) and remain in Newgate Prison "during the Queen's pleasure," or indefinitely.

As part of his sentence he was ordered to find securities for his good behavior during the next seven years, which precluded publication of anything that could be construed as inflammatory. The harshness of Defoe's sentence has been explained by the personal resentment of the Old Bailey judges whom he had satirized in scathing terms in *Reformation of Manners*, a pamphlet published the previous year. Public exposure in the pillory was considered to be the most humiliating punishment in English law, and was potentially fatal. By the time Defoe stood in the pillory, however, he had become a hero for many Dissenters. Rather than pelting him with stones or garbage, the mob threw flowers.

Through the influence of the moderate Tory Robert Harley, an astute politician who was speaker of the House of Commons and had recently become a secretary of state, Defoe was released from Newgate in November 1703. He had spent more than six months behind bars. Harley had obtained a pardon for him and insured the payment of his fine and court costs. However, while Defoe had languished in prison, his brick-and-tile factory had failed and his debts had mounted. He was forced to declare bankruptcy.

Defoe's arrest and public humiliation is regarded by biographers as the most significant event of his life. The residue of bitterness and anger over the incident colored Defoe's attitudes and beliefs. He was never again able to free himself from debt. For the next 11 years Defoe served his benefactor Robert Harley secretly as a political spy and confidential agent, and he wrote in Harley's support for the rest of Harley's political career.

Despite the threat of further action against him if he should offend the government, while imprisoned at Newgate Defoe defiantly published *More Reformation*, a bitter satire lambasting two of his judges, and a poem, *A Hymn to the Pillory*. While he stood in the pillory, the poem was circulated on the streets below: "Let all Mankind be told for what: /Tell them t'was because he was too bold, /And told those Truths which shou'd not ha' been told." Defoe wrote in 1705 that the poem "was the Author's declaration, even when in the cruel hands of a merciless as well as unjust ministry, that the treatment he had from them was unjust, exorbitant, and consequently illegal."

FURTHER READINGS

Backscheider, Paula. *Daniel Defoe: His Life*. Baltimore: Johns Hopkins University Press, 1989.
Earle, Peter. *The World of Defoe*. New York: Atheneum, 1977.
Levy, Leonard W. *Blasphemy: Verbal Offense Against the Sacred, from Moses to Salman Rushdie*. New York: Alfred A. Knopf, 1993.
Moore, John Robert. *Defoe in the Pillory and Other Studies*. New York: Octagon Books, 1973.
Richetti, John J. *Daniel Defoe*. Boston: Twayne Publishers, 1987.
Sutherland, James. *Daniel Defoe: A Critical Study*. Cambridge, Mass.: Harvard University Press, 1971.

THE SOCIAL CONTRACT

Author: Jean-Jacques Rousseau
Original date and place of publication: 1762, Holland
Literary form: Political-philosophical treatise

SUMMARY

The Social Contract outlines the influential political theories of the Swiss-French philosopher Jean-Jacques Rousseau. One of the most quoted remarks in political philosophy is the opening sentence of its first chapter: "Man is born free and everywhere he is in chains." The chains Rousseau refers to are those of government. His concern is to explain why people should submit to the bondage of government. "What can render it legitimate?" he asks.

To Rousseau, government is a social contract that determines distribution of power along lines dictated by the general will and for the common good. It is law rather than anarchy that makes people free. Freedom consists of voluntary submission by the individual to the general will, which is what rational citizens would choose for the common good. The government exists only to carry out the general will of the people.

The act of association "produces a moral and collective body, composed of as many members as the assembly contains votes, and which receives from this same act its unity, its common identity, its life and its will." This public person is the republic, or body politic.

The contract between a ruler and the people is just in that it entails reciprocal rights and obligations. Because citizens in association constitute the sovereign ruler, the social contract works only if every individual gives up all rights. "That which man loses by the social contract is his natural liberty and an unlimited right to everything he attempts to get and succeeds in getting; that which he gains is civil liberty and the proprietorship of all he possesses."

However, might does not create right, and people are obliged to obey only legitimate powers. "The undertakings binding us to the social body are obligatory only because they are mutual and their nature is such that in fulfilling them we cannot work for others without working for ourselves." When the social compact is violated, people regain their original rights and natural liberty. "There is in the State no fundamental law that cannot be revoked, not including the social compact itself; for if all the citizens assembled of one accord to break the compact, one cannot doubt that it would be very legitimately broken." At the heart of Rousseau's political philosophy is a moral theory, which begins with the assumption that human beings are by nature good. By substituting justice for instinct in their conduct, people pass from the state of nature to the civil state.

Among the most controversial elements of *The Social Contract* was Rousseau's promotion of a "civil religion" which would support the idea of the common good and provide one basic faith for everyone. For citizens to live peacefully there can be only one source of authority; the church should be subordinate to the state. Because Christianity "preaches only servitude and dependence," it should not be a state religion. If there is no longer an exclusive national religion, tolerance can be granted to all religions that tolerate others, so long as their dogmas contain nothing contrary to the duties of citizenship.

Although Rousseau hoped that *The Social Contract* would be "a book for all times," he did not expect to reach a wide audience. In a letter to his printer in Holland, he admitted that it was "difficult material, fit for a few readers." Because it was published in Holland, censors were able to refuse its entry and impede its circulation in France. But at the time of the French Revolution, it became well known and exerted a profound influence. As one of Rousseau's contemporaries wrote in 1791, "Formerly it was the least read of Rousseau's works. Today all the citizens think about it and learn it by heart."

CENSORSHIP HISTORY

See ÉMILE.

FURTHER READINGS

Collinson, Diané. *Fifty Major Philosophers: A Reference Guide*. London: Routledge, 1988.

Green, Jonathon. *The Encyclopedia of Censorship*. New York: Facts On File, 1990.

Haight, Anne Lyon. *Banned Books: 387 BC to 1978 AD*. Updated and enlarged by Chandler B. Grannis. New York: R. R. Bowker, 1978.

Mason, John Hope. *The Indispensable Rousseau*. London: Quartet Books, 1979.

Reill, Peter Hanns, and Ellen Judy Wilson. *Encyclopedia of the Enlightenment*. New York: Facts On File, 1996.

Scott-Kakures, Dion, Susan Castegnetto, Hugh Benson, William Taschek and Paul Hurley. *History of Philosophy*. New York: HarperCollins, 1993.

THE SORROWS OF YOUNG WERTHER

Author: Johann Wolfgang von Goethe
Original date and place of publication: 1774, 1787, Germany
Literary form: Novel

SUMMARY

The Sorrows of Young Werther is the first novel of the great German poet, playwright and novelist Johann Wolfgang von Goethe. This epistolary romance about a hopeless love affair and a young man's suicide achieved immediate and lasting success and won fame for its 25-year-old author. First published in German in 1774 and translated into every major European language soon after, it was one of the literary sensations of the century. The novel's romantic sensibilities struck a chord among the youth of Europe, who admired it with a cult-like fervor.

The story is told in the form of letters sent by a young man named Werther to a friend, Wilhelm, over the 18 months between May 1771 and December 1772. Book One collects Werther's letters over an idyllic spring and summer in the rural hamlet of Wahlheim. He describes his pleasure at the natural beauties of the area, his peaceful existence in a secluded cottage surrounded by a garden and his delight in the simple folk he meets.

"I am experiencing the kind of happiness that God dispenses only to his saints," he writes on June 21. At a ball he has met a young woman named Charlotte (Lotte), the beautiful and charming daughter of a judge. Though he realizes that she is engaged to be married to Albert, who is away, Werther becomes deeply infatuated with Lotte, to the point of obsession. He visits her daily and begins to object to the time she spends with other acquaintances. At the end of July, Albert returns and the joyous idyll with Lotte must come to an end.

He spends a miserable six weeks in the couple's company in the throes of a hopeless and frustrating passion. In August he writes: "My full, warm enjoyment of all living things that used to overwhelm me with so much delight and transform the world around me into a paradise has been turned into unbearable torment. . . ." In early September he leaves the area to escape the tensions of the situation.

Book Two covers the remaining 13 months of Werther's life. He becomes a secretary to an ambassador whom he dislikes. Expressing his boredom at the social aspirations of the "horrible people" with whom he must associate, he chafes at the responsibilities of his position. When he hears the news that Lotte and Albert have married, he resigns his post to become companion to a prince at his country estate, but remains discontented. Returning to Wahlheim, he begins to see Lotte and Albert again. His letters become more depressed, speaking of feelings of emptiness and the wish that he might go to sleep and not wake up again.

After Werther's letter of December 6, 1772, an unnamed editor takes over to fill in the account of the last weeks in Werther's life, referring to letters and notes left behind. Werther had become more depressed, exhausted and anxious. Lotte suggested that he visit her less frequently. One night when Albert was away, Werther went to Lotte's house. After he seized her in a wild embrace she fled in fear and locked herself in her room. The next day he sent his servant to Albert to borrow a brace of pistols to take on a journey. After writing in a final letter to Lotte that "it has been given to only a few noble beings to shed their blood for those they love, and by their death to create a new life a hundred times better for their friends," Werther shot himself in the head. He died the next day without regaining consciousness. The workmen of the village carried his body to its resting place under the trees at Wahlheim and "no priest attended him."

Goethe once remarked on the autobiographical nature of much of his fiction, saying that all his works were "fragments of a great confession." *The Sorrows of Young Werther* was inspired by two incidents in Goethe's life. Werther's relationship with Lotte is based on Goethe's unhappy infatuation with Charlotte Buff, the fiancee of his friend G. C. Kestner. Suffering from depression over the unfulfilled relationship with Charlotte, Goethe was also deeply affected by the suicide of Karl Wilhelm Jerusalem, a friend from Wetzlar who was secretary to the Brunswick ambassador. Snubbed by aristocratic society and in love with the wife of a colleague, he shot himself.

Goethe wrote in his memoirs, *My Life: Poetry and Truth*, "Suddenly I heard of Jerusalem's death and hot upon the general rumors, an exact and involved description of the entire incident. In that moment, the plan of Werther was found, the whole thing crystallized, like water in a glass that is on the point of freezing and can be turned to ice immediately with the slightest motion." Goethe said that he breathed into the work all the passion that results when there is no difference between fact and fiction.

CENSORSHIP HISTORY

Upon its publication in 1774, *The Sorrows of Young Werther* was greeted with enthusiasm by readers throughout Europe. The 20th-century German writer Thomas Mann, whose novel *Lotte in Weimar* was based on the central situation of *The Sorrows of Young Werther*, wrote, "As for Werther, all the riches of [Goethe's] gift were apparent. . . . The extreme, nerve-shattering sensitivity of the little book . . . evoked a storm of applause which went beyond all bounds and fairly intoxicated the world." It was "the spark that fell into the powder keg causing the sudden expansion of forces that had been awaiting release."

By proclaiming the rights of emotion, the book expressed the creed of youth protesting against the rationalism and moralism of the older generation. Goethe became the spokesman for his generation. The novel was a grand expression of the spirit of the Age of Sentiment and the first great achievement of what would later be called confessional literature.

The knowledge that Goethe's story was based on real events, particularly the suicide of young Karl Wilhelm Jerusalem, added to the "Werther fever" that swept the continent and was to last for decades after the novel's publication. There were sequels, parodies, imitations, operas, plays, songs and poems based on the story. Ladies wore Eau de Werther cologne, jewelry and fans. Men sported Werther's blue dress jacket and yellow vest. Figures of Werther and Lotte were modeled in export porcelain in China. Within 12 years, 20 unauthorized editions were issued in Germany. In England, by the end of the century there were 26 separate editions of a translation from French. Napoleon told Goethe that he had read the novel seven times. Pilgrims came from all over Europe to visit Karl Wilhelm Jerusalem's grave, where they made speeches and left flowers. A 19th-century English travel book guided visitors to the spot.

Werther's suicide inspired some young men and women in Germany and France to take their own lives, with copies of Goethe's novel in their pockets. Though it is not clear whether the suicides would have occurred anyway in the absence of Goethe's novel, Goethe was assailed by critics who saw the novel as having a corrupting influence and encouraging a morbid sensibility. Clergy preached sermons against the book. The Leipzig theological faculty applied for a ban of the novel on the grounds that it recommended suicide. Within two days, the city council imposed the prohibition. In Denmark in 1776, a proposed translation was forbidden as not being in accordance with Lutheran doctrine, established by the crown as the orthodox faith of the nation.

Goethe wrote of the novel in his memoirs: "I had saved myself from a situation into which I had been driven through my own fault. . . . I felt like a man after absolute confession, happy and free again, with the rights to a new life. But just as I had felt relieved and lighthearted because I had succeeded in transforming reality into poetry, my friends were confusing themselves by believing that they had to turn poetry into reality, enact the novel and shoot themselves! What actually took place among a few, happened later *en masse*, and this little book that had done me so much good acquired the reputation of being extremely harmful!"

During the years 1783–87, Goethe revised the novel. In the definitive text of 1787 he added material intended to emphasize Werther's mental disturbance and dissuade readers from following Werther's example of suicide. The note to readers that precedes Book One reads "And you, good soul, who feel a compulsive longing such as his, draw consolation from his sorrows, and let this little book be your friend whenever through fate or through your own fault you can find no closer companion."

The Sorrows of Young Werther was censored again 163 years after its publication. In 1939, the government of Spanish dictator Francisco Franco ordered libraries purged of works by "such disgraceful writers as Goethe."

FURTHER READING

Friedenthal, Richard. *Goethe: His Life and Times*. New York: World Publishing Co., 1963.

Goethe, Johann Wolfgang von. *The Sorrows of Young Werther*. Trans. and intro. by Michael Hulse. London: Penguin Books, 1989.

———. *The Sorrows of Young Werther and Selected Writings*. Trans. by Catherine Hutter. Foreword by Hermann J. Weigand. New York: New American Library, 1962.

———. *The Sufferings of Young Werther*. Trans. and intro. by Bayard Quincy Morgan. New York: Frederick Ungar Publishing Co., 1957.

THE SPIRIT OF LAWS

Author: Charles-Louis de Secondat, baron de la Brède et de Montesquieu
Original date and place of publication: 1748, Switzerland
Literary form: Political treatise

SUMMARY

The Spirit of Laws is generally considered the greatest work of the French jurist and political philosopher Montesquieu. The fruit of more than 20 years of research and writing, *The Spirit of Laws* was dictated to secretaries after Montesquieu had become blind in his old age. It became a fundamental guide to political thinking in the 18th century. Montesquieu's political theories influenced moderate leaders in the early days of the French Revolution, as well as the framers of the United States Constitution, who adopted Montesquieu's recommendations on the separation of legislative, executive and judicial powers in government.

"Laws in their widest meaning are the necessary relations which derive from the nature of things," Montesquieu declared in the famous first sentence of *The Spirit of Laws*. The law cannot be considered as the result of the arbitrary will of one man or of a nation. All beings have their laws. All laws are relative and vary according to the type of government, whether democracy, monarchy or tyranny, and the material and geographical conditions, cultural context and historical experience of each society. The guiding spirit of each type of political system is different. In a democracy it is virtue; in an aristocracy, moderation; in a monarchy, honor; and under despotism, fear.

Attempts to discover laws must begin with the study of facts, the "nature of things," rather than in the realm of ideas or abstractions, Montesquieu believed. In *The Spirit of Laws* Montesquieu studied three types of government: republic, monarchy and despotism. A republic can be either a democracy, in which the body of the people possess supreme power, or an aristocracy, in which only a part of the people hold power. In a monarchy, a prince governs in accordance with fundamental laws, while under despotism, the ruler governs without law. Denouncing the abuses of the French monarchy, Montesquieu determined that the powers of government should be separated to guarantee freedom of the individual.

"Power should be a check to power," Montesquieu recommended. When the legislative and executive powers are united in the same person or the same body of magistrates, there can be no liberty. The same monarch or senate could enact tyrannical laws and execute them in a tyrannical manner. If the judiciary power is not separated from the legislative and executive, the life and liberty of subjects would be exposed to arbitrary control. If the judiciary is joined to the executive power, a judge might behave with violence and oppression. "A government may be so constituted, as no man shall be compelled to do things to which the law does not oblige him, nor forced to abstain from things which the law permits."

Montesquieu warned of the dangers of despotism and encouraged humanization of the law. The rules governing the structure and powers of government should be separated from the civil and criminal law applying to private citizens. If the government interferes with civil law, the person and property of citizens are endangered. Likewise, religious law should be kept entirely separate from politics and secular law. Religious belief cannot be compelled by force.

CENSORSHIP HISTORY

Fearing French censorship, Montesquieu had *The Spirit of Laws* published in Geneva in 1748. It was distributed in France with neither the consent nor the interference of the state censor. Though it was published anonymously, Montesquieu was known to be its author. By the end of 1749, at least 22 editions, some in translation, were in print. The volume was widely read and well received throughout Europe. Most of the world's constitutional governments are indebted to it.

Montesquieu's spirit of moderation and toleration, his rejection of absolutism, denunciation of the abuses of the French monarchial system and advocacy of the use of reason and the empirical method in his analysis of political theory, were seen as challenges to ecclesiastical authority. Though *The Spirit of Laws* was soon recognized as a work of major importance, both Jesuits and their enemies, the Jansenists, attacked it as expressing profound indifference to Christianity, and urged secular authorities to take action against the book.

The Jansenist *Ecclesiastical News* wrote, "The parenthesis that the author inserts to inform us that he is a Christian gives slight assurance of his Catholicism; the author would laugh at our simplicity if we should take him for what he is not." Jesuit critics accused Montesquieu of following the pernicious materialistic philosophy of Spinoza and Hobbes. By assuming laws in history as in natural science, he left no room for freedom of the will. Truth and justice are absolute and based on God-given universal principles, the Jesuits argued, rather than on diversities of climate, soil, custom or national character.

Many of Montesquieu's Enlightenment colleagues, such as Voltaire and Helvétius, on the other hand, attacked the book as being too conservative, moderate in its reforms and halfhearted in its concept of religious toleration.

Responding publicly to his critics, in 1750 Montesquieu published his *Defense of the Spirit of Laws*, in which he reaffirmed his Christianity and disclaimed atheism, materialism and determinism. Religious authorities in Paris and Rome, however, unconvinced by his defense, began investigations of the book. A government order forbade its distribution in France until Malesherbes, the director of the book trade, removed the prohibition in 1750.

From July 1750 until July 1754, the Sorbonne, the theological faculty of the University of Paris, formally considered its condemnation. Five different accusations were drawn up and made public but none were ratified. In 1751, the book, like his satirical novel THE PERSIAN LETTERS, was placed on the Catholic church's Index of Forbidden Books. *The Spirit of Laws* remained on the Index through its final edition, in effect until 1966.

The censorship of *The Spirit of Laws* served only to enhance Montesquieu's fame. In 1753 he was named director of the French Academy. When Montesquieu died in 1755, he was regarded internationally as one of the most important writers of the century. *The Spirit of Laws* continued to be praised as a masterpiece and as a seminal influence on political thinking that has lasted for more than two centuries.

FURTHER READINGS

Conroy, Jr., Peter V. *Montesquieu Revisited*. New York: Twayne Publishers, 1992.

Curtis, Michael. *The Great Political Theories*. Vol. 1. New York: Avon Books, 1981.

Durant, Will, and Ariel Durant. *The Age of Voltaire*. New York: Simon and Schuster, 1965.

Haight, Anne Lyon. *Banned Books: 387 BC to 1978 AD*. Updated and enlarged by Chandler B. Grannis. New York: R. R. Bowker, 1978.

Shklar, Judith N. *Montesquieu*. Oxford: Oxford University Press, 1987.

SPIRITS REBELLIOUS

Author: Khalil Gibran
Date and place of publication: 1908, United States (in Arabic); 1947, United States (in English)
Original U.S. publisher in English: The Philosophical Library
Literary form: Short stories

SUMMARY

Spirits Rebellious is a collection of short stories by the Lebanese-American writer and artist Khalil Gibran. Gibran is better known for *The Prophet*, a book of 28 poetic essays that has sold millions of copies worldwide since its publication in 1923. A Maronite Christian, Gibran was a leader of the Arab-American community and published several periodicals that influenced literary development in the Arab world. Gibran's short stories about oppressive social conditions in 19th-century Lebanon originally appeared in a New York Arab-language newspaper, *Al-Mohajer*.

In "Madame Rose Hanie," the narrator visits his friend Rashid Bey Namaana in Beirut, finding him depressed because the woman whom he had rescued from poverty and made wealthy, and to whom he was a sincere companion and faithful husband, has left him for another man. A few days later the author meets the woman, Madame Rose Hanie, living in a hovel surrounded by flowers and trees. She recounts her involvement with her husband, who married her when she was 18 and he 40 years old. The husband brought her to his magnificent home, where he exhibited her as a strange rarity. Though she was at first seduced by the material wealth she acquired through the marriage, she felt imprisoned in his mansion. She fell in love with a poor young intellectual. "I comprehended the secrets of her protest against the society which persecutes those who rebel against confining laws and customs," Gibran writes. "For the first time in my life I found the phantom of happiness standing between a man and a woman, cursed by religion and opposed by the law."

In the allegorical story "The Cry of the Graves," Gibran recalls the brutal and ruthless injustice of 19th-century Lebanon. The narrator observes as the malevolent emir sentences three prisoners to death. As the background of each criminal is revealed, the crimes are shown to be society's responsibility. A murderer sentenced to be decapitated turns out to be a man who had protected a woman's honor by killing a rapacious tax collector. A woman stoned to death for committing adultery is revealed to have been wrongly accused. A thief sentenced to hang was a poor man who had stolen two sacks of flour from a monastery's overflowing granaries to feed his starving family. "When a man kills another man, the people say he is a murderer," Gibran writes, "but when the Emir robs him of his life, the Emir is honorable." After the three are executed, they are secretly buried by their loved ones. Above their graves are placed a sheathed sword, flowers and a cross, symbols of man's salvation by courage, love and the words of the Christ.

"Khalil the Heretic" is set in a village in North Lebanon, where Sheik Abbas lives in luxury in a mansion amid the huts of the poor. The huts and the fields the poor peasants till belong to him. In reward for their toil, the farmers are compensated with only a small portion of the crop, which keeps them on the brink of starvation. Rachel, a widow, and her daughter find a youth lying outside in the cold, bring him to their hut and care for him. He has been expelled from the monastery because he could not rest easy in the comfortable rooms built with the money of poor farmers. "Since the beginning of the creation and up to our present time, certain clans, rich by inheritance, in cooperation with the clergy, had appointed themselves the administrators of the people. . . . The Clergyman erects his temple upon the graves and bones of the devoted worshippers," Gibran writes.

Sheik Abbas arrests the youth, who defends his rebellion against the monastery. "The monks deceived your ancestors and took all the fields and vineyards," he says. "Your souls are in the grip of the priests and your bodies are in the closing jaws of the rulers." Khalil, the youth, reminds the villagers of their usurped rights and the greed of their rulers and monks. The villagers stage a bloodless rebellion, creating a utopian community free of oppression.

A fourth short story, "The Bridal Couch," was included in the Arabic edition but did not appear in the 1947 English-language edition. It tells the story of a desperate bride who kills her lover and herself on the eve of a forced marriage to a man she does not love.

CENSORSHIP HISTORY

Spirits Rebellious is a bitter denunciation of political and religious injustice in 19th-century Lebanon suffering under oppressive Turkish rule. Gibran's impassioned defense of the right of women to marry freely, his attacks on corrupt clergy and incitement to resistance against unjust tyranny were met with fury by church and state officials in Lebanon. The book was termed poisonous and dangerous to the peace of the country. The story of Khalil the Heretic, in particular, offended the sultan and his emirs. Soon after its publication the book was publicly burned in the Beirut marketplace. The book was also suppressed by the Syrian government, although 200 copies were smuggled into the country.

Gibran was exiled from Lebanon and excommunicated from the Maronite church. He escaped harm because he was in Paris at the time of the book's publication. When he learned of the destruction of the book, he said merely that it was a good reason for the publication of a second edition. In 1908, the government rescinded his exile from Lebanon, and he was ultimately embraced by the Maronite church.

FURTHER READINGS

Gibran, Jean, and Kahlil Gibran. *Kahlil Gibran: His Life and Work*. New York: Interlink Books, 1981.

Gibran, Kahlil. *Spirits Rebellious*. Trans. by Anthony Rizcallah Ferris. New York: Philosophical Library, 1947.

THE STORY OF ZAHRA

Author: Hanan al-Shaykh
Original date and place of publication: 1980, Lebanon; 1994, United States
Original publisher: Dar al-Nahar, Lebanon; Anchor Books, United States
Literary form: Novel

SUMMARY

The Story of Zahra is a highly praised novel by Hanan al-Shaykh, a Lebanese writer who lives in London, about a young woman's struggle to find personal fulfillment in a society that undervalues and constricts her. Zahra, the novel's memorable protagonist, is a Shi'ite Muslim from a middle-class Muslim family in Beirut, Lebanon, in the late 1970s. She is haunted by harrowing childhood memories in which sex, fear, guilt and love are tangled together. From a young age, Zahra had accompanied her mother to secret assignations with a lover. Her tyrannical father, suspecting his wife's affair, had beat both Zahra and her mother.

When the reader meets Zahra, she has arrived in West Africa to stay with her uncle Hashem, a political exile. As she recounts the story of her ill-fated sojourn, the details of the life she fled in Beirut emerge. She had drifted into an unsatisfying affair with a manipulative married man, had two abortions, a surgical "repair" of her virginity and a nervous breakdown treated with electric shock therapy.

With emotional problems, plain looks and a face scarred by acne, Zahra is not a particularly good marriage prospect. Her parents, fearing she will be an old maid, pressure her to marry a friend of her brothers's. But she refuses, swearing to remain single forever. Deeply depressed, in a state of passive rebellion against the limitations of her existence, she escapes into sleep and silence.

Zahra's flight to Africa provides no solution to her alienation. Her uncle Hashem is lonely and stranded, almost forgotten by his political party. His correspondence with Zahra was the only link with his homeland, and her arrival breathes life into his fading sense of connection to his family and culture. His longings are expressed as a powerful attraction for Zahra. When he begins to make sexual advances, the feelings of disgust or fear that mark Zahra's relationships with all the men in her life are transferred to her uncle.

To escape, Zahra suddenly agrees to marry her uncle's friend Majed, a fellow Lebanese whom she barely knows. Eager to save the trouble of returning to Lebanon to find a wife, Majed welcomes this ready-made bride. "Here I was, married at last," he says, "the owner of a woman's body that I could make love to whenever I wished." Revolted by her husband, Zahra realizes her terrible mistake. "I wanted my body to be mine alone," she cries. "I wanted the place on which I stood and the air surrounding me to be mine and no one else's." She leaves her husband and returns to Beirut, now in the throes of civil war.

As rockets shriek and street battles rage, Zahra sleeps too much and overeats. She dreads ceasefires, since they deprive her of an excuse to stay in bed. In war-torn Beirut normalcy and sheer terror are coupled. Yet Zahra hopes the war will go on. The traditional order of things has been upset and a new kind of personal freedom has emerged.

After her parents flee to the south, Zahra embarks on an erotic adventure with a rooftop sniper whom she meets on the landing of an abandoned apartment building. In this semi-anonymous relationship she approaches her lover on her own terms, and feels sexual pleasure for the first time. When she becomes pregnant, her sniper lover offers to marry her. On her way home, however, she is shot down in the street, most likely at the hands of her lover.

CENSORSHIP HISTORY

More than 15 years after its publication, *The Story of Zahra* is still banned in Saudi Arabia and other Arab countries because of its explicit portrayal of a woman's sexuality and its unsparing indictment of social and political hypocrisy in a contemporary Arab society. Premarital and extramarital sex, masturbation, incest, illegal abortion, fake repair of virginity and domestic violence are the forbidden subjects that scandalized the religious authorities in Saudi Arabia and the conservative Gulf states where the novel was censored.

Hanan al-Shaykh's work is considered by Islamic authorities to be antireligious in its subversion of patriarchy and its rejection of social and religious strictures that limit women's rights. Despite its censorship, the book has received wide circulation in the Middle East. Critics in Egypt and Lebanon, as well as in the United States and Britain, have praised the book for its strength, sensitivity and lyrical realism, as well as for its penetrating portrayal of aspects of sexuality as they relate to social and political problems. Hanan al-Shaykh is recognized as a forerunner among young writers expanding the scope of the contemporary Arab novel.

FURTHER READING

Accad, Evelyne. "Rebellion, Maturity and the Social Context: Arab Women's Special Contribution to Literature." In *Arab Women: Old Boundaries, New Frontiers*. Ed. by Judith Tucker, 240–245. Bloomington: Indiana University Press, 1993.

A TALE OF A TUB

Author: Jonathan Swift
Original date and place of publication: 1704–10, England
Literary form: Satire

SUMMARY

A Tale of a Tub: Written for the Universal Improvement of Mankind is the first important work of the Anglo-Irish satirist Jonathan Swift, author of *GULLIVER'S TRAVELS*. Written about 1696 but not published until 1704, when it appeared anonymously, *A Tale of a Tub* is a buoyant and good-humored prose satire on "corruptions in religion and learning." Regarded as among the greatest satires in the English language, it burlesques the historical development of the major contemporary Christian denominations: the Roman Catholic, Lutheran and Anglican churches and the various Protestant Dissenters.

Though its main theme is the allegory satirizing the abuses of religion, Swift added to later editions several "Digressions" discussing critics, the prevailing dispute between the respective merits of ancient and modern learning and madness. In its fifth edition, published in 1710, the digressions represented two-thirds of the book.

Swift explains in the preface the meaning of his title. The custom of sailors upon encountering a whale is to throw out an empty tub to divert it from attacking the ship. "The wits of the present age being so very numerous and penetrating," he writes, "it seems the grandees of church and state begin to fall under horrible apprehensions lest these gentlemen during the intervals of a long peace should find leisure to pick holes in the weak sides of religion and government." Swift's satire is the tub intended to divert the wits of the age from "tossing and sporting with the commonwealth."

The allegory traces the story of a father who leaves a legacy to his three sons: Peter (Saint Peter), Martin (Martin Luther) and Jack (John Calvin). Each receives a new coat with directions that the coats are to be kept clean and unaltered. The father further commands that the brothers live together in one house as friends. The sons disobey the injunctions, adding decorations to their coats according the latest fashion. They fall in love with three ladies: the duchess of money, the madame of grand titles and the countess of pride. Finally Martin and Jack quarrel with the arrogant Peter and then with each other, and then separate.

A Tale of a Tub offers a critique of hypocrisy, fanaticism, superstition, priestly greed and corruption. Swift, who was a loyal Anglican clergyman, reserves his most scathing comments for the Roman Catholic church, its papal bulls and dispensations, the doctrine of transubstantiation, the use of holy water or "universal pickle," and its devotion to rites and relics. Catholics, like the Protestant Dissenters, were regarded as enemies of the established Anglican church and threats to the British government.

"In short Peter grew so scandalous that all the neighborhood began in plain words to say he was no better than a knave," Swift writes. "And his two brothers, long weary of his ill usage, resolved at last to leave him, but first they humbly desired a copy of their fathers' will, which had now lain by neglected time out of mind. Instead of granting this request he called them damn'd sons of whores, rogues, traytors, and the rest of the vile names he could muster up."

Swift characterizes Protestant Dissenters as excessively devoted to Holy Scriptures. "He had a way of working it into any shape he pleased, so that it served him for a night-cap when he went to bed and for an umbrella in rainy weather. He would lap a piece of it about a sore toe; or when he had fits, burn two inches under his nose. . . ."

Swift's own Anglican church is also treated irreverently. In the fifth edition he makes particular sport of the criticisms of William Wotton, scholar and notable Church of England clergyman whose pedantry he had satirized. In his digressions it becomes clear that Swift regarded his book as more than a satire of corruptions in religion. He is criticizing the abandonment of practical reality and common sense in favor of false learning—the conflict between "right reason" and blind allegiance to one's own private illusions.

"But when a man's faculty gets astride on his reason; when imagination is at cuffs with the senses, and common understanding, as well as common sense, is kicked out of doors; the first proselyte he makes is himself; and when that is once compassed, the difficulty is not so great in bringing over others; a strong delusion always operating from without as vigorously as from within."

CENSORSHIP HISTORY

The first edition of *A Tale of a Tub* was published in 1704—anonymously, as were most of Swift's writings. The book contained irreverent and bawdy passages to which Swift, a clergyman, "could not becomingly put his name," as one critic observed. It soon became known, however, that Swift was the author. The book was well received by the public, and two new editions were printed during its first year alone. William Wotton, an object of the book's satire, admitted that it was "greedily bought up and read," and another contemporary declared that it "has made as much noise, and is as full of wit, as any book perhaps that has come out these last hundred years."

However, *A Tale of a Tub* offended powerful Church of England prelates such as Wotton, a notable church rector and chaplain to the earl of Nottingham. He saw the book as sacrilegious and lewd, espousing a contemptible opinion of Christianity. "The rest of the book which does not relate to us is of so irreligious a nature, is so crude a banter upon all that is esteemed as sacred among all sects and religions among men," Wotton declared.

In his *Apology* defending the work, Swift wrote: "Why should any clergyman of our church be angry to see the follies of fanaticism and superstition exposed, tho' in the most ridiculous manner, since that is perhaps the most probable way to cure them or at least to hinder them from farther spreading?" Swift "solemnly protests he is entirely innocent" of "glancing at some tenets in religion." Swift insisted the *Tale* celebrated "the Church of England as the most perfect of all others in Discipline and Doctrine."

After the publication of the *Tale*, Swift said, he was suspected within his church of "the sin of wit." One of Swift's great disappointments was his failure to be appointed a bishop in England. He was awarded, instead, the deanship of Saint Patrick's cathedral in Dublin in 1713. The widely shared opinion of Queen Anne that *A Tale of a Tub* was blasphemous was reputedly instrumental in dashing his chances for further advancement within the Church of England.

Two decades later, in 1734, the Catholic church made known its disapproval by placing *A Tale of a Tub* on the Index of Forbidden Books. It remained listed until 1881, when the ban was lifted by Pope Leo XIII.

FURTHER READINGS

Haight, Anne Lyon. *Banned Books: 387 BC to 1978 AD*. Updated and enlarged by Chandler B. Grannis. New York: R. R. Bowker, 1978.

Swift, Jonathan. *The Portable Swift*. Ed. and intro. by Carl Van Doren. New York: Penguin Books, 1978.

———. *A Tale of a Tub and Other Satires*. Intro. by Lewis Melville. New York: E. P. Dutton & Co. 1955.

———. *A Tale of a Tub: Written for the Universal Improvement of Mankind*. Foreword by Edward Hodnett. New York: Columbia University Press, 1930.

THE TALMUD

Original date and place of composition: Palestine and Mesopotamia, ca. A.D. 200–500

Literary form: Religious text

SUMMARY

The Talmud, a collection of teachings set down by the Jewish scholars of antiquity, is the compendium of the oral law and tradition of Judaism. The word *Talmud* comes from the Hebrew word meaning "instruction." The collection has two main components: the Mishnah, the book of law written in Hebrew, and the commentaries on the Mishnah, known as the Talmud or Gemarah, written in Aramaic. Talmudic sages believed that God revealed two Torahs to Moses. One was the Scriptures, or written books. The other, the

Mishnah, was preserved in oral traditions handed down through many centuries and compiled toward the end of the second century. The material of the Mishnah is arranged in six groups, called orders, that deal with agriculture, the sabbath and festivals, marriage, civil and criminal law, ritual sacrifices and cleanliness. The orders are subdivided into 63 tracts or books.

Oral explanations and commentaries that developed around the Mishnah over the centuries were later put into written form and called the Gemarah. The Mishnah serves as text and the Gemarah as a series of comments and notes. Two versions of the Gemarah exist: one compiled in the fourth century by the scholars of Palestine, and the other in the fifth century by the scholars of Babylonia, which became the authoritative work. The Talmud is considered, with the Hebrew Bible, as a central pillar of Judaism and the most important book in Jewish culture. It is the accepted religious authority among all Orthodox Jews.

CENSORSHIP HISTORY

The history of suppression of the Talmud is many centuries long. Early attempts to ban it date at least to the seventh and eighth centuries. During the Middle Ages, with the revival of learning and the appearance of books of theological speculation, the Catholic church began to adopt a more severe attitude toward suspect books. It began to examine Jewish literature and the Talmud more intensively.

In 1144 in Paris, the Talmud was burned by the Catholic church on charges of blasphemy and immorality. Other incidents of censorship were recorded during the next hundred years. The anti-Talmudic campaign reached its height in 1239, when Pope Gregory IX ordered all Jewish books to be burned. He acted on allegations of heresy in the Talmud brought by Jewish converts to Christianity. Gregory sent letters to the kings and prelates of England, France, Navarre, Aragon, Castile and Portugal, ordering that on a Sabbath during the following Lent, while Jews worshipped in their synagogues, the books should be seized and delivered to the mendicant friars for examination, and that these books deemed heretical should be destroyed. The order was carried out fully only in France.

In 1244, Pope Innocent IV ordered Louis IX of France to burn all copies of the Talmud. This order was repeated in 1248, when 20 wagonloads of books were burned in Paris, and again in 1254. In 1264 in Rome, Pope Clement IV appointed a committee of censors to expunge all passages from the Talmud that appeared derogatory to Christianity, allowing Jews to keep only expurgated versions. Three years later, Clement IV instructed the king of Aragon to force Jews to deliver Talmuds to inquisitors.

Numerous instances of official burnings of the Talmud were recorded in France in the 14th century, as the anti-Jewish polemic continued. In 1415, Pope Benedict XII ordered all copies of Talmudic books delivered to bishops for preservation subject to papal instructions. Jews themselves were forbidden to possess copies of any material considered antagonistic to Christianity, and could not ready or study the Talmud. A church synod in Basel in 1431 reaffirmed the stringent ban.

Because so many copies of the Talmud had been lost over the centuries, there was great interest among Jews in the new 15th-century technology of the printing press. The first printed edition of the Talmud appeared in Guadalajara, Spain, in 1482. But the Talmud soon became a target of the Spanish Inquisition. In 1490 in Spain, the Grand Inquisitor Torquemada burned Hebrew books by order of Ferdinand and Isabella; he later conducted at Salamanca an auto-da-fe of more than 6,000 volumes described as books of magic or infected with Jewish errors. When the Jews were expelled from Spain and Portugal, all Jewish books were confiscated.

In 1509, Johannes Pfefferkorn, a priest and Jewish convert to Christianity, advocated destruction of Hebrew books in all countries under the rule of the Holy Roman Emperor. Emperor Maximillian requested the opinion of another priest, Johann Reuchlin. Reuchlin, who had published the first Hebrew grammar for Christians, argued that to understand the Old Testament it was necessary to collect and study Hebrew manuscripts rather than destroying them. He suggested that Jews be required to furnish books for the universities and that chairs of Hebrew learning be instituted in every university in Germany. His recommendation was met by intense opposition, to which he responded in *Augenspiegel* (Mirror of the Eye) in 1511. He distinguished anti-Christian polemics from classical works in Hebrew, which he believed should be preserved. A sustained controversy developed between the humanists who supported Reuchlin and the clerics and leaders of the Inquisition who supported Pfefferkorn. In 1521, the Roman curia suppressed Reuchlin's writings against Pfefferkorn.

In 1520, Pope Leo X gave permission for the publication and printing of the Talmud in Venice, and several editions appeared in the next few decades. In the 1530s, Martin Luther, convinced that Christians in Moravia were being induced to convert to Judaism, urged that Jews be deported to Palestine, forbidden to practice usury, their synagogues burned and their books destroyed. German principalities expelled Jews from certain localities and suppressed their books. In other German cities, such as Frankfurt and Worms, Jews were tolerated.

As the Counter-Reformation and the church's battle against heresy and the power of the printing press intensified, Pope Julius III in 1553 halted the printings of the Talmud allowed by Pope Leo X. In 1555, the houses of Jews were searched, and Jews were ordered under pain of death to surrender all books blaspheming Christ. Princes, bishops and inquisitors were instructed to confiscate the Talmud. The books were collected and burned on the first day of Rosh Hashanah, the Jewish New Year. Christians were forbidden under threat of excommunication to possess or read Jewish books or to aid

Jews by producing copies in script or by printing. Jewish books, including rare rabbinic manuscripts, were burned by the thousands in Italian cities. Some 12,000 volumes of Hebrew texts were burned after the inquisitor Sixtus of Siena destroyed the library of the Hebrew school at Cremona. The Talmud was not published again in Renaissance Italy.

The harshness of Julius III's decree was somewhat alleviated by Pope Pius IV in 1559, who allowed distribution of the Talmud only if those sections that offended Christianity were erased. As a result of this decision, a truncated and expurgated edition was printed in Basel under the supervision of Catholic monks. Subsequent editions were often similarly expurgated. In many European countries, where the Talmud could be printed only with official permission, licensing was confined to Christian printers.

The church's first Index of Forbidden Books in 1559 included the Talmud. Under the revised Index prepared by the Council of Trent in 1564, all works of Jewish doctrine were banned, except those permitted by the pope after the Jewish community offered a substantial financial "gift."

In 1592, Pope Clement VIII issued a bull forbidding either Christians or Jews from owning, reading, buying or circulating "impious talmudic books or manuscripts" or writings in Hebrew or other languages that "tacitly or expressly contain heretical or erroneous statements against the Holy Scriptures of the Old Law and Testament." Any such work, whether expurgated or not, was to be destroyed. In 1596, this ruling was modified when the publication of the Machsor, the basic Hebrew prayer book, was permitted, but only in Hebrew.

Active suppression of the Talmud by the Catholic church lasted through the 18th century. In 1629, an Italian cardinal boasted of having collected 10,000 outlawed Jewish books for destruction. As late as 1775, Pope Clement XIV confirmed the prohibitions of previous papal bulls. No Hebrew books could be bought or sold until examined and approved by the church.

In the 20th century, the most extensive censorship of the Talmud was reported in Europe under the Communist Party in the Soviet Union and under the Nazis during the Holocaust. In 1926, the government of the Soviet Union ordered that religiously dogmatic books such as the Talmud could be left in the large libraries but must be removed from the small ones. Virtually no printing of the work was allowed after that time. A Russian translation, the first in any language to be permitted since the 1917 revolution, was recently undertaken under the sponsorship of the Russian Academy of Sciences. In 1939, most of the schools of Jewish learning in Europe were totally destroyed by the Nazis. Innumerable copies of Jewish religious texts were lost during the Holocaust.

For Western Christianity, a change in attitudes toward the Talmud was brought about by the Second Vatican Council in 1965, which deplored anti-Semitism and the persecution of Jews, emphasizing the church's biblical connection to Judaism and the common religious heritage of Christians and Jews.

FURTHER READINGS

Bainton, Roland. *Here I Stand: A Life of Martin Luther*. New York: Penguin Group, 1995.

Burman, Edward. *The Inquisition: Hammer of Heresy*. New York: Dorset Press, 1992.

Green, Jonathon. *The Encyclopedia of Censorship*. New York: Facts On File, 1990.

Haight, Anne Lyon. *Banned Books: 387 BC to 1978 AD*. Updated and enlarged by Chandler B. Grannis. New York: R. R. Bowker, 1978.

Hertzberg, Arthur. "Swimming without Drowning: New Approaches to the Ocean of the Talmud." *The New York Times Book Review* (March 27, 1994): 12–14.

Lea, Henry Charles. *History of the Inquisition of the Middle Ages*. Vol. 1. New York: Russell & Russell, 1955.

Levy, Leonard W. *Blasphemy: Verbal Offense Against the Sacred, from Moses to Salman Rushdie*. New York: Alfred A. Knopf, 1993.

Peters, Edward. *Inquisition*. New York: Free Press, 1988.

Putnam, George Haven. *The Censorship of the Church of Rome*. Vol. 1 New York: G. P. Putnam's Sons, 1906–07.

Steinsaltz, Adin. *The Essential Talmud*. New York: Basic Books, 1976.

THEOLOGICAL-POLITICAL TREATISE

Author: Baruch (Benedict) Spinoza
Original date and place of publication: 1670, Holland
Literary form: Philosophical treatise

SUMMARY

Theological-Political Treatise is the only work expressing the philosophical ideas of the eminent Dutch rationalist Baruch Spinoza to be published during the writer's lifetime. Already notorious for his radically skeptical views, having been excommunicated from the Jewish community of Amsterdam in 1656, Spinoza published the work anonymously under a fictitious imprint in 1670.

In the preface to *Theological-Political Treatise*, Spinoza declares the purpose of his book to be the defense of freedom of opinion. Freedom of thought is not only compatible with public order, it is necessary to it. "Everyone should be free to choose for himself the foundation of his creed, and that faith should be judged only by its fruits; each would then obey God freely with his whole heart; while nothing would be publicly honored save justice and charity," writes Spinoza. A rational government requires enlightened and tolerant citizens, he believed, just as free men require an enlightened and tolerant government.

Spinoza proposed that political and social problems should be studied scientifically and dispassionately, and that moral and religious exhortations have no place in political science. Appeals to supernatural causes are expressions of ignorance. The natural light of reason, for those skillful in its use, is sufficient to show "the true way of salvation."

Unlike his contemporaries, who insisted that revelation provided knowledge inaccessible and superior to reason, Spinoza held that reason alone was a sufficient path to truth. The Bible cannot be accepted as a reliable source of knowledge, because it contains many contradictions. It is "faulty, mutilated, tampered with and inconsistent." Moreover, Spinoza observed, the authors, circumstances or dates of many biblical books are unclear: "We cannot say into what hands they fell, nor how the numerous varying versions originated; nor, lastly, whether there were not other versions, now lost."

Belief in the Bible "is particularly necessary to the masses whose intellect is not capable of perceiving things clearly and distinctly," who must learn morality from easily understood stories or examples. Spinoza contended that there is no special revelation, or knowledge revealed directly from God to man. The Ten Commandments "were not intended to convey the actual words of the Lord, but only his meaning," and the story of the Ten Commandments itself is questionable because it implies that God has a form.

According to Spinoza, the acceptance of prophetic reports and stories of miracles as sources of knowledge represents superstition and is an "utter mistake." "I care not for the girdings of superstition," he wrote, "for superstition is the bitter enemy of all true knowledge and true morality." To Spinoza, religious superstition was a dangerous and all too real cause of prejudice and violence. Not only had it disrupted his own life and prevented the publication of his works, but it had also devastated Europe with religious wars and persecutions.

The free man, Spinoza believed, should criticize any religious dogma when it is represented as philosophical truth or when it leads to intolerance. "What greater evil can there be for a republic," he wrote, "than that honorable men be thrust into exile like criminals, because they hold dissenting views and know not how to conceal them?" In his view of the primacy of individual liberty, freedom of opinion and religious tolerance, Spinoza was a precursor of the liberal thinkers of later centuries.

CENSORSHIP HISTORY

See ETHICS.

FURTHER READINGS

Gerber, Jane S. *The Jews of Spain: A History of the Sephardic Experience*. New York: Free Press, Macmillan, 1992.

Hampshire, Stuart. *Spinoza: An Introduction to His Philosophical Thought*. London: Penguin Books, 1988.

———. ed. *The Age of Reason: The 17th Century Philosophers*. New York: New American Library, 1956.

Scott-Kakures, Dion, Susan Castegnetto, Hugh Benson, William Taschek and Paul Hurley. *History of Philosophy*. New York: HarperCollins, 1993.

THREE-PART WORK

Author: Meister Eckhart
Original date and place of publication: 1311, Germany
Literary form: Theological treatise

SUMMARY

Johannes Eckhart, known as Meister Eckhart, was an influential medieval German theologian and preacher and the founder of German mysticism. He studied and taught in Paris, Strasbourg and Cologne, and held administrative positions in the Dominican order of friars. In his writings Eckhart for the first time used German as a vehicle for religious ideas that had before been expressed only in Latin.

In 1311, he began an ambitious project, a systematic theological treatise in Latin, the *Three-Part Work*, which was never completed and survives only in fragments. Eckhart had planned the treatise to consist of a Work of Propositions, a Work of Questions and a Work of Commentaries. The first part was to include 1,000 propositions divided into 14 sections in which synthesis was presented through axioms or propositions organized according to opposed terms. The only part of the *Three-Part Work* that remains is the general prologue to the Work of Propositions. Eckhart completed other parts, but these were lost over the centuries.

In the *Three-Part Work*, Eckhart attempted to awaken Scholastic theology to the possibility of direct and unmediated experience of God, incorporating personal revelation into systematic religious life. Eckhart accepted Thomas Aquinas's views that God is known through both reason and revelation. But he added a third means of knowledge of God: God's direct revelation to the inner soul. His first proposition in the *Three-Part Work* is that God and existence are the same, alluding to the words of the book of Exodus, "I am who am." All essence is God and apart from God there is no being.

Because God is outside all experience he cannot be known within nature or described in any terms available to human beings: "God is nameless; his Infinity cannot be expressed or conveyed by words, as everything touching the human soul can be recognized but in finite terms. . . . God is inexpressible, because all Being in him is infinite."

In a formulation that was regarded with suspicion by church censors as implying that God was not good, Eckhart declared: "If anyone said that God was good, he would do him as great an injustice as if he had said that the sun was black." Ecclesiastical investigators also suspected that by claiming that "every distinction is alien to God, whether in Nature or in Persons," Eckhart was challenging the correct interpretation of the doctrine of the Holy Trinity.

Eckhart proposed that God is present everywhere and in the human soul; but human beings in their sinful state are unaware of the divine presence. To prepare oneself for mystical insight, the mind should be emptied of all content by withdrawing as much as possible from experience. Only in this way can the soul be made ready for mystical union with God, the ultimate aim of human existence.

CENSORSHIP HISTORY

In 1323, the general chapter of the Dominican order in Venice received complaints about sermons in the German provinces that might lead simple people astray. During the following year the archbishop of Cologne, referring to the immense popularity of Eckhart's sermons, filed a formal complaint against Eckhart with the papal court in Avignon, France, charging that he had "incited ignorant and undisciplined people to wild and dangerous excesses." The archbishop was unfriendly to the Dominicans and targeted Eckhart, the order's most distinguished and respected member.

The Dominican order's own investigation ended with a declaration of Eckhart's innocence. Without waiting for the papal investigator's verdict, the archbishop set up an independent investigating commission consisting of two Franciscan monks, who were avowed enemies of the Dominicans. They assembled 100 propositions taken from Eckhart's Latin treatises and German sermons, which they viewed as evidence of heresy. They suspected him of connection with the Beghards, a heretical religious association condemned by the church for teaching that those who gain perfection in this life cannot commit sin.

On September 26, 1326, Eckhart submitted a detailed defense of his work, declaring his loyalty to the church. "They think that everything they do not understand is an error and that every error is a heresy," he wrote, "when only obstinate adherence to error makes heresy and a heretic. . . ." The commission summoned both the papal investigator and Eckhart to appear before the archbishop's court in January 1327. Eckhart proclaimed his innocence and requested permission to make a direct appeal to Pope John XXII, challenging the authority of the archbishop and his inquisitors. On February 13, 1327, Eckhart declared in a public sermon that he was prepared to refute any errors the judges might find in his writings and sermons and that he had not deliberately departured from the faith on any point. A week later the archbishop's court refused permission for a direct appeal to the pope.

The official documents of the archbishop's court were forwarded to the pope, who ordered an investigation of their heretical character. Twentieth-century scholars who compared the condemned statements with the original works from which they were extracted found that the Cologne commission had distorted decisive points in Eckhart's writings.

The papal investigation affirmed the verdict of Cologne, and on March 27, 1329, the pope issued a bull condemning as heresy 28 statements from Eckhart's works. The bull was sent to the archbishop of Cologne bidding him to publicize the condemnation in all his parishes and to instruct the faithful that they could not consider themselves obedient children of the church if they continued to maintain Eckhart's false teachings. By the time the bull was issued, however, Eckhart had died.

The pope's decree said that Eckhart had been deceived "by the Father of Lies who often turns himself into an angel of light in order to replace the light of truth with a dark and gloomy cloud of the senses . . . and presented many things as dogma that were designed to cloud the true faith in the hearts of many . . .," particularly uneducated people. The pope also stated that Eckhart had retracted his errors on his deathbed, "insofar as they could generate in the minds of the faithful a heretical opinion or one erroneous and hostile to the true faith." Eckhart did not admit, however, that he accepted the church's judgment that his writings were heretical.

Eckhart's disciples tried in vain to have the pope's decree set aside. In 1330, his works were condemned by the University of Heidelberg. Though he had a considerable influence on the piety of the 14th and 15th centuries, by the end of the Middle Ages Eckhart was almost forgotten, condemned to obscurity by the stigma of heresy attached to his work and by the abstract and difficult nature of his writings. Though his disciples passed on his spiritual doctrine, most of his original works had disappeared. Only a handful of men were aware of the existence of his theological works written in Latin, among them the 15th-century German cardinal, papal legate and humanist philosopher Nicholas of Cusa, who found some of Eckhart's writings and in 1444 preserved them by having them copied for his own use.

Five centuries later, in the early 19th century, Eckhart's writings were rediscovered thanks to a revived interest in mysticism and pre-Reformation religious history. Twentieth-century editions of Eckhart's writings have been published under the Catholic church's imprimatur, indicating church approval of the religious doctrine contained in them.

FURTHER READINGS

Christie-Murray, David. *A History of Heresy*. Oxford: Oxford University Press, 1989.

Colledge, Edmund, and Bernard McGinn, eds. and intro. *Meister Eckhart: The Essential Sermons, Commentaries, Treatises, and Defense*. New York: Paulist Press, 1981.

Copleston, Frederick. *A History of Philosophy*. Vol. 3, *Late Medieval and Renaissance Philosophy*. New York: Doubleday, 1993.

Eckhart, Meister. *Meister Eckhart: A Modern Translation*. Trans. and intro. by Raymond Bernard Blakney. New York: Harper & Row, 1941.

———. *Meister Eckehart Speaks.* Trans. by Elizabeth Strakosch. Ed. and intro. by Otto Karrer. New York: Philosophical Library, 1957.

Wilcox, Donald J. *In Search of God and Self: Renaissance and Reformation Thought.* Boston: Houghton Mifflin Company, 1975.

THE VEIL AND THE MALE ELITE: A FEMINIST INTERPRETATION OF WOMEN'S RIGHTS IN ISLAM

Author: Fatima Mernissi
Original date and place of publication: 1987, France; 1991, United States
Original publisher: Editions Albin Michel S.A., France; Addison Wesley Publishing Co., United States
Literary form: Religious history

SUMMARY

The Moroccan sociologist, Koranic scholar and feminist Fatima Mernissi is the author of five highly regarded books on Islam, including *The Veil and the Male Elite*, a study of women's status under Islam. Examining the foundations of Islam, Mernissi advances the thesis that Islamic tradition does not oppose women's emancipation. If some modern Muslim men block women's rights, it is not because of the teachings of the Koran or the Prophet Muhammad: It is because those rights conflict with the interests of a male elite.

The motivation of those who are against women's rights in Muslim societies, Mernissi writes, is profit. But to find a source to justify exploitation of women it is necessary to go back to the shadows of the past. Mernissi says there are no grounds for the claim that women in Muslim states cannot be granted full enjoyment of human rights because their religion forbids it. "They are simply betting on our ignorance of the past, for their argument can never convince anyone with an elementary understanding of Islam's history."

She cites historical evidence that the quest for women's full participation stems not from imported Western values, but from Muslim tradition. Women fled tribal Mecca by the thousands to enter seventh-century Medina, the Prophet Muhammad's city. Islam promised equality and dignity for all—for men and women, masters and servants. Every woman who came to Medina when the prophet was political leader could gain access to full citizenship. Mohammed revolutionized life for women, granting them the right to divorce, to pray in mosques and to participate in the management of military and political affairs.

How, Mernissi asks, did the schism come about between the egalitarian origins of Islam and the misogynistic practices of Muslim societies today? Islam broke with pre-Islamic practices, calling into question the customs that ruled relations between the sexes, New laws of inheritance deprived men of privileges and women entered into competition with men for the sharing of fortunes. The Prophet's companions reacted negatively to these new laws and during his lifetime tried unsuccessfully to pressure him to change them. In desperation, Mernissi says, religious leaders took to manipulating the interpretation of sacred text.

In the opening chapter of the book, Mernissi relates an encounter with her grocer. "Can a woman be a leader of Muslims?" she asked. Another customer responded with the *hadith*, or saying of the Prophet, "Those who entrust their affairs to a woman will never know prosperity." This *hadith* is the definitive argument used to exclude women from politics.

The *hadith* collections record in minute detail what the Prophet said and did and constitute along with the Koran both the source of law and the standard for distinguishing the permitted from the forbidden. The science of establishing the *hadith* collection consists of presenting not only its content before the reader, but also the information about the informants, so that the reader can judge whether they are credible. In investigating the origins of this particular *hadith*, Mernissi went directly to texts usually probed only by religious authorities and found that its veracity has been hotly disputed. Other well-known misogynistic *hadith* were found to be equally suspect. Mernissi contends that the sacred texts were distorted and that their manipulation is a structural characteristic of the practice of power in Muslim societies. Less than two centuries after the death of the Prophet, there were already more than a half a million false *hadith* in circulation.

The skepticism that guided the work of the founders of religious scholarship has disappeared today, Mernissi says. She sees the phobic attitude toward women represented by the *hijab*, or segregation of the sexes and the veiling of women, as a violation of the Prophet's beliefs. He encouraged his adherents to renounce it as representing the superstitious attitudes of the *jahiliyya*, the pre-Islamic mentality.

A famous Muslim woman who resisted the *hijab* was Sukayna, one of the Prophet's great-granddaughters through his daughter Fatima. She attended meetings of the Qurayshi Tribal Council. Sukayna had a successive total of five or six husbands, stipulated in her marriage contracts that she would not obey her husband and refused to acknowledge his right to practice polygamy. The image of the Muslim woman will change, writes Mernissi, when the Muslim man feels the pressing need to root his future in a liberating memory, such as that of Sukayna. Women can help him to do this through daily pressure for equality.

CENSORSHIP HISTORY

Regarded as Mernissi's masterpiece, *The Veil and the Male Elite* has been praised by critics and scholars for its original and scrupulous research, wit and clarity. In her book *Islam and Democracy: Fear of the Modern World* (1992), Mernissi commented on the censorship of the book: "In *The Veil and the Male Elite*, I explained that in the course of its egalitarian revolution Islam allowed women to emerge as subjects, whereas in the *jahiliyya* [pre-Islamic period] they had the status of objects inherited and passed on like livestock. . . . With the advent of the Umayyad despotism, however, women sank back into a slavelike status like that which they had in the *jahiliyya*. This theory is apparently disputed because the book was banned in Morocco several months after its publication in French." (The book was also prohibited in the Gulf States and Saudi Arabia.)

Mernissi's contention that the sacred texts have been manipulated and employed as political weapons and that commonly accepted *hadith* are based on falsehood was viewed as particularly threatening to religious and political authorities in theocracies such as Saudi Arabia. Saudi Arabia is ruled by Muslim divine religious law, or *shari'a*, which encompasses the *hadith*. Moroccan legal family codes are also based on the *shari'a*.

"Delving into memory, slipping into the past, is an activity that these days is closely supervised, especially for Muslim women," Mernissi writes. "The sleeping past can animate the present. That is the virtue of memory. Magicians know it and the imams know it too."

"The [Moroccan] state can stop me," Mernissi told an interviewer. "They stopped *The Veil and the Male Elite*. But I made such *un grande scandale*, that they've never bothered me since." Fatima Mernissi lives in Morocco and teaches at University Mohammed V in Rabat. *The Veil and the Male Elite*, however, remains banned in Morocco.

FURTHER READINGS

Bardach, Ann Louise. "Tearing Off the Veil." *Vanity Fair* (August 1993): 123.

Mernissi, Fatima. *Islam and Democracy: Fear of the Modern World*. Trans. by Mary Jo Lakeland. Reading, Mass.: Addison-Wesley, 1992.

———. *The Veil and the Male Elite: A Feminist Interpretation of Women's Rights in Islam*. Trans. by Mary Jo Lakeland. Reading, Mass.: Addison-Wesley, 1991.

VOYAGES TO THE MOON AND THE SUN

Author: Savinien Cyrano de Bergerac
Original date and place of publication: 1657, 1662, France
Literary form: Fiction

SUMMARY

Savinien Cyrano de Bergerac is most often remembered today as the dueling libertine with a long nose—the legendary protagonist of the romantic drama written in the 19th century by Edmond Rostand. The real Cyrano was a 17th-century writer, playwright, scientist and soldier, well known as a wit and a freethinker. He satirized the customs and beliefs of his time in two science fiction narratives about imaginary journeys to the moon and the sun: *Voyage to the Moon* and *Voyage to the Sun*. In the modern English translation of the two books, they are published together as *Voyages to the Moon and the Sun*.

In his fanciful *Voyages*, Cyrano speculated on the possibility of life on other planets and on the eternal nature of the earth. His purpose was both to entertain and to comment on philosophical, social and political issues that could not easily be discussed in other formats. Although his imaginary travels are sometimes described as utopian, Cyrano does not offer for consideration an ideal political system. Like Swift's *Gulliver's Travels*, which was influenced by Cyrano's work, *Voyages* uses the device of a traveler's tales to satirize existing institutions and prejudices and to expose to ridicule fundamental flaws in the human character.

In *Voyages*, Cyrano is propelled to the moon by means of little bottles filled with dew strapped to his body. The heat of the sun draws the bottles into the clouds, but he falls to ground in New France, Canada, rather than on the moon. He then uses rockets to boost himself to the moon; where he lands in a garden of Eden populated by giant beast-men with human faces and bodies who walk on four legs. The opening sections of his first voyage parody the Old Testament and mock literal belief in the Scriptures.

On the moon, Cyrano meets a philosopher who originally came from the sun and was sent to colonize the earth. The philosopher had left the earth for the kingdom of the moon and decided to remain there, because the moon's beast-men are lovers of truth and there are no pedants among them. "The philosophers allow themselves to be convinced by reason alone and neither the authority of a learned man or numbers can overwhelm the opinion of a corn-thresher if the corn-thresher reasons powerfully."

Cyrano is held by the royal court of the beast-men as an entertaining curiosity. The queen believes that Cyrano is the female partner of her little animal, who turns out also to be a man from earth, a native of Spain. He tells Cyrano that the real reason he was obliged to wander the earth and abandon it for the moon was that he could not find a single country where even the imagination was free. "Observe," he says, "unless you wear a square cap, a chaperon or a cassock, whatever excellent things you may say, if they are against the principles of those diplomated doctors, you are an idiot, a madman or an atheist." He fell into the queen's hands because she had taken him for a monkey, for all the monkeys on the moon are dressed in Spanish clothes.

When they hear that Cyrano, who is thought to be an animal, can talk, the clergy on the moon publish a decree forbidding anyone to believe that he has the faculty of reason and commanding, instead, that any intellectual thing Cyrano does be regarded as a product of instinct. The quandary over the definition of Cyrano's being—is he man or animal?—divides the town into two factions. An assembly of the Estates of the realm is called to resolve the religious dispute.

Cyrano is examined by the court of justice, which finally declares that he is indeed a man; as such, he is set free on the proviso that he must make "shameful amends." He must publicly disavow having taught that the moon was a world, "and this on account of the scandal the novelty of the opinion might have caused the souls of the weaker brethren."

Cyrano meets two philosophers in the town who discuss with him theories of the origin of the universe and the immortality of the soul. "When we try to go back to the origin of this Great All," one of the philosophers says, "we are forced to run into three or four absurdities. . . . The first obstacle that stops us is the Eternity of the World. Men's minds are not strong enough to conceive it and, because they are not able to imagine that so vast, so beautiful, so well regulated a Universe could have made itself, they take refuge in Creation. . . . This absurdity. . . ."

Back on earth, Cyrano is harassed by critics of the tale of his first voyage to the moon. The parson of Colignac, in particular, circulates ridiculous tales of Cyrano's sorceries. Cyrano is dragged into jail by a mob and eventually imprisoned in a tower. One day his tower rises high into the sky above Toulouse, transporting him after four months of travel to one of the little worlds that fly around the sun. He perceives on his trip that it is indeed the earth that turns around the sun from east to west, and not the sun that turns about the earth.

He eventually arrives at the sun, a luminous land like burning snowflakes, a weightless world with no center. He comes into the kingdom of the birds, where he is indicted and put on trial in the parliament of birds, charged with being a man. Cyrano's indictment lists various criticisms of man, including his disturbing of peace, lack of equality and barbarity in his conduct. "They are so inclined to servitude," the indictment reads, "that for fear of failing to serve, they sell their liberty to each other. . . ."

Cyrano is sentenced to death for man's crimes, but is saved by turtle doves at the request of Caesar, his cousin's pet parrot. He then passes through the land of talking trees and the Kingdom of Love. Here the book ends abruptly, before Cyrano's return to earth.

CENSORSHIP HISTORY

Voyage to the Moon was written in 1648; *Voyage to the Sun* was begun in 1650, but left unfinished. Cyrano privately circulated *Voyage to the Moon* in manuscript form, but did not dare publish it during his lifetime because of ideas in it that would have been viewed as subversive and antireligious and could have exposed him to imprisonment or exile.

In 1654, a collection of Cyrano's works that included a theatrical tragedy, *The Death of Agrippina*, and his *Letters* was printed in two quartos. His *Letters*, which were popular for half a century after their publication, were heavily censored by their publisher, who eliminated philosophical or satirical arguments directed against government or the church.

After Cyrano's death in 1655, *Voyage to the Moon* was prepared for publication by his friend, Henry Le Bret. However, fearing punishment by the authorities, Le Bret expurgated the manuscript of material that could be construed by the church as offensive. The version that was published in 1657 eliminated many of the most daring passages, notably the pages satirizing the book of Genesis, with some of the omissions marked with ellipsis or the word *hiatus*. The censored version of *Voyage to the Moon* was the only one available in French until the discovery of the original manuscript in the late 19th century. Until 1962, English translations were also based on the expurgated edition.

Fourteen of the 96 pages that appeared in the first unexpurgated French edition had been deleted by Le Bret. In many cases, the effect of the deletions of essential words, sentences, paragraphs or whole pages was not only to blunt Cyrano's sarcasm, but also to make Cyrano's writing sound nonsensical and absurd. *Voyage to the Sun* was published separately in 1762, but because the original manuscript was never found, the extent of its deletions cannot be estimated.

Cyrano's posthumous reputation as an insane person, or, at the least, as an eccentric, was due in part to the impression created by the non sequiturs in his writing. But "he was not mad," his modern English translator claims, "he was simply heavily censored." Though the Catholic church condemned his writing as pagan heresy, his reputation as a madman had a more significant impact on suppressing interest in his work.

"What wretched works are those of Cyrano de Bergerac!" a 17th-century critic commented. "When he wrote his *Voyage to the Moon*, I think he had one quarter of the moon in his head." The 18th century saw a further decline in his reputation. The influential Voltaire, standard-bearer of the Enlightenment, referred to him as "a madman." No new editions of *Voyages to the Moon and the Sun* appeared in France between 1699 and 1855. Cyrano was virtually forgotten until he was revived as a legendary figure by Rostand in 1897.

FURTHER READINGS

Cyrano de Bergerac. *Voyages to the Moon and the Sun*. Trans., intro. and notes by Richard Aldington. New York: Orion Press, 1962.

Harth, Erica. *Cyrano de Bergerac and the Polemics of Modernity*. New York: Columbia University Press, 1970.

ZOONOMIA

Author: Erasmus Darwin
Original date and place of publication: 1794–96, England
Literary form: Scientific treatise

SUMMARY

The English physician and poet Erasmus Darwin was among the most eminent literary figures of his time. Sixty-five years before his grandson, Charles Darwin, wrote ON THE ORIGIN OF SPECIES and revolutionized biological science, Erasmus Darwin formulated an evolutionary system of world order in *Zoonomia*, his treatise on animal life.

Darwin ran a successful practice as a family physician, but was more prominent as a scientific poet. His book-length poem, *The Botanic Garden*, published in two parts—*The Loves of the Plants* in 1789 and *The Economy of Vegetation* in 1792—was immensely popular and influenced the English Romantic poets Blake, Wordsworth, Coleridge, Shelley and Keats.

In 1794, Darwin published the first volume of *Zoonomia*, a voluminous and difficult 1,400-page prose work directed to a professional medical audience, which reiterated in technical detail the theories on the physical nature of human life expounded in his poems. The second volume, a medical casebook with treatments for all known diseases, appeared in 1796. Four years later, he published *Phytologia, or the Philosophy of Agriculture and Gardening*, the counterpart to *Zoonomia* on plant life.

In *Zoonomia*, Darwin described the laws of organic life and analyzed the mechanism of all aspects of animal life. He posited a force or phenomenon in nature possessed by all living matter: "animal motion," or the spirit of animation. He divided animal motion into four different types: irritative, sensitive, voluntary and associative, each with its own definition and description. He then explained how "all our ideas are animal motions of the organs of sense."

The most important section of *Zoonomia* was the long chapter, "Of Generation," in which he described descent with modification and expounded his theory of what is now called biological evolution. Darwin had been convinced of the truth of evolution for more than 20 years. In the preface to *Zoonomia*, he wrote: "The great CREATOR of all things has infinitely diversified the works of his hands, but at the same time stamped a certain similitude on the features of nature, that demonstrates to us, that *the whole is one family of one parent*."

He argued that animals were able to pass on physical changes to their offspring and that such continual regeneration had produced all varieties of life from one original life source. He pointed to changes produced in animals through domestic breeding and naturally, "as in the production of the butterfly with painted wings from the crawling caterpillar; or of the respiring frog from the subnatant tadpole." He also noted that "monstrosities," or mutations, are often inherited.

Discarding the traditional biological notion of fixed species, he replaced it with a description of continual generation over time. "Would it be too bold to imagine," he asked, "that in the great length of time since the earth began to exist, perhaps millions of ages before the commencement of the history of mankind, would it be too bold to imagine that all warm-blooded animals have arisen from one living filament. . . ."

Darwin also proposed that a struggle for existence related to the generation and the survival of the fittest: "The final cause of this contest amongst the males seems to be, that the strongest and most active animal should propagate the species, which should thence become improved." Though Erasmus Darwin's account of evolution was incomplete and, unlike the work of Charles Darwin, based on speculation rather than observation, he did define the theory associated with his grandson and considered many of the subjects that were later studied more intensively by Charles Darwin.

CENSORSHIP HISTORY

Darwin began his work on *Zoonomia* in 1771 but did not publish it until more than 20 years later. He had considered delaying its publication until after his death, for fear of the negative reaction it might arouse from religious quarters. However, encouraged by the change in the intellectual climate in Europe after the French Revolution, he went forward with his project.

In *Zoonomia*, Darwin stressed that evolution proceeds "by its own inherent activity," or without divine intervention. He had considered the concept of adaptation without the bias common in 18th-century scientific investigation, which saw a purpose in all the creator's works for the immediate benefit of mankind. The response to *Zoonomia* was similar to that faced by Charles Darwin upon the publication of *On the Origin of the Species* two generations later. Although Erasmus Darwin's work was lauded by many for its great contribution to scientific thought, his theories were immediately denounced by the religious establishment and others who were shocked by the implications of a self-generated, godless universe. Darwin discards "all the authority of revelation in favour of the sports of his own imagination," one critic wrote. "He dwelt so much and so exclusively on secondary causes, he forgot that there is a first," wrote another.

A 560-page book, *Observations on the Zoonomia of Erasmus Darwin*, written by Thomas Brown, lambasted Darwin's medical and philosophic ideas. A government minister, George Canning, wrote a parody, "The Loves of the Triangles," ridiculing both Darwin's style and his belief that humans evolved from lower animals. The poet Samuel Taylor Coleridge described Darwin's philosophy in *Zoonomia* as the "State of Nature or the Orang Outang theology of the human race, substituted for the first chapters of the Book of Genesis."

Zoonomia's notoriety caused the Catholic church to place it on the Index of Forbidden Books in 1817. Despite the fact that it was rarely read after the late 19th century, the work remained on the Index through the last edition, in effect until 1966. Ironically, while the ponderous and difficult work of Erasmus Darwin, long ago superseded by that of his grandson, was forbidden to Catholics, Charles Darwin's *On the Origin of Species*, which firmly established evolutionary theories dealt with by his grandfather in embryonic form and aroused even greater controversy, was never listed on the Index.

FURTHER READINGS

Browne, Janet. *Charles Darwin: Voyaging, Volume I of a Biography*. New York: Alfred A. Knopf, 1995.

Darwin, Charles. *The Autobiography of Charles Darwin: 1809–1882*. Ed. by Nora Barlow. New York: W. W. Norton & Company, 1993.

Hassler, Donald M. *Erasmus Darwin*. New York: Twayne Publishers, 1973.

King-Hele, Desmond. *Erasmus Darwin and the Romantic Poets*. New York: St. Martin's Press, 1986.

CENSORED WRITERS ON RELIGIOUS CENSORSHIP

I have replied to the Louvain slanders modestly, of course, but not without salt and vinegar and even mustard.

—Henricus Cornelius Agrippa

But I take courage from the words of Daniel . . . assuring us that the defenders of the truth are shielded by divine power. . . .

—Dante Alighieri

I am of a constitution so general that it consorts and sympathizeth with all things. . . . All places, all airs, make unto me one Countrey; I am in England every where, and under any Meridian.

—Sir Thomas Browne

I borrow not the rules of my Religion from Rome or Geneva, but the dictates of my own reason.

—Sir Thomas Browne

I have ever expounded philosophically and according to the principles of Nature and by its light . . . although I may have set forth much suspicious matter occasioned by my own natural light . . . never have I taught anything directly contrary to the Catholic religion. . . .

—Giordano Bruno

[W]e regard those as heretics with whom we disagree . . . so that if you are orthodox in one city or region, you must be held for a heretic in the next.

—Sebastian Castellio

To kill a doctrine is not to protect a doctrine, but it is to kill a man. When the Genevans killed Servetus, they did not defend a doctrine, but they killed a man.

—Sebastian Castellio

I would have made the book more amusing, had it not been for the Holy Office.

—Miguel de Cervantes Saavedra

I am known not only as a writer, but also as a feminist. Feminists generally annoy fundamentalists of all ilk, and I have been no exception.

—Lindsey Collen

Observe, unless you wear a square cap, a chaperon or a cassock, whatever excellent things you may say, if they are against the principles of those diplomated doctors, you are an idiot, a madman or an atheist.

—Savinien Cyrano de Bergerac

I could not employ my life better than in adding a little to natural science. This I have done to the best of my abilities, and critics may say what they like, but they cannot destroy this conviction.

—Charles Darwin

Let all Mankind be told for what: Tell them t'was he was too bold, and told those Truths which shou'd not ha' been told.

—Daniel Defoe

Some men, who produced a silly work which imbecile editors botched further, have never been able to pardon us for having planned a better one. These enemies to all good have subjected us to every kind of persecution. We have seen our honor, our fortune, our liberty, our life endangered within a few months' time.

—Denis Diderot

To abandon the work is to turn one's back on the breach, and do what the rascals who persecute us desire.

—Denis Diderot

They think that everything they do not understand is an error and that every error is a heresy, when only obstinate adherence to error makes heresy and a heretic....

—Meister Eckhart

A disobedient woman writer is doubly punished, since she has violated the norm of her fundamental obligation to home, husband and children.

—Nawal El Saadawi

I might perhaps do better to pass over them [quibbling Scholastic theologians] in silence without stirring the mud of Camarina or grasping that noxious plant, lest they marshal their forces for an attack and force me to eat my words. If I refuse they'll denounce me as a heretic on the spot, for this is the bolt they always loose on anyone to whom they take a dislike.

—Desiderius Erasmus

Had I believed the majority of English readers were so fondly attached even to the name and shadow of Christianity, had I foreseen that the pious and the timid and the prudent would feel or affect to feel such exquisite sensibility, I might perhaps have softened the two individious chapters, which would create many enemies, and conciliate few friends.

—Edward Gibbon

To prohibit the reading of certain books is to declare the inhabitants to be either fools or slaves.

—Claude Adrien Helvétius

The King is a mortall man and not God, [and] therefore hath no power over the immortall soules of his subjects to make lawes and ordinances for them to set spirituall Lords over them.

—Thomas Helwys

Do not when a poor soul by violence is brought before you to speak his conscience in the profession of his religion to his God—do not first implore the oath ex officio. *Oh, most wicked course! And if he will not yield to that then imprison him close. Oh, horrible severity! . . . Let these courses be far from you, for there is no show of grace, religion, nor humanity in these courses.*

—Thomas Helwys

In the first place, I think I am too deeply engaged to think of a retreat. In the second place, I see not what bad consequences follow, in the present age, from the character of an infidel.

—David Hume

At Thy Tribunal Lord, I make my appeal. You have execrated me, Holy Fathers; I bless you. I pray that your conscience may be as clear as mine and that you may be as moral and religious as I am.

—Nikos Kazantzakis

I've always been amazed at the narrow-mindedness and narrow-heartedness of human beings. Here is a book I wrote in a state of deep religious exaltation, with a fervent love of Christ; and now the Pope has no understanding of it at all. . . .

—Nikos Kazantzakis

The greater the freedom of thought the more will faith be awakened in the sincerity of those who are devoted to scientific research.

—Johannes Kepler

It is true that the Index has been abolished and another name given to the Roman Inquisition. But there are still inquisitional processes against troublesome theologians. . . .

—Hans Küng

They say that some articles are heretical, some erroneous, some scandalous, some offensive. The implication is that those which are heretical are not erroneous, those which are erroneous are not scandalous, and those which are scandalous are not offensive. . . . It is better that I should die a thousand times than that I should retract one syllable of the condemned articles.

—Martin Luther

Heretics should be vanquished with books, not with burnings.

—Martin Luther

One idea can only be opposed by another idea.

—Naguib Mahfouz

Delving into memory, slipping into the past, is an activity that these days is closely supervised, especially for Muslim women. The sleeping past can animate the present. That is the virtue of memory. Magicians know it and the imams know it too.

—Fatima Mernissi

If all mankind minus one were of one opinion, and only one person were of the contrary opinion, mankind would be no more justified in silencing that one person, than he, if he had the power, would be justified in silencing mankind.

—John Stuart Mill

No proposition astounds me, no belief offends me, however much opposed it may be to my own.

—Michel de Montaigne

To forbid us anything is to make us have a mind for it.

—Michel de Montaigne

Those who publicize a novel proposition are at first called heretics. But no one is a heretic unless he wishes to be, for he needs only to split the difference and to offer some subtle distinction to his accusers, and no matter what the distinction is, or whether it is intelligible or not, it renders a man pure as snow and worthy of being called orthodox.

—Charles-Louis de Secondat de Montesquieu

Some people have found certain remarks excessively bold, but they are advised to regard the nature of the work itself. . . . Far from intending to touch upon any principle of our religion, he did not even suspect himself of imprudence. The remarks in question are always found joined to sentiments of surprise and astonishment, never to a sense of inquiry, and much less to one of criticism. . . .

—Charles-Louis de Secondat de Montesquieu

The problem is the intolerance of the fundamentalists. I fight with my pen, and they want to fight with a sword. I say what I think and they want to kill me. I will never let them intimidate me.

—Taslima Nasrin

I am convinced that the only way the fundamentalist forces can be stopped is if all of us who are secular and humanistic join together and fight their malignant influence. I, for one, will not be silenced.

—Taslima Nasrin

My own mind is my own church.

—Thomas Paine

It was in vain, too, that you obtained from Rome the decree against Galileo, which condemned his opinions regarding the earth's movements. It will take more than that to prove it keeps still, and if there were consistent observations proving that it is the earth that goes round, all the men in the world put together could not stop it from turning, or themselves turning with it.

—Blaise Pascal

My prison shall be my grave before I will budge a jot, for I owe my conscience to no mortal man.

—William Penn

Criticism knows no infallible texts; its first possibility is to admit the possibilities of error in the text which it examines.

—Ernest Renan

Neither the burning nor the decrees will ever make me change my language. The theologians, in ordering me to be humble, will never make me false and the philosophers, by taxing me with hypocrisy, will never make me profess unbelief.

—Jean-Jacques Rousseau

What is freedom of expression? Without the challenge to offend, it ceases to exist. Without the freedom to challenge, even to satirize all orthodoxies, including religious orthodoxies, it ceases to exist. Language and the imagination cannot be imprisoned, or art will die, and with it, a little of what makes us human.

—Salman Rushdie

Everyone should be free to choose for himself the foundation of his creed, and that faith should be judged only by its fruits; each would then obey God freely with his whole heart; while nothing would be publicly honored save justice and charity.

—Baruch Spinoza

What greater evil can there be for a republic than that honorable men be thrust into exile like criminals, because they hold dissenting views and know not how to conceal them?

—Baruch Spinoza

There is no freedom either in civil or ecclesiastical [affairs], but where the liberty of the press is maintain'd.

—Matthew Tindal

Lord, open the King of England's eyes.

—William Tyndale

There is no other remedy for this epidemic illness [religious fanaticism] than the spirit of free thought, which, spreading little by little, finally softens men's customs, and prevents the renewal of the disease.

—Voltaire

If there are a dozen caterers, each of whom has a different recipe, must we on that account cut each other's throats instead of dining? On the contrary every man will eat well in his fashion with the cook who pleases him best.

—Voltaire

It is shameful to put one's mind into the hands of those whom you wouldn't entrust with your money. Dare to think for yourself.

—Voltaire

Those churches cannot be truly Christian . . . which either actually themselves, or by the civill power of kings and princes . . . doe persecute such as dissent from them or be opposite against them.

—Roger Williams

BIOGRAPHICAL PROFILES

PIERRE ABELARD (1079–1142)

French theologian, poet and teacher who shifted the theological argument from reliance on authority to analysis by logic and reason. His *Introduction to Theology* (1120) was condemned and burned by the church in 1121. In 1140, he was charged with heresy, confined to a monastery and forbidden to continue writing. In the first Index of Forbidden Books in 1559 and in the Tridentine Index of 1564, all of his writings were prohibited.

HENRY CORNELIUS AGRIPPA (1486–1535)

German Catholic scholar, allied with the humanists and reformers in Europe. *Of the Vanitie and Uncertaintie of Artes and Sciences* (1530), a satire on religion, morals and society, was denounced and banned by the theological faculties of Louvain and the Sorbonne. His book on the occult, *De occulta* (1531), was banned in Cologne and Rome.

JEAN LE ROND D'ALEMBERT (1717–83)

French mathematician and philosopher, coeditor with Denis Diderot until 1758 of the most important literary endeavor of the Enlightenment, the *Encyclopédie* (1751–72), which was censored repeatedly during the 21 years of its publication and placed on the Catholic church's Index of Forbidden Books. He wrote the work's *Preliminary Discourse* (1751) and contributed articles on mathematics, philosophy and literature.

DANTE ALIGHIERI (1265–1321)

Florentine poet and author of the literary classic, *The Divine Comedy*. In *On Monarchy* (1310–13), his treatise on political philosophy, Dante argued against papal control over secular authority. The book was condemned by the pope and publicly burned in the marketplace of Bologna. In the 16th century, it was banned by the Spanish Inquisition and listed on the Catholic church's first Index of Forbidden Books, where it remained until the 19th century.

ARISTOTLE (384–322 B.C.)

One of the greatest of the ancient Greek philosophers. Born in Macedonia, he studied for 20 years under Plato at the academy in Athens. In 335 B.C., he founded his own school, the Lyceum. Fifty of his works survived as notes or summaries of his lectures made by his students. In the 13th century, the reading or teaching of the natural philosophy or metaphysics of Aristotle was forbidden as heretical by the provincial council of Paris and by the pope. The bans on Aristotle were impossible to enforce and were gradually lifted.

AVERROËS (IBN RUSHD) (1126–98)

Spanish-Arab philosopher and physician from Córdoba who was among the outstanding figures of medieval philosophy. His extensive *Commentaries* (1168–90) on the works of Aristotle influenced the development of medieval Scholasticism. His writings were banned by church authorities between 1210 and 1277 for proposing that philosophy could claim truth outside established religious sources. Nevertheless, his interpretation of Aristotle remained influential throughout the later Middle Ages and Renaissance.

FRANCIS BACON (1561–1626)

English philosopher, scientist and statesman. Educated at Trinity College in Cambridge, he practiced law and served in Parliament. *The Advancement of Learning* (1605), which advocated the inductive method of modern science, was placed on the Index of Forbidden Books by the Vatican. All of his works were condemned by the Spanish Inquisition.

ROGER BACON (ca. 1214–94)

Franciscan friar and English scientist and philosopher who came under suspicion of heresy for advocating the experimental method. His great encyclopedic work, *Opus Maius* (1268), was regarded as heretical. He was sent to prison and may have spent as many as 14 years behind bars.

PIERRE BAYLE (1647–1706)

French historian and philosopher, a notable advocate of religious toleration. His greatest work was his four-volume *Historical and Critical Dictionary* (1697), a compendium of historical biographies with comprehensive marginal notes viewed as subversive of religious orthodoxy. In the 18th century, as authorities fought the influence of Enlightenment thinking, the *Dictionary* was censored. It was burned in Germany and placed by the Vatican on the Index of Forbidden Books, where it remained through the first two-thirds of the 20th century.

JEREMY BENTHAM (1748–1832)

English jurist, philosopher and social reformer, known as the father of utilitarianism. His *Introduction to the Principals of Morals and Legislation* (1789), a scientific attempt to assess the moral content of human action by focusing on its results and consequences, won him recognition throughout the Western world. His writing was placed by the Catholic church on the Index of Forbidden Books, remaining listed through its last edition in effect until 1966.

HENRI BERGSON (1859–1941)

French philosopher and Nobel Prize winner, among the most influential thinkers of his time. In *Creative Evolution* (1907), he proposed a dynamic vision of the universe to reconcile evolutionary theory with Christian traditions of creation. In 1907, the Vatican condemned "modernist" views, and in 1914, *Creative Evolution* was placed on the church's Index of Forbidden Books. Bergson died of pneumonia in German-occupied Paris after standing in line to be registered as a Jew.

GEORGE BERKELEY (1685–1753)

Anglo-Irish philosopher and Anglican bishop, regarded as among the outstanding British classical empiricists. *Alciphron, or the Minute Philosopher* (1732), aimed at vindicating Christianity against the views of freethinkers and atheists, was placed on the Catholic church's Index of Forbidden Books for anti-Catholic views. It remained listed through the Index's last edition in effect until 1966.

LEONARDO BOFF (1938–)

Brazilian Catholic theologian and former Franciscan priest, a leading exponent of liberation theology. In 1985, Boff was interrogated and censured by the Vatican for his views regarding the church's abuse of hierarchical power expressed in *Church: Charism and Power: Liberation Theology and the Institutional Church* (1981). Boff was sentenced to an "obedient silence," forbidding him to write, publish or teach, which was lifted after ten months. In 1991, Boff resigned from the priesthood.

SIR THOMAS BROWNE (1605–82)

English Oxford-educated physician and writer. He expressed views of religious tolerance in *Religio Medici* (1643), a popular collection of his reflections on faith. In 1645, it was placed on the Index of Forbidden Books for its skeptical, rationalist perspective and its allegiance to the Anglican church. The book remained listed until 1966.

GIORDANO BRUNO (1548–1600)

Italian philosopher, expelled from the Dominican religious order when he was charged with heresy. His major metaphysical work, *On the Infinite Universe and Worlds* (1584), refuted the traditional cosmology of Aristotle. He was arrested by the Inquisition in Venice and tried on charges of blasphemy and heresy. After seven years in prison, he was executed in 1600. All of his writings were placed on the Index of Forbidden Books and listed through the first two-thirds of the 20th century.

JOHN CALVIN (1509–64)

French Protestant theologian of the Reformation. He wrote the first systematic and logical exposition of reform belief in *Institutes of the Christian Religion* (1536–59). In Calvin's French translation from the Latin it was the first theological treatise written in French prose. Calvin's writing was banned from England in 1555 and condemned on the Catholic church's first Index of Forbidden Books in 1559 and on the Tridentine Index in 1564.

SEBASTIAN CASTELLIO (1515–63)

French Protestant theologian, wrote the most important book favoring religious toleration to be published on the Continent during the 16th century, *Concerning Heretics* (1554). Prompted by the execution by Calvinists of Spanish heretic Michael Servetus, Castellio protested persecution by Christians carried out in the name of doctrine. In 1563, he was put on trial for heresy, but died during the proceedings.

MIGUEL DE CERVANTES SAAVEDRA (1547–1616)

Self-educated son of a Spanish apothecary-surgeon who created one of the greatest and most enduring classics of European literature, *Don Quixote* (1605, 1615), a burlesque of the popular romances of chivalry. In 1640, the novel was placed on the Spanish Index of Forbidden Books for a single sentence: "Works of charity performed negligently have neither merit nor value." In 1981, the Chilean military junta banned the novel for supporting individual freedom and attacking authority.

LINDSEY COLLEN (1948–)

South African writer and feminist who lives in Mauritius. Her second novel, *The Rape of Sita* (1993), won a 1994 Commonwealth Writers Prize for the best book from Africa but was banned by the Mauritian government and temporarily withdrawn by its publisher after protests by Hindu fundamentalists.

AUGUSTE COMTE (1798–1857)

French philosopher and social reformer, founder of the school of philosophy known as positivism. His six-volume *Course of Positive Philosophy* (1830–42) substituted a new religion of humanity and sociological ethics for metaphysics and revealed religion. It was placed on the Catholic church's Index of Forbidden Books and remained banned through the last edition of the Index in effect until 1966.

CONFUCIUS (551–479 B.C.)

China's greatest philosopher, founder of the ethical and religious system of Confucianism which was influential in China for millennia. *The Analects*, a collection of sayings and short dialogues compiled by his disciples during the third and fourth centuries B.C., was burned by Emperor Shih Huang Di in 221 B.C. During the Cultural Revolution in China in 1966–74, possession of Confucian writings again became dangerous.

NICHOLAS COPERNICUS (1473–1543)

Celebrated Polish astronomer. In *On the Revolution of Heavenly Spheres* (1543), he was the first person to propose the theory that the earth moves around the sun. The church viewed the Copernican theory as a challenge to orthodoxy. In 1616, the book was placed on the Catholic church's Index of Forbidden Books. The general prohibition against Copernicus's theories remained in effect until 1753, and his name was not removed from the Index until 1835.

THOMAS CRANMER (1489–1556)

English religious reformer. He was appointed archbishop of Canterbury by King Henry VIII in 1533 and shaped the doctrine and liturgical transformation of the Church of England during the reign of Edward VI. He was responsible for the writing of most of the first Book of Common Prayer in 1549, brought into compulsory use in the Church of England by act of Parliament, and for the 1552 revision of the book. In 1553, the Catholic Queen Mary banned the use of the Prayer Book. Cranmer was convicted of treason and heresy and executed.

SAVINIEN CYRANO DE BERGERAC (1619–55)

French writer, playwright, scientist and soldier, later the protagonist of Edmond Rostand's 19th-century romantic drama. Cyrano satirized the customs and beliefs of his times in two science fiction narratives, *Voyage to the Moon* (1657) and *Voyage to the Sun* (1662). It was considered too dangerous to publish the material during his lifetime. After Cyrano's death his publisher expurgated the manuscripts so that his writing sounded nonsensical, lending credence to his posthumous reputation as insane or eccentric.

CHARLES DARWIN (1809–82)

British naturalist, who in his *On the Origin of Species* (1859) introduced the concept of "descent with modification" to science. His book unleashed one of the most dramatic controversies of the era. A resurgence of opposition to Darwin's theories began in the 1920s in the U.S. and led to laws prohibiting the teaching of evolution in schools. Battles about the teaching of evolution have continued, especially at the local school board level. In the 1930s the book was banned in Yugoslavia and in Greece.

ERASMUS DARWIN (1731–1802)

English physician and poet, one of the most eminent literary figures of his time. Sixty-five years before his grandson Charles Darwin revolutionized biological science, Darwin formulated an evolutionary system in his treatise on animal life, *Zoonomia* (1794–96). *Zoonomia*'s notoriety caused it to be placed on the Catholic church's Index of Forbidden Books, where it remained listed until 1966.

DANIEL DEFOE (1660?–1731)

English novelist and journalist. He was one of the most prolific writers in the English language, with more than 500 works to his credit. In 1703, Defoe was jailed, fined and pilloried for his parody of religious intolerance, *The Shortest Way with the Dissenters* (1702). His *Political History of the Devil* (1726), about the influence of Satan in the world, was the only one of Defoe's works to be placed on the Catholic church's Index of Forbidden Books. It remained listed until 1966.

RENÉ DESCARTES (1596–1650)

French philosopher and scientist, the founder of modern philosophy and mathematics. By applying the methods and concepts of mathematical and natural sciences to philosophic inquiry in his *Discourse on Method* (1637) and *Meditations on First Philosophy* (1641), he launched an intellectual revolution. Descartes's philosophy was condemned by church, state and universities in both France and Holland. All of his writing was placed on the Catholic church's Index of Forbidden Books in 1663, remaining listed until 1966.

CHARLES DICKENS (1812–70)

English author. He was the most popular and most widely read writer of his time. Dickens's portrayal of the Jewish character Fagin, in his novel *Oliver*

Twist (1838), has been the object of protest since the time of the novel's publication. In 1949, Jewish parents in Brooklyn, New York, contending that the book violated their children's rights to an education free of religious bias, sued to prevent study of the novel in public high schools. The Kings County Supreme Court ruled against the banning of the book.

DENIS DIDEROT (1713–84)

French philosopher, dramatist and critic, the primary editor of the *Encyclopédie* (1751–72), the greatest single work of the Enlightenment. Diderot was imprisoned for more than three months for flagrant disregard of religious orthodoxy in *Letter on the Blind* (1749), an analysis of the impact of the senses on moral and metaphysical ideas. The *Encyclopédie* was censored repeatedly during the 21 years of its publication. In 1804, it was placed on the Catholic church's Index of Forbidden Books, where it remained listed until 1966.

JOHN WILLIAM DRAPER (1811–82)

One of the greatest American scientists of the 19th century. He worked on early experiments in photography, taught physiology to medical students and spoke out in favor of the theory of evolution. In the last 20 years of his life, he sought to apply Charles Darwin's theories of biological evolution to human history and politics. His *History of the Conflict Between Religion and Science* (1874) was the first American book to be listed on the Catholic church's Index of Forbidden Books.

MEISTER (JOHANNES) ECKHART (ca. 1260–ca. 1328)

Influential German mystical theologian and preacher. He studied and taught at Paris, Strasbourg and Cologne and held administrative positions in the Dominican order of friars. His systematic theological treatise, *Three-Part Work* (1311), never completed, was declared heretical by the pope.

JOHN ELIOT (1604–90)

Puritan clergyman. He was among the first settlers to minister to the Indian tribes in Massachusetts. In *The Christian Commonwealth* (1659), Eliot laid out his plans for running a society according to the precepts of Mosaic law. The Algonquian Indians of Natick, Massachusetts, welcomed Eliot's ideas and governed their town according to his principles. In 1661, Eliot's book was banned in Massachusetts for stating that even royal authorities owed their power to a higher source.

NAWAL EL SAADAWI (1931–)

Medical doctor, sociologist, novelist and author of essays and books on women's issues; currently a visiting professor at U.S. universities. She is one of the most widely translated Egyptian writers and a prominent feminist. After publishing *Women and Sex* (1972), she was dismissed from the Egyptian Ministry of Health and her book was recalled by its publisher. The Egyptian government refused a permit to publish *The Hidden Face of Eve* (1977). A Lebanese edition was barred from Egypt and many Arab countries. She was blacklisted from Egyptian radio and television and has been the target of death threats by fundamentalists.

DESIDERIUS ERASMUS (1466?–1536)

Dutch writer, Catholic priest and biblical scholar. He was an influential proponent of Christian humanism and a critic of abuses within the Catholic church. His *Colloquies* (1518–33) and *The Praise of Folly* (1511) were condemned by the Sorbonne and the Parlement of Paris for allegedly heretical sympathies with Lutheranism. All of Erasmus's works were listed on the first Index of Forbidden Books established in 1559, a ban that remained until the 1930s.

ANATOLE FRANCE (JACQUES ANATOLE THIBAULT) (1844–1924)

One of the most popular and influential French authors in his lifetime, awarded the Nobel Prize in literature in 1921. His novel *Penguin Island* (1908), a satirical history of France attacking the hypocrisies of organized religion and the Socialist party, was placed on the Catholic church's Index of Forbidden Books, along with all of his works. They remained on the Index until 1966.

SIGMUND FREUD (1856–1939)

The creator of psychoanalysis. He brought the scientific method into the study of everyday mental life. *Introductory Lectures on Psychoanalysis* (1933) was Freud's most widely read book considered dangerous by the Catholic church, which opposed psychoanalysis, because of its popularity. In 1934, Pope Pius XI published a statement criticizing psychoanalysis and Freud's ideas on religious belief. Freud's writings were considered off-limits to Catholics as dangerous to faith and morals according to canon law. Freud's works were censored in the Soviet Union after 1930 and were among those burned by the Nazis in 1939.

GALILEO GALILEI (1564–1642)

Italian astronomer, mathematician and physicist who laid the foundations for the development of modern experimental science. His *Dialogue Concerning the Two Chief World Systems* (1632) supported the Copernican sun-centered system, determining that the earth was not the center of creation. In 1663, Galileo was put on trial by the Inquisition in Rome for heresy. He was convicted to an indefinite prison sentence and ordered to formally abjure his errors. *Dialogue* was banned along with all of his work. In 1824, the church announced its acceptance of modern astronomy, and in 1992 Pope Paul II formally rehabilitated Galileo.

EDWARD GIBBON (1737–94)

English historian and Enlightenment thinker. His epic six-volume *History of the Decline and Fall of the Roman Empire* (1776–88) was one of the most widely read historical works of modern times. The Catholic church viewed the two chapters on the rise of Christianity as contradicting official church history, and placed the work on the Index of Forbidden Books. It remained listed through the last edition of the Index.

KAHLIL GIBRAN (1833–1931)

Lebanese-American writer and artist, best known for *The Prophet*, a book of poetical essays that has sold millions of copies worldwide. Gibran was a leader in the Arab-American community and published periodicals that influenced literary development in the Arab world. His *Spirits Rebellious* (1908), a collection of short stories protesting religious and political tyranny, was publicly burned in the Beirut marketplace and suppressed by the Syrian government. Gibran was exiled from Lebanon and excommunicated from the Maronite church.

JOHANN WOLFGANG VON GOETHE (1749–1832)

German poet, dramatist, novelist and scientist. He achieved lasting fame at the age of 25 when he published *The Sorrows of Young Werther* (1774, 1787), an epistolary romance about a young man's hopeless love affair and suicide. His novel became the literary sensation of the century. The Leipzig city council banned the book on the grounds that it recommended suicide. In Denmark, a proposed translation was forbidden for conflicting with Lutheran doctrine. In 1939, the dictatorship of Francisco Franco in Spain ordered libraries purged of Goethe's work.

GRAHAM GREENE (1904–91)

English novelist and author of short stories, essays and reviews. Greene, a convert to Catholicism, often portrayed sinful and despairing characters with sympathy and understanding. In 1953, after protests about his portrayal of the whiskey priest in his novel *The Power and the Glory* (1940), the Vatican requested that he change the book's text. Greene refused. A pastoral letter was read to churches in Britain condemning the book. Four other Greene novels were banned in Ireland as offensive to Catholics.

HUGO GROTIUS (1583–1645)

Dutch statesman, jurist and theologian, regarded as the founder of modern international law. His *On the Law of War and Peace* (1625), which proposed a policy of religious toleration, was the first definitive text on the subject. In 1662, the States-General of the Netherlands banned the book. All of his books were condemned by the Spanish Inquisition and in the 18th century his complete works were placed on the Index of Forbidden Books, where they remained until 1966.

CLAUDE ADRIEN HELVÉTIUS (1715–71)

French Enlightenment philosopher and contributor to the *Encyclopédie*. He held the lucrative post of farmer-general, or tax collector. His utilitarian theories, as expressed in his first major work, *De l'esprit* (1758), influenced the British philosophers Jeremy Bentham, James Mill and Adam Smith. Banned by the archbishop of Paris, the pope, the Parlement of Paris and the Sorbonne, the book became an underground bestseller.

THOMAS HELWYS (?–1616)

English Separatist who withdrew from the Church of England and founded with John Murton the first permanent Baptist church in England. His *Short Declaration of the Mistery of Iniquity* (1612) was the first work published in English to advocate tolerance of all religions. Helwys was imprisoned on the orders of King James I for defending the ideas of religious freedom.

THOMAS HOBBES (1588–1679)

English philosopher, among the greatest 17th-century philosophers. His most important work, *Leviathan* (1651), was placed on the Catholic church's Index of Forbidden Books and banned in Holland because of its frank materialism. Hobbes was forbidden thereafter by the British government from publishing his philosophic opinions. His complete works were listed on the Index until 1966.

DAVID HUME (1711–76)

Scottish philosopher and historian, one of the great empiricists of the Enlightenment. His *Inquiry Concerning Human Understanding* (1748) recommended the application of the scientific experimental method to the study of man and cast doubt on the veracity of miracles. Because of the furor over his writing, Hume's *Dialogues Concerning Natural Religion* (1779) did not appear until after his death. In 1827, all of his historical and philosophical works were placed on the Catholic church's Index of Forbidden Books, where they remained until 1966.

JOHN HUS (1369?–1415)

Czech priest, theologian, religious reformer and forerunner of the 16th-century Protestant Reformation. He was influenced by the views of English heretic John Wycliff. In *De Ecclesia* (1413), he denied the pope's infallibility and proposed that the state should supervise the church. Put on trial at the church Council of Constance, he was convicted of heresy. His books were destroyed and he was burned at the stake.

IMMANUEL KANT (1724–1804)

German philosopher, considered to be among the most important philosophers in Western culture. *The Critique of Pure Reason* (1781) marked the birth of the critical philosophy of transcendental idealism. In *Religion within the Limits of Reason Alone* (1793), he proposed a philosophy of ethical theism. He was forbidden by the king to write on religion, and his *Religion* was banned by the Lutheran church. The *Critique* was placed on the Vatican's Index of Forbidden Books. All of Kant's writing was banned in the Soviet Union in 1928.

NIKOS KAZANTZAKIS (1883–1957)

Greek novelist, poet, dramatist and translator. Born on Crete, he studied in Paris under the philosopher Henri Bergson. His novel *The Last Temptation of Christ* (1953), an unorthodox portrait of Jesus, was placed on the Catholic church's Index of Forbidden Books, and Kazantzakis was excommunicated from the Eastern Orthodox church. A 1988 film of the novel by Martin Scorsese was censored in many countries, including the U.S.

JOHANNES KEPLER (1571–1630)

German astronomer and mathematics professor who developed the first significant improvement of the astronomical theories of the 16th-century astronomer Nicholas Copernicus. His *New Astronomy* (1609) is considered the most important book on astronomy ever published. The Vatican banned this book and his astronomy textbook under a general prohibition on reading or teaching heliocentric theory. The ban on his theories remained in effect until 1753.

HANS KÜNG (1928–)

Swiss priest, prominent Catholic theologian and professor of ecumenical theology of the University of Tübingen in Germany. He rejected the doctrine of papal infallibility in *Infallible? An Inquiry* (1970). In 1979, the Vatican withdrew his permission to teach in the name of the church and prohibited Catholic institutions from employing him.

JOHN LOCKE (1632–1704)

English philosopher known as the intellectual ruler of the 18th century, and a founder of the school of philosophy known as British empiricism. Suspected of radicalism by the British government, he fled to Holland in 1683, where he completed *An Essay Concerning Human Understanding* (1690), one of the most important works in modern philosophy. The Latin version was prohibited at Oxford, and in 1700, a French translation of the essay was placed by the Catholic church on the Index of Forbidden Books, where it remained until 1966.

MARTIN LUTHER (1483–1546)

German theologian and monk, the founder of the Protestant Reformation. His *Ninety-Five Theses* (1517) challenged Catholic church doctrine on indulgences and was banned by the pope in 1520. His writings attacking papal authority and rejecting the priesthood and the sacraments led to his excommunication and the destruction and banning of his works throughout Europe.

NAGUIB MAHFOUZ (1912–)

Egyptian author of 35 novels and more than a dozen collections of stories. Among them are the three novels of his masterpiece, *The Cairo Trilogy*, written between 1945 and 1957. In 1988, Mahfouz was the first Arab writer to win the Nobel Prize. His novel *Children of the Alley* (1959) was banned for 35 years in Egypt for blasphemy against Islam. Since 1959, Mahfouz has been threatened by religious fundamentalists offended by his novel. In October 1994, he was stabbed by an Islamist terrorist.

MOSES MAIMONIDES (1135–1204)

Court physician, jurist and leader of Egypt's Jewish community; the most important Jewish medieval philosopher. In his principal philosophical work, *The Guide of the Perplexed* (1197), he sought to reconcile Judaism with Aristotle's teaching. In 1232 in France, the work was banned from Jewish homes under penalty of excommunication. At the request of French rabbis, friars confiscated and burned copies of the book. Three hundred years later, it was condemned by the Yeshiva of Lublin, Poland, and it still faced bans in the 19th century.

BERNARD MANDEVILLE (1670–1733)

Dutch physician who lived in London; his *Fable of the Bees* (1714–28) was one of the most controversial and widely read books of the time. His moral fable about the symbiotic relationship between vice and national greatness was the target of attacks in the press, pulpits and courts that lasted through most of the century. The book was presented twice by an English grand jury for blasphemy, and in France it was ordered burned. It was listed on the Catholic church's Index of Forbidden Books, where it remained until 1966.

FATIMA MERNISSI (1941–)

Moroccan sociologist and Koranic scholar, author of highly regarded books on Islam. She teaches at Mohammed V University in Rabat, Morocco. Her study of women's status under Islam, *The Veil and the Male Elite* (1987), was banned in Morocco, Saudi Arabia and the Gulf States.

JOHN STUART MILL (1806–73)

British philosopher, economist and social reformer. Mill was one of the leading intellectual figures of the 19th century. His *System of Logic* (1843), the standard philosophical text of the time, and *Principles of Political Economy* (1848), his treatise on economic theory, were placed on the Catholic church's Index of Forbidden Books for reflecting modernist and liberal theories. They remained listed until 1966.

MICHEL DE MONTAIGNE (1533–92)

French humanist writer, the originator of the personal essay as a literary form. In his *Essays* (1580), he set out to test his judgment on a wide range of subjects, revealing his inner life and personality. His book was confiscated on a trip to Rome, and a papal censor ordered revisions in the *Essays*. In 1595, an unauthorized Protestant version expurgated the book. *Essays* was condemned by the Spanish Inquisition, and in 1676 the work was placed on the Roman Index of Forbidden Books, where it remained for almost 300 years.

CHARLES-LOUIS DE SECONDAT DE MONTESQUIEU (1689–1755)

French novelist, jurist and political philosopher. His bestselling satirical novel on French institutions, *The Persian Letters* (1721), and his influential treatise on political theory, *The Spirit of Laws* (1748), circulated underground in France. Both were condemned by the Catholic church and remained on the Index of Forbidden books until 1966.

TASLIMA NASRIN (1962–)

Bangladeshi physician, novelist, journalist and poet. She is the author of more than 20 books. Her novel *Lajja* (*Shame*) (1993), about the persecution of Hindus by Muslims in Bangladesh, was banned in Bangladesh and a death decree was proclaimed against her by a Muslim cleric. When a warrant was issued for her arrest, she went into exile in Europe.

THOMAS PAINE (1737–1809)

Anglo-American political theorist and revolutionary pamphleteer. He was indicted by the British government on the charge of seditious libel for *The Rights of Man* (1791–92), a work defending the French Revolution. *The Age of Reason* (1794–95), an attack on Christianity based on the principles of deism and rationalism, was banned by British authorities. For 25 years, the British government pursued publishers and booksellers of *The Age of Reason*, prosecuting and imprisoning them on blasphemy charges.

BLAISE PASCAL (1623–62)

French scientist, mathematician and religious philosopher. He was a convert to Jansenism, a reform movement within Catholicism. His defense of Jansenism in *The Provincial Letters* (1656–57) made a mockery of Jesuit theological disputes. *Letters*, an underground bestseller, was ordered burned by King Louis XIV, and it became too dangerous to continue its publication. Both *Letters* and a 1776 edition of *Pensées*, his thoughts in defense of religious belief, with an introduction by Voltaire, were placed on the Index of Forbidden Books. They remained listed until 1966.

WILLIAM PENN (1644–1718)

English-born religious reformer and founder of Pennsylvania. He was an early convert to the Society of Friends, also known as Quakers. His frequent pleas for religious tolerance and freedom of conscience earned him the enmity of English religious and secular authorities. After publishing *The Sandy Foundation Shaken* (1668), which refuted Presbyterian views of the Trinity, he was imprisoned for eight months in the Tower of London on charges of blasphemy.

PIERRE-JOSEPH PROUDHON (1809–65)

French social theorist, anarchist philosopher and reformer. He became notorious with a series of pamphlets and books in which he condemned abuses of private property and church and state absolutism. Proudhon's books were seized and he fled to Belgium to avoid arrest. All of his works were placed by the Catholic church on the Index of Forbidden Books, remaining there until 1966.

WILLIAM PYNCHON (1590?–1662)

English colonist and fur merchant. After arriving in Massachusetts in 1630, he founded the cities of Roxbury and Springfield. He began writing theology in 1650, and his long-hidden unorthodox religious ideas surprised and angered his Puritan neighbors. His *Meritorious Price of Our Redemption* (1650) was the first book to be burned publicly in the British colonies in North America. Facing punishment for his writings, he returned to England.

ERNEST RENAN (1823–92)

French historian, critic and philologist. Renan studied religion from a historical, rather than a theological, perspective. His *Life of Jesus* (1863), the first biography of Jesus to use modern historical methods, was condemned by the Catholic church. It was placed on the Index of Forbidden Books along with 19 other works by Renan and remained listed until 1966.

JEAN-JACQUES ROUSSEAU (1712–78)

Swiss-French philosopher and novelist who expressed the visionary theories that generated the romantic movement in literature. His two most influential works were *Émile* (1762), a novel about his ideas on education, and *The Social Contract* (1762), about his political philosophy. *Émile* was condemned by the archbishop and Parlement of Paris, the Sorbonne and the Inquisition. Rousseau fled France to avoid arrest. In 1763, *Émile* and *The Social Contract* were banned in Geneva. Both books were placed on the Spanish and Roman Index of Forbidden Books and remained forbidden to Catholics until 1966.

SALMAN RUSHDIE (1947–)

British writer who was born in India; the most censored author of the 20th century. His fourth novel, *The Satanic Verses* (1988), was banned in many countries throughout the world for its perceived offenses against the Islamic faith. In 1989, Iran's clerical leader, the Ayatollah Khomeini, issued a death decree against Rushdie, forcing him to go into hiding under protection of the British government. Acts of terrorism against publishers and translators of the book continued through 1993. Only in 1995 was Rushdie able to make public appearances, still under police protection.

GIROLAMO SAVONAROLA (1452–98)

Dominican monk, Italian religious reformer and charismatic preacher. He became the spiritual leader of Florence after the fall of the Medici in 1494 and organized the censorious "bonfires of the vanities." In his *Compendium Revelationum* (1495), he claimed a divine calling to convert Florence to the life of the spirit. He was excommunicated by the pope and forbidden from preaching. In 1498, he was convicted of heresy and schism, hanged and burned with all of his writings.

MICHAEL SERVETUS (1511–33)

Spanish theologian and physician. He became notorious at the age of 20 for *On the Errors of the Trinity* (1531). His book was banned, and he was hunted by the Spanish and French Inquisitions as well as by the Protestants. In *Christianity Restored* (1552), published secretly, Servetus attacked the doctrine of the Trinity and the practice of infant baptism. He was arrested in Geneva on John Calvin's orders and burned at the stake for heresy. Servetus's death sparked the first important controversy over the issue of toleration within Protestantism.

HANAN AL-SHAYKH (1943–)

Novelist born in Lebanon and educated in Egypt; she worked as a journalist in Beirut and now lives in London. Her novel *The Story of Zahra* (1980) is still banned in Saudi Arabia and other Arab countries more than 15 years after its publication for offending religious authorities by its explicit portrayal of sexuality and its indictment of social hypocrisy in contemporary Arab society.

BARUCH (BENEDICT) SPINOZA (1632–77)

Dutch rationalist philosopher who was expelled from Amsterdam's Jewish community for questioning traditional tenets of Judaism. His *Theological-Political Treatise* (1670), setting out foundations for a rational interpretation of religious doctrine, was the only book he could publish during his lifetime. Spinoza's writing, including his masterpiece, *Ethics* (1677), was widely banned in Holland as atheistic and subversive, and in 1679 all of his work was placed on the Catholic church's Index of Forbidden Books, remaining listed until 1966.

STENDHAL (HENRI MARIE BEYLE) (1783–1842)

French author, considered among the greatest French novelists of the 19th century. His novel *The Red and the Black* (1831), which lacked a religious world view and was bitterly critical of the Jesuits, was placed by the Vatican on the Index of Forbidden Books, listed until 1966. In 1850, the novel was banned in czarist Russia, and in 1939 it was prohibited by the dictatorship of Francisco Franco in Spain.

EMANUEL SWEDENBORG (1688–1772)

Swedish scientist and theologian whose writings form the doctrine of the Church of the New Jerusalem. His most notable scientific volume, *Principia* (1721), which proposed a rational mathematical explanation of the universe, was placed on the Catholic church's Index of Forbidden Books and remained listed for over two centuries. His mystical theological works, including *Arcana Coelestia* (1747–58), were banned by the Swedish government as heretical for contradicting Lutheran doctrine.

JONATHAN SWIFT (1667–1745)

Anglo-Irish satirist, novelist and Anglican clergyman. Swift burlesqued the historical development of the Christian religions in *A Tale of a Tub* (1704–10). The controversy over the book dashed his chances for further advancement in the Anglican church. In 1734, the book was placed on the Catholic church's Index of Forbidden Books. It was listed until 1881.

MATTHEW TINDAL (1655–1753)

English deist who belonged to the Church of England. His *Rights of the Christian Church Asserted* (1706), which favored the subordination of the church to state authority, established his notoriety as a freethinker. In 1707, an English grand jury made a presentment against the book, and in 1710 it was proscribed by Parliament and burned.

JOHN TOLAND (1670–1722)

Irish deist who earned his living as a writer and publicist for radical Whig causes. He wrote some 200 works, including *Christianity Not Mysterious* (1696), asserting that neither God nor revelation is above the comprehension of human reason. The book was presented by an English grand jury and ordered burned for heresy by the Irish Parliament. Toland escaped arrest by fleeing to Holland.

WILLIAM TYNDALE (1494?–1536)

Protestant reformer and linguist. He was the first person to translate the Bible into English from the original Greek and Hebrew and the first to print the Bible in English. Tyndale's 1526 translation of the New Testament was burned in England. Arrested in Belgium in 1535, he was convicted on charges of heresy and executed. Tyndale's translations were incorporated in later Bible editions, including the Authorized King James Version of 1604.

POLYDORE VERGIL (ca. 1470–1555)

Italian humanist. Vergil lived in England, where he served as the archdeacon of Wells. His three-volume *De Inventoribus Rerum* (1499), a reference book tracing the inventions of civilization, was among the most popular books of the 16th and 17th centuries. It was condemned by the Sorbonne, the Spanish Index of Forbidden Books, the Liège Index and the Roman Index. The Catholic church published an expurgated edition in 1576 removing criticisms of the church, and an English translator rewrote another edition of the book to give it a more Protestant flavor.

VOLTAIRE (FRANÇOIS MARIE AROUET) (1694–1778)

French author and philosopher, the chief standardbearer of the Enlightenment. His *Letters Concerning the English Nation* (1733) was printed clandestinely, banned by the French parlement, burned by the public executioner and placed on the Catholic church's Index of Forbidden Books, along with 38 other books by Voltaire. His *Philosophical Dictionary* (1764) was banned and burned in France, Geneva, the Netherlands and Rome.

ROGER WILLIAMS (1603–82)

Puritan minister and founder of the Massachusetts Bay Colony. Williams was exiled from Salem to the wilderness of Rhode Island for his belief in freedom of worship. His tract, *The Bloudy Tenent of Persecution* (1644), favoring separation of church and state and denouncing religious repression, was burned by order of the English Parliament in 1644.

JOHN WYCLIFF (1328–84)

English religious scholar and reformer. Wycliff studied and taught theology at Oxford. He was the most eminent heretic to challenge the Catholic church before the 16th-century Protestant Reformation. His treatise, *On Civil Lordship* (1376), was condemned by the pope. A council at Oxford prohibited his work as heretical and forbade him from preaching or lecturing. In 1415, a church council in Germany ordered his bones exhumed and burned and his ashes thrown into a running stream.

LAURENCE YEP (1948–)

Author and university professor from San Francisco who has written more than 20 books. His novels about Chinese-Americans for children and young adults have won numerous prizes. The Newbery Honor award-winner *Dragonwings* (1975), about a boy who emigrates from China to San Francisco in 1905, was the target of censorship in Pennsylvania in 1992. A Pentecostal minister who objected to allusions to Eastern religion in the book brought suit to prevent it from being used in the eighth-grade curriculum of a public school. The county court denied the request to ban the book.

Bibliography

BOOKS

Accad, Evelyne. "Rebellion, Maturity and the Social Context: Arab Women's Special Contribution to Literature." In *Arab Women: Old Boundaries, New Frontiers*. Ed. by Judith Tucker, 240–245. Bloomington: Indiana University Press, 1993.

Appelbaum, David. *The Vision of Kant*. Rockport, Mass.: Element Books, 1995.

*Appignanesi, Lisa, and Sara Maitland, eds. *The Rushdie File*. Syracuse, New York: Syracuse University Press, 1990.

Armytage, Frances, and Juliette Tomlinson. *The Pynchons of Springfield: Founders and Colonizers* (1636–1702). Springfield, Mass.: Connecticut Valley Historical Museum, 1969.

Bachman, Albert. *Censorship in France from 1715–1750: Voltaire's Opposition*. New York: Burt Franklin, 1971.

Backschneider, Paula R. *Daniel Defoe: His Life*. Baltimore: Johns Hopkins University Press, 1989.

Bacon, Francis. *Francis Bacon: A Selection of His Works*. Ed. by Sidney Warhaft. Indianapolis: Odyssey Press, 1981.

Bahr, Lauren S., editorial director, and Bernard Johnston, editor-in-chief. *Collier's Encyclopedia*. New York: Macmillan Educational Company, 1992.

Bainton, Roland. *Here I Stand: A Life of Martin Luther*. New York: Penguin Group, 1995.

———. *Hunted Heretic. The Life and Death of Michael Servetus*. Gloucester, Mass.: Peter Smith, 1978.

Barker, George F. *Memoir of John William Draper, 1811–1882* (reprint ed.). New York: Garland Publishing, 1974.

Baumgardt, Carola. *Johannes Kepler: Life and Letters*. Intro. by Albert Einstein. New York: Philosophical Library, 1951.

Bentham, Jeremy. *The Principles of Morals and Legislation*. Buffalo: Prometheus Books, 1988.

* Key sources

Berkeley, George. *The Works of George Berkeley*. Vol. 2, *Philosophical Works, 1732–33*. Preface by Alexander Campbell Fraser. Oxford: Clarendon Press, 1931.

Boase, Alan M. *The Fortunes of Montaigne: A History of the Essays in France 1580–1669*. New York: Octagon Books, 1970.

Boff, Leonardo. *Church: Charism and Power: Liberation Theology and the Institutional Church*. New York: Crossroad, 1985.

* Bokenkotter, Thomas. *A Concise History of the Catholic Church*. New York: Doubleday & Company, 1977.

The Book of Common Prayer. New York: Seabury Press, 1977.

* Boorstein, Daniel J. *The Discoverers: A History of Man's Search to Know His World and Himself*. New York: Random House, 1983.

Boulting, William. *Giordano Bruno: His Life, Thought and Martyrdom*. New York: Books for Libraries Press, 1972.

Boyle, Kevin, ed. *Article 19: World Report 1988*. New York: Times Books, 1988.

Brombert, Victor, ed. *Stendhal: A Collection of Critical Essays*. Englewood Cliffs, N.J.: Prentice-Hall, 1962.

Browne, Janet. *Charles Darwin: Voyaging, Volume I of a Biography*. New York: Alfred A. Knopf, 1995.

Browne, Sir Thomas. *The Religio Medici and Other Writings of Sir Thomas Browne*. Intro. by C. H. Herford. New York: E. P. Dutton & Co., 1906.

Burgess, Walter H. *John Smith, Thomas Helwys and the First Baptist Church in England*. London: James Clarke & Co., 1911.

* Burke, Redmond A. *What Is the Index?* Milwaukee: Bruce Publishing Co., 1952.

* Burman, Edward. *The Inquisition: Hammer of Heresy*. New York: Dorset Press, 1992.

* Burne, Peter. *Natural Religion and the Nature of Religion: The Legacy of Deism*. London: Routledge, 1991.

Burress, Lee. *Battle of the Books: Library Censorship in the Public Schools, 1950–1985*. Metuchen, N.J.: Scarecrow Press, 1989.

Burt, Henry M. *The First Century of the History of Springfield: The Official Records from 1636 to 1736*. Springfield, Mass.: Privately Printed, 1898.

Cassirer, Ernst. *Kant's Life and Thought*. Trans. by James Hader. Intro. by Stephan Korner. New Haven: Yale University Press, 1981.

Castellio, Sebastian. *Concerning Heretics, Whether They Are to Be Persecuted and How They Are to Be Treated*. Trans. and intro. by Roland H. Bainton. New York: Columbia University Press, 1935.

Chadbourne, Richard M. *Ernest Renan*. New York: Twayne Publishers, 1968.

Chadbourne, Richard M. *Ernest Renan as an Essayist*. Ithaca, N.Y.: Cornell University Press, 1957.

Chappell, Vere, ed. *The Cambridge Companion to Locke*. Cambridge: Cambridge University Press, 1994.

* Christie-Murray, David. *A History of Heresy*. Oxford: Oxford University Press, 1976.

Clark, Ronald W. *Freud: The Man and the Cause*. London: Jonathan Cape; Weidenfeld and Nelson, 1980.

Colledge, Edmund, and Bernard McGinn, eds. and intro. *Meister Eckhart: The Essential Sermons, Commentaries, Treatises, and Defense*. New York: Paulist Press, 1981.

Collen, Lindsey. *The Rape of Sita*. Portsmouth, N.H.: Heinemann Educational Books, 1995.

* Collinson, Diané. *Fifty Major Philosophers: A Reference Guide*. London: Routledge, 1988.

Conroy, Jr., Peter V. *Montesquieu Revisited*. New York: Twayne Publishers, 1992.

Cook, Richard I. *Bernard Mandeville*. New York: Twayne Publishers, 1974.

* Copleston, Frederick. *A History of Philosophy*. 6 vols. New York: Doubleday & Company, 1993–94.

Costigan, Giovanni. *Sigmund Freud: A Short Biography*. New York: Macmillan Company, 1965.

Covey, Cyclone. *The Gentle Radical: A Biography of Roger Williams*. New York: Macmillan Company, 1966.

Cox, Harvey. *The Silencing of Leonardo Boff: The Vatican and the Future of World Christianity*. Oak Part, Ill.: Meyer Stone Books, 1988.

Cragg, G. R. *Reason and Authority in the Eighteenth Century*. Cambridge: Cambridge University Press, 1964.

Craig, Alec. *Suppressed Books: A History of the Conception of Literary Obscenity*. Cleveland: World Publishing Co., 1963.

Curtis, Michael, ed. and intro. *The Great Political Theories*. Vol. 1. New York: Avon Books, 1981.

Cyrano de Bergerac, Savinien. *Voyages to the Moon and the Sun*. Trans., intro. and notes by Richard Aldington. New York: Orion Press, 1962.

Daniell, David. *Let There Be Light: William Tyndale and the Making of the English Bible*. London: British Library, 1994.

———. *William Tyndale: A Biography*. New Haven: Yale University Press, 1994.

Dante. *On Monarchy and Three Political Letters*. Trans. and intro. by Donald Nicholl. London: Weidenfeld and Nicholson, 1954.

Dargan, Edwin Preston. *Anatole France*. New York: Oxford University Press, 1937.

* Darnton, Robert. *The Business of Enlightenment: A Publishing History of the Encyclopédie 1775–1800*. Cambridge, Mass.: Belknap Press of Harvard University Press, 1979.

Darwin, Charles. *The Autobiography of Charles Darwin: 1809–1882*. Ed. by Nora Barlow. New York: W. W. Norton & Company, 1993.

Defoe, Daniel. *The Political History of the Devil, as Well Ancient as Modern (reprint ed.)*. New York: AMS Press, 1973.

Delatorre, Joan. *What Johnny Shouldn't Read: Textbook Censors in America.* New Haven: Yale University Press, 1992.

Demac, Donna A. *Liberty Denied: The Current Rise of Censorship in America.* New York: PEN American Center, 1988.

Descartes, Rene. *Discourse on Method.* Trans. and intro. by Laurence J. Lafleur. Indianapolis, Ind.: Bobbs-Merrill Company, 1956.

———. *Meditations on First Philosophy.* Trans. and intro. by Laurence J. Lafleur. New York: Bobbs-Merrill Co., 1960.

Dickens, Charles. *Oliver Twist.* Intro. by Irving Howe. New York: Bantam Books, 1982.

Diderot, Denis. *Diderot's Selected Writings.* Ed. and intro. by Lester G. Crocker. Trans. by Derek Coltman. New York: Macmillan Company, 1966.

Dinwiddy, John. *Bentham.* Oxford: Oxford University Press, 1989.

Donaghy, Henry J., ed. *Conversations with Graham Greene.* Jackson, Miss.: University Press of Mississippi, 1992.

* Doyle, Robert P., *Banned Books 1996 Resource Guide.* Chicago: American Library Association, 1996.

Draper, John William. *History of the Conflict Between Religion and Science* (reprint ed.). Westmead, Farnbrough, Hants., England: Gregg International Publishers Limited, 1970.

* Dunham, Barrows. *Heroes and Heretics: A Political History of Western Thought.* New York: Alfred A. Knopf, 1964.

Dunn, Mary Maples, and Richard S. Dunn, eds. *The Papers of William Penn.* Vol. 1, *1644–1679.* Philadelphia: University of Pennsylvania Press, 1981.

Dunn, Richard S., and Mary Maples Dunn, eds. *The World of William Penn.* Philadelphia: University of Pennsylvania Press, 1986.

Durant, Will, and Ariel Durant. *The Age of Voltaire.* New York: Simon and Schuster, 1965.

Durnbauld, Edward. *The Life and Legal Writings of Hugo Grotius.* Norman, Okla.: University of Oklahoma Press, 1969.

Earle, Peter. *The World of Defoe.* New York: Atheneum, 1977.

Eckehart, Meister. *Meister Eckehart Speaks.* Trans. by Elizabeth Strakosch. Ed. and intro. by Otto Karrer. New York: Philosophical Library, 1957.

Eckhart, Meister. *Meister Eckhart: A Modern Translation.* Trans. and intro. by Raymond Bernard Blakney. New York: Harper & Row, 1941.

Eliot, John. *The Christian Commonwealth: Or, the Civil Policy of the Rising Kingdom of Jesus Christ* (reprint ed.). New York: Arno Press, 1972.

El Saadawi, Nawal. *The Hidden Face of Eve: Women in the Arab World.* Foreword by Irene L. Gendzier. Boston: Beacon Press, 1982.

———. *The Hidden Face of Eve: Women in the Arab World.* Preface by Nawal El Saadawi. Trans. by Sherif Hetata. London: Zed Books, 1980.

Endy, Melvin B., Jr. *William Penn and Early Quakerism.* Princeton, N.J.: Princeton University Press, 1973.

Erasmus, Desiderius. *The Colloquies of Erasmus*. Trans. and intro. by Craig R. Thompson. Chicago: University of Chicago Press, 1965.

———. *The Praise of Folly*. Trans. by John Wilson. Ann Arbor: University of Michigan Press, 1958.

———. *Ten Colloquies of Erasmus*. Trans. and intro. by Craig R. Thompson. New York: Liberal Arts Press, 1957.

Erlanger, Rachael. *The Unarmed Prophet: Savonarola in Florence*. New York: McGraw Hill Book Company, 1988.

Farah, Caesar E. *Islam: Belief and Observances*. New York: Barron's Educational Services, 1987.

Fleming, Donald. *John William Draper and the Religion of Science*. Philadelphia: University of Pennsylvania Press, 1950.

Foner, Eric. *Tom Paine and Revolutionary America*. London: Oxford University Press, 1976.

* *For Rushdie: Essays by Arab and Muslim Writers in Defense of Free Speech*. New York: George Braziller, 1994.

Frame, Donald M., trans. and intro. *The Complete Essays of Montaigne*. Stanford, Calif.: Stanford University Press, 1958.

———, trans. and intro. *The Complete Works of Montaigne*. Stanford, Calif.: Stanford University Press, 1967.

France, Anatole. *Penguin Island*. Trans. by A. W. Evans. New York: Dodd, Mead & Co., 1909.

Freidel, David, Linda Schele and Joy Parker. *Maya Cosmos: Three Thousand Years on the Shaman's Path*. New York: William Morrow and Company, 1993.

Freud, Sigmund. *The Complete Introductory Lectures on Psychoanalysis*. Ed. and trans. by James Strachey. New York: W. W. Norton, 1966.

Friedenthal, Richard. *Goethe: His Life and Times*. New York: World Publishing Co., 1963.

Gallenkamp, Charles. *Maya: The Riddle and Discovery of a Lost Civilization*. New York: David McKay and Company, 1976.

Garraty, John A., and Peter Gay. *The Columbia History of the World*. New York: Harper & Row, 1972.

Gaustad, Edwin S. *Liberty of Conscience: Roger Williams in America*. Grand Rapids, Mich.: Wm. B. Eerdmans Publishing Co., 1991.

Gay, Peter. *Freud: A Life for Our Times*. New York: W. W. Norton and Company, 1988.

* ———. *The Enlightenment: An Interpretation. The Rise of Modern Paganism*. New York: W. W. Norton & Co., 1995.

Gellinek, Christian. *Hugo Grotius*. Boston: Twayne Publishers, 1983.

George, Leonard. *Crimes of Perception: An Encyclopedia of Heresies and Heretics. New York: Paragon House, 1995.*

* Gerber, Jane S. *The Jews of Spain: A History of the Sephardic Experience*. New York: Free Press, 1992.

Gibbon, Edward. *Memoirs of My Life*. Ed. and intro. by Betty Radice. London: Penguin Books, 1984.

Gibran, Jean, and Kahlil Gibran. *Kahlil Gibran: His Life and Work*. New York: Interlink Books, 1981.

Gibran, Kahlil. *Spirits Rebellious*. Trans. by Anthony Rizcallah Ferris. New York: Philosophical Library, 1947.

Goethe, Johann Wolfgang von. *The Sorrows of Young Werther*. Trans. and intro. by Michael Hulse. London: Penguin Books, 1989.

———. *The Sorrows of Young Werther and Selected Writings*. Trans. by Catherine Hutter. Foreword by Hermann J. Weigand. New York: New American Library, 1962.

———. *The Sufferings of Young Werther*. Trans. and intro. by Bayard Quincy Morgan. New York: Frederick Ungar Publishing Co., 1957.

Gould, Stephen Jay. *Ever Since Darwin: Reflections on Natural History*. New York: W. W. Norton and Company, 1977.

Grane, Leif. *Peter Abelard: Philosophy and Christianity in the Middle Ages*. Trans. by Frederick and Christine Crowley. New York: Harcourt, Brace & World, 1970.

* Green, Jonathon. *The Encyclopedia of Censorship*. New York: Facts On File, 1990.

Greene, Graham. *A Sort of Life*. New York: Simon and Schuster, 1971.

———. *The Power and the Glory*. New York: Penguin Books, 1971 (orig. pub. 1940).

———. *Ways of Escape*. New York: Simon and Schuster, 1980.

* Haight, Anne Lyon. *Banned Books: 387 BC to 1978 AD*. Updated and enlarged by Chandler B. Grannis. New York: R. R. Bowker, 1978.

Hall, Constance Margaret. *The Sociology of Pierre Joseph Proudhon (1809–65)*. New York: Philosophical Library, 1971.

Hampshire, Stuart, ed. *The Age of Reason: The 17th Century Philosophers*. New York: New American Library, 1956.

———. *Spinoza: An Introduction to His Philosophical Thought*. London: Penguin Books, 1988.

Harrison, James. *Salman Rushdie*. New York: Twayne Publishers, 1992.

* Harris, William H., and Judith S. Levy, eds. *The New Columbia Encyclopedia*. Fourth Edition. New York: Columbia University Press, 1975.

Harth, Erica. *Cyrano de Bergerac and the Polemics of Modernity*. New York: Columbia University Press, 1970.

Harvey, Sir Paul, ed. *The Oxford Companion to English Literature*. 3d Ed. Oxford: Oxford University Press, 1955.

Hassler, Donald M. *Erasmus Darwin*. New York: Twayne Publishers, 1973.

Hays, Denys. *Polydore Vergil: Renaissance Historian and Man of Letters*. Oxford: Clarendon Press, 1952.

Hazard, Paul. *European Thought in the Eighteenth Century: From Montesquieu to Lessing*. Cleveland: World Publishing Co., 1973.

Heilbroner, Robert. *The Worldly Philosophers: The Lives, Times and Ideas of the Great Economic Thinkers*. New York: Simon & Schuster, 1986.

* Heins, Marjorie. *Sex, Sin and Blasphemy: A Guide to America's Culture Wars.* New York: New Press, 1993.

Hentoff, Nat. *Free Speech for Me, but Not for Thee*. New York: HarperCollins, 1992.

Hoffman, Eleanor. *Realm of the Evening Star: A History of Morocco and the Lands of the Moors*. Philadelphia: Chilton Books, 1965.

Hoffman, Robert L. *The Social and Political Theory of P.-J. Proudhon*. Urbana, Ill.: University of Illinois Press, 1972.

Hollier, Denis. *A New History of French Literature*. Cambridge, Mass.: Harvard University Press, 1989.

* Hornstein. Lillian Herlands., ed. *The Readers' Companion to World Literature*. New York: New American Library, 1956.

Hume, David. *An Inquiry Concerning Human Understanding*. Ed. and intro. by Charles W. Hendel. Indianapolis, Ind.: Bobbs-Merrill Co., 1979.

———. *On Human Nature and the Understanding*. Ed and intro. by Anthony Flew. New York: Macmillan Publishing Co., 1975.

Hyams, Edward. *Pierre-Joseph Proudhon: His Revolutionary Life, Mind and Works*. New York: Taplinger Publishing Company, 1979.

Jaspers, Karl. *The Great Philosophers*. Vol. 3. New York: Harcourt Brace & Company, 1993.

Jefferson, Carter. *Anatole France: The Politics of Skepticism*. New Brunswick, N.J.: Rutgers University Press, 1965.

Jenkinson, Edward B. "The *Bible*: A Source of Great Literature and Controversy." In *Censored Books: Critical Viewpoints*. Ed. by Nicholas J. Karolides, Lee Burress and John M. Kean, 98–102. Metuchen, N.J.: Scarecrow Press, 1993.

Jolley, Nicholas. "The Reception of Descartes' Philosophy." In *The Cambridge Companion to Descartes*. Ed. by John Cottingham, 393–423. Cambridge: Cambridge University Press, 1992.

* Jordan, W. K. *The Development of Religious Toleration in England*. Vols. 3 and 4. Gloucester, Mass.: Peter Smith, 1965.

Kant, Immanuel. *The Critique of Pure Reason*. Trans. by N. Kemp Smith. New York: St. Martin's Press, 1965.

———. *The Philosophy of Kant: Immanuel Kant's Moral and Political Writings*. Ed. and intro. by Carl J. Friedrich. New York: Modern Library, 1993.

Kaplan, Fred, ed. *Oliver Twist: A Norton Critical Edition*. New York: W. W. Norton & Co., 1993.

Kazantzakis, Helen. *Kazantzakis: A Biography Based on His Letters*, Trans. by Amy Mims. New York: Simon & Schuster, 1968.

Kazantzakis, Nikos. *The Last Temptation of Christ*. Trans. and afterword by P. A. Bien. New York: Simon & Schuster, 1960.

Kilcullen, John. *Sincerity and Truth: Essays on Arnauld, Bayle and Toleration.* Oxford: Clarendon Press, 1988.

King-Hele, Desmond. *Erasmus Darwin and the Romantic Poets.* New York: St. Martin's Press, 1986.

Kolakowski, Leszek. *Bergson.* Oxford: Oxford University Press, 1985.

The Koran. Trans. and intro. by N. J. Dawood. Baltimore: Penguin Books, 1968.

Kundera, Milan. *Testaments Betrayed.* Trans. by Linda Asher. New York: HarperCollins, 1995.

Küng, Hans. *Infallible? An Unresolved Inquiry.* Preface by Herbert Haag. New York: Continuum, 1994.

Landau, Rom. *Morocco.* New York: G. P. Putnam's Sons. 1967.

* Larson, Edward J. *Trial and Error: The American Controversy Over Creation and Evolution.* New York: Oxford University Press, 1985.

* Lea, Henry Charles. *History of the Inquisition of the Middle Ages* Vols. 1 and 2. New York: Russell & Russell, 1955.

Leaman, Oliver. *Moses Maimonides.* Cairo: American University in Cairo Press, 1993.

* Levy, Leonard W. *Blasphemy: Verbal Offense Against the Sacred, from Moses to Salman Rushdie.* New York: Alfred A. Knopf, 1993.

Lippman, Thomas W. *Understanding Islam: An Introduction to the Muslim World.* New York: Penguin Books USA, 1990.

Lofmark, Carl. *What Is the Bible?* Buffalo, N.Y.: Prometheus Books, 1992.

Mahfouz, Naguib. *Children of Gebelawi.* Trans. by Philip Stewart. Washington, D.C.: Three Continents Press, 1988.

———. *Children of the Alley.* Trans. by Paul Theroux. New York: Doubleday, 1996.

Malti-Douglas, Fedwa, and Allen Douglas. "Reflections of a Feminist." In *Opening the Gates: A Century of Arab Feminist Writing.* Ed. by Margot Badran and Miriam Cooke, 394–404. Bloomington, Ind.: Indiana University Press, 1990.

Mandeville, Bernard. *The Fable of the Bees.* Intro. by Philip Harth. London: Penguin Books, 1970.

Manguel, Alberto. *A History of Reading.* New York: Viking, 1996.

Markman, Roberta, and Peter Markman. *The Flayed God: The Mythology of Mesoamerica.* New York: HarperCollins, 1992.

Mason, John Hope. *The Indispensable Rousseau.* London: Quartet Books, 1979.

McIntyre, Ruth A. *William Pynchon: Merchant and Colonizer.* Springfield, Mass.: Connecticut Valley Historical Museum, 1961.

Mernissi, Fatima. *Islam and Democracy: Fear of the Modern World.* Trans. by Mary Jo Lakeland. Reading, Mass.: Addison-Wesley, 1992.

———. *The Veil and the Male Elite: A Feminist Interpretation of Women's Rights in Islam.* Trans. by Mary Jo Lakeland. Reading, Mass.: Addison-Wesley, 1991.

Mill, John Stuart. *Essential Works of John Stuart Mill*. Ed. and intro. by Max Lerner. New York: Bantam Books, 1971.

Montaigne, Michel de. *Essays*. Ed. and intro. by J. M. Cohen. Middlesex, England: Penguin Books, 1958.

Montesquieu. *The Persian Letters*. Trans. and intro. by George R. Healy. Indianapolis, Ind.: Bobbs-Merrill Company, 1964.

Moore, John Robert. *Defoe in the Pillory and Other Studies*. New York: Octagon Books, 1973.

Morgan, Edmund S. *Roger Williams: The Church and the State*. New York: Harcourt, Brace & World, 1967.

Nasrin, Taslima. *Lajja (Shame)*. New Delhi: Penguin Books, 1994.

Nauert, Charles G., Jr. *Agrippa and the Crisis of Renaissance Thought*. Urbana, Ill.: University of Illinois Press, 1965.

*New York Public Library. *Censorship: 500 Years of Conflict*. New York: Oxford University Press, 1984.

Noyes, Alfred. *Two Worlds for Memory*. Philadelphia: J. B. Lippincott Co., 1953.

Numbers, Ronald L., ed. *Creation-Evolution Debates*. New York: Garland Publishing, 1955.

Olsen, Tillie. *Silences*. New York: Dell Publishing Co., 1978.

O'Neil, Robert M. "The Bible and the Constitution." In *Censored Books: Critical Viewpoints*. Ed. by Nicholas J. Karolides, Lee Burress and John M. Kean, 103–08. Metuchen, N.J.: Scarecrow Press, 1993.

O'Prey, Paul. *A Reader's Guide to Graham Greene*. New York: Thames and Hudson, 1988.

Osborne, Richard. *Philosophy for Beginners*. New York: Writers and Readers Publishing, 1991.

Paine, Thomas. *The Age of Reason*. Introduction by Philip S. Foner. Secaucus, N.J.: Citadel Press, 1974.

Parker, T. H. L. *John Calvin*. Batavia, Ill.: Lion Publishing Corporation, 1975.

Pascal, Blaise. *The Provincial Letters*. Ed. and intro. by J. Krailsheimer. Harmondsworth, Middlesex, England: Penguin Books, 1967.

Penelhum, Terence. *David Hume: An Introduction to His Philosophical System*. West Lafayette, Ind.: Purdue University Press, 1992.

Perrin, Noel. *Dr. Bowdler's Legacy: A History of Expurgated Books in England and America*. New York: Anchor Books, 1971.

Peters, Edward. *Inquisition*. New York: Free Press, 1988.

Pipes, Daniel. *The Rushdie Affair*. New York: Carol Publishing Group, 1990.

Polishook, Irwin H. *Roger Williams, John Cotton, and Religious Freedom: A Controversy in New and Old England*. Englewood Cliffs, N.J.: Prentice-Hall, 1967.

*Popkin, Richard, and Avrum Stroll. *Philosophy Made Simple*. New York: Doubleday, 1993.

Price, John V. *David Hume*. New York: Twayne Publishers, 1968.

* Putnam, George Haven. *The Censorship of the Church of Rome*. 2 vols. New York: G. P. Putnam's Sons, 1906–07.

Redman, Ben Ray, ed. and intro. *The Portable Voltaire*. New York: Penguin Books, 1977.

Reill, Peter Hanns, and Ellen Judy Wilson. *Encyclopedia of the Enlightenment*. New York: Facts On File, 1996.

Renan, Ernest. *The Life of Jesus*. Intro. by John Haynes Holmes. New York: Modern Library, 1955.

Rex, Walter. *Pascal's Provincial Letters: An Introduction*. New York: Holmes & Meier Publishers, 1977.

Richetti, John J. *Daniel Defoe*. Boston: Twayne Publishers, 1987.

Ridley, Jasper. *Thomas Cranmer*. Oxford: Clarendon Press, 1962.

Ritvo, Lucille B. *Darwin's Influence on Freud: A Tale of Two Sciences*. New Haven: Yale University Press, 1990.

Rogers, Donald J. *Banned! Book Censorship in the Schools*. New York: Julian Messner, 1988.

Roth, Cecil. *The Spanish Inquisition*. New York: W. W. Norton & Co., 1964.

Rummel, Erika, ed. *The Erasmus Reader*. Toronto: University of Toronto Press, 1990.

* Rushdie, Salman. *Imaginary Homelands: Essays and Criticism 1981–1991*. New York: Penguin Books, 1991.

———. *The Satanic Verses*. New York: Viking Penguin, 1989.

Ruthven, Malise. *A Satanic Affair: Salman Rushdie and the Wrath of Islam*. London: Hogarth Press, 1991.

* Scammel, Michael. "Censorship and Its History: A Personal View" in *Article 19: World Report 1988*. Edited by Kevin Boyle, 1–18. New York: Times Books, 1988.

* Scott-Kakures, Dion, Susan Castegnetto, Hugh Benson, William Taschek and Paul Hurley. *History of Philosophy*. New York: HarperCollins, 1993.

al-Shaykh, Hanan. *The Story of Zahra*. New York: Anchor Books, 1994.

Sherry, Norman. *The Life of Graham Greene*, Vol. 2, *1939–1955*. New York: Viking Penguin, 1994.

Shklar, Judith N. *Montesquieu*. Oxford: Oxford University Press, 1987.

Sigmund, Paul E. *Liberation Theology at the Crossroads: Democracy or Revolution?* New York: Oxford University Press, 1990.

Simon, Edith. *The Reformation*. New York: Time-Life Books, 1966.

Smith, D. W. *Helvétius, A Study in Persecution*. Oxford: Clarendon Press, 1965.

* Smith, George H. *Atheism, Ayn Rand, and Other Heresies*. Buffalo: Prometheus Books, 1991.

Smith, Joseph H., ed. *Colonial Justice in Western Massachusetts (1639–1702): The Pynchon Court Record*. Cambridge, Mass.: Harvard University Press, 1961.

Spence, Jonathan D., *The Search for Modern China*. New York: W. W. Norton & Co., 1990.

*Spitz, Lewis W., ed. *The Protestant Reformation*. Englewood Cliffs, N.J.: Prentice-Hall, 1966.

Standley, Arline Reilein. *Auguste Comte*. Boston: Twayne Publishers, 1981.

Steinsaltz, Adin. *The Essential Talmud*. New York: Basic Books, 1976.

Stendhal. *Red and Black: A Norton Critical Edition*. Trans. and ed. by Robert M. Adams. New York: W. W. Norton & Company, 1969.

Stuart, Gene S., and George E. Stuart. *Lost Kingdoms of the Maya*. Washington, D.C.: National Geographic Society, 1993.

Sullivan, Robert E. *John Toland and the Deist Controversy: A Study in Adaptations*. Cambridge, Mass.: Harvard University Press, 1982.

Sutherland, James. *Daniel Defoe: A Critical Study*. Cambridge, Mass.: Harvard University Press, 1971.

Swift, Jonathan. *The Portable Swift*. Ed. and intro. by Carl Van Doren. New York: Penguin Books, 1978.

———. *A Tale of a Tub and Other Satires*. Intro. by Lewis Melville. New York: E. P. Dutton & Co. 1955.

———. *A Tale of a Tub: Written for the Universal Improvement of Mankind*. Foreword by Edward Hodnett. New York: Columbia University Press, 1930.

Synnestvedt, Sig. *The Essential Swedenborg*. New York: Twayne Publishers, 1970.

Talbot, Emile J. *Stendhal Revisited*. New York: Twayne Publishers, 1993.

Tedlock, Dennis, trans. *Popol Vuh: The Definitive Edition of the Mayan Book of the Dawn of Life and the Glories of Gods and Kings*. New York: Simon & Schuster, 1985.

Tetel, Marcel. *Montaigne: Updated Edition*. Boston: Twayne Publishers, 1990.

Thilly, Frank. *The History of Philosophy*. Rev. by Ledger Wood. New York: Holt, Rinehart and Winston, 1957.

Thompson, David, and Ian Christie, eds. *Scorsese on Scorsese*. London: Faber and Faber, 1989.

Toksvig, Signe. *Emanuel Swedenborg: Scientist and Mystic*. Freeport, N.Y.: Books for Libraries Press, 1972.

*Toulmin, Stephen. *Cosmopolis: The Hidden Agenda of Modernity*. Chicago: University of Chicago Press, 1990.

Trowbridge, George. *Swedenborg, Life and Teaching*. New York: Swedenborg Foundation, 1938.

Urvoy, Dominique. *Ibn Rushd (Averroës)*. Trans. by Olivia Steward. Cairo: American University in Cairo Press, 1993.

Van Hollthoon, F. L. *The Road to Utopia: A Study of John Stuart Mill's Social Thought*. Assem, Netherlands: Van Gorcum & Company, 1971.

Veidmanis, Gladys, "Reflections on 'the Shylock Problem,' " In *Censored Books: Critical Viewpoints*. Ed. by Nicholas J. Karolides, Lee Burress and John M. Kean, 370–78. Metuchen, N.J.: Scarecrow Press, 1993.

Voltaire. *Philosophical Dictionary*. Ed., trans. and intro. by Theodore Besterman. New York: Penguin Books, 1972.

Weatherby, W. J. *Salman Rushdie: Sentenced to Death*. New York: Carroll and Graf Publishers, 1990.

Weinstein, Donald. *Savonarola and Florence: Prophecy and Patriotism in the Renaissance*. Princeton, N.J.: Princeton University Press, 1970.

Welsby, Paul A. *A History of the Church of England 1945–1980*. Oxford: Oxford University Press, 1984.

*Wilcox, Donald J. *In Search of God and Self: Renaissance and Reformation Thought*. Boston: Houghton Mifflin Company, 1975.

Wildes, Harry Emerson. *William Penn*. New York: Macmillan Publishing Co., 1974.

Winslow, Ola Elizabeth. *John Eliot, "Apostle to the Indians."* Boston: Houghton Mifflin Company, 1968.

*Wippel, John F., and Allan B. Wolter, eds. *Medieval Philosophy: From St. Augustine to Nicholas of Cusa*. New York: Free Press, 1969.

Wolff, Robert Paul, ed. *Ten Great Works of Philosophy*. New York: New American Library, 1969.

Yep, Laurence. *Dragonwings*. Afterword by Laurence Yep. New York: Scholastic, 1990.

Yutang, Lin, ed. *The Wisdom of Confucius*. New York: Modern Library, Random House, 1966.

PERIODICALS

*Alrawi, Karim. "Fiction's Freedom: The Government and Its Islamic Opponents Join Forces to Cripple Egyptian Publishing." *Index on Censorship* 25.2 (March/April 1996): 172–75.

American Library Association. *Newsletter on Intellectual Freedom* 42.1 (January 1993): 18.

*Aronsfeld, C. C. "Book Burning in Jewish History." *Index on Censorship* 11.1 (February 1982): 18.

Atwood, Margaret. *Women's Review of Books* 12.10–11 (July 1995): 28.

Bardach, Ann Louise, "Tearing Off the Veil." *Vanity Fair* (August 1993): 123.

Barnes, Julian. "Staying Alive." *The New Yorker* (February 21, 1994): 99–105.

*Birley, Robert. "Freedom of the Press." *Index on Censorship* 5.1 (Spring 1976): 32.

Collen, Lindsey, "The Rape of Fiction." *Index on Censorship* 12.4–5 (September/October 1994): 210–12.

Crossette, Barbara, "A Cry for Tolerance Brings New Hatred Down on a Writer." *New York Times* (July 3, 1994): 7.

El Saadawi, Nawal. "Defying Submission." *Index on Censorship* 19.9 (October 1980): 16.

Hertzberg, Arthur. "Swimming without Drowning: New Approaches to the Ocean of the Talmud." *New York Times Book Review* (March 27, 1994): 12–14.

Moore, Celia, "Banned in Mauritius." *Ms.* (November/December 1995: 89.

Nugent, Philippa. "Of Such Is Reputation Made." *Index on Censorship* 25.2 (March/April 1996): 160.

Piggott, Jill. "Rage Deferred." *Women's Review of Books* 12.10–11 (July 1995): 28.

Riaz, Ali. "Taslima Nasrin: Breaking the Structured Silence." *Bulletin of Concerned Asian Scholars* 27.1 (January–March 1995): 21–27.

Stanley, Alessandra. "Freud in Russia: Return of the Repressed." *New York Times.* (December 11, 1996): 1,10.

Tax, Meredith. "Taslima Nasrin: A Background Paper." *Bulletin of Concerned Asian Scholars* 25.4 (October–December 1993): 72–74.

Tinguet, Margaret. "Ethiopia: Destroy the Muslims." *Index on Censorship* 16.4 (April 1987): 33–35.

Weaver, Mary Anne. "A Fugitive from Justice." *The New Yorker* (September 12, 1994): 47–60.

Weaver, Mary Anne. "The Novelist and the Sheikh." *The New Yorker* (January 30, 1995): 52–59.

Whyatt, Sara. "Taslima Nasrin." *Index on Censorship* 23.4–5 (September/October 1994): 202–07.

WORKS DISCUSSED IN THE OTHER VOLUMES OF THIS SERIES

WORKS DISCUSSED IN *BANNED BOOKS: LITERATURE SUPPRESSED ON POLITICAL GROUNDS* BY NICHOLAS J. KAROLIDES

ABOUT DAVID
Susan Beth Pfeiffer

THE AFFLUENT SOCIETY
John Kenneth Galbraith

THE AGE OF KEYNES
Robert Lekachman

ALL QUIET ON THE WESTERN FRONT
Erich Maria Remarque

AMERICA IN LEGEND
Richard M. Dorson

AMERICAN CIVICS
William H. Hartley and William S. Vincent

THE AMERICAN PAGEANT: A HISTORY OF THE REPUBLIC
Thomas A. Bailey

ANDERSONVILLE
MacKinlay Kantor

ANIMAL FARM
George Orwell

AREOPAGITICA
John Milton

BLACK BOY
Richard Wright

BLOODS: AN ORAL HISTORY OF THE VIETNAM WAR BY BLACK VETERANS
Wallace Terry

BORN ON THE FOURTH OF JULY
Ron Kovic

BOSS: RICHARD J. DALEY OF CHICAGO
Mike Royko

BURGHER'S DAUGHTER
Nadine Gordimer

BURY MY HEART AT WOUNDED KNEE
Dee Brown

BY WAY OF DECEPTION: THE MAKING AND UNMAKING OF A MOSSAD OFFICER
Victor Ostrovsky and Claire Hoy

CANCER WARD
Aleksandr Solzhenitsyn

THE CASE FOR INDIA
Will Durant

CAT'S CRADLE
Kurt Vonnegut Jr.

THE CHINA LOBBY IN AMERICAN POLITICS
Ross Y. Koen

THE CIA AND THE CULT OF INTELLIGENCE
Victor Marchetti and John D. Marks

CITIZEN TOM PAINE
Howard Fast

THE COMMERCIAL RESTRAINTS OF IRELAND CONSIDERED
John Hely Hutchinson

COMPARATIVE POLITICS TODAY: A WORLD VIEW
Gabriel A. Almond, general ed.

CRY AMANDLA!
June Goodwin

DAS KAPITAL
Karl Marx

DAUGHTER OF EARTH
Agnes Smedley

THE DAY THEY CAME TO ARREST THE BOOK
Nat Hentoff

DECENT INTERVAL: AN INSIDER'S ACCOUNT OF SAIGON'S INDECENT END
Frank Snepp

DOCTOR ZHIVAGO
Boris Pasternak

THE DRAPIER'S LETTERS
Jonathan Swift

A DRY WHITE SEASON
André Brink

DU PONT: BEHIND THE NYLON CURTAIN
Gerald Colby Zilg

EL SEÑOR PRESIDENTE
Miguel Angel Asturias

FAIL-SAFE
Eugene Burdick and Harvey Wheeler

FIELDS OF FIRE
James Webb

A FLEET IN BEING: NOTES OF TWO TRIPS WITH THE CHANNEL SQUADRON
Rudyard Kipling

THE FRAGILE FLAG
Jane Langton

THE FUGITIVE
Pramoedya Ananta Toer

A GLOBAL HISTORY OF MAN
Leften S. Stavrianos

THE GRAPES OF WRATH
John Steinbeck

THE GULAG ARCHIPELAGO 1918-1956
Aleksandr Solzhenitsyn

GULLIVER'S TRAVELS
Jonathan Swift

HANDBOOK FOR CONSCIENTIOUS OBJECTORS
Robert A. Seeley, Editor

A HERO ON A DONKEY
Miodrag Bulatovic

THE HOAX OF THE TWENTIETH CENTURY
Arthur R. Butz

I AM THE CHEESE
Robert Cormier

INSIDE RUSSIA TODAY
John Gunther

INSIDE THE COMPANY: CIA DIARY
Philip Agee

IN THE SPIRIT OF CRAZY HORSE
Peter Matthiessen

AN INTRODUCTION TO PROBLEMS OF AMERICAN CULTURE
Harold O. Rugg

THE INVISIBLE GOVERNMENT
David Wise and Thomas B. Ross

IT CAN'T HAPPEN HERE
Sinclair Lewis

JOHNNY GOT HIS GUN
Dalton Trumbo

A JOURNEY FROM ST. PETERSBURG TO MOSCOW
Aleksandr Nikolaevich Radishchev

JULIE OF THE WOLVES
Jean Craighead George

THE JUNGLE
Upton Sinclair

KEEPING FAITH: MEMOIRS OF A PRESIDENT
Jimmy Carter

THE LAND AND PEOPLE OF CUBA
Victoria Ortiz

LAND OF THE FREE: A HISTORY OF THE UNITED STATES
John W. Caughey, John Hope Franklin and Ernest R. May

LAUGHING BOY
Oliver LaFarge

LES MISERABLES
Victor Hugo

MANIFESTO OF THE COMMUNIST PARTY
Karl Marx and Friedrich Engels

MARXISM VERSUS SOCIALISM
Vladimir G. Simkhovitch

MEIN KAMPF
Adolf Hitler

MEN AND NATIONS
Anatole G. Mazour and John M. Peoples

MY BROTHER SAM IS DEAD
James Lincoln Collier and Christopher Collier

MY NAME IS ASHER LEV
Chaim Potok

MY PEOPLE: THE STORY OF THE JEWS
Abba Eban

NELSON AND WINNIE MANDELA
Dorothy Hoobler and Thomas Hoobler

NINETEEN EIGHTY-FOUR
George Orwell

NOVEL WITHOUT A NAME
Duong Thu Huong

OIL!
Upton Sinclair

ONE DAY IN THE LIFE OF IVAN DENISOVICH
Aleksandr Solzhenitsyn

ONE PEOPLE, ONE DESTINY: THE CARIBBEAN AND CENTRAL AMERICA TODAY
Don Rojas

OUR LAND, OUR TIME
Joseph Robert Conlin

PARADISE OF THE BLIND
Duong Thu Huong

THE PRINCE
Niccolò Machiavelli

PRINCIPLES OF NATURE
Elihu Palmer

PROMISE OF AMERICA
Larry Cuban and Philip Roden

RED STAR OVER CUBA
Nathaniel Weyl

REPORT OF THE SIBERIAN DELEGATION
Leon Trotsky

THE RIGHTS OF MAN
Thomas Paine

RUSSIA
Vernon Ives

SECRECY AND DEMOCRACY: THE CIA IN TRANSITION
Stansfield Turner

SLAUGHTERHOUSE-FIVE OR THE CHILDREN'S CRUSADE
Kurt Vonnegut Jr.

SPYCATCHER
Peter Wright

THE STATE AND REVOLUTION
Vladimir I. Lenin

STRONG WIND
THE GREEN POPE
Miguel Angel Asturias

THE STRUGGLE IS MY LIFE
Nelson Mandela

A SUMMARY VIEW OF THE RIGHTS OF BRITISH AMERICA
Thomas Jefferson

SYLVESTER AND THE MAGIC PEBBLE
William Steig

TEN DAYS THAT SHOOK THE WORLD
John Reed

THE THINGS THEY CARRIED
Tim O'Brien

THIS EARTH OF MANKIND
CHILD OF ALL NATIONS
Pramoedya Ananta Toer

365 DAYS
Ronald J. Glasser

TODAY'S ISMS: COMMUNISM, FASCISM, CAPITALISM, SOCIALISM
William Ebenstein

THE UGLY AMERICAN
William J. Lederer and Eugene Burdick

UNCLE TOM'S CABIN
Harriet Beecher Stowe

UNITED STATES VIETNAM RELATIONS, 1945–67 ("THE PENTAGON PAPERS")
U.S. Department of Defense

WHY ARE WE IN VIETNAM?
Norman Mailer

WORDS OF CONSCIENCE: RELIGIOUS STATEMENTS OF CONSCIENTIOUS OBJECTORS
Shawn Perry, ed.

WORKS DISCUSSED IN *BANNED BOOKS: LITERATURE SUPPRESSED ON SEXUAL GROUNDS* BY DAWN SOVA

AN AMERICAN TRAGEDY
Theodore Dreiser

THE ARABIAN NIGHTS
Sir Richard Burton, trans.

THE ART OF LOVE
Ovid (Publius Ovidius Naso)

BESSIE COTTER
Wallace Smith

THE BLUEST EYE
Toni Morrison

BOY
James Hanley

CANDIDE
Voltaire (François Marie Arouet)

CANDY
Maxwell Kenton

THE CARPETBAGGERS
Harold Robbins

CASANOVA'S HOMECOMING
Arthur Schnitzler

THE CHINESE ROOM
Vivian Connell

CHRISTINE
Stephen King

THE CLAN OF THE CAVE BEAR
Jean Auel

CONFESSIONS
Jean-Jacques Rousseau

THE DECAMERON
Giovanni Boccaccio

THE DEER PARK
Norman Mailer

THE DEVIL RIDES OUTSIDE
John Howard Griffin

THE DIARY OF SAMUEL PEPYS
Samuel Pepys

DROLL STORIES
Honoré de Balzac

DUBLINERS
James Joyce

FANNY HILL: OR MEMOIRS OF A WOMAN OF PLEASURE
John Cleland

THE FIFTEEN PLAGUES OF A MAIDENHEAD
Anonymous

FLOWERS FOR ALGERNON
Daniel Keyes

THE FLOWERS OF EVIL
Charles Baudelaire

FOREVER
Judy Blume

FOREVER AMBER
Kathleen Winsor

FROM HERE TO ETERNITY
James Jones

THE GENIUS
Theodore Dreiser

THE GILDED HEARSE
Charles Gorham

THE GINGER MAN
James Donleavy

GOD'S LITTLE ACRE
Erskine Caldwell

THE GROUP
Mary McCarthy

HAGAR REVELLY
Daniel Goodman

THE HANDMAID'S TALE
Margaret Atwood

THE HEPTAMERON
Queen Margaret of Navarre

THE HISTORY OF TOM JONES
Henry Fielding

HOMO SAPIENS
Stanley Przybyskzewski

IF IT DIE
André Gide

ISLE OF PINES
Henry Neville

JANET MARCH
Floyd Dell

JUDE THE OBSCURE
Thomas Hardy

JURGEN
James Cabell

JUSTINE, OR THE MISFORTUNES OF VIRTUE
JULIETTE, HER SISTER, OR THE PROSPERITIES OF VICE
Marquis de Sade

THE KAMA SUTRA *OF VATSAYANA*
Sir Richard Burton, F. F. Arbuthnot, trans.

THE KREUTZER SONATA
Leo Tolstoy

LADIES IN THE PARLOR
Jim Tully

LADY CHATTERLEY'S LOVER
D. H. Lawrence

LA TERRE (THE EARTH)
Émile Zola

LOLITA
Vladimir Nabokov

THE LUSTFUL TURK
Anonymous

MADAME BOVARY
Gustave Flaubert

MADELEINE
Anonymous

MADEMOISELLE DE MAUPIN
Théophile Gautier

MAID OF ORLEANS
Voltaire (François Marie Arouet)

MEMOIRES
Giovanni Casanova de Seingalt

MEMOIRS OF A YOUNG RAKEHELL
Guillaume Apollinaire

MEMOIRS OF HECATE COUNTY
Edmund Wilson

THE MERRY MUSES OF CALEDONIA
Robert Burns

MOLL FLANDERS
Daniel Defoe

MY LIFE AND LOVES
Frank Harris

A NIGHT IN A MOORISH HAREM
Anonymous

NOVEMBER
Gustave Flaubert

THE 120 DAYS OF SODOM
Marquis de Sade

OUR LADY OF THE FLOWERS
Jean Genet

PAMELA, OR VIRTUE REWARDED
Samuel Richardson

PANSIES
D. H. Lawrence

THE PERFUMED GARDEN
Sir Richard Burton, trans.

PEYTON PLACE
Grace Metalious

THE PHILANDERER
Stanley Kauffmann

POEMS AND BALLADS
Algernon Charles Swinburne

POINT COUNTER POINT
Aldous Huxley

RABBIT, RUN
John Updike

THE RAINBOW
D. H. Lawrence

REPLENISHING JESSICA
Max Bodenheim

SANCTUARY
William Faulkner

THE SATYRICON
Gaius Petronius Arbiter

SEPTEMBER IN QUINZE
Vivian Connell

SERENADE
James M. Cain

SEXUS
Henry Miller

SIMON CALLED PETER
Robert Keable

1601—A FIRESIDE CONVERSATION IN YE TIME OF QUEEN ELIZABETH
Mark Twain

SLEEVELESS ERRAND
Norah Jacobs

A STORY TELLER'S HOLIDAY
George Moore

THE STUDS LONIGAN TRILOGY
James T. Farrell

SUSAN LENOX: HER FALL AND RISE
David Graham Phillips

SWEETER THAN LIFE
Mark Tryon

TEN NORTH FREDERICK
John O'Hara

TESS OF THE D'URBERVILLES
Thomas Hardy

THEN AGAIN, MAYBE I WON'T
Judy Blume

THE THIEF'S JOURNAL
Jean Genet

THREE WEEKS
Elinor Glyn

TOBACCO ROAD
Erskine Caldwell

TRAGIC GROUND
Erskine Caldwell

TRILBY
George du Maurier

TRIUMPH OF DEATH
Gabriele D'Annunzio

TROPIC OF CANCER
TROPIC OF CAPRICORN
Henry Miller

ULYSSES
James Joyce

VENUS AND TANNHAUSER (UNDER THE HILL)
Aubrey Beardsley

THE WILD PALMS
William Faulkner

WOMEN IN LOVE
D. H. Lawrence

A YOUNG GIRL'S DIARY
Anonymous

WORKS DISCUSSED IN *BANNED BOOKS: LITERATURE SUPPRESSED ON SOCIAL GROUNDS* BY DAWN SOVA

THE ADVENTURES OF HUCKLEBERRY FINN
Mark Twain

THE ADVENTURES OF SHERLOCK HOLMES
Sir Arthur Conan Doyle

THE ADVENTURES OF TOM SAWYER
Mark Twain

ALICE'S ADVENTURES IN WONDERLAND
Lewis Carroll

THE AMBOY DUKES
Irving Shulman

THE AMERICAN HERITAGE DICTIONARY OF THE ENGLISH LANGUAGE

AND STILL I RISE
Maya Angelou

ANNE FRANK: THE DIARY OF A YOUNG GIRL
Anne Frank

ANNIE ON MY MIND
Nancy Garden

ANOTHER COUNTRY
James Baldwin

APHRODITE
Pierre Louÿs

APPOINTMENT IN SAMARRA
John O'Hara

AS I LAY DYING
William Faulkner

THE AUTOBIOGRAPHY OF BENJAMIN FRANKLIN
Benjamin Franklin

THE AUTOBIOGRAPHY OF MALCOLM X
Malcolm X, with Alex Haley

THE AUTOBIOGRAPHY OF MISS JANE PITTMAN
Ernest J. Gaines

BEING THERE
Jerzy Kosinski

THE BELL JAR
Sylvia Plath

THE BEST SHORT STORIES BY NEGRO WRITERS
Langston Hughes, ed.

BLACK LIKE ME
John Howard Griffin

BLESS THE BEASTS AND CHILDREN
Glendon Swarthout

BLUBBER
Judy Blume

BRAVE NEW WORLD
Aldous Huxley

BRIDGE TO TERABITHIA
Katherine Paterson

CAIN'S BOOK
Alexander Trocchi

CAMILLE
Alexander Dumas Jr.

THE CANTERBURY TALES
Geoffrey Chaucer

CATCH-22
Joseph Heller

THE CATCHER IN THE RYE
J. D. Salinger

THE CHOCOLATE WAR
Robert Cormier

A CLOCKWORK ORANGE
Anthony Burgess

THE COLOR PURPLE
Alice Walker

CUJO
Stephen King

DADDY'S ROOMMATE
Michael Willhoite

A DAY NO PIGS WOULD DIE
Robert Newton Peck

DELIVERANCE
James Dickey

A DICTIONARY OF AMERICAN SLANG
Harold Wentworth

DICTIONARY OF SLANG AND UNCONVENTIONAL ENGLISH
Eric Partridge

DOCTOR DOLITTLE
Hugh John Lofting

DOG DAY AFTERNOON
Patrick Mann

DOWN THESE MEAN STREETS
Piri Thomas

DRACULA
Bram Stoker

EAST OF EDEN
John Steinbeck

ELMER GANTRY
Sinclair Lewis

END AS A MAN
Calder Willingham

ESTHER WATERS
George Moore

FAHRENHEIT 451
Ray Bradbury

A FAREWELL TO ARMS
Ernest Hemingway

THE FIXER
Bernard Malamud

FRUITS OF PHILOSOPHY
Charles Knowlton

GARGANTUA AND PANTAGRUEL
François Rabelais

GO ASK ALICE
Anonymous

GO TELL IT ON THE MOUNTAIN
James Baldwin

GONE WITH THE WIND
Margaret Mitchell

GORILLAS IN THE MIST
Dian Fossey

GRENDEL
John Gardner

HEATHER HAS TWO MOMMIES
Leslea Newman

A HERO AIN'T NOTHIN' BUT A SANDWICH
Alice Childress

HOWL AND OTHER POEMS
Allen Ginsberg

I KNOW WHY THE CAGED BIRD SINGS
Maya Angelou

IN THE NIGHT KITCHEN
Maurice Sendak

INVISIBLE MAN
Ralph Ellison

JAMES AND THE GIANT PEACH
Roald Dahl

JAWS
Peter Benchley

JUNKY
William S. Burroughs

KINGSBLOOD ROYAL
Sinclair Lewis

LAST EXIT TO BROOKLYN
Hubert Selby Jr.

LEAVES OF GRASS
Walt Whitman

LITTLE BLACK SAMBO
Helen Bannerman

LITTLE HOUSE ON THE PRAIRIE
Laura Ingalls Wilder

LITTLE RED RIDING HOOD
Charles Perrault

LORD OF THE FLIES
William Golding

MANCHILD IN THE PROMISED LAND
Claude Brown

MARRIED LOVE
Marie Stopes

MERRIAM WEBSTER COLLEGIATE DICTIONARY

MY HOUSE
Nikki Giovanni

THE NAKED APE
Desmond Morris

NAKED LUNCH
William S. Burroughs

NANA
Émile Zola

NEVER LOVE A STRANGER
Harold Robbins

NEW DICTIONARY OF AMERICAN SLANG
Robert Chapman

OF MICE AND MEN
John Steinbeck

OF TIME AND THE RIVER
Thomas Wolfe

ONE FLEW OVER THE CUCKOO'S NEST
Ken Kesey

ORDINARY PEOPLE
Judith Guest

THE OX-BOW INCIDENT
Walter Clark

THE RED PONY
John Steinbeck

THE SCARLET LETTER
Nathaniel Hawthorne

A SEPARATE PEACE
John Knowles

SISTER CARRIE
Theodore Dreiser

SOUL ON ICE
Eldridge Cleaver

STEPPENWOLF
Hermann Hesse

STRANGE FRUIT
Lillian Smith

STRANGER IN A STRANGE LAND
Robert A. Heinlein

THE SUN ALSO RISES
Ernest Hemingway

TO HAVE AND HAVE NOT
Ernest Hemingway

TO KILL A MOCKINGBIRD
Harper Lee

WELCOME TO THE MONKEY HOUSE
Kurt Vonnegut Jr.

THE WELL OF LONELINESS
Radclyffe Hall

WOMAN IN THE MISTS
Farley Mowat

WORKING
Studs Terkel

A WORLD I NEVER MADE
James T. Farrell

Index

T

U